Not Working

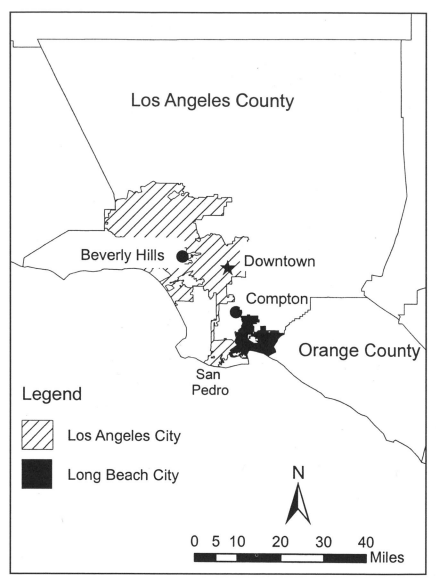

Los Angeles-Long Beach Metropolitan Area. *Daniel Burrough*.

Not Working

Latina Immigrants, Low-Wage Jobs, and the Failure of Welfare Reform

Alejandra Marchevsky *and*
Jeanne Theoharis

NEW YORK UNIVERSITY PRESS
New York and London

NEW YORK UNIVERSITY PRESS
New York and London
www.nyupress.org

© 2006 by New York University
All rights reserved

Library of Congress Cataloging-in-Publication Data
Marchevsky, Alejandra.
Not working : Latina immigrants, low-wage jobs, and the failure of
welfare reform / Alejandra Marchevsky and Jeanne Theoharis.
p. cm.
Includes bibliographical references and index.
ISBN–13: 978–0–8147–5709–3 (cloth : alk. paper)
ISBN–10: 0–8147–5709–X (cloth : alk. paper)
ISBN–13: 978–0–8147–5710–9 (pbk. : alk. paper)
ISBN–10: 0–8147–5710–3 (pbk. : alk. paper)
1. Welfare recipients—Employment—United States.   2. Public wel-
fare—Political aspects—United States.   3. Mexican American
women—California—Long Beach—Social conditions.   4. Mexican
American women—California—Long Beach—Economic conditions.
5. Immigrants—California—Long Beach—Social conditions.   6.
Immigrants—California—Long Beach—Economic conditions.   7.
Temporary Assistance for Needy Families (Program)   8. United
States. Personal Responsibility and Work Opportunity Reconciliation
Act of 1996.   I. Theoharis, Jeanne.   II. Title.
HV95.M2737   2006
362.5'84—dc22   2005029382

New York University Press books are printed on acid-free paper,
and their binding materials are chosen for strength and durability.

Manufactured in the United States of America

10 9 8 7 6 5 4 3 2 1

Contents

Acknowledgments

We live in a society where dependency is treated as a social pathology and an individual failing. To confess one's dependencies is to forfeit one's individuality and rights in the American state. This book interrogates and rejects this discourse of dependency, imagining instead a society where relying on help from others and the state is seen as good common sense and an act of responsible citizenship.

The academic profession is not immune to the discourse of dependency. We acknowledge the influence of others on our work but fall back on a model of rugged independence where scholarship is most valued when it is a singular enterprise. This is especially true in the humanities where coauthored work is viewed with trepidation, where ideas are believed to be diluted and rigor comprised when academic work is produced jointly. We too are guilty of picking up a coauthored book only to search for clues of who did what and who should get the real credit. And yet, when we read through this book, it is impossible to mark where Jeanne's ideas end and Alejandra's begin. Written too often with four hands on the keyboard, this book confirms for us that scholarship is enriched when two people wade chin-deep in the minutiae and expanse of social inquiry. This book grew through interdependency, and we hope that it is all the better for it.

Our work also stands on the shoulders, backs, actions, and words of many other people. It was born out of a collaborative process, out of the history of struggle that produced ethnic studies, out of the collective fight for welfare and immigrant rights being waged today by groups like Californians for Justice, the Kensington Welfare Rights Union and the University of the Poor, and the Los Angeles Metropolitan Alliance, out of a community of friends, activists, and scholars where the individual ownership of ideas is secondary to the larger task of social justice and transformative knowledge.

The Latinas who participated in this research project trusted Alejandra to translate their stories and ideas and dedicated hundreds of hours to talk with her at a time in their lives when even a half an hour of sleep, with their children, or by themselves, was a precious commodity. They did so because they knew that theirs was a story that needed to be at the heart of public discourse and social policy. We dedicate this book to women like Myrna, Zoraida, and Maria, not in celebration of their strength and resiliency in the face of devastating poverty, but as a testament to their courage to insist that resiliency is not the foundation of justice. *A las mamas y trabajadoras de Long Beach, gracias por su ejemplo.*

This work is also dedicated to numerous other Long Beach residents who convinced us that there was a crucial, ignored story to tell in the periphery of L.A. County. Amelia Nieto and her battalion of volunteers at Centro Shalom, Maria Nuñez at Burnett Elementary School, Colleen Triesch from the Family Literacy Program, and Hope Troy from Mark Twain Library all saw the importance of telling the story of Central Long Beach, and amidst their impossible schedules and myriad commitments made time for our novice questions and needs. We hope that this book will in some way assist in the struggle for social change that these community workers wage daily in the homes, churches, community institutions, and schools of Long Beach.

Roderick Harrison, Alice O'Connor, Elizabeth Gonzalez, and Sanford Schram generously read and provided feedback on the last part of the book, testifying to the need and critical importance of detailed analyses of poverty research. Mark Wild, Kaye Briegel, and the Special Collections staff at Cal State Long Beach all gave invaluable expertise on Long Beach history. Daniel Flaming and others at the Economic Roundtable shared their research on welfare reform implementation in L.A. County and their perspectives on the poverty research industry. We are grateful to Daniel Borough in the Department of Geography at Cal State L.A. for producing the two maps that appear in this book. We are also grateful to MDRC for their financial and logistical support of the ethnographic research that appears in this book and, more recently, to Gordon Berlin for meeting with Jeanne to talk about the Urban Change Project.

We also want to thank the Rockefeller Foundation, the CUNY Scholar Incentive Award Program, and the PSC-CUNY Research Award that enabled us to have a year to work on this book in the same city and to hire two fabulous graduate research assistants. Dawn Rizzo and Juily Phun brought unflagging enthusiasm, creative sleuthing, and keen minds to the last stages of this project and sifted undaunted through hundreds of articles and reports on the effects of PRWORA and the history of Long Beach and its redevelopment. Dawn and Juily juggled this research—and Juily the index—alongside their own scholarship, work, and family commitments because they saw the urgency in making this story to the public. Thanks to Debbie Gershenowitz at NYU Press for expressing an early interest and excitement in this book and introducing us to Ilene Kalish who saw the urgency of a book on immigrants and welfare reform. Ilene shared our enthusiasm for the subject, understood the need for this to be a broadly interdisciplinary study, and encouraged our efforts at every stage. We are also grateful to Despina Papazoglou Gimbel for the tremendous care and attention she put into producing this book.

—JT and AM

I am deeply to a wide community of friends and colleagues who sustained me during the long journey that produced this book. Over the past decade I have been graced with the friendship and support of Frances Aparicio, whose intellectual and political vision and commitment to students has served as a model for how to be an excellent scholar-activist-teacher. Ruth Behar, Alexandra Stern, and Matthew Countryman also championed this project in its early stages, helping to mold its contours and tease out the intricacies of my ideas. Abel Valenzuela generously made a place for me at UCLA's Center for the Study of Urban Poverty; he and other Urban Change researchers—Karen Quintanillia, Elizabeth Gonzalez, Gil Contreras, Lisette Islas, and Earl Johnson in L.A., and later Carol and Alex Stepick in Miami—embodied the spirit of collaborative ethnography, helping me to find my way through the chaos that is both ethnographic research and welfare reform. I also send a bouquet of thank you's to friends at Cal State L.A.—especially John Ramirez, Patrick Sharp, Micol Siegel, Rob DeChaine, Jennifer Faust, Thu-Hung Nguyen-vo, and faculty and students in the Rockefeller Humanities Residency Program and the Center for the Study of Gender and Sexualities—who have provided a dynamic, interdisciplinary home for my scholarship and teaching. My students at Cal State L.A. have left their mark all over this book; the enumerable sacrifices they make in order to pursue a college degree and their unshakable belief in the transformative power of knowledge remind me over and over again why I do the work that I do.

In moments when my faith faltered, numerous friends kept in sight the personal and political significance of this project and urged me on with a powerful brew of patience and insistence: Isabella Alcaniz, Carolina Briones, Ernesto Calvo, Brenda Cardenas, Mike Chavez, Scott Dexter, Beti Gonzalez, Lupe and Paco Gonzalez and their now-grown children, Krupskaia, Arlen, and Anton, John Heathcliff, Sheri Ozeki, and Rafael Pizarro. Eve Oishi took her keen mind to various drafts of this work, brought her laptop over to my house to break the solitude of writing, and encouraged me to get the book done because she wanted to assign it to her class. During the writing of this book, the Theoharis family became my own, and I thank Liz and Nancy in particular for their contagious excitement about this project and their daily example in the fight against poverty and social injustice. I am forever grateful to Joaquina Martinez for applying her marvelous talents to caring for baby Emilio, affording me the time and peace of mind to create this book.

I want to celebrate my parents, Liliana and Alberto Marchevsky, who sowed the seeds of this project by shaping me into an independent thinker and teaching me to engage in the world with responsibility and compassion. *Mami y papi, gracias por tu amor sin fondo,* for caring for Emilio so that I could have time to write, for nourishing me, both literally and figuratively, for taking me in when I was paralyzed and always throwing me back into the world when I could walk again. My sister, Miriam Marchevsky, lovingly listened to me rant about this project and, together with Justin Magana, knew when to ask about my progress and when to distract me with architectural talk, all the while cheering each step that took me closer to its completion. This book was still a jumble of words and ideas when Emilio arrived, and just as these pages took form and character so has he grown into a formidable force of curiosity and determination, infusing my life with hilarity and marvel. Finally, I send infinite love and respect to Jason Elias for building the scaffolding for this book, for taking Emilio and Mochi on long treks through Silver Lake so that I could think in silence and appearing at my office window with gifts of food and stolen flowers, for putting up with my idiosyncratic work habits, and for always, always testifying to the power of my voice and the need for this type of scholarly and political intervention. Jason's lived commitment to worker's rights and economic justice in Los Angeles is a source of inspiration for my own work, and I hope that this book approximates the convictions that we continually strive to put into action.

—AM

My first gratitude goes to my students at Brooklyn College who remind me regularly of why I do the work that I do—of the steadfastness that committed scholarship takes and the value of new knowledges in the service of justice. The friendship and support from a community of friends and colleagues—Jennifer Bernstein, Julie Cooper, Paisley Currah, Gaston Alonso Donate, Jason Elias, Lauren Fox, Debbie Gershenowitz, Stephanie Melnick Goldstein, Roderick Harrison, Amy Schmidt Jones, Robin Kelley, Barbara Krauthamer, Steve Lang, Alberto and Liliana Marchevsky, Jennifer McCormick, Karen Miller, Mojubaolu Olufunke Okome, Brian Purnell, John Ramirez, Corey Robin, John Rogers, Alfio Saitta, Pete Sigal, Kelly Stupple, Harrod Suarez, Mark Ungar, Sam Vong, Mark Wild, and Lisa Woznica—nourished me and this work in its longest and richest moments. They embroidered the shapes of my thoughts, refracted the angles of my vision, and leavened my life with patience and prodding, generosity and wisdom.

Arnold Franklin walked by my side throughout this period, bringing a magical combination of hard questions, intense listening, and inspired delight to the journey. Komozi Woodard's intellectual companionship over the past many years has been a blessing beyond measure; Komozi models daily the politically engaged scholar, expansive friend, and intellectual collaborator that I aspire to emulate. Scott Dexter understood how much I had committed to when I embarked on this project. Unwavering in his support of this work, he continued to gather my pieces and give them back to me in all the right order and never let me doubt the possibility and importance of this book.

Finally, I consider it my life's greatest fortune to be part of a family who loves justice and practices kindness. My parents, Nancy and Athan Theoharis, and my siblings, George Theoharis, Liz Theoharis, Julie Causton Theoharis, and Chris Caruso, all make this work possible through their daily efforts to make this a more just and fair society and through their unwavering belief that the work would be splendid so I should just get it out there where it was most needed. In the course of this project, three new members of my family announced their presence to the world: Emilio Elias Marchevsky, Ella Josephine Theoharis, and Samuel Athan Theoharis already embody the orneriness, determination, and joy that this world needs more of.

—JT

Introduction

Latinas on the Fault Lines of Citizenship

Myrna Cardenas and her three children live in a one-bedroom garden apartment in central Long Beach. With its collection of single-story row apartments organized around a communal courtyard landscaped with flowering bushes and imported palms, the "garden apartment complex" is a quintessential Southern California architectural form. Regional developers and architects of the early twentieth century drew upon the California landscape as a metaphor for the transformative power of this new American city, a classless society where newcomers could reinvent themselves and where even the most modest apartment renters, shut out of the dream of the single-family home, could enjoy a small patch of green outside their front door.[1]

The courtyard complex where Myrna lives is located on the outskirts of Long Beach's renovated downtown shopping district and a few miles from one of the nation's busiest ports. This Spanish-style apartment complex was likely built to house sailors during the navy's heydays in Long Beach in the 1920s. Now, all of Myrna's neighbors in this apartment complex are migrants from Mexico, Guatemala, and El Salvador. During the weekdays, the courtyard feels abandoned; the muffled sounds of *rancheras* or midday *telenovelas* the only signs of life behind bolted doors and drawn curtains. In the evenings, however, the concrete walkway comes alive as residents open their doors to let in the ocean air, and sit on their front steps watching young children ride tricycles up to the front gate and back again.

In the 500-square-foot apartment that Myrna rents for $650 a month, a full-sized mattress is pushed up against the far wall of the living room for twelve-year-old Ana and five-year-old Jasmine. Their brother, James, a fourth-grade "citizen of the month" at Jefferson Elementary School, sleeps on a cot under the front window. Working 40-hour weeks at an Or-

1

ange County plastics factory, along with a part-time graveyard shift stocking inventory at a discount department store, Myrna is lucky when she can sleep for three or four hours in a 24-hour period. Usually she crashes out alongside her daughters for the few hours that separate her night shift from her day shift. Myrna is saving to buy a dresser at a second-hand furniture store; in the meantime, the family sofa is piled high with clothing. At the beginning of the week, the sofa is neatly stacked with pressed and folded clothing fresh from the laundromat. By Thursday morning at 5 A.M., as Myrna frantically rushes to get her children dressed and to her mother's house all in time to make her 9 A.M. shift at the factory 25 miles east in Orange County, the apartment has devolved into what Myrna calls a "un desmadre" (slang for a mess, literally translated as "unmotherly").

If we looked into most homes in America, we might find this same tangled mess of socks, jeans, and sweaters on the sofa, and perhaps a pile of dirty dishes in the sink. But, in Myrna's case, a messy home or an empty refrigerator could cost her her children because Myrna is on welfare. Twice, in fact, the government has inspected her home, checking for food in the refrigerator and men's clothing in the closet. There are only three populations in the United States whose privacy is not protected under "probable cause" rules: prisoners, undocumented immigrants, and welfare recipients. As one of the latter, Myrna must allow government inspectors into her home, or she will be labeled "noncompliant," a designation that strips her of her welfare benefits and possibly results in criminal prosecution. While Myrna had little choice but to cooperate with welfare officials during these surprise inspections, she did not passively accept the system's criminalization of her as a welfare cheat and unfit mother. Rather, like most of the Mexican immigrant women interviewed in Long Beach, she agreed to participate in a nationwide ethnographic study of welfare reform because she saw it as an opportunity to refute the stereotypes that society imposes on her and other welfare mothers.[2]

"They can't say that people on welfare are lazy, because I do work. When there's hours, I work over 40 hours." With this statement Myrna opened her first interview for this study in March 1997, directly disputing the notion that people on welfare do not want to work or that they do not know how to get and keep a job. At thirty-five years old, Myrna Cardenas has worked nearly continuously for the past 12 years but has never earned enough to lift her family above the poverty line. For five of those years, Myrna worked *and* was on welfare. She first applied for

AFDC in 1991 after her husband returned to Mexico, leaving her behind with three young children. At the time, Myrna did not qualify for aid because she was not a lawful permanent resident. Myrna had always known that she was born two months premature while her mother, a lawful U.S. resident, was visiting an aunt in Tijuana. Yet, she had always believed that her mother had "fixed" her paperwork soon upon returning to Los Angeles. While she was growing up in Long Beach, Myrna's immigration status was never under question. Her unaccented English and light complexion led public schoolteachers and, later, employers to presume that she was a U.S. citizen. Myrna had lived her entire life in the United States, attended American public schools, and given birth to two U.S. citizens, yet she could be deported at any moment. When the caseworker at the welfare office demanded to see Myrna's green card and she could not produce one, Myrna was deemed ineligible for public assistance. Still, her U.S. citizen children were eligible, and Myrna began receiving cash assistance and food stamps on their behalf. For two years, she cut corners and worked odd jobs to stretch a welfare check for three into a livelihood for a family of four.

When her residency application was approved by the INS, Myrna returned to the welfare office to be added to her family's welfare grant. The caseworker took one look at her newly issued green card, and "she said, 'No, no, it's a fake. What you need to do is look for a job.'" Myrna spent the next four years trying to track down a caseworker that would take the time to call the INS to verify that her green card was valid. In the meantime, she found a part-time job at Target, counting and reshelving inventory from 10 P.M. to 6 A.M. for $4.25/hour. Because Myrna and her coworkers were classified as part-time employees, despite the fact that some months they worked over 40 hours per week, Target did not pay their medical benefits or overtime pay. Myrna was working and reported her wages to the welfare office, yet it did not take long for her to realize that this job was not a pathway off welfare. During the holiday rush season, from late September through December, Myrna worked 30 to 40 hours per week and earned a monthly paycheck of $760. However, once the store's Christmas decorations came down, her work hours dwindled to as few as ten per week and her monthly paycheck shrunk to less than $170, which was only marginally corrected by a slight increase in her children's food stamps and cash assistance.

In November 1997, Myrna's persistence finally paid off as she managed to convince a new caseworker that her green card was legitimate and that she was eligible for welfare. She was officially added to her family's case the following month, which raised their monthly benefits by a total of $100—enough to get their phone reconnected and buy an extra bag of groceries. But as Myrna explained,

> I didn't get no check in the following year, in February [two months later]. And I called my [caseworker], "Why am I not getting a check? You told me that if I could get more money, that I could get childcare, and this and that. And now you're cutting me off?" [. . .] And so I called her and she told me, "Oh it's because you work and you made more than $790, that's more than enough. So you're not getting nothing."

Encouraged by the welfare system to get a job, Myrna was now told she no longer qualified for aid because her December paycheck was slightly above the County's eligibility threshold (but still below the poverty line for a family of four). By the time she secured a face-to-face meeting with a caseworker three weeks later, Myrna had already registered with a temporary employment agency and had been assigned to an assembly line, where she attached handles onto plastic buckets for $6.50/hr. with no benefits. At this meeting, yet a different caseworker explained to Myrna the new welfare rules that had been imposed by Congress in August 1996. Each day that she received welfare (even if she was also working) would be counted against a five-year lifetime maximum. Because Myrna was already working the required 35 hours per week, she was advised not to apply for welfare and to "save those five years for a rainy day, when things get really bad."

By March 1998, Myrna was off welfare and juggling two jobs—a full-time shift at the plastics factory along with a few nights per week on the graveyard shift at Target—yet her family's economic security was shakier than ever before. It had been over a year since the family had health insurance, because their Medi-Cal coverage had been cancelled when their TANF file closed. She had lost over 25 pounds because some of the factories she works at are "like 10 to 20 degrees hotter than what it is outside" but was trying to avoid having to go to the doctor. And, with a monthly income of $900, or a yearly income of $15,600, Myrna and her children continued to fall below the poverty line. Moreover, working an average of 50 hours per week, Myrna was lucky when she could spend an hour or two each day with her children. The morning of the interview, Myrna had even more reason to worry. The supervisor of the temp agency had called to say that she and several other employees had been placed on a week-long suspension, punishment for their refusal to work on Labor Day. As Myrna explained, "She said that if I kept up this bad attitude, I wouldn't get no more work." Less than a year later, Myrna was laid off at the factory and had reapplied for welfare.

Down and Out in Long Beach

Myrna was one of 14 Mexican immigrant women in Long Beach, California, who had received welfare and participated in a nationwide ethnographic study of the effects of welfare reform. Passed by Congress and signed by President Bill Clinton in 1996, the Personal Responsibility and Work Opportunity Reconciliation Act (PRWORA, Public Law 104-193) dismantled the 60-year-old federal cash assistance program, Aid to Families With Dependent Children (AFDC), and replaced it with Temporary Assistance to Needy Families (TANF)—block grants to states governed under a new set of time limits and restrictions.[3] Welfare was no longer a social safety net but a temporary program designed to encourage marriage and other "family values" among the nation's poor and to move welfare recipients as quickly as possible into the workforce. Along with a five-year lifetime limit on cash benefits and new work requirements, the PRWORA implemented strict restrictions on welfare eligibility, banning large sectors of the American public (including legal immigrants, teenage mothers, and convicted felons) from receiving public assistance. This study sought to investigate how people were faring under the new rules.

Ranging in age from twenty-four to forty-eight, these *mexicanas* had migrated to the United States as young children and as grown mothers from Tijuana, Uruapan, Guadalajara, Chihuahua, and Mazatlan. They had sold *gorditas* in Cuidad Juarez, cleaned kitchens in Mexico City, sewn skirts in the factories of Los Angeles, picked strawberries in the Imperial Valley, welded computer chips in Huntington Park, and canned tuna in Long Beach. Many had followed their husbands and parents to Long Beach, while others were drawn to this coastal suburb in the southwest corner of L.A. County by cheap rents and jobs in the city's new hotels. At the time that they joined this study, all were legal residents of the United States, although most had spent some time as undocumented immigrants. Living with husbands and boyfriends, parents and siblings, they cared for newborns, toddlers, teenagers, and some even grandchildren. And all relied on AFDC to feed and shelter their families.

Four years after Congress passed welfare reform, this new legislation had produced tremendous instability and insecurity for these women and their children. Over two-thirds were either forced off of welfare or they chose voluntarily to disenroll from public assistance because they were tired of the surveillance and harassment from the welfare office, or the minimal benefits they were receiving no longer seemed worth the work of meeting the continually changing requirements. Those who found employment were working low-wage jobs, did not have health care or job stability, and continued to fall below the poverty line. None of the families in this study were living above the poverty line. Moreover, because very few women received the childcare assistance promised under the PRWORA, they were constantly relying on their older children, other family members, neighbors, and babysitters to watch their children while they were at work. Indeed, welfare reform proved to be a profound disappointment for this group of Mexican immigrant mothers. Initially excited about the legislation's promise of education, training, and help finding good-paying jobs, these women instead discovered a welfare system designed to thwart their educational and career ambitions and to track them into the same low-wage work they had been doing for most of their lives.

These immigrant women's perspectives on welfare reform, and their framings of their experiences in both the welfare system and the labor market, provide an important window into the racial politics of citizenship in the contemporary moment. In this book we trace the growing symbolic power of citizenship in American politics and the concurrent whittling away at the social rights and protections that have been the hallmark of U.S. citizenship in the twentieth century. We analyze the ways that welfare reform calls on immigrant women to be good mothers and self-determining workers while simultaneously restricting them to the periphery of American citizenship. Finally, we consider how Latina immigrants as social thinkers and actors narrate and navigate this new system of public entitlements, and how they frame the salience of citizenship and its denial in the post-welfare era.

Over and over again in the ethnographic interviews, Latina immigrants voiced a tremendous sense of dislocation and marginalization. This marginalization went beyond the common rupture that accompanies the process of migrating and adapting to a new country. Rather, it was more firmly rooted in their experiences of living in a nation where their presence was heavily policed—by the state, by employers, by the media—at the same time that their perspectives and daily needs were cast aside. They spoke of longer work days, shrinking paychecks, and growing stacks of bills at the end of each day, of increased surveillance in the streets of Long Beach, in the workplace, in schools, welfare offices, and public hospitals. Their commentary ranged from the most local spaces, like public schools and neighborhood clinics, to national arenas like welfare reform and immigrant rights, to the global terrain of multinational corporations and U.S. hegemony. Most struggled to convey the schizophrenic experience of living in a country that welcomes and profits from the labor of Latino immigrants, yet continually treats them as racial threats and undeserving interlopers within the national community.

Myrna: A Welfare Success Story?

This book is about welfare queens and hardworking, self-sacrificing immigrant mothers, the two most pervasive representations of Latinas in contemporary U.S. society. In the early 1990s, images of women like Myrna Cardenas—undocumented immigrants and black and brown single mothers on welfare—drove the passage of California's Proposition 187 and led to a draconian overhaul of the national welfare system. Derided for their laziness and promiscuity, these women came to symbolize the pitfalls of American liberalism—lax immigration rules, morally corrupt and overly generous welfare policies, broken families, and disintegrating communities. Claiming that these women needed a "hand up, not a handout" Congress approved the PRWORA, which created a new system of time-limited and work-based welfare, imposed strict moral regulations over access to benefits, and greatly reduced or eliminated the eligibility of legal immigrants to most public entitlements. As the nation's welfare rolls dropped from 12.2 million in 1996 to 5.3 million in 2001, another image of Myrna surfaced in public discourse—the "welfare success story."[4] Hailed by Democratic President Bill Clinton and his Republican successor George W. Bush as proof of the soundness of welfare reform, such stories of poor mothers "trading a welfare check for a paycheck" are today regularly cited by politicians, journalists, and researchers as the personification of American values of personal responsibility and self-reliance.

Myrna is a recognizable trope in American political discourse: the illegal Mexican immigrant and her flock of children, who drain public coffers and overcrowd welfare offices and hospitals. She is the high school dropout and teenage mother, abandoned by a dead-beat dad to become a burden on the government and hardworking taxpayers. She is the urban single mother, with too many children, too little values, and a string of no-good men in her life. She is the reformed ex-welfare recipient who, with the push of new rules and incentives introduced under welfare reform, finally confronts her dependency and starts down the path to self-sufficiency. She is a new version of the American Dream, an immigrant "welfare-to-worker" who manages to pull herself up by her bootstraps by working two low-wage jobs in order to provide a better future for her children.

When examined more closely, however, Myrna's story is less familiar. Whereas dominant ideas represent work as the antidote to welfare dependency, Myrna in fact had worked a series of low-paying jobs since her teenage years and yet had never risen above the poverty line. Like for millions of low-income women across the nation, work was not sufficient to provide for her family, and she also needed state assistance to be able to support her three children. However, welfare did not mean a generous or regular government handout every month and afternoons spent watching soap operas. Wrongly told by welfare officials that she did not qualify for aid because she is not a U.S. citizen, Myrna had to fight to get on welfare and, once on, had to continue working because the benefits she received each month barely covered two weeks of groceries and utilities. Myrna's story challenges the dichotomous construction of welfare and work, informing us that alone neither is adequate for families to survive in a society with an increasingly elusive social safety net and an economy that profits from poverty wages and disposable workers. Her story also serves as a powerful counterpoint to the near-universal, bipartisan celebration of welfare reform as a success. Two years following the passage of PRWORA, Myrna was "working hard and playing by the rules," yet her family was still poor, now had no health insurance, and insufficient childcare. Another two years later, Myrna had lost her job and had little choice but to reapply for welfare.

Myrna's story not only illustrates the interdependency between welfare and work in poor women's lives, but it also dispels the prevailing wisdom that identifies welfare as a program for sexually loose and irresponsible women. In many regards, Myrna is the living embodiment of the family values that conservatives claim are lacking among the nation's welfare recipients. Married to her high school sweetheart, Myrna did not have her first child until she was in her early twenties, and all three of her children were born to the same father. As their family grew, she and her husband both worked to "save money," but like many other working couples, their marriage dissolved under the pressure of financial insecurity and conflicting plans for the future. Contrary to the assumption that single motherhood is to blame for poverty, Myrna's family was poor before she and her husband separated. And contrary to assertions that welfare leads to family dissolution, welfare in fact helped to keep Myrna's family together. Indeed, had it not been for AFDC, Myrna alone would not have been able to support herself and her three children on a part-time salary, and were it not for AFDC, she would have been at risk of losing her children to the foster care system.

If Myrna does not fit the stereotype of the unmarried welfare queen with a brood of illegitimate children, she also stands in stark contrast to that of the pregnant illegal alien who sneaks across the border in order to cash in on American entitlements. Although Myrna was technically "undocumented" in the eyes of the U.S. government, her parents were legal immigrants and low-wage workers who had not relied on welfare while Myrna was growing up. Myrna herself had worked as a teenager and an adult and only turned to welfare in her mid-twenties when work was not enough to make ends meet. Myrna lived her entire life in the United States, attended public schools, worked and paid taxes—it was not until she entered into the welfare system that she assumed the official label of "illegal alien." A bilingual and bicultural mother of three U.S.-born children, Myrna blurs the line between legal and illegal, citizen and stranger, complicating the binary divisions that permeate the contemporary debate over immigration.

In many regards Myrna looks like the vast majority of poor women on welfare across the United States. Studies show that most welfare recipients live in overpriced working-class suburbs, not in the inner-city public housing projects that predominate in popular representations of poverty. Most have children that excel in school. Most have men in their lives that help with child-raising and family finances. Most have long employment histories, and many, like Myrna and other *mexicanas* in this study, combine welfare and work in order to make ends meet.[5] For most, work means pleading with supervisors for full-time hours, waiting in line at temp agencies, constantly juggling childcare and transportation to meet an ever-changing work schedule, and shuffling between dead-end jobs that are physically and psychically exhausting and rarely last for more than a few months. Most turn to the welfare system for basic necessities they cannot find in the labor market, like health insurance, utilities, and food supplements for themselves and their children. And most struggle daily to keep their footing in a social and political minefield of overly laden representations of welfare recipients that tell them who they are, who they should be, and what their place is in the nation.[6]

The End of Welfare

Despite the mountain of evidence presented during congressional debates in the mid-1990s that provided a much more complicated picture of welfare recipients and poverty, the legislation approved in 1996 was nevertheless based on the *idea* of the welfare mother as an economic sycophant and cultural pariah in need of "help" and discipline. As sociologist Sharon Hays notes, Americans overwhelmingly supported welfare reform not because they believed that AFDC was costing taxpayers too much money, but because they believed that welfare encouraged people to "adopt the wrong lifestyle" and that people were "overly dependent."[7] Thus, PRWORA targeted the individual recipient as the object of reform with strict work requirements, time-limited welfare, family caps, and marriage incentives. The legislation left in place those structural conditions—declining wages and eroding worker protections, racism and the dismantling of civil rights, unaffordable and inadequate childcare, underfunded public schools, and diminished access to higher education—responsible for the reproduction of poverty and social inequality in U.S. society.

Because welfare reform was designed to push people off of welfare and teach them the "right values," it was declared a success from the moment President Clinton signed the legislation. Six years later, as Congress began debating its reauthorization, the sharp drop of seven million people from the welfare rolls was proof positive of the law's soundness; few politicians stopped to question the tautological nature of celebrating a drop in the rolls because people were being dropped from the rolls. Nor did they raise questions when the federal government's own studies showed that no more than half of the people who had left welfare were working at any given time. Among recent welfare recipients nationwide, only 28 percent were working by March 2003, and more than half of these workers had below poverty wages. Food stamp participation had increased significantly between 1997 and 2002 for former welfare recipients.

As many critics had pointed out in debates around welfare reform, work was not an antidote to poverty within the U.S. economy. In 2002, more than four million families had earnings below the poverty level, even though the head of the family worked. Five out of ten families that used food pantries had a working parent.[8] The vast majority of "welfare leavers" were still living in poverty. Following a short-lived, but much touted, economic boom in the mid-1990s, poverty has risen steadily since 1999. According to the Census Bureau, 35.9 million people (or 12.5 percent of the nation's population) were living below the poverty line in 2003, up 1.3 million from 2002.[9] The data shows that Americans today are more likely to live in deep poverty than prior to 1996, and that work for most former welfare recipients means average earnings of $8,000 to $10,800 per year,[10] far below the poverty line for a family of four, which in 2005 was $18,850.

One 1999 study by the Urban Institute showed that "nearly one-third of those that had left public assistance since August of 1996 had returned at least once, and that one-fourth of those who had left welfare are not working and have no working partner."[11] The study also found that health insurance, which had formerly been provided to recipients through the Medicaid program, had been severely impacted by the 1996 reforms. Only a small minority, 23 percent, of those who had moved from welfare to work reported receiving health insurance through their employment—nearly 50 percent below the national average of all workers.[12] In its nationwide survey of wages earned by former welfare recipients who had moved into work, the congressional General Accounting Office found that mean hourly wages fell between $5.60 and $6.60, leaving a full-time worker with two children below the poverty line.[13] Moreover, one 1999 study of former recipients who are employed found that most do not have full-time, year-round jobs. Thus, their annual earnings average between $8,000 and 9,500.[14]

With some of the poorest counties in the United States, California was home to the largest number of welfare recipients in the nation and half lived in L.A. County. Poverty in Los Angeles was nearly triple the national average—36 percent of the city lived below the poverty line in 2003. More than 30 percent of immigrant families in Los Angeles lived below the poverty line and 61 percent had incomes that fell below 200 percent of the poverty level. Immigrants, and especially Latinos, were more likely to be poor, despite high levels of work (75 percent versus 58 percent of low-income native-born families). Yet since the passage of welfare reform, fewer immigrants in Los Angeles accessed public assistance. One-third of immigrants who were receiving food stamps in 1996–1997 had lost all their food stamp benefits by 1998, and 55 percent had lost all by 2000 (more than half of those immigrants who still received food stamps found their allotment reduced).[15] Indeed, part of the large initial drop in the welfare rolls was due to the anti-immigrant provisions of the legislation. A study by the Center for Law and Social Policy found that the immigrant caseload decline accounted for over half of the welfare savings accrued in the first year of reform.[16]

Research conducted on immigrant households shows that the effects of welfare reform have been devastating. Between 1994 and 1999, there were substantial declines in legal immigrants' participation in all major benefit programs: TANF (–60 percent), food stamps (–48 percent), SSI (–32 percent), and Medicaid (–15 percent). Low-income legal immigrant families with children had lower rates of usage for TANF and food stamps than low-income citizen families with children. Yet, almost one-fifth of low-income immigrant families in Los Angeles and over one-quarter in New York reported problems paying their rent, mortgage, or utilities during the prior year. One-third of all immigrant families in Los Angeles and 31 percent in New York are food insecure, compared to families composed of native-born citizens at 12 percent in Los Angeles and 11 percent in New York.[17] These figures are even more staggering in states with large numbers of immigrants. In Illinois, between January 1998 and April 1999, the number of noncitizens receiving TANF declined by 42 percent, while the number of native-born fell by 25 percent. Food stamp participation among naturalized citizens and noncitizens fell by 30 percent.[18] Similar patterns were documented in Texas, where the number of noncitizens receiving TANF dropped 40 percent between August 1996 and September 1998, and food stamp receipt declined by over half.[19]

Despite these alarming figures, welfare reform continues to enjoy near-unanimous acclaim among conservatives and liberals. In his recent best-selling account of PRWORA, *New York Times* reporter Jason DeParle proclaims, "the country knows now what it didn't know a decade ago: that anti-poverty policy can enjoy a measure of success."[20] However, the standards used to evaluate the efficacy of welfare reform are not very demanding. As political scientists Sanford Schram and Joe Soss point out,

"Compared to improving material conditions in poor communities, it is relatively easy to pare the welfare rolls and push the poor into low-wage work."[21] Because the PRWORA was never intended to save money nor to eradicate poverty, but to send the "right message," its success was untarnished by the fact that TANF was costing the federal government more than AFDC had, that most who left the roles for work were making poverty wages with no health insurance, and that many who left the rolls had not found work.[22] Absent any national conversation or rigorous assessment of PRWORA, debates on reauthorization have affirmed the success of welfare reform and largely focused on increasing hourly work requirements and setting aside millions more federal dollars for marriage incentives.

Reauthorization has also been propelled by the mainstream media, which over the past seven years has nearly universally celebrated the success of the legislation by persistently and exclusively focusing on sharp decline in the welfare rolls. Although most major news outlets have separately reported rising poverty, increased food insecurity, and declining health coverage rates, few have attributed these alarming trends to the effects of the PRWORA. Instead media coverage of welfare reform has been limited to moving accounts of individuals who have left welfare for work. Professing to shed light on the "human face" of welfare reform, these newspaper articles and television news segments have in fact delimited the humanity of welfare recipients by narrating their lives in voyeuristic detail. Often reduced to two-dimensional morality plays, poor women's lives are narrated as inspirational stories, in which lifelong recipients struggle to adjust to the "culture" of the workplace, and newly employed single mothers buy their family's first Christmas tree. These "success stories" are especially troubling because they persuade the American public to see hard working and dedicated mothers like Myrna as the *outcome* of welfare reform, as proof of the rehabilitative power of a public policy based on zero-tolerance and tough love. We cannot see that Myrna worked hard and made sacrifices for her children *before* being "reformed," and that she continues to do so in spite of a new barrage of laws that require her to work long hours for insufficient pay, to settle for inferior childcare, and to submit to constant monitoring by the welfare state. By looking narrowly at Myrna's individual path off of welfare, the media-circulated "success story" also intimates that people who continue to rely on government aid have no one to blame but themselves and, as such, they deserve to be permanently ousted from the safety net after five years.

While seemingly opposite, the two images of Myrna as welfare queen and welfare success story are in fact dialectical, resting on a set of long-standing, mutually reinforcing American ideologies regarding hard work and meritocracy, gender norms and appropriate motherhood, race and culture, the deserving and undeserving poor. Certainly the belief that poor people are personally responsible for their own life conditions, and the adjoining view of women of color as sexually licentious, is an old theme in American attitudes toward welfare. Nor is the nativist agenda of PRWORA exceptional in the course of U.S. history, for nativity and race have long driven the nation's distinctions between citizens and outsiders. Notwithstanding its historical resonance, however, the passage of the 1996 legislation marks a dramatic reversal of American social welfare policy and a new intertwining of race, gender, and immigration in late twentieth-century America. Not simply an attempt to rework public assistance, welfare reform fundamentally engaged the questions of what is America and who is an American. Its response to these questions signals a troubling shift in American ideas of citizenship.

Part of a frontal attack on the rights and protections of workers in the U.S. economy, welfare reform solidified a neoliberal model of civil society, in which the social functions of the state are increasingly privatized and tied to corporate interests. Devolving federal power to state and local government, and institutionalizing time-limited and work-based welfare, PRWORA abandoned the federal government's commitment to universal entitlement and social citizenship symbolized by President Franklin Roosevelt's New Deal and strengthened in the 1960s by President Lyndon Johnson's civil rights legislation and the War on Poverty. As historian Michael Katz asserts, by dismantling the social safety net and forcing people to take any job regardless of the pay and working conditions, PRWORA ushered in a new private model of citizenship, under which "the responsibility for economic security [no longer rests] on charity, employers and the state, but with autonomous individuals taking charge of their lives."[23]

At the same time, this legislation further legitimated a category of second-class citizenship for welfare recipients, carving away at their civil liberties through increased information sharing between government agencies, new reporting requirements, and limiting of due process. This retrenchment of American civil liberties was brought into sharp relief by PRWORA's ban on food stamp benefits and Supplemental Security Income (SSI) for most legal immigrants, and its imposition of a five-year waiting period on all new immigrants, regardless of their immigration status or financial need, before they could apply for public assistance. Along with the Immigration Reform Act of 1996, this legislation also expanded the government's surveillance of the immigrant population by imposing stricter "public charge" standards, and by requiring welfare officials to investigate and report any "suspicious aliens," in effect, transforming the welfare system into a semiautonomous arm of the INS. Whereas throughout the twentieth century immigrants had slowly gained many of the same political and social rights as citizens, welfare reform dramatically reversed this trend by widening the gap between these two groups and creating a new category of permanently disentitled persons inside the body politic.[24] Enacted at a time when the vast majority of immigrants arriving to the United States are nonwhite, the assault on immigrant rights under the PWRORA was part of a broader attack on civil rights. As legal scholar Dorothy Roberts argues, with its anti-immigrant provisions and its assault on the reproductive freedom of poor black and brown women, welfare reform "sent a powerful message about who is worthy to add their children to the future community of citizens."[25]

In the first part of this book, we argue that welfare reform garnered nationwide popularity and marked the ascendancy of post–civil rights politics because it braided together three themes that had dominated the American political stage since the 1970s: the anti-federalist, anti-tax movement that galvanized white suburbanites and gave rise to the New Right; the backlash against the radical civil rights and women's movements; and a "new nativism" directed at immigrants from Asia and Latin America. In the wake of the freedom struggles of the 1960s, conservatives could no longer draw on overtly racist justifications for denying people of color full and equal citizenship. Instead, they turned to a covert discourse that associated urban blacks and new immigrants with cultural pathology and economic dependency. This discourse on urban crisis gained full legitimacy under the Democratic presidency of William Jefferson Clinton, who ascended to the White House partly on his 1992 campaign promise to "end welfare as we know it." Indeed, it would take a New South Democrat like Bill Clinton—celebrated by African-American novelist Toni Morrison as the nation's "first black president"—to ring in America's post–civil rights era and its triumphal event, the dismantling of welfare.

The Triumph of Post–Civil Rights Politics

Advocates of welfare reform strategically linked two groups together in public discourse—blacks and nonwhite immigrants—who were constructed as freeloaders and threats to the national community. Yet, while drawing on age-old ideologies about people of color, welfare reform ultimately rested on a post–civil rights paradigm that distinguished hardworking immigrants from lazy ones, successful African Americans from their underclass brothers and sisters. Blacks, Asians, and Latinos who had "made it" were now held up as proof that race no longer determines individual life chances in U.S. society, and thus that poverty and racial inequality now resulted from the dysfunctional "culture" and behavior of urban blacks and immigrants.

Along with the token celebration of exemplary minorities (and a concurrent demonization of the black and brown masses), post–civil rights discourse invoked a narrative of absolution and reconciliation in which America's tragic history of racism—reduced to flashpoints like slavery, Chinese exclusion, Jim Crow laws—stood as proof of the nation's contemporary rebirth as a "colorblind" society. Racism in the past was represented as undeniable and regrettable and juxtaposed to the present where racial problems were complex and morally murky. It was now racist to draw attention to race and to privilege group rights over individual rights. Racial disparities in employment and education did not bespeak ongoing discrimination, but rather revealed the "different aptitudes" of different racial groups. It was now racist *not* to talk about the "dysfunction within" black and Latino communities, and few public figures felt the need to scrutinize the way that contemporary images of welfare recipients called up age-old stereotypes of black and Latina women as lazy, irresponsible, and promiscuous. Civil rights legislation and liberal programs from the 1960s, like affirmative action and bilingual education, were not only obsolete in this new colorblind society, but they were also racist because they discriminated against whites and stigmatized people of color. Welfare was no longer a hard-won program that protected the rights of workers and families, but an unjust system that extended special favors to undeserving minorities at the expense of America's "working families."

The nativism that swept contemporary American politics in the 1990s resonated with post–civil rights ideology in a number of ways. While decrying the history of Asian exclusion acts and racist immigration quotas, politicians, journalists, and ordinary citizens characterized post-1965 immigration law as nondiscriminatory, while they drew on racialized images of hordes of Latino and Asian immigrants to argue that America's "open door policy" had gone too far. Whereas nativism in the past had been driven by irrational xenophobia, calls for immigration reform in the present were justified by a "realistic" assessment of the nation's inability to absorb more newcomers. And while immigrants continued to be symbolically celebrated as the personification of American freedom and opportunity, they were simultaneously blamed for everything from unemployment to pollution to rising taxes to the decline of the English language.

The "new nativism" of the 1990s was characterized by a tactical shift to a gendered discourse that targeted immigrant women as rampant biological reproducers and depleters of public resources. As recently as the 1970s, immigrants had been primarily attacked as cheap workers who undercut wages and stole American jobs. Less than two decades later, when the recession of the early 1990s devastated federal and state budgets and led to major cutbacks in public spending, nativist discourse shifted from a focus on immigrant labor (understood as male) to the arena of public entitlements and social services (as represented by immigrant women). In the years preceding the passage of welfare reform, polarizing images of poor, nonwhite immigrant women and children (particularly Mexicans) overcrowding welfare offices, emergency rooms, maternity wards, and schools dominated national debate about the public cost of immigration. Major newspapers perpetuated the association between immigrants and welfare with sensationalist headlines like "Why Immigrants get More Welfare: Family Size a Key Factor, Study Says," and "Study Backs Fears About Immigrants: Report Shows Higher Welfare Dependence."[26] The linking of new immigration to welfare dependency to rampant reproduction to an erosion of the social fabric of the United States played on white fears of a demographic and political takeover by people of color. Unlike their native-born black and Latino counterparts, new immigrants were perceived to have arrived in this country without the "baggage" of historical racism, and because they were competing in an even playing field, they had no need for or claim to the social protections born out of civil rights struggles. This message was echoed by President Clinton in 1993: "We must not—we will not—surrender our borders to those who wish to exploit our history of compassion and justice."[27] The portrayal of immigrants as welfare cheats who were getting a "free ride" on the nation's liberal social policies resonated with post–

civil rights ideas about race. It also facilitated the rolling back of civil rights more broadly as immigrant access to "benefits" (like affirmative action, welfare, and voting rights) became further evidence of the bankruptcy of liberal public policy.

Central to post–civil rights discourse was the value of work, not only fiscally but also psychically uplifting—and particularly liberating for Third World immigrant women. Many Americans argued that wage labor would lead to growing freedom for women from repressive patriarchal cultures by giving them more autonomy and economic power in the household.[28] Unlike immigrant women's home countries, which remained mired in traditional sex roles, the United States had emerged from the turmoil of the 1960s as a gender equal society in which women were no longer limited by their sex. Calls for immigrant women to liberate themselves from their culturally defined gender roles, however, conveniently corresponded to the nation's growing demand for immigrant domestic labor. In the post-feminist era, immigrant women's domestic labor in their own homes was characterized as oppressive, but this same labor when performed in other people's homes was seen as an act of independence.

Whether targeted at immigrant or native-born welfare recipients, the work-first provisions of PRWORA were justified not merely as a punishment for laziness, but also as a way to help poor women to transform themselves by overcoming their "dependency" and building their "self-esteem." Welfare-to-work initiatives taught women participants to understand all facets of their lives—from economic hardship to limited educational opportunities to domestic violence and substance abuse—as personal "traumas" and shortcomings that could be overcome by the improved self-esteem that comes from getting off of welfare and into a job. Work was cast as a form of female self-empowerment, regardless of the low pay and onerous and often humiliating conditions that recipients had to withstand at the bottom of the labor market. It also became a symbolic marker of good motherhood, as welfare recipients were encouraged to be "working role models" for their children, but were provided with very few supports to effectively juggle full-time employment with their mothering responsibilities. With its psychologizing of poverty and its call for poor women to fix themselves (without a correlative effort to fix the structural problems that reproduce female poverty), welfare reform echoed the broader ideology of post-feminism in U.S. society, which appropriated the consciousness-raising component of 1960s feminism but stripped it of its radical political overtones. American women were now instructed to look to their own behavior and psychology as contributors to gender inequity. Through welfare-to-work programs and best-selling books, workshops, and television programs on "women who love too much," "reclaiming your self-esteem," and "overcoming codependency," the obstacles and problems faced by women were treated as individual, not collective, and the solution lay in women changing themselves rather than changing society.

Toward a New Poverty Knowledge

Almost a decade ago we embarked on a research collaboration that sought to better understand the linking of African Americans and immigrants in anti-welfare discourse. As graduate students at the University of Michigan, Jeanne in African American Studies and Alejandra in Latino Studies, we were concerned that liberal social science's embrace of underclass theory, while aiming for better conditions for communities of color, was contributing to the growing consensus in American politics that cultural pathology and dependency were the main problems facing poor Americans.[29] With its focus on poor people's behavior and downplaying of political, economic, and historical analysis, research on the underclass had contributed to the dangerous belief that American cities were facing an unprecedented moral breakdown. Our fears about the dangers of this scholarship were confirmed in 1996 with the passage of PRWORA—and thus our first project was to chart the ways that liberal social science research had produced the paradigms on which welfare reform was built.

In 1998, Alejandra was invited to contribute to an ethnographic study of welfare reform being directed by Manpower Demonstration Research Corporation (MDRC), one of the leading research organizations in the field of poverty and welfare policy. Entitled "The Project on Devolution and Urban Change," MDRC's three-year, multimethod study proposed to research the effects of welfare reform on poor families and neighborhoods across racial groups in four metropolitan counties across the nation, Miami-Dade, Philadelphia, Cleveland-Cuyahoga, and Los Angeles. Having spent the previous year and a half conducting ethnographic research on Mexican and Central American immigrants in Long Beach, Alejandra had witnessed firsthand the crucial role that government programs like AFDC, Medi-Cal, and food stamps played in the survival of Latino immigrant families. Knowing that MDRC's evaluation of welfare reform would capture the attention of key policymakers, this constituted a rare opportunity to introduce the voices and experiences of Latina immigrants into the public debate over welfare reform.

Beginning in the fall of 1998, Alejandra worked to identify and recruit a group of Mexican immigrant welfare recipients in Long Beach to participate in the Urban Change study.[30] Given the research parameters laid out by MDRC, particularly the requirement that ethnographers only interview women who received cash benefits for themselves as well as their children, this task proved extremely difficult. As Alejandra discovered after working with local teachers, residents, and community leaders to identify participants for the study, most of the Mexican immigrant families who received welfare did so only for their children. The welfare recipient that MDRC wanted for its project was the exception, not the rule, in the city's Mexican immigrant community. It took nearly six months to find respondents who met the sampling criteria. For the next two years, she tracked these women's lives as they grappled with the new welfare rules, attended job programs, filled out employment applications, moved in and out of work, and struggled to find adequate childcare. Simultaneously, she watched these women as they helped their children with their homework, took care of sick family members, celebrated birthdays, went to church, shopped for groceries, and fought to keep their heads above water in the post-welfare era. Once a year, Alejandra conducted an extensive semistructured interview in Spanish with each woman, using an interview protocol designed by MDRC. This interview included questions about the new welfare requirements and paperwork, their experiences in the labor market, their monthly expenditures, and their family's health and well-being. In between these annual interviews, she kept in regular contact through phone calls and informal visits to their homes. Alejandra's ethnographic research, however, exceeded MDRC's study; she added more questions on their life and work histories and introduced a new set of questions on their ideas on American rights and entitlement. A great deal of time was spent in everyday conversation, where topics ranged from relationship issues to troubles finding work to parenting.

During the course of this ethnographic research, Alejandra discovered that these Latinas defied most popular images of immigrant welfare recipients and the success of PRWORA. Most of these women were pushed off of welfare into low-wage jobs without adequate childcare and thwarted in their attempts to seek out additional education and training. Yet pieces of their interviews began appearing in MDRC reports that affirmed the general soundness of welfare reform, and stories like Myrna's filled newspaper accounts celebrating the success of the 1996 legislation. This chilling discrepancy prompted us to come together to write this book. We realized it would not be enough just to tell a different story about Myrna. The myth-busting facts and real stories about poor families on welfare have been available to the American public for decades, and yet have not dislodged popular ideas about welfare. While MDRC's own study had yielded more complicated findings, the nature of MDRC's methods for analyzing and reporting date made it impossible for these more far-ranging accounts to make it into the organization's reports.

Our book had to be a different kind of ethnography—one that joined political economy, history, analysis of representation, and critique of social science research with rich detail about people's lives. It also had to provide ample space for Latinas to theorize their own experiences and the larger society around them. It needed the outsider perspective that Jeanne could provide to the ethnographic material and on the framework for the collection and interpretation of the data that MDRC had put forth. It drew on Alejandra's previous ethnographic work with undocumented immigrants in Long Beach. And it took years of sifting and resifting through the interviews, of arranging and rearranging the material, of doing extensive research on the history of Long Beach and Southern California's global economy, and considerable analysis of the limits of liberal social science and media reporting on welfare to create the book as it stands today.

This collaborative book thus aims to chart a different path for thinking about poverty. It rejects the values-and-attitudes framework for thinking about poor women's social position, examining the variety of forces at work that shape a person's place in American society and looking at the myriad and contradictory ways that women engage dominant ideology and formulate knowledge about themselves and the world. Women like Myrna appear in this book as a constellation of voices and ideas, not as fully drawn subjects, in part because of the fragmentary lens imposed by the Urban Change study, but primarily because ethnography is always fractured and incomplete. The power of this research lies, then, not in explaining these women or "telling their lives," but in elaborating on their explanations of the most pressing issues we face as a nation: the widening gap between rich and poor, the country's growing dependence on and concurrent rejection of its immigrants, ongoing racial inequality, and the dangerous abdication of societal responsibility for addressing these problems.

Our book places political economy at the center of an evaluation of poverty and welfare reform. It interweaves a critique of social science and the politics of representation with a ground-level study that engages Mexican immigrant women's ideas about social science and representation. It expands our vision from the domestic spaces of women's lives to the public arenas of the welfare state, the labor market, and social science research. While this book focuses on Mexican immigrant women, it does not treat them as a window onto "Mexican culture," but as racialized subjects in the welfare debate and society at large. Finally, we do not presume to construct full portraits of these women's inner lives, families, and histories, nor to convince the reader of their moral worthiness for the entitlements of citizenship.

The Latina mothers who appear in these pages agreed to participate in this study because they wanted to talk about welfare reforms, get-to-work rules, family caps, and government cutbacks. The same themes run throughout hours of audiotape: neither work nor welfare pay and I need both to get by; I am a good mother but am constantly asked to make choices that are not good for my children; welfare is not a "free ride" but takes work to get on and stay on; I believe that I should be personally responsible for myself and my family but so should the government; this is not an open and equal society, but rather one in which race determines your position in life, and your access to jobs, welfare, and education.

Indeed, these Latinas repeatedly moved the discussion away from questions about their budgets, mental health, and family relations to conversations about the government's spending priorities, racism in the welfare office, and the subordinate place of Latinos in the global economy. In doing so, they implicitly rejected their construction as solely domestic subjects, asserting their place alongside other experts in the domain of public discourse and government policy. Acutely aware of the ways that they were represented in U.S. society, they not only contested these images of themselves, their children, and their communities but also spoke to the faulty assumptions at play in welfare policy. These Latinas thus challenge the misconception that poor people are too busy surviving to create social theory.

However, at the same time that these women advanced a critique of dominant ideologies about work, welfare, and personal responsibility, they still recognized themselves in media portrayals of welfare recipients and drew on these same discourses when describing themselves, their choices, and those of other women on welfare. These women, thus, did not stand outside of social ideology. Many called up the myth of the welfare queen, attacking other women for being bad mothers and abusing the system, so as to stake their own identities as righteous mothers and lawful citizens. While pointing to the multiple constraints placed on their choices and opportunities, these Latinas still persisted in blaming themselves and their choices for their family's situation. Most agreed that welfare reform was a necessary measure to weed out dependency and fraud, even as they persistently worried about what would happen to poor families in the aftermath of reform and challenged the priorities of a society that would put children at risk. These women foregrounded the political and economic forces beyond their control that delimit their life chances, yet they simultaneously asserted their own responsibility in determining their family's future. Beneath these immigrant women's language of personal choice and self-blame is a claim to individual autonomy and citizenship. Still, because this claim lies too close to the public discourse of personal responsibility that undergirds welfare reform, it ultimately boomerangs back upon these women, holding them and only them responsible for their poverty. At a time when politicians and the mainstream press regularly cite welfare recipients' own support for welfare reform and personal responsibility as proof that these policies are necessary and sound, progressive scholars and activists must pay closer, more critical attention to the slippery role of ideology in ensuring social control.

Studying Immigrant Welfare Use

While some scholars have critiqued the construction of Latina immigrants as welfare abusers, few have researched the use of welfare among immigrants, understandably out of fear that this could inadvertently bolster the anti-immigration cause. Instead, most social scientists have focused on the "immigrant working poor," producing studies of the labor market effects of immigration, of workplace experiences and unionization drives among new immigrants, and of the settlement process and living conditions in poor immigrant communities.[31] This rich body of quantitative and qualitative research has provided us with an important understanding of "how the other half works" and of the centrality of immigrant labor in the post-Fordist economy.[32] However, much of this empiricist work accepts as given that immigrants *are* cheap labor, while failing to critically analyze the ways that immigrants are rendered "cheap" through racial, gender, and national ideologies, as well as through government policies like welfare reform.

Although feminist post-colonial studies has paid closer attention to the role of ideology in shaping global labor arrangements, few have considered the effects of the welfare state on these processes. Research on "the "feminization of labor" in the global economy has documented the experiences of female migrant workers in U.S. cities and Third World export-manufacturing zones, and the pivotal role of feminized labor in securing the global economic hegemony of the United States.[33] While this scholarship has yielded important insights about the centrality of gender and race in transnational migration flows, it has notably failed to address the relationship between immigrants and the welfare state.

Similarly, within a vast and rich body of scholarship on welfare, there is little treatment of immigrants on welfare. Most of this work focuses on African-American and white women inside the welfare system and posits the issues of race and welfare along a black-white continuum.[34] And, despite a growing literature on the "new immigration" to the United States, there are few qualitative works that analyze the experiences of immigrants on welfare.[35]

This gap is partly explained by the fact that immigrants comprise a small percentage of the national welfare population and are proportionally less likely to receive aid than their native-born counterparts. However, when we look at states with large immigrant populations, the welfare rate among noncitizens is significant; for example, prior to the passage of welfare reform, immigrants accounted for nearly a quarter of California's AFDC caseload.[36] Moreover, most figures on the welfare population refer only to AFDC/TANF, not the full array of anti-poverty programs like Medicaid and food stamps that immigrants use with more regularity.

In the current political climate, when conservatives closely associate new immigrants with skyrocketing taxes and welfare dependency, liberals have explained that *most* immigrants are not on welfare. This retort implicitly makes welfare shameful and ignores the reasons why immigrants would need public assistance. It perpetuates the idea that people who use welfare are deviant, reinforcing the distinction between good immigrants who eschew welfare and bad immigrants who use it. It also bolsters, however unintentionally, the construction of welfare as a behavioral problem—not a by-product of economic inequality.

Fundamentally, then, liberal silence around immigrant welfare use inadvertently divorces the struggle for welfare rights from that for immigrant rights. As we argue throughout this book, untrammeled access to the welfare safety net is essential to economic stability and social citizenship in the United States. An examination of immigrants and welfare is especially crucial today when welfare reform has reinforced the economic exploitation of immigrants in the laborforce. Strict new work requirements and welfare-to-work programs force immigrant welfare recipients to accept low-paying and unstable employment, while driving down wages, displacing workers, and eroding labor protections in industries where immigrant workers are most heavily concentrated.

PRWORA has also transformed the welfare state into a key vehicle for the design and implementation of immigration policy. Because most immigration scholarship focuses on the macrolevel of federal law and policy, it offers a very limited understanding of the process by which public policies take shape at the local level. Scholars too often assume that the INS is the main state agency to shape immigrant lives, and therefore ignore other public institutions like schools, welfare offices, hospitals, and neighborhood clinics through which immigrants—and particularly immigrant women—have regular interaction with the state. This myopic focus on the INS not only misses the fundamental influence of other state agencies in immigrant communities, but it also fails to capture the gendered dimensions of immigrant settlement. Sociologist Pierrette Hondagneu-Sotelo's research has shown how Mexican immigrant women facilitate the settlement process by acting as mediators between their families and the state.[37] While research has focused on immigrant women's participation in public schools and community-based organizations, it has paid less attention to their interactions within welfare offices and other social service agencies.

This study also seeks to intervene in current debates about citizenship and nation building in the era of globalization. In the 1990s, critics from across the political spectrum predicted that globalization would erode the significance of nation-based citizenship.[38] Our book challenges this view, asserting that globalization has given renewed importance to citizenship in contemporary American life. The surge of nationalism that peaked in the 1990s reasserted the symbolic power of citizenship in American politics at the same time as nativist laws like PRWORA restricted a greater number of rights and entitlements to citizens only. Citizenship has indeed become a prized possession and an increasingly powerful marker of personhood in the national community.

This can be seen in the historic boom in naturalization applications in the past decade as immigrants moved to safeguard the rights now restricted to citizens and to claim their voice in U.S. society. Whereas naturalization had steadily declined during the postwar period, in 1996 alone, the United States gained a record one million new citizens with Southern California home to more than one-third of the nation's new citizenry.[39] Equally unprecedented was the sharp increase in Latino applications for U.S. citizenship, particularly among Mexicans who have historically had one of the lowest naturalization rates of immigrant groups. These two phenomena—the rise of anti-immigrant politics targeting public entitlements and the dramatic increase in newly naturalized citizens—exemplify different responses to the instability brought about by globalization. Yet both turn to citizenship, in practice and in theory, as a central site for the negotiation of opposing visions of nationhood and individual and group identities.

Focusing on the experiences of Mexican immigrant women in welfare-to-work programs, this book takes up welfare reform as a window onto emergent immigration control tactics in post-Fordist America. Alongside the increased policing of welfare recipients, we have witnessed the monumental expansion of what cultural geographer Joseph Nevins calls the "border control industry," a set of discursive practices and government programs that further the criminalization of immigrants in U.S. society.[40] Yet, while framed in a language of national sovereignty and security, "immigration control" is not designed to stop undocumented immigration. Instead, these policing practices manage transnational labor flows that fuel the U.S. economy, while they simultaneously erect higher borders to the entitlements of U.S. citizenship by *producing* distinctions among people based on national origin, immigration status, class, race, and gender.[41]

While there has been sporadic public outcry over the most dramatic consequences of this policing—legal residents deported without due process, migrants shot down by the Border Patrol or dying in the desert—there has been little attention to the far more pervasive and mundane "immigration control tactics" which are normalized and exercised within the welfare state. Today, as local welfare offices increasingly work in collaboration with (and sometimes autonomous from) the INS, they function to monitor and discipline poor immigrants. The place where many immigrant women have their most concrete and regular experience with the state, welfare offices become a stage for daily struggles over entitlement, citizenship, and rights.

Indeed, for Latinas in Long Beach, immigrant life entails a constant negotiation with the disciplinary welfare state. Their experiences within this system shed light on a fundamental dimension of "immigration control" —one that aims not to keep immigrants out, but rather to regulate and relegate them into a class of flexible workers that sits outside the boundaries of full membership in U.S. society. Under welfare reform, power operates externally through punitive rules and sanctions and internally by getting welfare recipients to engage in a process of self-management and rehabilitation. By training recipients to link their own empowerment to getting off welfare (while also purging people from the rolls) the state diverts broad-based anger against repressive social policy by making the decision to leave welfare an individual one. By teaching poor women that personal responsibility means taking any job at any wage (while also forcing them to do so), welfare policy promotes worker docility and availability by promoting the decision to take a low-paying job as an act of self-improvement.[42]

However, this is not an absolute system of social control. Rather, the Latina immigrants who participated in this study were located on the fissures of these practices of power. As they called for real education and job training that would link them to high-paying and satisfying jobs, and accessible and quality childcare, they highlighted the gap between welfare reform's spectacle of empowerment and the "real goods" of citizenship in a democratic society.

These women's experiences in the welfare system and the labor market tell us that pragmatic reforms like increased childcare and transportation vouchers are useful and necessary to their family's well-being (indeed, most asserted that without more support they could not meet the minimum work requirements of TANF). But they do not get to the heart of the problem. Testifying to widespread discrimination and disentitlement within the welfare state, these women stressed the dangers of devolution and reaffirmed the importance of federal oversight and standards in social welfare provision. Speaking of the sharp racial segmentation of the labor market and the preponderance of unstable, poverty-wage jobs, their interviews remind us of the structural context of poverty and the need for a radical revisioning of the economic paradigms and social priorities that guide U.S. welfare policy. While they reaffirm the ideology of individual responsibility at the heart of welfare reform, they simultaneously bring into sharp relief the ongoing salience of race and citizenship in constraining the choices and opportunities open to different groups of individuals in U.S. society.

Organization of the Book

The book is organized into two parts. Part I sets the historical, political-economic, and geographic stage for the ethnographic writing that follows. The first chapter traces the history of racialized ideas about public entitlement in the United States. It focuses on two concurrent transformations in the 1980s and 1990s that made welfare reform possible: shifting racial ideologies and the "new nativism" in the post–civil rights era; and globalization and the restructuring of U.S. cities and suburbs. Broad in scope, this chapter foregrounds a number of themes that run throughout the book, including the racialization of Latino immigration, the role played by liberal social science in the passage of welfare reform, the relationship between welfare reform and the new labor demands of the post-Fordist economy, and the emergence of a neoliberal model of citizenship.

The second chapter moves from the national and global arenas to look at how these processes play out on the local level in Southern California and the city of Long Beach, in particular. This chapter uses Long Beach as an illustrative example of the emergent "global suburb" and the ways that local actors shape the racialized path of globalization. By focusing on Long Beach, which is today a port of entry for new immigrants and boasts one of the highest poverty rates in L.A. County, this chapter challenges long-held views of suburbs as a postwar refuge for the white middle class. The epitome of dependency on federal funds, Long Beach had flourished throughout the twentieth century through federal subsidies in ports, housing, highways, and defense. By the 1980s, as defense jobs and white residents left the city, Long Beach had gained national notoriety as a casualty of the end of the Cold War and an unwitting magnet for non-white immigrants, especially from Latin America and Asia. Today, Long Beach is celebrated as a model for urban renewal, as the city has invested billions of dollars in razing low-income areas for downtown redevelopment. This chapter, then, critically examines the history of Long Beach's redevelopment and the role of municipal policy in redeveloping poverty and segregation.

Part II focuses on our ethnographic study of Mexican immigrant women in Long Beach, as they navigate the new mandates of welfare reform. This part is organized into three interlocking chapters: an account of the implementation and effects of welfare reform in L.A. County; an analysis of how these women's paths through work and welfare disrupt the discourse behind welfare reform and the methods used to push people off of welfare; and a critical look at the ideology of "personal responsibility" (and its two subdiscourses of "self-esteem" and "choice") that undergirds welfare reform.

Although L.A. County's welfare-to-work program, GAIN (Greater Avenues for Independence), has been held up as a model for other cities to follow, we contend that GAIN has been largely unsuccessful in helping these welfare recipients to achieve "self-sufficiency." While claiming to open up social mobility to culturally deprived groups, GAIN fundamentally revolves around soft skills training, rather than substantive education and structural change. By ideologically reconditioning welfare recipients to accept "any job at any wage," and to link their empowerment to getting off of welfare, the program helps to produce low-wage and compliant workers for the post-Fordist economy. Perhaps the strongest theme that emerged from our research with Latina recipients was the contrast between the welfare state's language of individual opportunity and self-improvement and the lack of opportunity they were given to pursue their personal goals. Most entered L.A. County's welfare-to-work program with specific ideas about what type of education and training they needed, and the types of jobs that they would most excel at, but in fact none were encouraged or assisted in the pursuit of these aspirations. Part II, thus, foregrounds the ways that these *mexicanas* engage with and reformulate ideologies of work, welfare, personal responsibility, and citizenship as they make their way through the new welfare-to-work regime.

The concluding chapter of the book critically reflects on the problems and politics of poverty research through a systematic analysis of this ethnographic study of Mexican immigrant welfare recipients. The ethnographic data that appears here was originally collected as part of a larger nationwide evaluation of welfare reform, the Urban Change Project, commissioned by MDRC. But the ethnography we present in Part II and the questions it raises about the failure of welfare reform is startlingly different from the more positive story being put forth about welfare reform in MDRC's reports on Urban Change findings. MDRC's research has and will continue to have a deep impact on public understandings of welfare reform and on the shape of welfare reauthorization. Mirroring the work of many other researchers, MDRC's reports have contributed to a widespread celebration of the success of the 1996 legislation and a modest set of improvements and cautions for TANF reauthorization. The Urban Change Project, thus, provides an illuminating case study of the myopia of post-1996 evaluations of welfare reform and the ways this has delimited public debates over reauthorization and anti-poverty policy.

PART I

Neither a Hand Up
nor a Handout

1

Ending Welfare

New Nativism and the Triumph of Post–Civil Rights Politics

The passage of PRWORA in August 1996 heralded the success of a "post–civil rights consensus" in American politics. Americans had come to embrace the idea that race no longer determines individual success or failure, and that the government should only help those who help themselves. The emerging consensus among liberal politicians, scholars, and journalists around the *cultural* nature of welfare reflected a confidence that the nation had moved past its own history of denigrating the "cultures" of nonwhite people. With his set of black friends and New South background, President Bill Clinton was well situated to usher in a post-welfare world that played on racial imagery and ensured a racially bifurcated workforce while disavowing that race had anything to do with it. Indeed, the PRWORA sent a stark message about race and citizenship in late twentieth-century America. By marking who would have and who would be denied access to state protection and public benefits, welfare reform was a form of civic disfranchisement that had long roots in the racialized politics of American entitlements.

Equally historic was the PRWORA's intervention in the arena of U.S. immigration policy. Welfare reform served as a "back door" to immigration reform as it widened the gap between citizens and legal immigrants, created immigrant categories entirely new to U.S. law, and opened up new channels of surveillance and information-sharing between social service agencies and the Immigration and Naturalization Service (INS). Riding on the political momentum of California's Proposition 187, the 1994 ballot initiative that sought to bar undocumented immigrants from most social services, welfare reform signaled the emergence of an anti-immigrant agenda markedly different from other periods of nativism in U.S. history.[1]

This "new nativism" represents immigrants from Latin America and Asia not so much as threats to American workers, as in previous decades, but increasingly as threats to the civic and fiscal community.[2] Accompanying this shift in focus is a gendered language for immigration that vilifies immigrant women as welfare cheats and overly fertile breeders, who are responsible for the "browning of America." Yet, although the new nativism deploys a racial-nationalist discourse, policies like Proposition 187 and PRWORA ultimately further a neoliberal agenda, in which the state serves the interests of global capital by ensuring the availability of a foreign-born and female low-wage workforce in the United States.[3]

Despite evidence of a shortage of jobs with living wages for welfare recipients to get out of poverty, the PRWORA accepted the labor market as is: recipients were the ones needing fixing, not the economy.[4] The legislation's "work-first" approach required welfare recipients to accept any job, regardless of pay, work conditions, and childcare considerations. Those recipients who cannot secure paid employment were placed in "workfare" assignments, performing work in the public sector in order to receive their monthly welfare stipends. However, workfare assignments did not have to be new jobs, workfare workers were not accorded the labor protections other workers have under national law, and there were no requirements for job training or higher education. Passed amidst a resurgence of labor activism in the United States, and particularly at a time when service sector unions like the Service Employees International Union (SEIU) had made significant gains in organizing female and immigrant workers, welfare reform unleashed a frontal assault on organized labor. Not only did this policy force millions of low-skilled workers into a deregulated labor market, but it also did not require states to keep records on what happens to recipients once they leave the welfare rolls. Thus, there were few safeguards to protect individuals as states seek to reduce their rolls by any means available, and as employers capitalize on the vulnerability of this new workforce.

The dismantling of the American social welfare system provides a revealing window into the role of the nation-state under late twentieth-century capitalism. On the one hand, welfare reform represents an attempt to tighten the reigns of state authority and to reassert U.S. sovereignty in the face of global economic integration. The second most significant piece of legislation of the 1990s, following the 1994 North American Free Trade Agreement (NAFTA)—passed at a time when Ford cars and Sears clothing are manufactured in Third World "free trade zones" and when the gospel of free trade is used to undermine the power of workers around the world—the PRWORA offered American voters insulation against the tide of globalization. Vilified as an affront to American values of family, individualism, and self-reliance, black and Latina welfare mothers confirmed the voting public's sense of Americanness precisely by serving as its antithesis.[5]

Yet, although framed by a moralistic discussion of the psychosocial benefits of work and "self-reliance," the actual rewards of welfare reform were to be found in the economic benefits of an enlarged low-wage workforce within the United States. Through its work-first approach, the PRWORA ensured a plentiful workforce vulnerable to the demands of global capital. By imposing time limits on welfare, welfare reform eradicated social subsidies as an alternative or supplement to low-wage work, shifting more power to employers to set wage levels and working conditions. Welfare reform followed from NAFTA's paradigms—removing the national fetters on work and trade while erecting higher boundaries to entitlement and state protection.[6] Supporters sold both NAFTA and PRWORA through the neoliberal logic of free trade, arguing that lifting trade restrictions and social subsides would elevate all workers. Yet, the economic effects of both policies have hardly been elevating for those at the bottom of the economic ladder. Indeed, the PRWORA provides a telling window on the centrality of race within the ideologies fueling globalization: by playing on faulty assumptions about the cultures and values of people of color, such ideologies legitimate economic policies that maintain, if not exacerbate, racial hierarchies.

The War on Welfare: From Deserving Mothers to Welfare Queens

AFDC had its roots in the mother's pensions programs instituted by most states in the 1910s and 1920s that sought to reinforce women's domestic role and keep mothers out of the workplace by giving "deserving mothers"—white women with children—a small subsidy.[7] In 1935, in the midst of a savage depression and mounting political unrest, Congress passed the Social Security Act, creating five new programs to provide a safety net for Americans if they were to come on hard times: unemployment compensation, old-age insurance, Aid to the Blind, Old Age Assistance, and Aid to Dependent Children (ADC, changed to AFDC in 1962).

ADC benefits were "designed to release from the wage earning role the person whose natural function is to give her children the physical and affectionate guardianship necessary."[8] Yet, because states had control over most New Deal programs, and because, particularly in the South, white politicians feared losing black women's agricultural and domestic labor, black women were largely deemed ineligible for ADC benefits, barred during the cotton harvesting season, or intimidated from even applying.[9] "Suitable home" provisions found in the statute were often enforced on a racial basis; caseworkers disqualifying black children if their mothers did apply.[10] In the Southwest, local relief agencies shut their doors to immigrant and U.S.-born Mexican applicants, using federal welfare dollars instead to assist police and immigration authorities in "repatriating" over one million ethnic Mexicans during the 1930s. Thus, welfare was largely not accessible to African-American and Mexican-American families.

Turned away from their entitlements as mothers, women of color were also denied their rights as workers. Both the Social Security Act and the Wagner Act enacted special exemptions for agricultural workers and domestic servants, leaving the majority of Mexican and black workers ineligible for the minimum wage and unprotected under Old Age and Unemployment Assistance and union legislation. Forged by a powerful coalition between southern politicians and white organized labor, the New Deal created what historian Jill Quadagno calls a "racial welfare state regime," one that denied people of color "the full perquisites of citizenship," while ensuring their availability as a flexible, low-wage workforce for U.S. employers.[11] At the close of the twentieth century, this racial regime would be revived under the PRWORA's welfare-to-work mandate.

Indeed, although AFDC had never been a very popular program, the backlash against welfare began when women of color began demanding access to the entitlements that had long been the prerogative of whites. In the late 1960s, growing activism in communities of color, particularly the formation of the National Welfare Rights Organization (NWRO) in 1967, led to change in the welfare system, and as historian Michael Katz notes, "for the first time, social welfare policy became one strategy for attacking the consequences of racism in America."[12] Civil rights activists pushed to open AFDC to all those who met means-tested standards and lobbied to increase benefits to ensure that they met poor families' basic needs. Framing welfare as a right and a matter of equality, the NWRO took its message to the streets, into welfare offices, in front of state legislatures, and before the courts on behalf of the rights of poor women. By

1969, its membership reached 25,000 with thousands more participating in NWRO-sponsored events. As Johnnie Tillmon, the first chairwoman of the NWRO and a black welfare recipient herself, argued:

> There are a lot of other lies that male society tells about welfare mothers: that AFDC mothers are immoral, that AFDC mothers are lazy, misuse their welfare checks, spend it all on booze and are stupid and incompetent. If people are willing to believe these lies, it's partly because they're just special versions of the lies that society tells about all women.[13]

Civil rights lawyers and NWRO activists challenged these stereotypes as they successfully fought to overturn "man in the house" rules, establish a right to a fair hearing to maintain or obtain welfare benefits, and ensure enforcement of little-known provisions in welfare regulations, outlining minimum standards for people on welfare.[14]

Chicana activists both in the NWRO and in separate Mexican-American organizations also challenged their exclusions from welfare and fought to oppose Nixon's support for work-based welfare. On November 7, 1967, over 75 Mexican-American welfare recipients gathered in East L.A. to protest cuts to medical, fight for access to full benefits, and form a new organization: the East Los Angeles Welfare Rights Organization.[15] In 1973, Chicanas spearheaded opposition to the Talmadge Amendment to the Social Security Act, which required mothers on public assistance with children over six to register with the state employment office and report every two weeks until they found work. As Sandra Ugarte wrote in *La Raza,*

> The taxpayers are not the only ones who want the poor to work—the poor also want to work. But at decent jobs with decent wages and without the stigma of welfare. . . . [Nixon's proposal] will force a cheap source of labor on the labor market at a time when job competition is already at a critical level. . . . Employers are already laying off their own employees and replacing them with welfare recipients at far reduced wage rates.[16]

Francisca Flores, founding director of the Chicana Service Action Center in Los Angeles, and Alicia Escalante, founder of the East Los Angeles Welfare Rights Organization that later became the Chicano National Welfare Rights Organization, led this opposition to Nixon's plan.[17]

These grassroots organizing efforts, along with President Lyndon Johnson's War on Poverty, opened welfare to those eligible, including women of color; by 1971, over 90 percent of eligible families were receiving AFDC, up from less than 33 percent in 1960. At the same time, increasing numbers of families faced extreme poverty in the late 1960s, particularly as a result of the mechanization of southern agriculture and deindustrialization in the North. By 1974, 10.8 million people were receiving AFDC, up from 3.1 million in 1961, and there was ample evidence that the expansion of AFDC and food stamp benefits was succeeding in reducing hunger and malnutrition in America.[18]

Although the AFDC rolls remained predominantly white in the 1960s, public discourse during this period almost exclusively associated welfare with unmarried and sexually irresponsible women of color. The large number of black women in the NWRO and the organization's ties to the civil rights movement inadvertently lent a black face to welfare. Moreover, an emergent liberal consensus flagged AFDC as a prime example of the "cultural deprivation" that plagued poor blacks and Latinos. Released in 1965, the influential Moynihan Report blamed the "Negro crisis" on black women who took jobs and status away from men, had babies without marrying, and formed matriarchal families dependent on government handouts. Published the following year, anthropologist Oscar Lewis's *La Vida: A Puerto Rican Family in the Culture of Poverty, San Juan and New York* legitimated the prevailing view of Latinos as culturally inferior with its thesis that poverty produces its own unique and self-defeating cultural patterns. Although intended to paint a sympathetic portrait of poor people by providing a rationale for their behavior, liberal tracts on the "culture of poverty" instead fueled public resentment toward irresponsible women of color and the liberal government programs that rewarded their bad choices.[19]

Equally pivotal in the war on welfare were the federal government's primary beneficiaries: middle-class whites. At the peak of the social revolts of the 1960s, white suburbanites launched a counterrevolution that propelled right-wing conservatism from the margins to the center of U.S. politics. Angered by the "lawlessness" of civil rights and student protests, and by what they perceived as the federal government's intrusion in their "private" affairs, white suburbanites mobilized to take back the nation from the Washington "establishment" of liberal intellectuals and radical minorities. Deploying the symbols of the McCarthy era, New Right conservatives forged a powerful social movement against state centralization, the spread of dangerous liberal ideas (like sex education and multiculturalism) in public school curricula, and the conspiracy to extend "special rights" to, as worded by one conservative newsletter, "the black and brown peoples of the world."[20]

High on the New Right's list of grievances were anti-poverty programs that redistributed middle-class tax dollars to "undeserving" minority groups. Introducing arguments that two decades later would dominate the welfare debate, conservatives in the 1960s and 1970s asserted that AFDC undermined free-market capitalism and American civil liberties. By providing individuals with a modicum of economic security, welfare produced "overly secure workers who are less likely to acquiesce to onerous working conditions," and violated the "freedom" of poor people by making them dependent on a centralized government. This argument was advanced in *The Socialist Plan for Conquest,* a political pamphlet published in 1966 by the California Free Enterprise Association (CFEA):[21]

> The difference between a free nation and a slave nation can be very simply stated. In a free nation, the people accept the responsibility for their own welfare; while in a slave nation the responsibility is turned over to the government. [. . .] They will want their government to guarantee minimum wages . . . full employment . . . good prices for their produce . . . good housing . . . medical care . . . such people are . . . choosing slavery rather than freedom . . . for this is the security of the penitentiary.[22]

The CFEA's association of welfare recipients with black slaves typified the New Right's effective strategy of disguising racist arguments in anti-communist and anti-federalist language. Avoiding the forthright (and politically unpopular) white supremacy typical of the Deep South, new conservatives couched their racist assault on welfare in a racially coded lexicon of "personal responsibility," "government intrusion," and "basic Americanism." For all its anti-government rhetoric, the New Right squarely located governmental power, public resources, and "basic rights" in the material and social interests of white citizens.

New Right ideology and organizations flourished in Sunbelt suburban locales like Orange County, California, and Scottsdale, Arizona, the bedrocks of "modern Americanism" that had been manufactured entirely by postwar federal policy and spending.[23] Historian Lisa McGirr's study of the New Right in Orange County, *Suburban Warriors,* illustrates this sharp contradiction in neoconservative politics. The wealthy white entrepreneurs and professionals, who formed the rank-and-file of Orange County's New Right, derived their privileges from a government that sent them to college, financed their homes and neighborhood schools, stimulated economic growth, and inflated their property values by zoning poor people and people of color out of their communities. Yet, these suburbanites obscured their profound dependency on the government by crediting their economic success to individual initiative and sacrifice, while attacking programs like AFDC and affirmative action for extending resources to undeserving blacks and other people of color.

This same contradictory ideology propelled Richard Nixon to the White House in 1968, through a platform that pitted working- and middle-class whites—America's "Silent Majority"—against radical minorities, criminals, and welfare recipients. Once in office, Nixon abolished Johnson's Equal Opportunity Office and then set out to reform the AFDC program, which he claimed discouraged able-bodied Americans from working and encouraged broken families and out-of-wedlock births. Painting AFDC and Great Society programs more generally as the special purview of minority groups, Nixon extended eligibility to low-wage white workers and shifted the emphasis in social service provision from reducing poverty to "enhancing human development and the general quality of life" through educational and "health-related" programs.[24] Recipients began receiving a smaller portion of their benefits as cash, whereas larger portions of federal and state welfare budgets went to public and private social service organizations charged with reforming the immoral behavior of poor people. The Nixon administration's limited expansion of the welfare state further entrenched a moral divide among the nation's poor—between hard-working whites and indolent blacks and Latinos—thus solidifying the link between whiteness and public entitlement.

White entitlement took a different turn with Reagan's arrival in the White House in 1980. In contrast to Nixon's strong working-class base, Reagan was elected governor of California in 1966 by cultivating close ties to private industry and the emergent power bloc of wealthy, conservative suburbanites. Reagan campaigned against "ultra-liberal" incumbent Governor Pat Brown for being soft on radicals, criminals and an inner-city "jungle . . . waiting to take over."[25] Pioneering the language that would later propel Nixon into the presidency, Reagan condemned civil rights legislation as a misguided attempt to "give one segment of the population a right at the expense of the basic rights of all our citizens," and threw his support behind the suburban-led Proposition 14 campaign to overturn the Rumford Fair Housing Act.[26] On the campaign trail, the first-time political candidate told a crowd in Southern California that he opposed open housing laws because in a free society all citizens have a "basic and cherished right to do as they please with their property. If an individual wants to discriminate against Negroes or others in selling or renting his house, then he has the right to do so."[27] Having championed the interests of big business and wealthy property owners in California, Reagan's challenge once in Washington was to continue advocating for the rich without alienating white working-class voters from the Republican Party.

Reagan's ingenious strategy was a two-pronged war against "big government" and "big labor." His administration attacked both Great Society programs and organized labor for inflating wages, discouraging foreign investment, and forcing U.S. corporations to move their operations overseas. Just as union "fat-cats" were lining their pockets with membership dues, opportunistic "welfare queens" were having babies just to collect a bigger government check. For Reagan, AFDC's shortcomings went beyond its fiscal cost to honest, hard-working (read "white") taxpayers. In his 1986 State of the Union address, the president openly denounced the AFDC system for propagating a "welfare culture" of "female and child poverty, child abandonment, horrible crimes, and deteriorating schools."[28]

The Shift to Post-Fordism

Reagan's strategic mix of libertarian and populist ideology widely appealed to white working-and-middle-class voters who were struggling to make sense of an economic crisis that shook the foundations of U.S. society. Beginning in the early 1970s, private divestment from manufacturing centers in the East and Midwest, coupled with the expansion of a low-wage service sector and light industry in the Sunbelt, profoundly transformed the U.S. labor market. In the 1970s, private divestment and capital flight cost over 38 million manufacturing jobs. Between 1979 and 1984, the poverty rate rose from 11.7 percent to 14.4 percent—a dramatic 23 percent increase.[29] The changing character of work began to erode public confidence in the Fordist promise of unrestrained economic growth and a rising national standard of living. The shift from manufacturing to service and high-tech information industries, and the deployment of just-in-time production techniques, made it easier for employers to replace full-time employment with part-time and temporary jobs and to "substitute lower-paid female labour for that of more highly paid and less easily laid-off core male workers."[30] As both real wages and publicly subsidized childcare shrank, the number of female-headed households living in poverty rose sharply. Between 1970 and 1978, the number of poor single mothers and their children grew by 38 percent, and by 1983, women accounted for two-thirds of all poor adults in the United States.[31]

By the mid-1980s, economic restructuring and globalization had profoundly altered the class and racial landscape of U.S. metropolitan centers. The transformation of industrial cities like New York and Chicago into global "command centers" for high finance, tourism, and technology produced what economists describe as an "hourglass economy," sharply divided between high-income and low-income workers.[32] Reindustrialization in Southwest cities like Los Angeles and Houston replaced unionized jobs in rubber and automobile manufacturing with sweatshop production in the growing garment and electronics industries. Economic restructuring disproportionately affected African-Americans and Latinos, who were concentrated in urban centers hit hard by corporate downsizing, factory shutdowns, and municipal cutbacks. "Last-hired, first fired" rules also contributed to massive lay-offs for black and Latino workers who, as a result of the anti-discrimination policies of the 1960s, had only recently gained entry into the skilled trades. In New York City, where manufacturing declined at three times the national rate, 40 percent of the city's Puerto Rican workers were unemployed by the mid-1980s. Also displaced from unionized blue-collar work, black workers were increasingly concentrated in low-wage clerical and service occupations in the private and public sectors (the latter devastated by the city's "fiscal restructuring" in the early 1990s, which cost 25,000 public jobs).[33] With similar patterns in cities across the nation, by 1985, the black unemployment rate had risen to a crisis level of 15.1 percent, followed by Latino unemployment at 10.5 percent.[34]

Beginning in the late 1960s, new immigration from Latin America and Asia also dramatically transformed American cities. In three decades following the passage of the 1965 immigration reforms, the percentage of Europeans among legal immigrants dropped from 80 percent to less than 20 percent, with the majority of non-European immigrants settling in coastal metropoles like New York, Miami, and Los Angeles.[35] The migration of highly educated Asian and South American professionals and venture capitalists contributed to the growth of the "informational city," and to the development of transnational economic linkages between the United States and newly industrializing nations. More significant, in sheer numbers, was the arrival of millions of working-class immigrants from Mexico, the Caribbean, and Southeast Asia, displaced from their homelands by U.S.-instigated wars, industrialization, and multinational development, and drawn to U.S. cities by jobs in the growing service and light manufacturing sectors.

In Los Angeles, for example, the Latino population grew by 71 percent between 1970 and 1980, with Mexican and Central American immigrant workers concentrated in producer services or export-competitive production—industries characterized by low-wages, low unionization rates, and unstable employment. By 1980, 61 percent of male workers and 66 percent of female workers in Los Angeles were employed in part-time, part-year jobs. Moreover, between 1967 and 1982, real average wages for L.A.'s unskilled workers (both native-born and immigrant) dropped by 8 percent.[36] While Los Angeles' Latino immigrants were "instrumental in the reindustrialization of certain low-wage industries,"[37] and thus central to the success of post-Fordist capitalism, the vast majority of Latino workers and their children lived in racially segregated, high poverty barrios.

Amidst the wave of capital flight and federal urban divestment in the 1970s and 1980s, mayors and city councils of job-starved cities began to employ a variety of strategies to restimulate the local economy. Tax incentives, convention centers, fee waivers for municipal services, relaxation of zoning approval processes, the underwriting of construction and maintenance costs for new business districts and industrial parks, and increased police services all constituted a customizable arsenal of "economic development" tactics used by city officials to attract new capital and jobs. Community redevelopment agencies partnered with private developers to bulldoze "urban blight" and refashion city centers as entertainment and leisure playgrounds for tourists and a new population of young professionals who had returned to the city in search of "diversity" and "alternative" lifestyles. With over $3 billion in urban renewal money from the federal government, state and local programs of "slum clearance" cut through historically black and Latino neighborhoods, displacing over one million people, half of whom were black.[38] As Urban Studies scholars Victor Valle and Rodolfo Torres note, although this process was enabled by federal policies of economic deregulation and increased funding for urban renewal, the accessibility and flexibility of local political machinery "allowed capital to appropriate more and more of local government's economic planning and regulatory functions."[39] More accessible to global enterprises than their state-level and large city counterparts, smaller cities and metropolitan and suburban counties would come to play an increasingly central role in the global economy.[40]

This was true in Southern California where the effects of economic restructuring and globalization were equally powerful, and the enticements equally palpable, in the archipelago of small cities that lay just outside the city boundaries of Los Angeles. As we will show in the next chapter, the city of Long Beach, located in the southwest corner of L.A. County, fiercely competed for capital investment during the 1980s and 1990s in a race to become the next Pacific Rim City. In the process, it became a key hub of immigration and a global command center for international trade and high technology. In Long Beach, as in many cities during this period, redevelopment strategies exacerbated economic distress, cultivating industries with large bases of low-wage, nonunion jobs and pushing poor people out of the downtown area into overcrowded, segregated neighborhoods. Moreover, because urban renewal was cast as an attempt to improve economic and social conditions within cities, the continuing presence of poor, segregated neighborhoods was blamed on poor people themselves and used as proof that government programs could not solve social problems.

Urban Dystopias: The Inner-City as Political Commodity

The story of Long Beach was writ large on the national stage during the 1980s when media coverage and political discourse on urban decline constructed an image of the inner-city, and its brown and black residents, as a world apart from the rest of America. Centuries-old racist and nativist beliefs intertwined in this portrait of a "Third World inside a First," of ghettos and barrios as incubators for alien cultural values, hypersexual and criminal behavior, broken marriages, and overly large families. In the face of the changing realities of post-Fordist America, President Reagan capitalized on the inner-city as a valuable political commodity. The genius of Reagan's strategy lay in his ability to link this portrait of a foreign and dangerous city to the "cultural struggle over the material and symbolic conditions of U.S. citizenship."[41] The city became the dystopian mirror to Reagan's Americanism. Calling on "ordinary citizens" to reclaim the nation from liberals, minority interest groups, and urban criminals, Reagan offered American voters a new private vision of the public sphere: citizenship embodied in the cosseted middle-class enclave of family and privatized community life.

Reagan's fetishization of privacy and individualism, however, did not extend to poor women and people of color whose behavior and family life came under intensified government surveillance during the 1980s. Painting welfare recipients alternately as threats to the national community and as victims of liberal government policy, Reagan moved to eradicate welfare "for the good of the poor." Calling for a return to the American tradition of self-help and voluntary associations,[42] Reagan abolished the public service jobs program, cut almost half a million people from the food stamp program, and reduced or eliminated funds for public housing and Medicaid for the working poor. Moreover, Reagan implemented more work requirements into AFDC and encouraged states to adopt welfare-to-work demonstration programs.[43] By 1983, "under complex new regulations, over 408,000 people had lost their eligibility for AFDC, and 299,000 had lost their benefits."[44]

In spite of the White House's rhetorical celebration of work as a means to self-reliance, low-income working mothers lost significant ground during the Reagan years. In 1980, 47 states used AFDC funds to supplement the wages of a single mother with three children who earned 50 percent of the poverty line; by 1984, only 24 states did so. During this period, the working mother described above lost 20 percent of her total food stamp and AFDC benefits, while her income taxes increased by over 400 percent, from a $91 credit to a $461 liability.[45] By 1987, as a result of Reagan's tax cuts, workers in the lowest tenth percentile of the wage ladder were paying an unprecedented 20 percent of their yearly income in taxes, whereas the wealthiest 1 percent of the U.S. population gained a net tax savings of 25 percent. Reagan's administration led the national trend toward part-time and contract labor, allowing federal and state agencies to hire temp workers at below union wages and legalized the practice of home work—in New York City alone, this led to a 500 percent increase in the number of children engaged in sweatshop labor.[46]

Revealing the new role of the American state under late capitalism, Reagan's laissez-faire ideology did not aim to do away with government but to shift its role—this was big government for another purpose. Cuts in social programs coincided with mammoth increases in law enforcement and military spending. In 1981, Reagan persuaded Congress to allocate a $1.2 trillion increase in military spending over five years. Reagan's War on Drugs gave the federal government new jurisdiction over crime, and in 1982, Congress authorized $125 million to hire a thousand new FBI and DEA agents. Armed with harsh mandatory minimum sentencing guidelines, federal drug prosecutions increased by nearly 100 percent from 1982 to 1988, far ahead of any actual increase in drug crimes. Welfare recipients were also increasingly suspected of fraud and subjected to escalating government surveillance. By the late 1970s, according to political scientist John Gilliom, "many states began intensifying the scrutiny of their AFDC clients, frequently shifting from income estimates to mandated monthly reporting and beginning the use of computer matching and other means of more closely inspecting their clients."[47] Reagan's Council on Integrity and Efficiency implemented a national computer system that tracked AFDC clients' income levels and cross-referenced these with Social Security, INS, and criminal databases. By the mid-1980s, as federal guidelines required states to prosecute "dead-beat dads," many county AFDC offices began holding "blood draw days," where dozens of children were subjected to DNA-typing so that the state could identify their fathers.[48] Thus, during the Reagan years, the state increasingly exercised its disciplinary power through what social theorist Christian Parenti calls "ritualized displays" of terror—SWAT teams, police sweeps, gang injunctions, mandatory DNA paternity testing, computerized welfare fraud databases—aimed particularly at low-income African-American and Latino populations.[49]

With its labor market approach to social policy and its criminalization of poverty, the Reagan Revolution created ripe conditions for the dismantling of the U.S. welfare state. However, although Reagan and his successor George Bush succeeded in abolishing some social programs and slashing the dollar amounts for others, neither president was able to build sufficient political support to do away entirely with the AFDC system. The "welfare reform" bill proposed by Reagan and passed under George H. W. Bush as the Family Support Act (FSA) of 1988 furthered the Right's assault on AFDC by introducing work requirements and incentives.[50]

The large-scale dismantling of AFDC, however, began in the early 1990s under the leadership of an aggressive coalition of Republican governors but was brought to fruition by the New Democratic presidency of Bill Clinton. Led by Tommy Thompson of Wisconsin, Richard Engler of

Michigan, and William Weld of Massachusetts, GOP governors slashed their states' general assistance programs, reducing benefit levels, and implementing stricter sanctions and eligibility requirements. By the mid-1990s, over 40 states had taken advantage of the federal waiver program first introduced by Reagan, and were running welfare-to-work demonstrations programs that eventually laid the groundwork for the federal TANF program.[51] In a calculated attempt to lure white voters back to the Democratic Party, a growing cadre of "New Democrats" led by Arkansas Governor Bill Clinton joined the attack on AFDC, endorsing federal waivers, time-limited welfare, and the privatization of "wasteful" government programs. Both Republicans and Democrats now dismissed the New Deal's vision of the welfare safety net as a fundamental right for low-income women and children as dangerously naïve. Rather, the task at hand was to find the quickest way of lowering the welfare rolls.

While most critics blame the Reagan Revolution for the dismantling of the welfare state, the PRWORA in fact would not have been possible without two other concurrent historical developments. The first was a vast body of social science produced by liberal scholars in the 1980s and 1990s, which legitimized a behaviorist analysis of poverty and identified welfare as a prime issue to be addressed through public policy. The second was a strategic shift among nativist groups from a focus on protecting American jobs to one of stripping immigrants of social entitlements like welfare, Social Security, and education. Both of these developments helped to solidify a post–civil rights consensus that equated poor urban blacks and immigrants with a menacing "underclass" and blamed this underclass for the decline of the American Dream.

Forging a "Post–Civil Rights" Consensus: Liberal Social Science and the Underclass

> Far from a triumph for poverty knowledge, the end of welfare was a humiliating defeat, less because politicians ignored than because they could find legitimation in liberal poverty expertise.
>
> —Alice O'Connor, *Poverty Knowledge*

In 1996, soon after President Clinton signed the PRWORA, two of his top welfare policy advisors quit in protest. The public resignation of David Ellwood and Mary Joe Bane, both Harvard professors and renowned poverty researchers, continues to be cited as evidence that the Clinton administration and welfare reform betrayed the liberal academy. But, as historian Alice O'Connor documents in her book *Poverty Knowledge,* the assumptions and tenets of the PRWORA, in fact, rested on the work of liberal academics like Ellwood, Bane, and William Julius Wilson, along with liberal think tanks like the Manpower Demonstration Research Corporation (MDRC) and the University of Wisconsin's Institute for Research on Poverty (IRP). Since the 1930s, liberal social science had abandoned an analysis of political economy and adopted a behavioral science approach that located the causes of poverty in the "culturally-based behaviors" of poor people. By the 1980s, both liberal researchers and policymakers had coalesced around the concept of a behaviorally defined "underclass," as an alien and nonwhite subpopulation at fault for its troubled position in society.

No work was more pivotal in legitimating this notion of an underclass than University of Chicago sociologist William Julius Wilson's 1987 *The Truly Disadvantaged.* Wilson took older conservative ideas about poverty, married them to a structural analysis, and recast them as liberal formulations on the underclass. He explicitly connected this new underclass to changes in the U.S. economy (notably deindustrialization and public and corporate divestment from U.S. cities) that improved the incomes of many blacks while leaving the rest of the black community unemployed and increasingly isolated. These structural changes in the economy, according to Wilson, precipitated behavioral and community change in black inner-city neighborhoods. As basic institutions declined, the social organization of inner-city neighborhoods—sense of community, positive neighborhood identification, and explicit norms and sanctions against aberrant behavior—likewise declined.[52]

Wilson contended that social dislocation and isolation were the defining traits of the underclass, the problems of poor blacks stemming from class rather than race.[53] The dissolution of the black community[54] and of black families, as men lost their jobs, led to the creation of a permanent underclass, whose "behavior contrasts sharply with that of mainstream America."[55] Wilson was particularly concerned with the proliferation of single-parent families and teenage pregnancy, even while citing statistics that showed that fertility rates for black teenagers have decreased since 1970. While Wilson took pains to distinguish his analysis from conservatives like Charles Murray by emphasizing the structural roots of black community decline, his focus on "the tangle of pathology in the inner city" legitimated the belief that an unusual destructive culture had emerged in the nation's inner cities.[56]

By the early 1990s, Wilson's theoretical formulations had overtaken American social science, forging what Coontz calls the "new consensus" that weak family ties and values were responsible for postwar black poverty.[57] Journalists and scholars followed Wilson's lead, traveling to the "other America" to portray how different inner-city blacks were from the rest of the nation.[58] Wilson's gendering of urban problems—his fixation on absent fathers and overly sexual mothers—lent academic credence to conservative political arguments not only by locating the causes of black poverty in black culture (a theme already well developed in the 1960s and 1970s), but also by explicitly establishing a structural link between black social pathology, rapid urban decline, and rising public expenditures. Moreover, Wilson's portrayal of an inner-city population forsaken by more successful, middle-class African Americans confirmed the idea that cultural "pathology" had replaced racial discrimination as the primary determinant of black life outcomes.

Wilson's underclass also set new parameters for social science research on Latino poverty, as sociologists and anthropologists rushed to test the applicability of his model to Chicano and Puerto Rican communities. Much of the resulting literature on "Latinos and the Underclass Debate," as labeled by an eponymous 1994 collection of essays, took for granted Wilson's portrait of the African-American underclass, contrasting it to low-income Latinos.[59] While broken families and community dissolution might account for black poverty, sociologists like Joan Moore and Nestor Rodriguez conceded, traditional family values and high employment rates among Latinos proved that structural forces like ongoing immigration and labor market segmentation, and not cultural pathology, were responsible for Latino poverty. However, by contrasting Latinos to blacks under the moralistic framework established by Wilson, such scholarship inadvertently validated the proposition that *some* groups were poor because of their cultural values.

Other scholars reiterated Wilson's underclass thesis as they developed "segmented assimilation theory" to explain growing economic and social disparities between different immigrant groups and across immigrant generations. Inverting the logic of assimilation theory, sociologists like Alejandro Portes and Min Zhou credited the economic success of certain immigrant groups in U.S. society, such as Cubans and Punjabi Sikhs, to the maintenance of tight-knit ethnic communities and the retention of "traditional values" from their countries of origin, such as belief in hard work, sacrifice, and family unity. In contrast, the authors argued, other immigrant groups like Mexicans and Haitians have assimilated into an "inner-city minority culture" that is characterized by "an adversarial stance towards the white mainstream" and a self-defeating cynicism about the possibility of upward social mobility.[60] By embracing "urban culture," which Portes and Zhou identify with rap music, hip-hop dress, and defiance toward school officials, the U.S.-born children of Mexican and Haitian immigrants place limits on their own educational and economic mobility.[61] In this paradigm, race was no longer a structural force that produces unequal outcomes for different groups, but rather a cultural costume and self-destructive *choice* that new immigrants and their offspring can put on or take off at will. By crediting positive cultural values and choices for the socioeconomic progress of some immigrant groups, segmented assimilation theory reinforced the moral assumptions of underclass theory. Once transported into mainstream debate, the image of the hard-working, self-sacrificing immigrant served to naturalize the exploitation of immigrant workers and to be held up as a model for African Americans and U.S.-born Latinos to follow.[62]

Perhaps the most compelling, and dangerous, aspect of social science literature on the "underclass" was that it included among its proponents scholars of color who claimed to break through "liberal silences" in their communities. In particular, Wilson self-consciously fashioned himself as bold and objective enough to break through the silences of the black community and liberal academia to address the cultural nature of poverty. In *The Truly Disadvantaged,* he asserted that liberals "can no longer afford to be timid in addressing these problems, . . . to look for data to deny the very existence of an underclass, or, finally, to rely heavily on the easy explanation of racism."[63] This was precisely the message that the Democratic Leadership Conference with William Jefferson Clinton at its head was also promoting. Clinton too sought to fashion himself as a new kind of Democrat willing to break with old truisms and make tough choices about what Americans needed. What made the work of Wilson and other liberal social scientists particularly attractive to the leadership of the DLC was the insistence that racism no longer mattered. Echoing Wilson's postulation that racial discrimination was primarily not responsible for post-1960s black poverty, conservatives and liberals converged around the idea that the civil rights era had successfully eradicated institutional racism and now low-income blacks and Latinos had no excuse for their personal failings.

Also crucial to the forging of a "post–civil rights consensus" were prominent African Americans and Latinos who trumpeted a "tough love" approach to urban problems—what Mike Davis has called the "Black-lash."[64] Public figures like Minister Farrakhan, Cornel West, Linda Chavez, and Edward James Olmos (and more recently Bill Cosby) openly condemned the "nihilistic" culture among inner-city youth and called on blacks and Latinos to assume more responsibility for their communities. In the 1980s and 1990s, many black and Latino intellectuals, politicians, and civil rights activists embraced self-help as a means to community empowerment. Yet, once co-opted into national debate, community self-help came to support a system where government and taxpayers were no longer responsible.

In this emergent "post–civil rights discourse," politicians could celebrate the achievements of Martin Luther King and Cesar Chavez in the same breath that they denounced civil rights protections like affirmative action, bilingual education, and public assistance. They could foreground the problems *with* low-income blacks and Latinos while denying that racism had anything to do with their intentions. Two decades of "well-meaning" inner-city educational outreach, job training, and anti-poverty programs had purportedly shown that government could not correct the problems of low-income, urban families; individuals and communities had to assume more personal responsibility. As President Clinton explained, "It's not racist for whites to assert that the culture of welfare dependency, out-of-wedlock pregnancy and absent fatherhood cannot be broken by social programs, unless there is first more personal responsibility." Indeed, when polled, nearly 60 percent of white Americans responded that blacks on welfare "could get along if they tried" and that if "blacks would only try harder, they could be just as well off as whites."[65] The racial histories behind these assumptions were palpable: welfare recipients were lazy, had too many babies and too little work ethic, cheated the system and squandered their benefits. But the cleverness of post–civil rights discourse was its deployment of polite racial code words—"inner-city," "welfare recipient," and "underclass"—which made the moral crisis of welfare dependency seem so new, so urgent, and so post-racial as to avoid the historical parallels.[66]

The New Nativism: Immigration Reform Meets Welfare Reform

Underclass theory also proved an ideal vehicle for nativist politicians and immigration reform groups who capitalized on suburban antipathy toward taxes and federal spending by blaming Third World immigration for urban decline and rising public expenditures. In the 1980s and early 1990s, mounting public outcry over illegal immigration and the growing visibility of nonwhite immigrants in public schools, hospitals, and social service agencies associated immigration with "urban problems" like crime, poverty, and welfare. Although the new nativism targeted all immigrants as a threat to the nation, Latinos—and particularly Mexicans— were frequently singled out as the crux of America's "immigration crisis." In public debate, Latinos were represented as "alien" not simply because of their national origins, but rather because, like blacks, they possessed a culture antithetical to the American way of life. Always already cast as newcomers and cultural outsiders and concentrated in metropolitan centers (often in or near black neighborhoods), low-income Latinos fit ideally into the cultural-behavioralist discourse at the heart of underclass theory.

This linking of blacks and immigrants in public discourse marks a unique characteristic of post–civil rights politics. In the 1960s and 1970s, immigrants had served as a foil to African Americans. Celebrated as exemplars of American values of family and hard work, second-generation European immigrants' assimilation into the suburban middle class—and later, the emergence of Asian Americans as "model minorities"—proved that with the right cultural values all ethnic groups could succeed in U.S. society.[67] The framing of immigrant success, then, obscured continuing racial discrimination by locating the causes for racial and class inequality in the cultural defects of African Americans. Indeed, as evidenced in attacks on immigrant men as "cheap labor" and "job stealers" during the recession years of the late 1970s and early 1980s, even *anti*-immigrant discourse accepted the notion that, unlike blacks, immigrants were hardworking and driven to get ahead.

Having celebrated immigrant success as proof that the system works, the slashing of immigrant welfare entitlements in the 1990s was only possible through the particular racialization of the "immigration problem." Implicit and explicit in calls for restricting immigration and denying welfare to noncitizens was the contention that post-1965 immigrants were racially inassimilable to the Anglo-Saxon core of American society. In his

1995 *Alien Nation* Peter Brimelow, senior editor at *Forbes Magazine* and the *National Review*, described new immigrants as "poor, ignorant desperate people" fleeing from "primate cities" like Mexico City, Cairo, or Calcutta.[68] Proclaiming that "race and ethnicity are destiny in American politics," Brimelow warned that unskilled Third World immigrants were "swelling the ranks of the welfare underclass."[69] *Chicago Tribune* writer Georgie Anne Geyer blamed Third World immigrants for undermining the American tenets of self-government and citizenship. Contrasting Latino and Asian immigrants to a nostalgic (and historically inaccurate) portrait of earlier European immigrants, Geyer concluded that new immigrants "lack the inclination to assimilate" and are pulled to the United States by economic desperation and government handouts.[70]

While some journalists like Brimelow and Geyer lumped together all new immigrants into one menacing "racial other," more moderate conservatives and liberals advanced similar views by drawing distinctions between "good" and "bad" immigrants.[71] Good immigrants learned English, became U.S. citizens, and never took government handouts. Bad immigrants included illegal aliens, day laborers, criminals, welfare queens, and bilingual speakers.[72] Immigrants who had made it without government help were proof that hard work and personal responsibility led to success. This moral typology resonated with the model of meritocracy and racial progress so central to underclass theory and provided native-born whites a lens for understanding Americanism in an increasingly global world.[73]

This cultural vocabulary for immigration signals the emergence of a new racism, which political scientist Etienne Balibar describes as "a racism without races . . . whose dominant theme is not biological heredity but the insurmountability of cultural differences."[74] Elaborating on this idea, historian Paul Gilroy writes:

> We increasingly face a racism which avoids being recognized as such because it is able to line up "race" with nationhood, patriotism, and nationalism. A racism which has taken a necessary distance from crude ideas of biological inferiority and superiority now seeks to represent an imaginary definition of the nation as a unified cultural community.[75]

Certainly, with the widespread discourse on birth and disease rates in nonwhite immigrant populations, biology was not far beneath the surface of late twentieth-century nativism. Yet, most nativists strategically distanced themselves from overtly biological theories of racial inferiority, contending instead that it was the inferior cultural values of nonwhite immigrants that made them a threat to America. Once race was recast as culture, and culture was tied to social and class position, liberals and conservatives could advocate for eliminating public entitlements for undeserving foreigners, while continuing to celebrate a "nation of immigrants" and "individual opportunity."

Just as the current generation of urban blacks was denounced for abandoning the cultural traditions of the old African-American community, so immigrant newcomers were represented as culturally different from the hardworking and humble European immigrants of previous generations. Public discourse on the welfare underclass invoked a mythic history of the values and motivations of early twentieth-century blacks and immigrants as proof of contemporary decline. In the "get tough" discourse of late twentieth-century America, blacks could no longer claim historical racism as an excuse for their personal failings; Latino and Asian newcomers had migrated "voluntarily," and thus had no legitimate claim to entitlement programs intended to correct past wrongs against African Americans, Chicanos, and Puerto Ricans.

Proposition 187: The Test-Case for Welfare Reform

The power of these ideas was proven in the passage of Proposition 187, the 1994 California ballot initiative that sought to cut most social services, including public education and health care, to the state's estimated 1.5 million undocumented immigrants.[76] The success of the campaign for Proposition 187 rested on its ability to tie social spending to immigration and to blame these for the massive economic changes California had experienced since the 1970s. In 1991, after eight years under Proposition 13 had produced crisis-level shortages in state and city budgets, California Governor Pete Wilson strategically released a report contending that Latinas received AFDC at a rate 23 percent higher than other women. As with most targeting of Latinas as a drain on public resources, Wilson's accompanying call for stiffer federal controls over illegal immigration conveniently ignored the facts that all undocumented immigrants are not Latino, that 70 percent of Latinos are not immigrants, and that undocumented immigrants are not eligible for AFDC.

The national press also propagated the myth that welfare is a magnet for illegal immigration. In 1994, the television news-magazine *60 Minutes* featured clips of hordes of pregnant women crossing the border from Mexico, accompanied by an interview with then–San Diego County supervisor, Brian Bilbray, who asserted that "4,800 people last year come to this country from a foreign country, illegally, to give birth to their child; 41 percent of them went immediately on welfare." In June of that same year, *Reader's Digest* reported "the exploitation of our welfare and social service system by illegal immigrants . . . a pattern of abuse, fraud, and official complacency costing taxpayers billions each year."[77] As the media, politicians, and anti-immigration groups like the Federation for American Immigration Reform (FAIR) circulated statistics linking rising AFDC rolls to high Latina birthrates, they fueled public hysteria over the "immigration time-bomb" that would bankrupt the government and direct public dollars away from "deserving" citizens.

The foundational ideology of "Save Our State (SOS)," the citizens' campaign for Proposition 187, melded cultural Moynihanism and bottom-line economics—a powerful combination that would later prove effective in passing the PRWORA. In order to justify the denial of health and educational services to workers and children within U.S. national borders, Proposition 187 proponents represented undocumented Mexicans as enemy aliens eating away at the national fabric. Yet, the racial message of this initiative was made palatable by its packaging as economic pragmatism. One San Fernando Valley SOS organizer was quoted in the *Los Angeles Times* as saying, "We have people who are flooding our borders with a very high fertility rate and a very low educational level. We're exporting jobs and importing poverty. And unless something is done, this state has nothing to face but fiscal havoc."[78] By deploying the threat of fiscal collapse linked to illegal immigration, SOS gained control of the state election. Furthermore, as it disguised its agenda in a narrative of impending economic disaster, SOS appealed to concerned California voters who did not have to think of themselves as racist.

Approved in November 1994, the proposition was immediately placed under a temporary court injunction after civil rights groups filed an appeal charging that it violated the 1986 Supreme Court ruling in *Plyer v. Doe* that undocumented children are constitutionally entitled to a public education. Federal District Court Judge Judy Pfaelzer finally ruled in 1998 that much of Proposition 187 was unconstitutional because it was

superseded by court precedent and federal law.[79] Pfaelzer's ruling, however, was a bittersweet victory for immigrant rights advocates as it followed from the success of the nativist agenda at the federal level. During
the four years of court battles over the California initiative, Proposition
187 was reborn at the federal level through two historic pieces of legislation: the PRWORA and the Illegal Immigration Reform and Immigrant
Responsiblity Act of 1996, which together barred undocumented immigrants from receiving all but emergency services and severely restricted
public assistance for legal immigrants.

The fact that none of these immigration reforms proposed to
strengthen or even enforce sanctions against employers who hire undocumented immigrants illustrates a tacit consensus in American politics
that the United States should import foreign labor, but need not be responsible for the social needs and well-being of these workers. This
agenda was made clear by Governor Wilson's enthusiastic campaigning
on behalf of Proposition 187 and his simultaneous lobbying in Washington, D.C. for a new guest worker program that would import temporary
workers from Mexico, deny them most political rights and social protections, and return them across the border once their labor was no
longer needed. Indeed, by distracting public attention away from employer sanctions and capital flight, Proposition 187 facilitated the
transnational flow of capital, peoples, and commodities that is the foundation of California's global economy. Simultaneously, by denying those
social services and legal networks that in part help to organize individual immigrants into political communities, the proposition metaphori-
cally exorcised "illegals" from the imagined community at the same time
that it literally safeguarded public monies and citizenship privileges for
the middle class.

Although most scholars have argued that globalization has led to a decline in the significance of citizenship, Proposition 187 instead suggests
that citizenship remains a crucial site for the contestation over nationhood, economics, and rights in the global era. This was not just true for
white supporters. Rather, the unintended effect of Proposition 187 was
the transformation of immigrants into an emergent voting block and political voice in American politics—as witnessed in the mobilization of immigrant rights groups, the forging of a historic alliance between organized labor and immigrant communities, the election of progressive Latinos to the California legislature, and the groundswell of citizenship
applications nationwide—which would ironically work to repeal some of

the harshest anti-immigrant provisions of welfare reform. By 1997, the state that had given birth to Proposition 187 just three years earlier would allocate state funds to partially restore cash aid and food stamps to legal immigrants cut off by federal law.

At the same time, Proposition 187 played a key role in forging the political path to welfare reform. Although targeted explicitly at undocumented immigrants, it opened the door to an assault on all immigrants and demonstrated to nativist organizations like FAIR that the issue of welfare was the ticket to advancing the anti-immigrant cause. Proposition 187 also buttressed an ongoing anti–civil rights movement that for the past three decades has held up people of color as the cause of the nation's social and economic fissures, while chipping way at the federal government's role as a watchdog over state and local government. Proposition 187 attempted and welfare reform more successfully enabled states to purvey entitlements outside of the regulation and oversight of the federal government. The economic motivations behind both of these policies were clear. Just as Proposition 187 was not about stopping undocumented immigration, the PRWORA was not about ending poverty. By stripping certain workers of social entitlements and protections, both laws provided American employers an expanded workforce of flexible, vulnerable laborers.

The End of Welfare as We Know It: An Overview of the PRWORA

By the mid-1990s, the national debate over "personal responsibility" focused nearly exclusively on the black and immigrant welfare poor—this in spite of the federal government's own statistics showing that poor whites made up the majority of the nation's welfare recipients.[80] Although families on welfare were slightly smaller than the average U.S. family and less than 9 percent of immigrant households received cash public assistance,[81] most politicians and journalists continued to promote the idea that blacks were making careers of having babies just to collect a larger welfare check and Latino immigrants with their overly large families were crossing the border illegally to cash in on American entitlements. While the immigrant population that used public assistance was a diverse sampling of immigrants from Europe, Asia, and Latin America, public images centered on Mexicans and Puerto Ricans (although Puerto

Ricans are citizens not immigrants).[82] Rather than describe a government program that kept women and children hovering at the poverty line, but had succeeded in combating widespread hunger in many communities, "welfare" had become a code word for race and the linchpin in a national debate over American culture and citizenship.

Media stories similarly highlighted the substandard work ethic among blacks and Latinos, who allegedly preferred waiting for their next welfare check instead of looking for a job. In reality, three-quarters of welfare recipients did not remain long on welfare but moved from welfare to underpaid work with great frequency.[83] In their comparative study of welfare recipients and single-mothers in low-wage jobs, sociologists Katherine Edin and Laura Lein found that the economic gap between working women and women on welfare (most of whom were also working) was insignificant. Based on their actual incomes and their labor market opportunities, work was not a route out of poverty for either group of women.[84] Edin and Lein's ethnographic findings were confirmed in national data that show that work in the 1990s often did not lift a family out of poverty. While a full-time, minimum-wage worker with two children in the 1970s lived above the poverty line, the same family made $8840 a year in 1995—far below the poverty line of $12,188.[85] For many parents in minimum-wage jobs, AFDC was a necessary means to supplement what they were denied in the private sector: an income they could survive on and health benefits for their family.

Rather than respond to the real demographics of poverty—an inadequate labor market, a lack of childcare and health benefits, urban divestment from social services and public education, and rising college costs—the authors of welfare reform drew upon two-dimensional caricatures of welfare recipients to shape a legislation that would slash welfare numbers and impose moral values on the poor.[86] Almost two-thirds of the 1996 welfare law involved a litany of rules and sanctions on family and sexual life. Already familiar with a punitive system that tracked their personal behavior, welfare recipients now had to navigate a more complicated system of eligibility standards and penalties: mothers under the age of eighteen must be living with an adult and enrolled in school or they lose all benefits; parents convicted of fraud or drug possession (no matter which drug or what quantity) face a lifetime ban on benefits; families who move to a higher benefit state are subject to the lower benefit levels of their home state; and parents who fail to immunize their children or send them to school will lose some or all of their cash benefits.

Alongside these "family values" provisions, the PRWORA established a maximum five-year lifetime limit on cash benefits and stipulated that at least 80 percent of each state's welfare recipients must be working a minimum number of hours within two years. Notably, federal work requirements operate from an "any job is better than welfare" philosophy. States were not required to provide basic education or skills development to their welfare clients or to track employment outcomes and wages through time. Welfare clients who cannot find a job were given a choice of losing all of their benefits or working in the public sector in exchange for a monthly welfare stipend (known as "workfare"). Under PRWORA, workfare participants were not protected under minimum wage provisions or national fair labor standards.

One of the most telling features of workfare has been the use of welfare recipients to replace unionized workers. Since workfare jobs did not have to be newly created jobs, workfare was often used to undermine the successes unions had been gaining in the service sector by replacing full-time salaried workers with part-time below-minimum-wage employees. In New York City, for example, Mayor Rudolph Giuliani fired 22,000 municipal workers and replaced them largely with workfare workers. Part-time workfare workers then constituted three-fourths of the labor-force in the Parks Department and one-third of the Sanitation Department. They also helped staff the city's welfare agency, housing authority, and public hospitals. The fiscal advantage to the city was clear: the average New York City clerical worker's hourly wage is $12.32 not including benefits but a workfare worker costs the city $1.80 an hour for a 20-hour work week and earns no benefits.[87]

This was not the outcome that the architects of the PRWORA put forth. The assumptions behind the work-first provisions of the PRWORA —like those of low-paid immigrant work more broadly—were that welfare recipients would take the jobs that no one else wanted. Reformers played on the racial antagonism of (imagined white) workers toward (imagined colored and free-loading) welfare recipients to distract workers from the economic ramifications of welfare reform and to prevent any alliances between recipients and workers.[88] Thus, workfare in practice not only ensured the public and private sectors of an available, cheap new workforce, but also threatened to drive down wages and force more Americans into poverty.

Welfare reform has also meant big profits for Wall Street. Under generous tax breaks implemented by the Clinton administration, private employers who hire former welfare recipients could deduct up to 50 percent of their employees' wages from their taxes.[89] Large corporations vied for more than $20 billion in federal and state grants to run welfare-to-work services. Maximus, the nation's largest company specializing in government-contracted welfare work, boasted an annual revenue of $127 million and over 1,600 employees nationwide who have taken over the duties of traditional caseworkers in the public sector.[90] Public support of the poor, then, had been replaced with a money trail for corporations.

The Anti-Immigrant Provisions of PRWORA

Alongside this attack on workers' rights, PRWORA also served as a covert means for immigration reform, as it created "new lines of stratification between citizens and noncitizens," making citizenship a requirement for most social entitlements in U.S. society.[91] Whereas in the past, permanent residents and citizens were by and large guaranteed equal access to public assistance, the 1996 law banned noncitizens from food stamp and old-age (SSI) assistance. Only certain refugees and asylees, veterans and their families, and legal immigrants who could provide proof of 40 quarters (or ten years) of work in the United States were exempt from the cut-offs.[92] On August 22, 1996, over one million legal immigrants became ineligible for food stamps, and half a million elderly and disabled immigrants became ineligible for SSI benefits. Although Congress partially restored noncitizen benefits in 1997, 1998, and 2002, the vast majority of legal immigrants remain ineligible for food stamp and old-age assistance.[93]

Along with citizenship status, PRWORA also established timing of arrival as a new criterion for public assistance. Legal immigrants who arrive after August 1996 became ineligible for all means-tested federal benefits (including cash assistance, food stamps, SSI, public health insurance, and public housing) for their first five years in the United States.[94] Even after they have met this five-year waiting requirement, immigrants now confront a system in which it is much riskier to apply, and harder to qualify, for assistance. New rules introduced in 1996 make immigrant sponsors legally responsible for their charges for up to five years, and also stipulate that when an immigrant applies for assistance, his or her income and resources be "deemed" to include the sponsor's income and resources.[95] In effect, federal law requires legal immigrants to demonstrate much higher levels of need than citizens in order to qualify for assistance.

A less-publicized feature of welfare reform was its frontal attack on illegal immigration. Under AFDC, undocumented immigrants were not eligible for public assistance, but their U.S.-born children were. While this distinction remains in place, all state agencies who receive federal funding are required "to furnish the INS with the name and address of, and any other identifying information about, any individual who the [agency] knows is unlawfully in the United States."[96] This reporting requirement was accompanied by a new system of information sharing between public service agencies and the INS. Previously prohibited by federal law, welfare caseworkers can now directly contact immigration agents for information about their clients. An undocumented mother who applies for public assistance for her U.S.-born child risks the threat, not only of deportation, but also of having to repay any public benefits that were improperly received (whether or not there is proven intent to deceive).[97] The implications of these new rules for undocumented immigrants move far beyond the sphere of the welfare system, transforming every public service agency into an arm of the INS.

The PRWORA's assault on immigrant rights was enhanced by two additional laws passed by Congress in the same year. The Illegal Immigration Reform and Immigrant Responsibility Act (IIRIA), ratified in September 1996, allocated billions of dollars to border enforcement, opened up new interagency collaboration between the INS and local police authorities, and greatly expanded the power of the state to arrest and deport "criminal aliens." Its companion bill, the Antiterrorism and Effective Death Penalty Act, passed in April 1996, expedited procedures for the removal of "alien terrorists," including providing state and local authorities access to confidential immigration and naturalization files through court order. Together these three laws stripped noncitizens of the right to due process (a cornerstone of American civil liberties) and created a heightened anti-immigrant climate that would pave the way for the intensified offensive against immigrant rights in the wake of September 11th.[98] The labor market benefits of this legislation should not be underestimated. As Parenti argues in *Lockdown America,* secret detentions, expedited deportations, and stepped-up INS raids of immigrant workplaces and neighborhoods provide an invaluable service to American employers by intimidating immigrant workers from demanding better wages, organizing unions, and protesting inhumane working conditions. Moreover, immigration scholars Philip Kretsedemas and Ana Aparicio note that the devolution of federal authority to local government and service providers has placed job creation "in the hands of local labor markets" and enabled a fine-tuning of welfare-to-work policy to the specific needs of local employers. As they conclude, "This policy regime has increased the pressures that poor immigrants already face to take immediate available work opportunities, often in the informal and lowest-paying sectors of the economy."[99]

Welfare's Missing in Action: Assessing the Aftermath of the PRWORA

No sooner had President Clinton signed the PRWORA into law, than Republicans and Democrats were jostling for airtime, eager to take credit for ending a morally corrupt entitlement system. Celebrants of welfare reform, from members of Congress to state governors to the mainstream press, rushed to publish statistics and rosy human interest stories of dropping welfare numbers as evidence of the success of "ending welfare as we knew it."[100] Between 1993 and 1997 (though the PRWORA had just passed in 1996), Clinton's Council of Economic Advisors reported, almost three million recipients had fallen off the rolls, a 20 percent drop nationwide.[101] By the summer of 1999, Clinton would once again declare welfare reform a success, citing new evidence that 35 percent of all welfare recipients had moved into work or "work-related activities."[102] And in 2002, the Bush Administration reported that the number of welfare recipients in the United States had dropped by 62 percent, or over nine million people, between 1993 and 2001.

As with much of the public debate that enshrouded welfare reform, these statistics were largely tautological. Poor families were leaving the welfare rolls because they were being pushed off of welfare.[103] As states rushed to secure federal block grants by reducing their welfare rolls, welfare review boards found that half of the cases they reviewed, where recipients had lost some or all of their benefits, were the result of erroneous state action.[104] By 2002, experts reported that at any given time about one-third of all recipients in the nation were under sanction for failing to comply with welfare regulations—a doubling of the sanction rate since 1996.[105] According to the Commission on Civil Rights, however, white recipients were less likely to be sanctioned: "There are disparities in access to and utilization of services, there is discrimination in the delivery of welfare benefits, whether intentional or not, and civil rights consider-ations are paramount."[106] Welfare politics in the United States had be-come a numbers game. Politicians could cite changes that happened be-fore the 1996 passage as evidence of the success of welfare reform, and states could count multiple exits by the same family as proof that they are reducing their rolls, yet did not keep records of return applications or ex-plain how applicants left the rolls or what happened to them once off public assistance.

The labor market effects of welfare reform have also been significant. Introducing a large body of low-wage workers into the labor market has driven up competition for low-wage jobs and driven down wages. A 1997 study of what kinds of jobs would be available to low-skilled welfare re-cipients in the Midwest, for example, found "twenty-two workers for each job that pays at least a poverty wage; sixty-four workers for every job that pays 150 percent of poverty ($18,417/year); and ninety-seven workers for each job at a living wage ($25,907/year for a family of three)."[107] Even in regions with significant job growth, rising employment rates have been accompanied by rising poverty rates and growing class polarization. Out of the 300,000 new jobs created in Los Angeles County between 1993 and 1999, for example, the vast majority pay less than $25,000 a year, and barely one in ten averages above $60,000. Los An-geles's transformation into a polarized economy is further evidenced by the fact the region's economic recovery has "yielded no net jobs in indus-tries that pay solid middle-class salaries."[108] With the fastest growing job category into the twenty-first century, according to the Bureau of Labor Statistics, being cashiers, job creation in most U.S. cities is concentrated in industries that specialize in poverty wages and flexible labor arrange-ments.[109] Moreover, larger economic trends confirm welfare reform's benefits to employers. In countries with narrowing social assistance—United States, Great Britain, Canada, Japan, and Australia—the relative wages of low-skilled workers fell, but in European countries with higher benefits, despite rising unemployment, wages remained stable. Within the United States "reform" has depressed wages. One Salt Lake City official told the *New York Times* that "without the welfare people . . . we would have had to raise the wage . . . maybe 5 percent."[110] Thus, the "economic miracle" of the New Economy looked more like a crisis from the vantage point of low-income families.

One of the untold stories of TANF (which has cost the federal govern-ment $4 billion more than AFDC) was the ways that states and private companies have gained financially since 1996. While framed within an anti-government discourse, welfare reform neither limited government spending nor government intervention in people's lives. Before the passage of PRWORA, states spent 80 percent of their welfare budgets on actual cash relief; by 2001, this dropped to 50 percent with the rest going to private companies, nonprofits, and the states themselves to administer programs and monitor poor women.[111] For instance, most of the money being collected from "deadbeat dads" is being kept by the state and not shared with the family—with the understanding that the state deserves child support collections because it has been "the Man" supporting these women. Maximus, Lockheed Martin IMS, Citigroup, Randstad, and Electronic Data Systems (Ross Perot's company), to name a few, all secured multihundred-million-dollar contracts and reaped significant profits in the PRWORA market. This despite evidence of fraud; accused of mismanagement and corruption in Los Angeles, New York, and Milwaukee, Maximus still received contracts to provide welfare services in all 50 states and every major city and county in the nation.

While private firms receiving millions in public contracts and employer tax breaks are subject to little oversight, people who continue to receive public assistance are required to negotiate an ever-more complicated maze of rules, regulations, and restrictions. Before a hungry family can apply for the food stamps they are entitled to under law, they must complete an application that averages 12 pages, eight pages longer than applications for a federal firearms permit or a school bus driver's license. Another study in Ohio concluded that a typical recipient would likely face "770 questions related to personal and financial circumstances" and regulations covered in 4,300 pages with another 2,000 pages of clarification.[112] Bureaucratic hurdles and stepped-up state surveillance of poor families have successfully produced a 33 percent decrease in food stamp applications—matched by what local charities and social service agencies report as a threefold increase in the demand for emergency food services. Such surveillance produces a climate of fear—by compromising poor women's access to privacy and due process, many recipients would "voluntarily" disenroll to escape this surveillance.

Equally alarming was the cynical shift in welfare discourse after 1996. Having created the much-maligned character of the welfare recipient, federal and state welfare agencies in partnership with private industry now needed to resuscitate the image of welfare recipients in order to get businesses to hire them. Across billboards and on the radio, these "welfare-to-work partnerships" launched advertising campaigns to promote welfare recipients as ideal employees by publicizing the same information that had been obscured in debates to reform welfare: welfare recipients want to work and have work experience, welfare recipients have on average two children and are conscientious about work and their children.[113] Yet, neither these portraits of welfare recipients as "ordinary Americans," nor the celebratory stories of former recipients as "heroic working mothers" that flooded newspapers and news magazines after 1996, tell the whole story of welfare reform. The same media sources that characterized welfare reform as a success also published separate findings showing that the number of families lacking health care was increasing precipitously, that food pantries and emergency shelters were reporting increased need, that childcare was a major problem for most families, and that children whose parents have workfare jobs (or have found other low-wage work) were watching more television, being supervised less, and not doing better in school. What is telling, then, is that this accumulation of data provided no significant momentum to undercut the fundamental consensus about the success of the legislation.

Conclusion: A Post-National, Post-Racial World?

Despite these alarming trends, American journalists as well as readers, politicians as well as voters, continue myopically to applaud the drop in welfare numbers by turning away from a broader analysis of the nature of work and poverty in the global economy. As recent studies of welfare reform show, job growth and rising employment rates are not reliable indicators of poverty reduction in this post-Fordist economy. Rather, poverty is today a product of work for those Americans at the bottom of the socioeconomic structure, as it is for the majority of workers around the world. The trends we see in the United States—the erosion of wages, benefits, and working conditions, the incorporation of greater numbers of women, racial minorities, and immigrants into the low-wage workforce, and widening class divisions—are magnified at the global level as multinationals migrate freely and continuously across national borders in search of bigger profits.

Welfare reform, like NAFTA, followed from the logic of global free trade: open the market, get rid of the artificial barriers and subsidies, and all will have the chance to prosper. Yet, neither PRWORA nor NAFTA dismantled the barriers to economic and racial equality so much as recast globalization through a mix of neoclassical economics and bootstrap individualism. Thus, while supporters of NAFTA proposed "to bridge the racial and cultural borders that divide the Americas," and to "empower" Mexican workers by granting them entry into a First World economy, NAFTA supporters tellingly never proposed opening the border or extending U.S. citizenship to Mexican migrants.[114] Similarly, proponents of the PRWORA celebrated American ideals of opportunity and responsibility, while chipping away at the labor protections that could provide former recipients with actual opportunity in the workplace.[115] The effect of these policies on both sides of the border is greater economic and social instability, as more than a million and a half Mexican workers lost their jobs through NAFTA, and as millions of recipients and their children in the United States race against the welfare clock in search of a sustainable livelihood.

Citing the expansive reach of multinational corporations and the increased mobility of people and commodities across national borders, critics across the political spectrum have charged that globalization has resulted in the decline of the power of the nation-state and meanings of American nationalism.[116] However, while framed through an anti-government discourse, neoliberal policies like welfare reform do not reduce government so much as reshape it. As the social state is "downsized" through the elimination and privatization of social services, schools, hospitals, and transportation, the positive public benefits that were once the hallmark of U.S. citizenship are increasingly accessible only to those who can afford them. At the same time, as states replace schools with prisons, cities rush to grow their police forces, and the Border Patrol doubles in size, the punitive arm of the state extends its surveillance over the nation's poor. The result is a federal government that actively facilitates the flexibility of capital by forcing millions of workers into a deregulated labor market, while it erects higher barriers to full citizenship in the national community. That contemporary efforts to circumscribe the benefits of citizenship continue to posit people of color, both immigrant and U.S.-born, as national outsiders further suggests that the symbolic power of white Americanism has not suffered under globalization.

In this newly privatized civil society, where U.S. citizens-qua-consumers are presumably "empowered" to choose their schools as well as their racial identities, those individuals who freely make the wrong choices are marked (workfare workers in NYC are required to wear a bright orange vest), punished, or "rehabilitated." Motivational counselors, job club programs, and individualized work plans all bombard welfare recipients with a post-feminist discourse of women's "self-sufficiency," and encourage them to associate their children's well-being with a minimum-wage paycheck. In this way, welfare recipients today report a decline in all indicators of family well-being—from income, to nutrition, to quality time with their children—and yet often still conclude that working has improved their self-esteem and made them better mothers. This individualization of free choice bolsters the ideology of meritocracy at the heart of post-1960s American politics by locating choice in the private, psychological terrain of the "self," thus obscuring the ways in which choices are themselves structured by political economy. The tautological nature of this ideology is evident in the equation of good and bad choices with class and racial position. In post–civil rights America, the nation can call upon welfare recipients to achieve "self-sufficiency" in a labor market that lacks adequate wages, safe childcare, decent medical coverage, and affordable housing, and, in the same breath, blame the continued marginalization of black and Latina workers on their self-defeating cultures and unfortunate lifestyle choices. The ideology of "choice" ultimately rests on racialized and gendered ideas about what kinds of work and remuneration different kinds of people deserve, while simultaneously ensuring that those on the losing end of the globalization equation are made responsible for their own failure and subjection.

2

Poverty in the Suburbs
Race and Redevelopment Policy in Long Beach

Set back from Anaheim Boulevard by a narrow patch of lawn, the Mark Twain Library is a mere 2,100 square feet. The smallest public branch library in Long Beach, it approximates the size of a generous living room and den with bookshelves placed at angles and squeezed into all corners. Over half of this small space is dominated by overstuffed shelves of children's books, most nonfiction so that Twain's young patrons can complete their school assignments. The most popular children's selections— *Goosebumps, Dr. Seuss, SpongeBob*—are conveniently stored in plastic baskets next to the librarian's desk in the center of the room. Lining the wall on the opposite side of the room stand the foreign-language holdings in Spanish, Vietnamese, and Khmer marked off by handwritten index cards taped to the shelves. The collection of Khmer books, the largest west of the Rockies, comprises three shelves mostly acquired by the librarians at local Cambodian markets.

A key hub of activity in the library is the computer center, consisting of six computers arranged in a circle less than ten feet from the librarian's desk. These computers are constantly in use for e-mailing, doing online research, working on homework, resumes, and letters by a rotating array of people. One Library Assessment Report found that the majority of the 35,000 residents in Mark Twain's service area do not have computers at home and thus rely heavily on the library for their computing needs.[1] The library's primary clientele are young people: teenagers working on the computers, packs of middle-schoolers giggling and reading in clusters, small children and their parents looking for books and videos. A table in one corner is reserved on Saturdays for a retired schoolteacher who volunteers her time and materials to run an informal tutoring workshop for

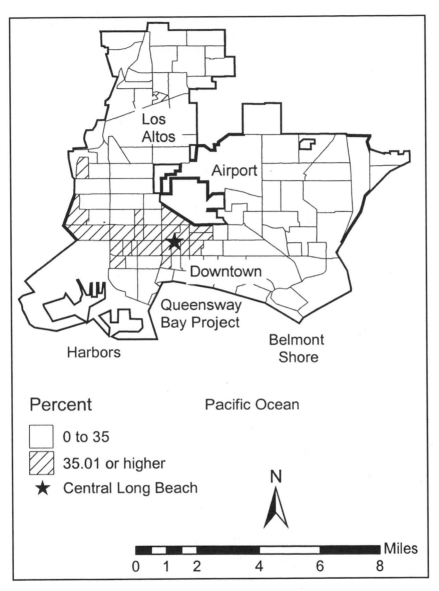

Long Beach Persons Below Poverty Level: 2000. *Daniel Burrough.*

children. In this library, Alphie the Bookworm shares space with a red Cambodian dragon, and garlands of multicolored paw prints festoon the space, bearing the carefully hand-printed names of the library's youngest readers. With signs posted throughout in English, Spanish, Khmer, and Vietnamese, Mark Twain serves one of the poorest and most multiethnic (though almost exclusively nonwhite) communities in the nation.

Mark Twain opened at its permanent location on Anaheim Boulevard on July 1, 1950, when this central Long Beach neighborhood was one of two areas where African Americans could buy or rent homes in the city. Indeed, the library's small size today stands as testament to the second-class status accorded to blacks throughout Long Beach's history. Since the 1960s, a growing number of Latino and Asian immigrants also moved into the Anaheim area, making this the densest core of the city. As one drives along this three-mile stretch of the boulevard, decades of economic and political neglect are visible in the aging housing stock, a mixture of small California bungalows, Spanish duplexes, and low-slung motel-style apartment buildings, and the predominance of liquor stores, cash-checking businesses, and boarded-up storefronts. Yet, there are numerous signs of community life and commercial vitality. Mark Twain sits in the heart of an area known as "Little Phnom Penh," where shoppers at H&H video can rent a Taiwanese love story with Cambodian subtitles or buy lotus rootlets and pickled catfish at Mekong Market. Two miles north on Atlantic Boulevard, past Long Beach's flagship Polytechnic High School, the Afrikan Cultural Center and Barber Shop sits across the street from Rudy's Casa de Muebles and the Tabernaca de Dios. In the shell of a former Denny's Restaurant, Mexican, Guatemalan, and Salvadoran customers crowd into red vinyl booths to enjoy King Taco's *tortas de asada* and *tacos al pastor*. Located just outside of the gentrified downtown business district, these Central Long Beach neighborhoods are home to the majority of the city's African-American, Asian, and Latino residents, including the women who participated in this study. In 1990, four out of ten families fell below the poverty line, with a per capita annual income of $5,750.

But this is not Chicago's Southside or the Lower East Side of Manhattan. Poverty takes on a suburban face here, sprawling across the landscape of tree-lined streets, single-family homes, backyards, and strip malls. In the midday heat, residents are either at work or shut up in their homes, and the streets are quiet as people hustle to and from bus stops, push strollers, and carry groceries. Behind this facade of postwar suburbia, two or three families crowd into small houses and converted garage units, often getting by without basic amenities like heating, running water, or telephone service. Located 20 miles south of Los Angeles, Long Beach is California's fifth-largest city, yet still holds onto its identity as a slow-paced and quiet refuge from its larger neighbor to the north.

Mark Twain Library pulls from five elementary schools where *all* of the children qualify for free lunch. These schools have grown so crowded that they have gone to a year-round schedule and house classrooms in trailers in order to accommodate the neighborhood's students, despite community calls for the School Board to construct a new school. Whereas other branch libraries are open until 8 P.M., Twain operates from noon to 5:30 because the librarians do not want children walking after dark. And with recent budget cuts, each branch library in the city has been forced to close an extra day so Twain is only open Tuesday, Wednesday, Thursday, and Saturday. In 2003, Mark Twain had only $12,199 to spend on acquiring children's books and $6,579 on adult books (with a bonus $5,500 contribution by Jet Blue Airlines when a local judge ordered them to donate to the library because they were increasing noise pollution in the city). A few years ago, the library received no money for new books, and librarian Hope Troy complained that the book budget was "less and less each year."

One of three librarians at Twain, Troy grew up in New Haven, Connecticut and is a classic northeastern transplantee. She and her husband came to Southern California for a visit in the 1970s, "loved it, and never went back." A white resident of Seal Beach, just across the border in Orange County, Troy wears a red cable-knit cardigan and proudly displays her library I.D. on a red-white-and-blue lanyard hanging from her neck. She has worked at this library for over 12 years, splitting a full-time appointment with another librarian. With over 30 years of experience in numerous libraries across Los Angeles and Orange Counties, Troy describes the diversity of the library as "wonderful" and Mark Twain as "the best place to work." The kids are "so motivated" and the parents "so appreciative," she explained. To illustrate this point, she compared Twain to a middle-class library in Long Beach where she had previously worked, noting that the parents there were either overly demanding or too busy to accompany their children to the library. Mark Twain, in contrast, "is like rolling back the clock": People walk to the library; they line up outside its doors on Saturday mornings; children do their homework and meet with tutors while their parents read or wait for them. She points to a group of Latina mothers in the children's section, who she and the other librarians have dubbed the "stroller brigade"—"they check out books like crazy!" Troy pulls out a folder where across the years she has collected snippets of Long Beach news and history. There is the newspaper clipping of "the day they brought snow to Long Beach"; a photograph of a teenage girl and regular patron who is now a student at UC Irvine; various funeral programs for young library users who had been shot and killed; and a "cheat-sheet" that Troy assembled with yearbook photos of middle-school girls who frequent the library so that she can remember their names. She tells a story of Ilene, a painfully shy Cambodian girl who came to the library every day to do her homework and now has blossomed into a confident middle-schooler. "Kids grow up here," she explains.

In many regards, the Mark Twain library *is* like rolling back the clock, calling up an idealized American past when librarians knew patrons by name, kids walked to the library every day after school, parents were involved in their children's education, and the library was a family and community space. This nostalgic image is today cherished as a relic of the past and lamented as proof that the American family and community are in crisis. Contemporary American culture is saturated with an alarmist discourse on broken families, working parents, and latchkey kids, on the loss of family time and shared rituals, and on the decline of community where neighbors do not know each other or look out for each other's children. While this language of crisis cuts across class and race lines, contributing to the widespread belief that the institution of the family is under threat, it is most excoriating when directed at poor nonwhite communities. It runs from sensational images of crack moms, felon dads, and gangster kids to the pervasive belief that lower-class parents do not have the time or wherewithal to be involved in their children's education and community life.

This nostalgia for better and simpler times neither accurately reflects the ways that families actually existed in the past, nor helps to see clearly the myriad and complicated ways that Americans create and experience "community" in the contemporary moment.[2] Public places like Mark Twain rarely appear in images of urban communities, the assumptions variously being that poor people of color have no appreciation for things like libraries, or that public spaces like libraries have been so overrun by gangs, graffiti, or neglect that they are either emptied of patrons or have been forced to shut down. And if we do catch a glimpse of Mark Twain, it is usually in an inspiring human interest story about dedicated librarians like Hope Troy or hardworking young people like Ilene, who are held up to show that anything is possible with perseverance and determination.

Yet to frame Mark Twain as an inspiring story of community self-help and resiliency ultimately curtails our imagination of what is possible and just for low-income communities. Because this library is cozy and structurally sound with enthusiastic librarians and parent volunteers, it is not hard to see why Long Beach Mayor Beverly O'Neil exalts Mark Twain as her "favorite library." But as Troy herself pointed out, "it's not all success stories." While Twain is a jewel of a place, there is a dangerous seduction in celebrating what people are able to do with little. Twain appears successful partly because the American public has grown accustomed to the most extreme and easily recognizable images of urban injustice—crumbling buildings, exposed electrical wires, bitter and racist civil servants, neglected children desperate for adult attention. Simultaneously, its success is marked as exceptional, in contrast to public beliefs about the kind of neighborhood in which it sits.

Indeed, the diverse Central Long Beach community that Twain serves has been the subject of much contestation and consternation within the city of Long Beach. In the 1980s, Long Beach residents, and particularly middle-class white homeowners, pointed to these Central Long Beach neighborhoods as evidence of the anti-American values and cultural habits that threatened the city's identity. Calling up a nostalgic image of Long Beach's past, middle-class residents complained that crime, gangs, day laborers, and slum housing had overrun their orderly and quiet suburban community. This talk of "community decline" served as a coded racial language for describing the broader macroeconomic processes underway in the city. Massive defense cuts and downsizing of the city's military-industrial economy had produced rising unemployment, falling real estate values, and white flight out of Long Beach.

City leaders responded to this economic downturn by investing millions of public dollars in economic development strategies that facilitated the growth of tourist, retail, and high-technology sectors. Downtown redevelopment razed affordable housing to make way for banks, high-rise office buildings, hotels, and luxury condominiums, pushing low-income residents into already overcrowded neighborhoods in Central Long

Beach. At the same time, redevelopment subsidized the growth of poverty through the proliferation of low-paid service positions in hotel and office cleaning, food preparation, restaurants, retail, landscaping services, and so on. The ballooning of Long Beach's economies of service and support has depended on the influx of a low-wage immigrant laborforce, transforming this coastal suburb into a key point of entry for new immigrants from Latin America and Southeast Asia. Yet, while these new immigrants have fueled the city's economic comeback, and while their cultures have been highly commodified to suit Long Beach's new image as an "International City," they remain largely marginalized in the city's social and political landscape. Vilified as a threat to the "quality of life" in the·city, Latino and Asian immigrants, along with their Chicano and African-American neighbors, became the target of new policing measures, such as gang and youth curfews and police sweeps, undertaken to control Long Beach's working-class population.

Ethnoburbs and the Landscape of Poverty

A suburban municipality that sits inside a large metropolitan county, Long Beach differs significantly from larger cities, like Chicago, New York, and Philadelphia, which typically are the focus of poverty and welfare research. The suburban city of Long Beach does not match the iconic image of poor immigrant ghettos in megametropoles like New York and Chicago, concrete urban jungles where people live cramped on top of each other, and self-contained ethnic enclaves where residents shop, socialize, and worship only with people of the same ethnicity. Whereas suburbs in the postwar era were predominantly home to middle-class whites and a refuge for second- and third-generation Americans to escape their immigrant compatriots, today suburban regions are often the first stop for new immigrants from Latin America and Asia. As suburbs have become "command centers" for transnational finance, industry, and services, they have been transformed into places where wealthy Americans and poor immigrants often live in close proximity and are increasingly dependent on one another. These "ethnoburbs" have introduced new conditions for immigrant settlement and adaptation, often producing explosive battles between long-term residents and recent settlers over the cultural character of their community and access to neighborhood services and resources.[3]

This changing landscape of American poverty is not exclusive to immigrants, but rather points to the need for more comprehensive research on suburban poverty and welfare use. In particular, although statistics show that the average welfare recipient lives in the suburbs, there is a dearth of research on suburban welfare receipt. According to the 2000 Census, 49 percent of all poor people resided in the suburbs in 2000, up from 46 percent in 1990. While poverty rates remained the same in central cities and rural areas, poverty rates in the suburbs rose from 7.8 percent in 2000 to 8.2 percent in 2001 (although the poverty rate was twice as large in central cities as in suburbs). Still, nearly all social science research on poverty in the contemporary era focuses on cities and assumes the economic and racial homogeneity of suburbs, despite recent evidence to the contrary. Myrna's Central Long Beach neighborhood, with its single-family homes, landscaped yards, and wide boulevards, makes us reconsider the landscape of poverty. It calls into question pervasive stereotypes of urban slums, immigrant barrios, and welfare homes, all of which associate poverty and the moral character of poor people with the physical decay of the city. This assumes not only that poverty is visible but also that it looks a particular way. Like their actual urban counterparts, low-income suburban neighborhoods like Central Long Beach refute accusations that poor people do not maintain their property and "lack pride" in their community. They also disassemble the social construction of suburbs as the antithesis of everything that has gone wrong in the American city. Orderly, homogeneous, private, and domestic, the suburb since World War II has come to symbolize the ideal form of American community. To see poverty in the suburb, then, is to bring into view the very contradictions of that form.

This book thus directs our gaze to the city's periphery, providing an ethnographic study of poor Mexican immigrants in Long Beach, a "global suburb" located in the southwest corner of Los Angeles County.[4] With its multiracial and international population, its multinational corporations and middle-American heritage, its residential sprawl and dense pockets of poverty, Long Beach disrupts most common-sense distinctions between suburbs and cities. Once a predominantly white bedroom community, Long Beach over the past three decades has grown into a global metropolis that is home to nearly half a million people and a key hub in Southern California's high-technology and tourism industries. As in "global cities" like Los Angeles and New York, Long Beach's economy is sharply divided between high-paying and poverty-wage jobs and increasingly dependent on an immigrant laborforce. Widening economic disparities among residents have made Long Beach home to some of the richest and poorest neighborhoods in L.A. County. With one of the most diverse populations in the nation, Long Beach remains intensely segregated with its residents of color marginalized economically and politically.[5]

Our analysis of Long Beach as a "global suburb" challenges top-down theories of globalization that portray local communities as passive objects of global forces outside their control. In this chapter, we stress the ways that Long Beach city government has facilitated and often determined the trajectory of globalization through urban renewal and redevelopment projects, zoning, tax abatement, workforce development, and lobbying for federal support and capital investment.[6] Indeed, government policy, particularly the city's redevelopment strategies, has encouraged the production of low-wage jobs and exacerbated poverty in Long Beach. While Long Beach has received millions of dollars of federal redevelopment funds which have attached requirements for jobs and housing for low-wage residents, the city has not consistently met these standards (let alone been proactive in setting living wage standards for new jobs created through redevelopment). Thus, Long Beach employers and their political allies in City Hall stand to benefit from welfare reform as L.A. County's work-first welfare program provides them with a ready supply of low-wage workers.

Relatedly, this chapter traces a history of racial inequity in the city in order to contest the pervasive belief that racism in the post–civil rights era is simply a matter of individual prejudice rather than government policy. Founded as a racially exclusive municipality, Long Beach became a racially segregated suburb through state policies during and after World War II, as African Americans and Latinos moved in larger numbers into the city. With aid to sustain Long Beach's defense industries, underwrite home loans and new suburban housing developments, and build highways to link the suburb to other parts of Southern California—federal welfare served the municipality's nearly all-white population. Long Beach's postwar economic growth rested on the racial hierarchies produced by state policies, and the city's economic "rebirth" in the 1980s and 1990s worked through these ongoing racial hierarchies. Part of Long Beach's economic renewal strategy—brought to public acclaim by Mayor Beverly O'Neil—was to encourage downtown redevelopment and tourism, selling the multicultural aspects of the city while attempting to contain the city's diverse population. This official celebration of multiculturalism worked hand in hand with redevelopment policy that spent billions of dollars in the name of city improvement with little actual benefit to the city's low-income, nonwhite residents. With its racially coded discourse and policy to combat crime and urban decay and its celebration of diversity and taking the name "International City," Long Beach thus provides a useful window onto the racial imperatives of welfare reform in the post–civil rights suburb.

Lastly, this chapter provides a historical and structural context in which to situate the ethnographic findings recounted in subsequent chapters. The Mexican women who appear in this book all lived in Central Long Beach at the time that they were interviewed for MDRC's Urban Change Project. Central Long Beach was selected as one ethnographic site for this nationwide study of welfare reform because it had some of the highest poverty and welfare rates in L.A. County and thus presumably represented a typical "welfare community." Most ethnographies of welfare recipients provide only a cursory look at the local history and political-economic conditions of the community in which they live. Place is too often treated as a passive setting or as a self-contained environment (the "housing project" or the "ghetto") that exists isolated from larger historical, political, and economic forces in the city. In these works, locale typically appears as a set of statistical figures and colorful descriptions that form the backdrop to the "real" ethnography of poor women's life histories and daily struggles. Yet, without accounting for how history and political economy structure poor people's life trajectories and choices, ethnographic portraits of the welfare poor fail to disrupt the view of poverty as an individual condition and moral failing.

These women's struggles to find stable and sustainable employment in Long Beach take on a different valence when they are contextualized in city redevelopment strategies that rest on the proliferation of low-wage jobs. Similarly, these women's first-hand accounts of a city, welfare system, and labor market that is deeply structured in racial inequality are all the more illuminating when placed alongside a long history of racial discrimination and segregation in Long Beach that has been directly subsidized and endorsed through federal policy.

Building a City of Brains, Wealth, and Respectability

> Thus, the suburb served as an asylum for the preservation of illusion.
> Here, domesticity could flourish, forgetful of the exploitation on which
> it was based.
>
> —Lewis Mumford, *The City in History*

Incorporated in 1897, Long Beach quickly assumed the unofficial moniker "Iowa-by-the-Sea" for its concentration of wealthy midwestern émigrés, who were drawn to this coastal city for its mild climate, small-town environment, and proximity to downtown Los Angeles, located just 25 miles to the northeast.[7] Local historians trace the city's birth to a land deal brokered in 1882 between Jotham Bixby, a wealthy industrialist who owned much of the land where Long Beach today sits, and William Wilmore, the Los Angeles branch manager of the California Immigrant Union (CIU).[8] Wilmore saw his promotion of Long Beach as furthering the aims of the CIU, an organization created by California industrialists and politicians to "encourage a good class of foreigners from Europe, Canada, and the eastern states [to come] to California."[9] Through the latter half of the nineteenth century, the CIU had labored tirelessly to create a White-only California, facilitating land division and sales to American-born whites and lobbying Sacramento to close the state's borders to Chinese immigrants and other "undesirable foreigners," including Irish, German, and later Southern and Eastern European immigrants. A charismatic speaker and evangelical believer in the superiority of "Aryan stock," Wilmore saw much potential in Long Beach's seaside location and mild climate. He paid several trips to the Midwest to recruit men with "brains, wealth, and respectability" to his city of Victorian amusements.[10] One strategy that Wilmore took to ensure that his city's population met these moral and class standards was to prohibit the use and sale of alcohol within the town's limits, making Long Beach one of two "dry" cities in all of California.[11]

Throughout the 1880s, city elites remained anxious about the encroachment of bad influences, despite the city's respectable reputation as a haven for the Protestant, American-born middle class. One 1888 guidebook described Long Beach as a place where "all objectionable elements are kept out."[12] Residents formed the Long Beach Improvement Society in 1895 to "clean up" the city and two years later filed for municipal incorporation. Long Beach's municipalization in 1897 served as an early precedent for the wave of city incorporations that swept the Los Angeles region in the 1920s and 1930s and continued throughout the twentieth century. Numerous studies of Southern California have documented the ways that forming municipalities gave middle-class elites control over land use and distribution, allowing them to zone out businesses and people they deemed undesirable. As Robert Fogelson explains in *The Fragmented Metropolis,* the white middle-class migrants who arrived in the Los Angeles region from cities and towns across the Midwest and Northeast firmly connected their vision of the "good life" to a system of spatial apartheid:

> [T]he native Americans came to Los Angeles with a conception of the good community which was embodied in single-family homes, located on large lots, surrounded by landscaped lawns, and isolated from business activities. . . . Their vision was epitomized by the residential suburb —spacious, affluent, clean, decent, permanent, predictable, and homogeneous—and violated by the big city—congested, impoverished, filthy, immoral, transient, uncertain, and heterogeneous.[13]

Whereas much of the nation in this period was moving toward urbanization, and cities like Chicago were exploding because of the proliferation of work, Long Beach staked its identity as a city on its *anti*-urbanness. As its population steadily grew, the majority of its residents were white midwesterners, who settled there not for employment but for a suburban lifestyle that offered refuge from "urban vices" like immigrants, non-whites, apartment buildings, and saloons. Intrinsic to Long Beach's founding and growth, this desire to zone out and reform immoral behavior, however shifting the definition, would remain a crucial priority over the next century.

With the 1902 opening of the Long Beach Pike, dubbed the "Coney Island of Southern California," Long Beach secured its reputation as the region's premier tourist destination.[14] However, Long Beach did not desire all tourists but a leisure class of significant means and character; accordingly, Victorian moral codes were enforced through a variety of city ordinances. Alongside the prohibition of alcohol, the city passed a 1920 ordinance requiring that all bathing suits completely conceal the body to the leg "one third of the way to the knee." Violation of this dress code was punishable with a $500 fine and up to six months in jail. Another ordinance in the 1920s made it unlawful for two persons of the opposite sex, attired in bathing suits, to touch each other in public.[15]

During the early decades of the twentieth century, thousands of white middle-class tourists swarmed to Long Beach from throughout California and the Midwest to soak in its seawater pools, visit the Japanese Tea Pavilion, and experience the "Chinaman" attraction at the Pike. As in other parts of the nation, the display and exoticization of nonwhite cultures were a central component of "good clean fun" in Long Beach. At the same time, keeping out nonwhites as tourists and residents ensured the city's appeal and respectability. One 1927 booster history asserted that Long Beach had proven that "the popularity, growth and prosperity of a beach municipality did not depend on a 'wide-open' policy."[16]

The city's industrial base and population also grew steadily during this period thanks to a strong infusion of federal defense money. By 1910, Long Beach was the fastest growing city in the United States and had emerged as a key player in the nation's military-industrial complex, a trend accelerated by the opening of the Long Beach–San Pedro port in 1911 and a U.S. Naval Station in 1919, both financed by the War Department.[17] The city's industrial base and population exploded further following the discovery of oil in Signal Hill on June 23, 1921. Two years later, the city was operating 238 oil wells and was home to 120,000 residents, double the population of pre-oil days. This growth would continue through the 1930s, when the U.S. Navy appointed Long Beach as its Pacific Fleet Headquarters—drawing an average of 40,000 sailors ashore each day.[18]

The arrival of a white working-class population to Long Beach was met with ambivalence, and often hostility, from city leaders and middle-class residents. While the fear of moral decline had long been present in Long Beach, public anxieties now focused on sailors and other working-class men, who were associated with "moral degeneracy" such as drinking and fighting in public, frequenting tattoo parlors and "girlie shows," and gay sex. In the 1920s, it was common for downtown shop owners to post flyers reading "No Dogs or Sailors Allowed" on their windows. The branding of downtown, and particularly the neighborhood of West Beach, as a place for working-class debauchery would continue through the postwar era. By the late 1960s, West Beach would become the first target for demolition and "renewal," described in a brochure published by the Long Beach Redevelopment Agency as "a neighborhood of honky-tonk bars, locker clubs, apartments and rooming houses. It was without question not the best part of town."[19]

The class-based, rather than race-based, nature of public fears derived from the city's prohibition on nonwhite residents; this anxiety would shift precipitously in the second half of the century as people of color slowly won access to housing and jobs in Long Beach. Until World War II, less than 1 percent of the city's population was nonwhite. As throughout Southern California, racial homogeneity in Long Beach was enforced through a variety of means, including restrictive covenants on property deeds, redlining practices by real estate agents and lenders, and scare tactics employed by local police and homeowners associations. A 1922 flyer promoting oil land warned readers that "purchasers of [these] Lots are restricted to the Caucasian or White Race." The city's largest developer, the Jonathan Bixby Company, enacted a similar set of "protective restrictions" for its newly constructed Bixby Knolls development, prohibiting sale or lease "to any person of African or Asiatic descent or to any person not of the white or Caucasian race."[20] Long Beach also made history in 1927 by becoming the first west coast city to host the Ku Klux Klan, as 30,000 people gathered along Ocean Boulevard to watch the Klan march to Bixby Park, the same park that hosted the city's famous annual Iowa Day Picnics.[21] A decade later, a report by the Long Beach Chamber of Commerce celebrated that the "town is singularly fortunate in having such a small portion of non-English speaking races."

Long Beach in the Boom Years

> Television antennas sprouted over Long Beach like the oil derricks of the 1930's. Rock and roll drifted from Hodys and Grissengers drive-ins and carhops on roller skates literally signaled the birth of "fast" food. . . . In Long Beach employment was up, construction was booming, especially in a new phenomena, the suburbs, and industry was growing steadily. [. . .] But it was our last quiet on the coastal front. The 1960's were just around the corner, and Long Beach, the International City, was forced to face that decade's urban upheaval head on.
> —The Junior League of Long Beach, *Long Beach Heritage*

The advent of World War II established Long Beach as a key hub in Southern California's defense-based economy. The city became a model for Fordist production and the quintessential Sunbelt military-industrial suburb. In the late 1930s, the city of Long Beach seized a plot of land through eminent domain and cleared ground for the construction of a plant for the privately owned Douglas Aircraft Company. In 1940, Douglas opened the doors to its first Long Beach plant, a 1.5-million-square-foot complex that included within its confines a company-owned store, school, restaurants, doctors, police, post offices, and clergy.[22] By 1943, at its wartime peak, Douglas was employing 43,000 workers, 23,000 of whom were women.[23] The U.S. military also directly invested over $150 million in Long Beach during the war years, opening the navy's Roosevelt Base and Naval Hospital in 1942 and the Naval Shipyard in 1943.[24]

Fueled by billions of dollars in government defense contracts and federally subsidized housing and highway construction, Long Beach grew into the prototypical postwar military suburb.[25] Between 1940 and 1950, the city's population grew from 164,271 to 250,000 residents, and the city added 34 new public schools between 1949 and 1958.[26] As Long Beach's largest employer, Douglas Aircraft not only dominated the city's economy but also reconfigured its physical landscape. Located in East Long Beach, the Douglas plant shifted the city's economy and population away from the downtown area, which became known as "the Jungle" because of its concentration of bars and locker clubs. With retail stores and services located in or near the factory, Douglas employees no longer traveled downtown to conduct their commerce. Through the infusion of federal money available through VA loans, new middle-class tract housing in East Long Beach multiplied exponentially. Long Beach was developing into two separate and unequal cities: Middle-class professionals concentrated in East Long Beach and along the shoreline, while working-class residents (still overwhelmingly white) lived in the remainder of the city. In 1960, in a city where over 95 percent of the population was white, the income differential between westside and eastside workers was in excess of $2,000.[27]

The centerpiece of eastside suburbanization was the Los Altos development, masterminded by lumber tycoon Lloyd Whaley.[28] Whaley hooked up with the Bixby family to build the Los Altos community, 25 tracts of housing built assembly-line-style, on curved streets with T-shaped intersections to control traffic. With land also set aside for schools, churches, access to the future 405 Interstate Freeway, and a large shopping complex on Bellflower Boulevard, Los Altos was the largest planned community in the nation.[29] Between 1947 and 1956, the neighborhood saw the construction of 10,000 new homes that sold as fast as they could be built.[30] Whereas other suburban developments enabled by the GI Bill opened up new housing for working-class whites, Whaley required a $450 up-front down payment on his houses in order to ensure the right class of residents. Regardless of their economic means, African Americans, Mexicans, and Asians were prohibited from buying homes in Los Altos, and despite the Supreme Court's ban on restrictive covenants in 1948 and ongoing protests against Los Altos, this neighborhood remained closed to people of color into the 1960s.

In the early 1950s, the completion of the 710 Interstate Freeway (followed in 1969 by the opening of 405 freeway which linked Long Beach with Orange County and Santa Monica) allowed middle-class residents to travel directly from the eastside to Los Angeles, bypassing downtown entirely. Throughout the postwar period, freeway construction and the demise of public transportation in Los Angeles County—marked most significantly by the closure of the Red Car system in 1961—increasingly made mobility a publicly subsidized privilege of the middle class. It also solidified the residential and psychological separation between the city of Los Angeles and outlying suburban cities like Long Beach.

In the postwar period, the physical landscape of the city developed through an infusion of public money that went to subsidize the suburban lifestyle of Long Beach's middle-class white residents but was concomitantly denied to people of color. While the navy brought black servicemen to Long Beach in the early half of the century, the majority of African Americans who worked in Long Beach were forced to live in the nearby city of Wilmington. One longtime black resident, Ernie McBride and his wife Lilian put a deposit via the mail on a modest rental home near Polytechnic High School in 1934. Upon seeing the McBrides, the landlord tore up their lease and refunded their deposit. Unable to move to Long Beach until 1938, Ernie McBride described the situation for blacks when he arrived in the city:

> When I first came to Long Beach, this little group, probably four or five hundred was in Martin Luther King [formerly California Ave.], that's where they put them. . . . So it began to expand, until they got this area all segregated. . . . In stores they had signs saying, "WE DON'T SERVE COLOREDS." . . . Then they had big stores along Ocean Front. You could go in there, but a black woman couldn't try on a hat, she couldn't try on shoes, she couldn't try on nothing."[31]

McBride took his first job shining shoes in front of city hall, one of the few jobs open to African Americans in Long Beach in the 1930s along with janitorial, domestic, and manual labor. In 1940, McBride and two other friends formed the Long Beach chapter of the NAACP, recruiting 50 members to fight residential segregation, police brutality, and educational inequality in the city.

Throughout the early half of the twentieth century, as Long Beach developed as a center for recreation and tourism, ethnic Mexicans were also drawn to the area by new employment opportunities as housekeepers, launderers, and dishwashers in facilities that catered to tourists; others worked in factories processing locally produced products such as fish, tomatoes, and wool. Outside the new town, there were settlements of Mexican agricultural workers who were employed at local ranchos and truck gardens that supplied local and metropolitan markets. By the 1930s, Mexican Americans were concentrated in areas like the Zaferia neighborhood near Anaheim and Redondo boulevards, home to the Mexican Methodist Church, and in the downtown area known as "The Jungle." In 1933, Jose Nieto, a descendant of Long Beach's original Spanish land grant holder Manuel Perez Nieto, founded Club Latino Americano de Long Beach y Signal Hill. Created initially to provide earthquake relief to the city's Mexican residents, the club soon turned its attention to police brutality and other civil rights issues. One pressing civil rights concern facing Chicanos and African Americans was the growing violence against young men of color during World War II. The hysteria over zoot suits which spread throughout Los Angeles moved south to Long Beach, as white servicemen physically assaulted young blacks and Chicanos (allegedly on a hunt for zoot suiters).[32] One local zoot suit incident took place on June 8, 1942, as a gang of white servicemen and civilians randomly attacked black and Chicano men in the downtown amusement zone.

Long Beach's Latino and African-American population grew exponentially during World War II.[33] For African Americans throughout the nation, the war had opened up many new employment opportunities. This was also true for Latinos in Long Beach, particularly women—nearly 15 percent of Latino men and over a quarter of Latina women workers in the city were employed in defense-related industries.[34] Yet, despite President Roosevelt's 1941 ban on racial discrimination in federal and defense employment, blacks continued to be segregated at the bottom of the war industries. Blacks in Long Beach were no exception—shut out of white shipyard unions, the city's African-American workers were relegated to the lowest-paying, most menial positions in the port and were largely excluded from jobs in the oil industry.[35] The growing number of black residents in Long Beach during the war years were met with public concerns about overcrowding, housing shortages, and juvenile delinquency. As the *Press Telegram* reported in 1944, the black population had grown

> ten times as large . . . with practically no increase in the area in which Negro citizens resided four years ago. This has forced a condition which finds each structure in the district housing many times the number for which it was planned. No increase in crime or delinquency has resulted. . . . The federal government should give immediate consideration to their housing problem.[36]

By the war's end, there were 15,000 African Americans living in Long Beach. The vast majority resided in the Cabrillo Homes War Emergency Housing Complex, a federal temporary housing compound located on the city's westside. This complex was divided into three tracts, and all African Americans were assigned to Cabrillo III. Despite protests throughout the war era calling for the desegregation of Cabrillo—many black residents asserted that they had left the South for California precisely to escape this state-sponsored segregation—blacks continued to be confined to Cabrillo III until the end of the war. As soon as African Americans were no longer needed to work the shipyards, the city of Long Beach along with the federal government designated the Cabrillo homes as "surplus housing" and marked the site for redevelopment. This decision led to the eviction of much of the city's black population living in Cabrillo. Over 5,000 black residents were then banished from Long Beach because most of the city's housing stock was off-limits to them due to racial covenants.

Indeed, although the U.S. Supreme Court ruled racial covenants unenforceable in 1948, fewer than 4,000 African Americans and approximately 5,000 Latinos lived in the city in 1950, constituting only 2.5 percent of the city's population. Those few middle-class African Americans who attempted to buy homes outside the city's black neighborhoods were harassed and threatened. In 1958, Dr. Charles Terry, a black surgeon working for the U.S. Airforce, bought a $50,000 house in the exclusive neighborhood of Bixby Knolls. Before his family could move in, segregationists had vandalized the home, causing $15,000 of damage. For many

African American residents in Long Beach, the attacks on the Terry home were a symbol of the virulent racism of the city. As one resident recalled, "[T]hose people harassed that man so much it was pathetic! They put the water hose in his window and flooded his home and everything! But the doctor didn't move out."[37] After the Terry family moved in, homeowners in Bixby Knolls organized a property owners protective association to prevent further black incursion into the neighborhood.[38]

As late as the mid-1960s, African Americans continued to be shut out of many neighborhoods and occupations in Long Beach. In 1963, the *Press Telegram* reported that "there are two 'open' neighborhoods in Long Beach—areas where Negroes can rent or buy living quarters."[39] Of the city's 15,000 African Americans, only six families were living outside these two areas, and nearly all black students were attending segregated public schools. As the public debate over fair housing raged throughout California in the early 1960s, the Long Beach chapter of the NAACP continued its decades-long effort to document and protest housing segregation in the city. In response to claims that blacks buying or renting homes in white neighborhoods would decrease property values and lead to general decline, local NAACP president Joseph Brooks responded:

> A Caucasian looks at a run-down Negro area and says, "See what they do when they move in." But the neighborhood already was run down when the Negroes moved in. That's why they were allowed to move in.[40]

A year following Brooks's statement, after California legislators passed the state's first Fair Housing Act, Long Beach homeowners and realtors assumed an active voice in statewide efforts to promote Proposition 14, which successfully sought to repeal this fair housing law. As one Long Beach realtor and chairman of the California Real Estate Association testified before a California State Sub-Committee on housing discrimination in 1964: "90% of Long Beach's Negro population prefer to live among themselves rather than to move into white neighborhoods."[41]

While African Americans in Long Beach had made some advances in federal and manufacturing employment, they continued to battle entrenched discrimination in the city's shipyards, small businesses, and city government. As Brooks testified at a state hearing, "Many city departments do not employ Negroes. But the sanitation department, particularly in rubbish collection, employs 60% of the Negroes holding city jobs."[42] By 1970, the vast majority of African-American workers in Long

Beach were concentrated in blue-collar occupations, with roughly 10 percent employed in professional, technical, and clerical positions (in the same year, these three occupations accounted for 40 percent of the city's total workforce). And, whereas the poverty rate for Long Beach as a whole was 8.2 percent, nearly a quarter of the city's black families fell below the federal poverty line.[43]

Economic circumstances were slightly better but still dire for the city's Latino residents. The 1970 Census counted 21,343 "Spanish Language Persons" living in Long Beach, the vast majority of whom were ethnic Mexicans.[44] In contrast to the black population, census figures for this year suggest that Latinos in the city comprised a bifurcated workforce. Over a third of Latino workers were employed in white-collar professions, whereas approximately half worked as craftsmen, machine operatives, laborers, and service workers.[45] Still, Latino families were surviving on 10 percent less income than the city average, and 11.8 percent fell below the poverty line. The vast majority of poor Latino families were extremely poor, reporting income at or below 75 percent of the poverty line.[46] As in Chicano communities across the Southwest during the civil rights era, Mexican American residents of Long Beach mobilized around issues like educational inequality, job discrimination, and police brutality. In the 1970s, the East Side Neighborhood Center on Anaheim Boulevard. in Central Long Beach became a hub for Chicano political and cultural activity, housing the Centro de la Raza, a youth center, and the local chapter of the League of Latin American Citizens. Still, as the nonwhite population of the city increased, Long Beach's postwar heyday continued to be out of reach for the vast majority of people of color.

Economic Crisis and Restructuring

As in much of Southern California, the 1970s marked a period of economic downturn for Long Beach. Cutbacks in federal military spending led to the loss of hundreds of thousands of defense-related jobs throughout the region. This corresponded with a major transformation in the industrial base of Southern California, as heavy manufacturing downsized its workforce or relocated entirely outside of the state and was replaced by low-wage jobs in the light manufacturing and service sectors.[47] Because Long Beach had been integrated into the regional economy, it was hard hit along with the rest of Southern California. But economic recession hit Long Beach the hardest because of the city's near-entire dependence on a defense-based economy. Whereas Long Beach in the postwar years was celebrated as the quintessential suburban success, by 1980 it had lost over 100,000 jobs and had one of the highest unemployment rates in the nation.

The city's postwar boom came to a halt in the 1970s as Long Beach lost its two major employers and could no longer rely on a steady stream of federal military dollars. In 1974, the closing of the Naval Station led to the evacuation of 19,000 military personnel and their families.[48] The dismantling of this military base, estimated to cost the Long Beach economy $400 billion a year, produced a loss of over 70,000 jobs and skyrocketing vacancy rates, devastated the downtown commercial district, and forced a number of ship-building companies to close their doors. Military cutbacks also hit the aerospace industry, as the city's other major employer, McDonnell Douglas, laid off 26,000 workers between 1968 and 1974. Throughout the decade, Long Beach continued on a course of economic decline briefly abated in the early 1980s, thanks to a new infusion of defense money during the federal largesse of the Reagan years. The navy returned to Long Beach, home-porting 38 ships and 16,000 people. McDonnell Douglas also enjoyed a comeback, employing close to 50,000 workers in its Long Beach plant in 1989.[49]

But the burst of federal defense money was short-lived. By 1990, 15 percent of the city's population was unemployed and 20 percent of its residents fell below the poverty line. These conditions would worsen throughout the decade as the navy once again began pulling personnel out of Long Beach, and the Naval Station officially closed on September 1, 1994. Defense cuts in the 1990s further retrenched the local aerospace industry with rippling effects throughout the city's entire economy. In 1990, McDonnell Douglas accounted for around a quarter of Long Beach's total employed workforce, and aerospace workers earned a total payroll of over $1.5 billion (over 30 percent of the city's total payroll).[50] By 1994, however, McDonnell Douglas had laid off 30,000 workers— over half of its 1989 workforce—producing a trickle-down effect in a wave of shutdowns among smaller subcontractors who had provided materials and services to the aerospace giant.[51] By the mid-1990s, Long Beach again had a higher unemployment rate than any other urban area in the nation[52] and became increasingly known throughout the nation as a casualty of the end of the Cold War, referred to by CNN as "the town the Navy left behind."[53] Many commentators blamed the decline of military suburbs like Long Beach to the loss of military bases and federal defense contracts without critiquing the larger political economy of such cities which, from their early development, had relied primarily on one industry rather than diversify their economic base.[54]

The loss of tens of thousands of jobs along with the 1978 passage of Proposition 13, which devastated the city's budget with the loss of property tax revenue, set Long Beach officials in a desperate search for a plan for economic recovery. Like many cities across the nation, Long Beach turned to an extensive redevelopment strategy that funneled millions of public dollars into private enterprise as a way to recover from this economic crisis.[55] The city's strategy—snappily called "3 T's and an R" (tourism, technology, trade, and retail)—aimed to entice large multinational hotel chains and global technology and trade firms to relocate to Long Beach. Local officials hoped to transform Long Beach into an "engaging and eclectic destination city" that would attract outsiders as tourists and consumers.[56]

In fact, redevelopment directed public money away from the city's most needy communities at the same time that it redeveloped poverty by grounding the city's economic base in low-wage, nonunion jobs. In the 1990s alone, the city redevelopment agency spent over $316 million, yet only 2 percent of these funds went to Central Long Beach where most of the city's low-income residents lived. A closer analysis of redevelopment in Long Beach challenges the pervasive discourse among city officials and business leaders who characterize the city as an unwitting casualty of outside forces, like defense cutbacks and globalization, beyond local control. To the contrary, economic and racial inequality is homegrown in Long Beach, in part the result of new initiatives implemented over the past three decades by city government in collaboration with the private sector.

Redeveloping Poverty

Leading the wave of "urban renewal" that swept through the nation's cities beginning in the 1960s, the Long Beach City Council approved the creation of a Redevelopment Agency at a packed meeting on September 26, 1961. In response to concerns by some residents that urban renewal infringed on individual property rights and was "Communist," the city adopted a policy declaration that emphasized the role of private enterprise in redevelopment.[57] When other residents voiced fears that "slum clearance" was actually a tactic to clear out black residents, city officials repeatedly insisted that they did not have a particular neighborhood in mind; yet within months, the Long Beach Redevelopment Agency (RDA) had unveiled its first project in West Beach, adjacent to downtown and one of two African-American neighborhoods in the city.[58]

Between 1964 and 1993, the RDA had designated eight redevelopment zones that comprised over half of the entire city territory. Most redevelopment concentrated on the downtown business district, starting in 1979 with a $69 million grant from the Carter administration to fund a mammoth downtown renewal plan (what one commentator called a "virtual Marshall Plan for a single American city").[59] Initiated by the Carter administration to encourage "public-private partnerships" in the redevelopment of troubled cities, these Urban Development Action grants required cities to recruit private investors and promised federal funds to help businesses relocate to distressed areas. However, this devolved into a system for funneling federal dollars for the development of private business in downtown, regardless of the benefit or detriment to the low-income residents of these areas. For city redevelopment agencies across the nation, including Long Beach's, the end game of urban renewal became profitability for these private partners, not the economic health of the city and its residents.[60]

The city's vision for "downtown renewal" was to reclaim downtown as a residential and leisure space for white middle-class tourists and consumers and remove the poor who stood in the way. As Long Beach's economic development specialist during the 1970s explained, "We want to include middle and upper class people into the downtown area if the downtown is going to resemble what it once was."[61] In a 1994 interview, another Redevelopment Agency employee noted that moving low-income people out of downtown was "definitely" a conscious goal of redevelopment.[62] The plan for downtown not only sought to attract outside tourists, but it also attempted to woo two different groups of white Long Beach residents. New entertainment and shopping amenities (like high-end retail shops, a top-of-the-line aquarium, and a 12-plex movie theater) would draw wealthy eastside families into downtown in the evenings and on weekends. At the same time, city officials recognized that in order to push the poor out of downtown they also had to recruit a new class of residents. Touting Long Beach's liberal image as pro-environmental and gay-positive, developers marketed the new downtown to young professionals in search of "city living" spiced with a taste of highly commodified multiculturalism. Throughout the 1980s and 1990s, the city's Redevelopment Agency transferred millions of public dollars to private developers, who refurbished artists' lofts, converted historic hotels into condominiums, and constructed an open-air pedestrian shopping district on Pine Street, lined with cafes, blues clubs, and upscale world-cuisine restaurants. The capstone of gentrification was the construction of the MTA Blue Line, a light-rail commuter train line that connected downtown Long Beach to the business district of downtown Los Angeles.

Between 1975 and 1981, a total $100 million in public funds went to redevelop downtown, $55 million in federal and state funds, and the rest provided by the city through revenue and tax allocation bonds. Throughout this period, the city seized hundreds of acres of "blighted" downtown land through eminent domain, relocating residents with 90-days notice and $500 for moving expenses. In an effort to entice business investment in this district, the Long Beach Local Development Corporation offered business loans up to $450,000 at a 4–6 percent reduction in prevailing interest rates, provided assistance to downtown developers in securing long-term multimillion-dollar loans through the U.S. Small Business Administration, and facilitated the distribution of tax-exempt bonds for industrial development. The Redevelopment Agency not only helped private businesses by enabling them to secure low-cost financing, but it also invested millions to construct a public infrastructure in downtown that would attract consumers to these new hotels, restaurants, and shopping malls. The city undertook a mammoth overhaul of public facilities in downtown, constructing a new city hall, public library, Convention Center, and Shoreline Park, while renovating the downtown Long Beach Marina and improving sewage, street, and transportation facilities in the 421-acre downtown redevelopment zone. By the mid-1980s, the downtown oceanfront was littered with high-rise buildings advertising corporate logos for ARCO, Hyatt, Home Savings, Ramada, and Southern California Edison.

Yet, downtown redevelopment did not produce the economic windfall predicted by city officials, and by the early 1990s, hotel and retail vacancy rates in the redevelopment area had approached pre-1975 levels. City officials responded by arguing that more redevelopment would give downtown an economic boost. Throughout the 1990s, the city invested an additional $111 million in public funds to expand the Convention Center. It also began clearing ground for a $650 million waterfront project that included a state-of-the-art Aquarium of the Pacific and the Queensway

Bay Project, a mixed-use development with an outdoor City Place mall, luxury hotels, and oceanview condominiums. Sold by the city as a way to "re-establish Long Beach as the premier waterfront designation in Southern California," this project was predicted to draw ten million visitors to the city, create over 1,000 new jobs, and boost convention and tourist business in downtown. Since its inception, however, the project was enmeshed in problems. In 1998, low-income residents in Long Beach filed a successful complaint against the city for its failure to meet state and federal requirements for targeted construction jobs and other economic opportunities in the Queensway Bay Project.[63] And two years after the Aquarium of the Pacific (financed with $120 million in public bonds) opened its doors, it was operating in the red and required to a $500,000 bailout from the state.[64] Nevertheless, the Queensway Bay Project continued to be acclaimed by city leaders as a successful model for "urban renewal" and earned an Award of Excellence in 2004 from the California Redevelopment Association.

By 1999, the city was operating with $297 million in long-term debt and six of the past seven years the Redevelopment Agency had shown operating losses. Despite mounting evidence that redevelopment was not generating income for the city, public officials continued to stand by this strategy. In a letter to the Long Beach City Council, one community leader described her frustration: "I have had conversations with many City officials regarding the acknowledged 'shot-gun' development methodology in Long Beach. The general consensus is 'bad development is better than no development at all.'"[65] One particularly glaring example was the city's ongoing commitment to attracting and keeping the Hyatt Regency Hotel in downtown. During the 1970s, the city embarked on a 12-year effort to recruit a luxury hotel to Long Beach with the belief that this would lend prestige and economic stability to the city, as the hotel would draw a superior class of visitors and inspire confidence for a new wave of investors. Following failed negotiations with the Sheraton Hotel Corporation, the city quickly turned to a partnership with the Hyatt Corporation for the construction of a 542-room hotel built on 8.5 acres of city land adjacent to the Convention Center. Long Beach initially committed $6.7 million (and secured an additional $3 million from federal grants) to the project, and signed a 50-year lease for the site that gave tremendous flexibility to the Hyatt Corporation regarding its financial responsibility to the city. While city officials recognized that this was a significant outlay of public funds, they praised the Hyatt deal as a huge coup for Long Beach—claiming that once opened, the hotel would generate $21 million in revenues to the city in the first ten years of operation. None of the projections were met, and by 1994, the hotel was in default and owed the city $27 million. In an effort to prevent foreclosure, the city of Long Beach signed a new restructured lease with Hyatt, which forgave the $27 million debt in exchange for an up-front cash payment of $2.7 million to go to the Tidelands Operating Fund and not the city's General Fund. In all, over $10 million in taxpayer dollars (local and federal), which could have gone directly to social services for Long Beach's low-income families, had gone to subsidize one of the nation's largest multinationals in a flawed investment that returned few tangible benefits to the residents of Long Beach.[66]

Several studies have cited Long Beach as a negative example of urban redevelopment because the city's strategies have failed to attract the consumer and tourist dollars that were promised, and because the city's Redevelopment Agency has been operating in the red since its inception.[67] However, as commentator James Elmendorf notes, "Failure . . . is a relative term. If, however, the city wanted simply to move out low-income residents to empty the space, then it has succeeded."[68] Moreover, if the goal of redevelopment is to enable private development with public money, then redevelopment in Long Beach has also been successful. The RDA on numerous occasions has bought property for redevelopment and sold it to developers at much lower costs. For instance, in promoting development alongside the coastline adjacent to downtown, the RDA directly invested $12,754,000 in Shoreline Square but sold the property for $6,000,000.

The cost of redevelopment to the city's low-income residents has been devastating. The scarcity of low-income housing throughout Long Beach is a direct result of public policies enacted at the local level. City officials, backed by homeowner's groups, sought exemptions from federal housing laws requiring that redevelopment projects include low-income housing —because, as they argued, such housing would turn Long Beach into a magnet for undesirable residents and "dependent households" from neighboring black Compton.[69] The razing of SROs and affordable housing in downtown pushed poor residents into outlying central city neighborhoods, further exacerbating housing shortages and overcrowding. Moreover, because the new jobs in the downtown area were mostly concentrated in retail and hotel and restaurant services and were overwhelmingly low-wage and nonunion, city-sponsored redevelopment did little to relieve (and in fact intensified) the widening gap between the city's rich and poor.

This is true of the city's economic development policies more generally, which have pinned Long Beach's hopes for financial revitalization and job creation on the expansion of the tourism, high technology, and retail industries. In addition to investing millions in the construction of a new convention center and hotels in the downtown area, the city during this period also began offering multimillion-dollar incentives and tax breaks to lure high-tech giants like Cim Vision, Covad Communications, and Cisco Systems to Long Beach. The city government's faith in high technology as an economic miracle was amply evident in the city's most recent partnership with Boeing Corporation in transforming the 230-acre site of the former Douglas aircraft plant into a high technology business park. When describing the city's plans for this redeveloped parcel, Long Beach City Manager Henry Taboada explained, 'We want anything in communication, satellite manufacturing, research and development, anything that has the potential to produce a high-tax and high-wage benefit."[70] Urban geographers like Allen Scott have challenged this, philosophy showing how high-tech firms generate a secondary labor market characterized by low wages and high rates of immigrant labor.

But the city was not just leaving offerings at the altars of tourism and high technology. Long Beach—like most cities in California in the aftermath of Proposition 13—also staked its future in shopping malls. One glossy newsletter published by the city of Long Beach titled "Retail rolls on" characterized retail development as "a locomotive . . . pumping new life into our community and dollars into our community."[71] In 1997, the city's Redevelopment Agency set its sights on the Los Altos mall, an Eastside suburban shopping center built in the 1950s, which had fallen into some physical disrepair but was still economically vibrant. Initial plans to tear down the mall and rebuild it were met with vocal concerns from community residents and leaders who worried that the Los Altos project would not only displace small business owners in the mall but also redirect city resources away from Westside neighborhoods most in need. Even the city manager expressed skepticism, "If you are going to conduct a redevelopment project, it has to be done in a blighted area. I think it would be difficult to show that Los Altos is a blighted area."[72] Indeed, at the same time as the Redevelopment Agency was pursuing the Los Altos project, the city was facing a lawsuit for failing to set aside mandated funds for low- and moderate-income housing in redevelopment areas.

Nevertheless the city barreled forward with its plans for the Los Altos project, claiming that a newer, expanded shopping center would double the sales tax revenue (even though a newer nearby mall in a different city was generating similar tax revenue to Los Altos before redevelopment).[73] In 2001, the city council approved the Los Altos Redevelopment Area and committed significant public funds to the project. Seventy-one percent of the acquisition, relocation, and interest costs for acquiring Los Altos for redevelopment were subsidized by the Redevelopment Agency without any obligation for the developer to repay the costs.[74] Moreover, in order to cover the growing cost of the Los Altos project, the city "borrowed" over $28,000 in redevelopment funds from the Westside Industrial Project area (which had been allocated to this predominantly nonwhite neighborhood with a per capita income of $17,000).

Yet, part of the Los Altos redevelopment—a $22 million mall makeover—required getting rid of old, primarily small family-owned businesses to pave the way for new corporate franchises and large department stores like Border's Books and Music, Circuit City, Bristol Farms, and Sears. As the owner of a small hardware store that was forced out by redevelopment noted, "I've fought big-box retailers, but I can't fight City Hall."[75] According to one study, the mall's redevelopment significantly reduced the number of better-paying managerial jobs and increased the number of jobs that pay minimum wages. "The Los Altos project, similar to many retail development projects that feature big name franchises, replaced dozens of small local businesses with a handful of large franchises, with only three spaces for small businesses. The resulting ratio of employees to managers significantly reduces the proportion of higher-pay wages."[76]

The ballooning of tourism, high technology, and retail in Long Beach over the past decade has worsened, rather than alleviated, economic disparities among city residents. As numerous economists have shown, these industries are fueled by a base of flexible low-wage workers, the vast majority of whom are women and immigrants—and yet these were the industries to which the city hitched its economic fortunes. Moreover, they provide workers at the bottom very few opportunities to move up the occupational ladder.[77] Thus, the city's official job creation strategy has resulted in the creation of a permanent population of working poor residents. It has transformed Long Beach into a key port of entry for new immigration from Latin America and Asia, as local employers and city coffers now depend on a constant influx of immigrant workers, who compete for jobs at the bottom of the city's expanding tourism and retail industries.

International City

Economic restructuring in Long Beach was accompanied by a major demographic transformation of its population. During the 1970s, a growing number of African Americans and Latinos had begun to settle in the city's westside, an area abandoned by white middle-class families in favor of new suburban developments in East Long Beach and neighboring cities like Lakewood. Economic downturn led to an intensification of white flight over the next two decades, and, by 1980, the city had lost nearly a third of its white population.[78] At the same time, high vacancy rates and falling property values created one of the most affordable renters' markets in the greater Los Angeles region and enticed larger numbers of African Americans and a wave of new immigrants from Asia and Latin America to the central core of the city. In 1990, Long Beach had a population of nearly 70,000 African-American residents, one of the largest black communities in Los Angeles County.[79] That same year, for the first time in Long Beach history, people of color comprised the numerical majority of the city, and seven out of every ten residents were black, Latino, or Asian. Whereas in 1960 whites had comprised 95 percent of the Long Beach population, by 2000, they had dropped to only a third of the city's population.

Not only a diverse city, Long Beach today is a city of immigrants. In 2000, immigrants comprised over one-quarter (28 percent) of the city's population, and nearly 45 percent of the city's residents reported speaking a language other than English at home. Long Beach also became home to the largest Cambodian community outside of Southeast Asia. Starting in 1979, an estimated 40,000 refugees fleeing the Khmer Rouge regime have resettled in Long Beach. By 1989, the city's Cambodian population was estimated at between 35,000 and 50,000 people. The vast majority (90 percent) of these Cambodian immigrants settled within two blocks of Anaheim Boulevard in Central Long Beach that became known as "Little Phnom Penh."[80] During the 1970s and 1980s, Central Long Beach also experienced an influx of immigration from Mexico and Central America, leading to a threefold increase in the city's Latino population. By 2000, Latinos constituted over 35 percent of the city's population and outnumbered any other racial group including non-Hispanic whites.[81] Ethnic Mexicans accounted for over two-thirds of the 165,000 Latino residents in the city, followed by Guatemalans, Salvadorans, and Hondurans.

The women who appear in this book formed part of this wave of new immigration that made Long Beach one of the fastest growing Latino communities in Southern California. These women had migrated to the United States from all over Mexico, from the border towns of Tijuana and Mexicali, small ranchos in Michoacan and Monterrey, and large capitals like Mexico City and Guadalajara. Many had migrated directly from Mexico to Long Beach in order to reunite with husbands and other relatives already living in the city. Herminia Hernandez and her children, for example, immigrated from Cuidad Juarez in 1986 in order to join her husband who had migrated to California for work in the 1970s and had settled in Long Beach, where he was seasonally employed as a construction worker. Conversely, Leticia Ramirez was the first in her family to arrive in Long Beach in 1989, where she worked for almost two years as a live-in nanny in order to finance her husband's passage across the border.

Others had come to Long Beach as a process of settling out, having first lived in Los Angeles and other cities in the region, and later relocating to Long Beach. Maria Sanchez, for instance, immigrated to Chicago in 1978, where she worked for nearly seven years in an auto factory before moving to Long Beach to live with an older sister. Lupe Jimenez was also drawn to Long Beach by family networks. Having grown up in the working-class suburbs of Southeast Los Angeles, Lupe dropped out of high school at age sixteen and later moved in with her father in Long Beach, where she eventually rented a small studio apartment for herself and her one-year-old son.

These women arrived in Central Long Beach in the 1980s and 1990s, when the Latino community was overwhelmingly comprised of recent immigrants, with over 60 percent of the immigrant population having arrived in the United States within the past ten years. Like many of their neighbors, nearly all of these women had lived for some time in the United States as undocumented immigrants. By the time they participated in this study in the late 1990s, all were legal permanent residents (most having been legalized after the passage of the Immigration Reform Control Act in 1986),[82] and all had lived in the United States for over ten years, with over a third having been in the United States for more than 25 years.[83] Reflecting the diversity of immigrant families in Central Long Beach, many of the women in this study lived in "mixed-status" households that included citizens, legal residents, and undocumented immigrants.

Like most of their neighbors, more than half of these Mexican immigrant women and their husbands worked in Long Beach's service sector, in low-wage jobs in construction, gardening, apartment and hotel maintenance, domestic work, and janitorial services. Others commuted to jobs in other parts of Los Angeles and Orange counties, where they typically labored on the assembly lines and stockrooms of garment, electronics, and other light industrial factories. Like hundreds of thousands of other immigrants from Mexico and Central America, these women and their families were drawn to Long Beach by the prospect of jobs in the city's tourist and service industries and by the relatively cheaper rents available in the central city neighborhoods. They instead found in Long Beach a tight labor and housing market, overcrowded schools, under-resourced hospitals, and a segregated city. By 2000, nearly 20 percent of the city's population lived in poverty.

Racial diversity in Long Beach has not meant racial or economic integration or equity. Rather, in the 1970s and 1980s, race became the principal dividing line between the east and west sides. Luxurious waterfront properties and lush public parks in East Long Beach contrasted starkly with the dilapidated housing stock, overcrowding, constant police surveillance, and inferior municipal services in Central Long Beach. In 2000, whites constituted nearly 90 percent of the residents of wealthy eastside communities like Naples and Belmont Shores, where homes regularly sold for nearly half a million dollars and the average family income was *four times* that of residents living in Central Long Beach. On the other side of the city, over 85 percent of the residents were nonwhites, and nearly half were immigrants.[84] In Central Long Beach, 38 percent of families fell below the poverty line, while more than half of these families were surviving on less than $25,000 per year.[85] And yet despite profound economic hardship, only 19 percent of these households were receiving any form of public assistance.

While housing in Central Long Beach is certainly more affordable when compared to Los Angeles, rents are by no measure cheap. In the late 1990s, one-bedroom apartments rented for $600–700 per month, and two-bedrooms (especially small houses) went for upward of a $1,000 per month. When we consider that the maximum TANF benefit for a family of three in California in 2002 was $679 per month, housing costs were prohibitive, eating up more than two-thirds of many families' incomes. Thus, several families were forced to rent rooms to boarders or double up with extended family. For instance, Teresa Barragan and her three children doubled up in a small three-bedroom bungalow with Teresa's brother, his wife, and their newborn baby. Similarly, Delia and Jose Villanueva rented one of the two bedrooms in their apartment to Jose's coworker, which meant that their two young children, ages two and three, slept on a sofa bed in the living room. Other families crowded into small living quarters; for the Nunez family this meant two adults and five children (ages six to eighteen) sharing a 900-square-foot, three-bedroom apartment.

Despite the focus on retail for other parts of the city, commerce is skimpy in Central Long Beach with a number of liquor stores, a few taquerias, and a smattering of Latino *ferreterias* (a mix between a housewares store and a corner market) and Cambodian produce markets. In the late 1990s, when this study was conducted, the closest shopping mall was four miles away at the downtown Long Beach Plaza, a run-down, increasingly vacant structure that housed a J.C. Penney's, a few 99-cent stores, and Miss Pearl's School of Beauty (the Plaza was eventually closed as part of yet another redevelopment effort). Two Catholic churches and a handful of storefront Pentecostal churches mark the neighborhood landscape. Very few community-based organizations exist to serve community needs. The city's only Latino community organization, Centro Shalom is run by Amelia Nieto, a longtime Long Beach resident and Chicana veteran of the farmworker struggles of the 1960s. The tiny storefront on Anaheim Boulevard down the street from the Mark Twain library is cramped with desks, papers, children's toys, canned goods, and bags of bread. Centro Shalom serves as a legal aid provider, immigration service center, food pantry, cultural center, and political advocate for the city's Latino immigrants.

Crowded into Long Beach's most underserved neighborhoods, Latinos, Asians, and African Americans also remain profoundly marginalized in the public life of the city. Until 1988, despite a number of candidacies including those of community leader Mary Butler and Superior Court Judge Huey Shepard, there had never been an African American or Latino on the board of the Long Beach School District;[86] in 1989, there were nearly 6,000 Cambodian students enrolled in Long Beach public schools, yet not a single certified bilingual teacher who spoke Khmer (despite a state law requiring 91 such teachers).[87] Most of the elementary schools that serve Central Long Beach are so overcrowded that they have had to resort to trailer classrooms or year-round schooling. And in 2000, a multiracial coalition of high school students walked out of their classrooms in protest of the inferior facilities and lack of college prep courses in central city schools.

The Backlash: Rising Slow-Growth and Anti-Crime Discourse

On April 29, 1992, as the world stood captivated by the civil rebellion unfolding in Los Angeles, another fire smoldered unnoticed south of South Central in "Iowa-by-the-Sea." In the three days following the acquittal of the four police officers accused of brutally beating Rodney King, thousands of Long Beach residents took to the streets in protest. As in neighboring Los Angeles, Long Beach's rebellion cut across racial and ethnic lines, drawing in white, black, Latino, and Asian residents of the city's central, downtown, and northside neighborhoods. In the aftermath of three days of rioting, Long Beach was left in shambles: one person was dead, 353 people injured, 30 businesses and homes destroyed, 380 businesses looted, with damages estimated at $40 million. The uprising would not only break apart the façade of tranquility in this coastal suburb, but also add further justification for many white residents to abandon parts of the central city. Longtime *Press-Telegram* writer Bill Hillburg concluded, "But the fear generated on the night of April 30–May 1, 1992, would linger as shoppers and visitors shunned the former riot areas."[88]

Urban rebellion came as a shock to Long Beach whose identity rested precisely in its *anti*-urban-ness. Despite being California's fifth largest city, Long Beach in 1992 continued to imagine itself as a quiet suburban town, a uniquely Californian hybrid of "Peyton Place" meets Pacific seaside resort. One component of downtown redevelopment had focused on fastidiously restoring the downtown's midwestern main street character. Teams of historical preservationists carefully restored the two-story redbrick buildings and art deco lampposts lining Pine Street. Behind Pine, a pedestrian promenade of quaint cafes, antique shops, and blues bars doubled as the site for the weekly Friday morning Farmer's Market. Even the Long Beach Police Department's downtown division, a small army of "cops-on-bikes" in shorts and polo shirts, evoked the nostalgia for small town America, where pedestrians outnumber automobiles and residents leave their doors unlocked at night. In the neighborhood of Naples (modeled paradoxically after the Italian city of Venice), white retirees and yuppies tended their million-dollar Victorian and Craftsman homes and picnicked in rowboats on the seawater canals.

This "simpler," slower pace of life, fiercely protected by a brigade of private and public security officers, became a rallying cry for Long Beach's homeowner movements during the 1980s and 1990s. "Long Beach is *not* Los Angeles," the city's white middle class insisted emphatically, as it protested the traffic congestion caused by new development and lobbied the police department for gang injunctions, youth curfews, and stiff fines for unlicensed street vendors. Yet, for those black and brown residents in the densely populated neighborhoods in the central core of the city, the distinction between Long Beach and Los Angeles is, at best, an exercise in semantics, and at worst, a familiar set of code words for race.

Up until 1960, the city had celebrated each surge in population—one 1956 headline extolled "Six Year Growth Boosts Population of City by 67,433." After 1960, reports of population growth were more met with alarm—a 1972 *Press-Telegram* headline forebode "Population Control: 40,000 Ceiling Proposed for the City." Amidst growing public discourse about the city's emergent "population and growth problems," a group of Long Beach residents formed a local chapter of Zero Population Growth and petitioned the city to provide financial support for sterilization clinics (after reviewing the proposal, the council decided that it was not feasible). Over the next two decades, homeowners organized to block several new proposed developments, including a mixed-use commercial and residential project on the westside, citing traffic gridlock and population density as their main concerns.

As with other homeowner movements across Southern California, citizen calls for slow growth in Long Beach were tied to a racialized discourse of "urbanization" and images of the poor and people of color as menacing criminals. Much of this hysteria focused on Asian and Latino youth gangs and the "relentless war for central city streets," as dubbed by the *Press-Telegram*.[89] California Attorney-General Dan Lungren blamed gangs for "most of the violent conduct" in the city, and the Long Beach police made the "Asian-Latino War" a main priority in the late 1980s and early 1990s. Indeed, there had been an escalating battle between the city's Asian and Latino gangs following the drive-by shooting of a Latino boy apparently by a Cambodian boy in 1989. This gang battle propelled Long Beach onto the national stage, prompting a front-page *New York Times* story by award-winning journalist Seth Mydans. This article was one of many such features the *Times* published on gangs in the 1990s, which served to illustrate the terrifying and increasingly foreign nature of inner city neighborhoods.[90] Since this gang dispute had begun, the "Asian-Latino" war had accounted for a total of 36 deaths. Yet, as James Elmendorf notes, "Though 36 murders is certainly too many, five percent of nearly 700 murders [that took place in the city between 1989 and 1994] hardly makes this battle responsible for this violence in the city."[91] And the cease-fire negotiated between Cambodian and Latino gangs in September 1994 went largely unnoticed by the local press.

In fact, crime in Long Beach had not increased—statistics show some decline in crime between 1990 and 1994. Nevertheless, citizen concern about crime ran rampant, echoing a previous hysteria among Long Beach elites and residents around spreading criminality in the early twentieth century. In the early 1990s, middle-class residents demanded and won increased policing, youth curfews, and drug sweeps in the central city district. The city created a "graffiti hotline" and began to mandate public school uniforms (white shirts and blue pants for boys, white blouses and blue skirts for girls), making the Long Beach School District the first in the nation to do so.

The widespread blaming of Long Beach's social and economic problems on people of color was evinced in a 1998 poll conducted by the *Los Angeles Times,* which ranked crime and drugs as the top two problems plaguing Long Beach. The paper reported that "one-third of [Long Beach] voters felt that the Asian and Latino lifestyles have worsened the city environment."[92] This popular sentiment was echoed by one Long Beach resident who asserted that, "[We] didn't have this trouble before the Third World moved in."[93] Long Beach city officials also perpetuated public hysteria over an ever-looming black and brown criminal mass. In 1987, the city manager asserted in the *Times* that the city's "rising" crime rate was "one result of the [nonwhite] population boom."[94] Five years later, another city official offered the following explanation for the ongoing white exodus from Long Beach: "They are leaving because of crime. When I was a kid, Long Beach was where all the white people lived, and in recent years this is starting to change."[95]

Others in city hall began promoting an alternately sunny discourse on Long Beach's future. While still foregrounding "urban problems" like crime and gangs in Central Long Beach, these city officials celebrated the city's "strength in diversity" and credited the entrepreneurial spirit and strong work ethic of new Southeast Asia and Latino immigrants for Long Beach's economic comeback. By the late twentieth century, "Iowa-by-the-Sea" had become the "International City"—an official title adopted by the Long Beach City Council in the 1990s and printed on banners that lined the city streets. The election of former educator and Democrat Beverly O'Neil as mayor of Long Beach in 1994 was the capstone of this movement. She explained, "I thought people weren't as proud of the city as I thought they should be, and I thought by running for mayor maybe I could instill some sense of pride in this wonderful town."[96]

Racialized images—whether of people of color as menacing savages and lazy dependents or of nonwhite immigrants as supplicant workers reviving the American Dream—worked hand in hand with the development of a post-Fordist economy in Long Beach. On the one hand, such racial ideologies functioned to naturalize the suitability of Asians and Latinos for the menial, low-wage work that fuels the city's new economy. Accustomed to hard work, naturally talented for physically arduous or manually detailed tasks, and grateful for any opportunity in their new country, Latino and Southeast Asian immigrants were represented as the ideal flexible laborforce for the "International City." On the other hand, concurrent images of blacks, Latinos, and Cambodians as drug dealers, gang members, and welfare queens produced a justification for the repressive measures (from police surveillance to cuts in social services) taken by local officials to contain those communities left behind by the city's redevelopment.

Implications for Poverty Research

The history and political economy of Long Beach provide a different starting point toward understanding welfare and citizenship in the twenty-first century. First, this chapter allows us to see contemporary concerns over immoral behavior as neither new nor particular to the groups being targeted today. From the city's incorporation in the 1890s, Long Beach public officials sought to shape who could live in the city and benefit from its resources. More than one hundred years of attempts to "clean up the city" and restrict its occupants present a much different window onto the ideological nature of contemporary fears about "the

Third World moving in." Whether sailors or African Americans, Southern Europeans or Mexican immigrants, public hysteria over immorality has a long and ignominious history in Long Beach and has often corresponded with white middle-class desires for exclusivity and containment. To treat today's concern with the decline of values among the urban poor as a real cataclysm in need of urgent reform is not only ahistorical but misses the ways such hysteria has often and continues to be used for larger political purposes.

Second, this chapter foregrounds how the shape of Long Beach's economy and physical design did not just naturally evolve but was made to happen through the actions of the federal government, Long Beach public officials, business representatives, and local citizens. The women who appear in this study did not simply end up poor and underserved by city public services, the Mark Twain Library unfortunately but unavoidably small and underfunded. These realities grew out a series of public actions taken over the course of the twentieth century. By the 1950s, the city's economy had grown exponentially through its municipal dependency on military contracts. As Long Beach developed into a company town—that company being the U.S. defense industry—the discrimination that pervaded the city's industries, housing, and schools was not accidental or de facto, but a publicly subsidized system of benefits for white middle-class residents at the expense of the rest of Long Beach's residents and the nation's taxpayers. Even in the city's postwar heyday, well-paying jobs, ample housing, and equal city services were never widely available to people of color in Long Beach, despite community protests that sought to open neighborhoods and unionized employment to people of color. The bifurcated economy and segregated housing patterns that we see today in Long Beach thus have long historical antecedents. Styling itself as a suburban refuge and the antithesis of urban poverty and blight, Long Beach has, for over a century, depended on underpaid workers to keep the city clean, homes well kept, and children cared for.

Beginning in the 1970s, when city fortunes started to slip and public attention focused on "blighted urban areas," Long Beach received hundreds of millions of state and federal dollars to help alleviate poverty, rebuild neighborhoods, and address urban problems of "crime, poverty, and neglect." Yet, this infusion of redevelopment funds has functioned largely as a strategy of transferring public money into private hands, and the neighborhoods and city residents it was intended to benefit have largely not profited. While proponents of redevelopment have promised big returns to the city through increased tax monies and new jobs, libraries like Mark Twain continue to be crippled by ongoing budget cuts, and more than a fifth of the city's residents continue to search for sustainable employment. The city has actively pursued redevelopment strategies in tourism and retail, industries that rest on a large base of low-wage workers—in a sense cultivating an economy that produces poverty wages. Decisions to increase city debt through countless unsuccessful redevelopment schemes and to continually cut back city services reflect not unavoidable budget realities but decisive city policy, as community leaders have consistently questioned the direction of urban renewal and redevelopment over the past 40 years. Long Beach, then, benefits from the work-first focus of welfare reform, which ensures a large base of workers forced to take "any job at any wage."

This chapter began with a description of the Mark Twain library in an attempt to raise more complicated ideas about poor and multiracial communities like Central Long Beach—about the tremendous value residents place on public spaces like Mark Twain, about the mundane, daily rituals of community and scholarship in poor communities, about shared family values and the "wonderful"-ness of diversity, *and* about the travesty of underfunding these services in the face of such desire and need. Looking at overcrowded and underfunded Mark Twain, and the "motivation" and "enthusiasm" of its patrons, provides a sharp rebuke to those who oppose services for immigrants on the belief that immigrants are ruining these cherished American institutions. With more funding, less than the city's redevelopment agency invested in the downtown shopping district last year, Mark Twain could be open more hours and all seven days a week, could have more than two full-time librarians and a bigger building, could comprise multiple rooms for children's and adult books with a computer center for adults along with a computer room for kids. While more computers, books, and librarians is not all that much to ask for, such requests are typically seen as impossible and unrealistic; the lack of adequate resources at libraries like Mark Twain is framed as an inevitable result of shrinking city budgets rather than the direct consequence of city spending priorities. A chart of the 2002 Long Beach budget makes the city's priorities immediately evident, with the line for police reaching near the top of the page, dwarfing social services like libraries. That the city was carrying a long-term debt of nearly $300 million due to failed redevelopment projects and investing tens of millions more of taxpayer dollars in risky new redevelopment initiatives, while slashing services like libraries, illuminates the political construction of "unavoidable cuts" versus "forward-thinking investments."

Mayor O'Neil refers to Twain as "her favorite" library, promising a new building whose completion has already been twice delayed. But such praise maintains the second-class status accorded to Twain and the community it serves. Public officials can celebrate the library's energy and diversity without seeing it as a repudiation of the city's priorities. Official multiculturalism serves to absolve public responsibility for profound racial inequalities in the city—at the same time that the mayor's recognition of Twain works to offset community calls for more resources. Celebrating what Twain's staff and patrons can accomplish with so little naturalizes the fact that such communities have so little—our attention drawn away from the structural inequalities that create Central Long Beach to the hard work and chutzpah of neighborhood residents (reinforcing the widespread belief that urban change rests with individual initiative).

Alongside this economic explanation for Mark Twain's perpetually shrinking resources, then, sits a cultural rationale for the library's low budgetary priority. Today libraries are seen as antiquated and alien and thus not crucial public concerns in a time of lean city budgets and privatization. Seen as antiquated in the face of home computers and big-box bookstores for middle-class Americans, they are cast as alien to poorer Americans who are "too busy surviving" to make time for books. Poor people—and particularly people of color—are believed not to hold the same value of education and learning as their middle-class counterparts, thus contributing to their lack of economic mobility and justifying the absence of well-apportioned libraries in places like Central Long Beach. Looking around the library on any of the four days it is open and the small crowd that sometimes forms in the morning before the doors are unlocked exposes this public fiction: people are busy reading and writing and researching and doing homework. But, if it can be publicly believed that poor people do not value learning, then they become responsible for their neighborhood's underresourced library. And mayors can celebrate special cases like Mark Twain without disrupting the prevailing view of poor communities as inherently culturally different and deficient.

In the face of white nostalgia for the good old days of Long Beach, part of what O'Neil attempts to do by celebrating Mark Twain is to instead assert diversity as one of the Long Beach's greatest assets. But such celebration obscures the city's long history of exclusion and racial inequity and evades responsibility for the structural inequalities that continue to define its economy, political structure, and school system in the present. And it obfuscates the craving for real opportunity and access to education that exists in these Central Long Beach neighborhoods. As we will show in the next section, this desire for education motivated the women in this study in their initial excitement about GAIN and drove their disappointment at the program's false promise.

PART II

Any Job at Any Wage

3

Tough Love in L.A. County
The Failure of Welfare-to-Work

Fieldnote #87

On an evening in March 1998, over one hundred parents, grandparents, and children crowded into the cafeteria of Burnett Elementary School in Central Long Beach, a mile north of Mark Twain Library. The meeting had been called by the L.A. County Department of Public Social Services (DPSS) to unveil California's new welfare program, known as "Cal-WORKs" (California Work Opportunity and Responsibility to Kids). Enacting the department's mission to create a more "client-positive environment," a small army of DPSS staff, along with volunteers from the school, local churches, and social services agencies, cheerily greeted arrivers. Inside, a long folding table was piled high with glossy CalWORKs brochures and flyers advertising job training programs and counseling services. Free refreshments of coffee, juice, and cookies were served.

Fidgeting apprehensively in their folding chairs, the women and men who attended the forum represented a cross-section of the surrounding community: Cambodian grandmothers cradled infants; African-American couples flipped through DPSS brochures; a group of Mexican and Central American mothers rotated a position at the door to keep an eye on their children outside in the playground. Mostly brown and black, with a handful of white faces, many in the audience had stopped at the meeting on their way to or from work. Their uniforms testified to the range of low-wage jobs that predominate in Central Long Beach: Alberto's Mechanics; Pic 'N' Save; Hilton Hotel Housekeeping; and Saint Mary's Hospital Food Services.

After 15 minutes of fiddling with the school's faulty P.A. system, a DPSS representative took the mike. "The government wants you to work in order to achieve self-sufficiency," the middle-aged Mexican-American speaker told the expectant audience first in English, next in Spanish, and finally translated into Khmer by the school's translator. "Welfare is no longer an entitlement for the rest of your life, but a temporary help for short periods of emergency. You can only get help for five more years. After your welfare clock runs out, you won't get any more help. The good news is that the government will help you to break your dependency on public assistance. You will be assigned to a job counselor who will help you to assess your skills and goals, and to develop a personalized plan to move you from welfare to work."

An African-American woman rose in her chair and interrupted the speaker. "I just got evicted from my home, and there's no space in the shelter. How am I supposed to look for a job when my kids don't even have a roof over their heads?" The DPSS official's smile shifted to a polished expression of empathy as she recited the phone number for emergency aid services. Then she continued enumerating a list of California's new welfare rules: Parents who do not produce their children's school attendance and immunization records will lose all or part of their cash benefits; single mothers under age eighteen must be living with a legal guardian and attending school full-time in order to receive welfare; if you've been convicted of a drug-related felony or of welfare fraud, you can no longer receive welfare; most adult legal immigrants are no longer eligible for food stamps . . .

This is post–civil rights California where welfare reform can be shown off like a new Florida time-share and there is no irony in serving free refreshments to inform people their food stamps are being cut off. Town hall politics, Clinton-style, meant that DPSS officials could "hear people's pain," but they did not have to take seriously the comments people were making to review or reformulate CalWORKs policy. Surrounded by a roomful of working people who were daily living with the reality that work does not protect a family from the vagaries of poverty, these officials stood as cheerful ambassadors of the new "empowerment" that comes from work. Structural problems endemic to poverty—from inadequate schools to low wages to substance abuse and domestic violence—were individualized, blamed on the welfare recipient's low self-esteem, motivation, and dependency problems. But, as these counselors promised, this could be cured through good old-fashioned work (admitting to having a problem and then applying oneself). The state had not stopped caring about its poor; but, following President Clinton's mandate that welfare be transformed into "a helping hand, not a hand-out," the poor now would be disciplined into helping themselves.

California's approach to welfare reform has earned it a reputation as one of the most generous welfare states in the nation. Thanks to a Democrat-controlled state legislature and powerful labor and immigrant rights lobbies, California managed to stave off some of the most draconian aspects of welfare reform. While states like Florida terminate the entire family's welfare benefits after two years, California continues to assist children under the age of eighteen, even if the parent has been cut off of TANF due to sanctions or time limits. Whereas legal immigrants in most states across the nation lost access to cash aid, food stamps, and medical benefits, California pledged its own state funds to provide cash aid to some legal immigrants who do not qualify for federal assistance. It also created a state-funded program to restore food stamps for 56,000 of the estimated 151,700 legal immigrants whose benefits were terminated under federal law.[1]

But, before we declare California a welfare wonderland, consider the following: Even prior to the passage of federal welfare reform, California was a vociferous advocate of work-first approaches. In the early 1990s the state began requiring long-term recipients (defined as three years or more) to get a job or lose their benefits. Assembly Bill 1542, signed by Governor Pete Wilson on August 11, 1997, imposed even stricter work requirements and time limits than those mandated under federal welfare reform; CalWORKs participants have 18 or 24 months to get a job, accept a workfare position, or lose their benefits;[2] they are subject to the maximum federal requisite of 32 hours per week of "work activities," which, with rare exceptions, do not include GED preparation or college courses. Although not required under federal law, California legislators imposed a "Maximum Family Grant" rule which denies benefits to children born to families already receiving welfare; thus, a mother of two who today applies for TANF in Los Angeles County will get a monthly check for $565, whereas a mother who has a second child while receiving TANF is expected to survive on $490.[3] Indeed, California's welfare policy only appears generous when viewed in the context of today's race to the bottom. In a neoliberal world, where "devolution" extends beyond a strengthening of state's rights to the dismantling of the most basic social rights, state budget battles rest on a choice of feeding children or providing them with textbooks.

While California's Welfare-To-Work Act of 1997 created the Cal-WORKs program and outlined state provisions that conform to federal mandates, it gave individual counties the responsibility for program design and implementation. For welfare administrators in Los Angeles County, home to the nation's third largest welfare caseload (behind the *states* of California and New York), this entailed the monumental task of moving over 100,000 adults into work or "work-related activities" in a regional labor market that was producing one-fifth the number of new jobs economists estimated as necessary to absorb the massive influx of welfare recipients.[4] Furthermore, according to DPSS's own figures, the majority of jobs available to TANF recipients in Los Angeles County paid the state minimum wage of $5.75, far below the hourly wage of $7.82 that is necessary for a family of three to become ineligible for public assistance.[5] In other words, even if DPSS managed the impossible feat of moving most welfare recipients into work, there was little guarantee that employment alone would produce the caseload declines demanded by the federal government. The design of L.A. County's welfare system, then, was not intended to succeed in the literal sense (indeed could not succeed in actually moving the vast majority of people into jobs that would pay enough to render them above the assistance threshold). But it could—and would by many accounts—succeed in the ideological sense of valorizing work and demonizing welfare to a point where more and more people would "choose" to leave the rolls (even if they had to return again or could not survive adequately without assistance).

In designing its welfare reform plan, DPSS also had to contend with a powerful alliance of legal advocacy organizations, community groups, and public sector unions that mobilized to block the most repressive policies adopted by other large metropolitan areas. In a political climate that cast welfare as the problem and work as the solution, most liberal and progressive organizations advanced the strategic position that recipients want to work but that they need more help in overcoming barriers to employment, and *good* jobs to lift them out of poverty. Grassroots groups like ACORN, AGENDA, Community Coalition, the Los Angeles Coalition Against Hunger and Homelessness, and the Human Services Network worked in tandem with city and county employee unions to repeal the most egregious workfare and sanctions proposals and to fight for additional funding for services like childcare and drug and alcohol treatment. They also fought for seats on the business-dominated governance councils responsible for administering billions in federal welfare funds. These tactics produced concrete political victories, from free bus and train passes for recipients to get to and from work, to more community oversight over the spending of welfare-to-work money. Most significantly, unlike in New York City and other large cities, union and community activists successfully blocked L.A. County from adopting a large-scale workfare program, and won an alternative small-scale City Jobs program that connects welfare recipients with full-time unionized employment with the city of Los Angeles.[6]

L.A. County's final plan for welfare reform, implemented in stages beginning in April 1998, downplays unpaid community service and on-the-job training in favor of a dual strategy that deters eligible families from applying for TANF, and facilitates the quick entry of existing recipients into the private sector labor market. In the words of former DPSS Director Lynn W. Bayer, this entailed the "evolution" of DPSS "from a traditional welfare department to an employment support agency."[7] The result, however, was not a total transformation of L.A. County's welfare system, but rather a more rigid delineation between two types of social welfare. Much like the "bad cop/good cop" routine from television police dramas, DPSS was divided into two functions, one punitive, the other rehabilitative—each with its own offices, administrative structure, bureaucratic procedures, and institutional culture.

Today, persons applying for TANF or inquiring about their existing benefits are directed to Eligibility Offices, officially known as "BAP" (Bureau of Assistance Payments) and referred to by most recipients as simply the "welfare office." In these prison-like structures, visitors often pass through metal detectors and armed security guards on their way to the clerk (in many offices cloistered behind Plexiglas windows), and then endure hours in the cheerless waiting room before they are seen by an Eligibility Worker. From an administrative standpoint, BAP offices have been redesigned to run like a well-oiled assembly line. No longer assigned to individual clients, BAP staff are "banked" into units of six eligibility workers, who are together responsible for managing between 2,500–3,000 cases at any given time. In a model that would make Frederick Winslow Taylor proud, cases are organized into separate processing streams: "Intake Units" handle new applications and determine eligibility for aid; "Approved Units" oversee existing cases where there is no outside income; and "Specialized Units" manage those cases where recipients are earning wages or receiving other forms of income.

When a person comes to apply for welfare, an Intake Eligibility worker collects information from them to enter into the Income and Eligibility Verification System (IEVS), which cross-checks this information with databases operated by the Social Security Administration, the State Tax

Board, the Internal Revenue Service, and, if the applicant is not a U.S. citizen, with the INS's Systematic Alien Verification for Entitlements (SAVE) system. If IEVS determines that the information provided by the applicant is true, then the computer will calculate the appropriate amount of cash and food stamp benefits for the applicant and generate a letter of approval. Once approved, an applicant must, under the threat of disqualification, have fingerprints and photograph taken, which are digitalized and stored in the statewide Fingerprint Imaging System.[8]

DPSS's internal reorganization and its growing reliance on computerized eligibility assessment and client tracking has resulted in the deskilling of the welfare caseworker. Once trained in social work techniques and expected to counsel clients in periods of crisis, eligibility workers have been retooled to act as the human interface between poor people and computer data management systems. This has significant consequences for the BAP worker and the welfare client. Because BAP workers are no longer assigned to individual cases, it is more difficult for them to become familiar with a client's case and to give each case the attention it deserves. This new organization also functions as an industrial speed-up and labor discipline within the DPSS workplace itself, as eligibility workers are required to do more work with less autonomy, under increased surveillance. The increased surveillance of eligibility workers further ensures that fewer will go out of their way for clients as their job now depends on working as quickly as possible to reduce the welfare rolls.[9]

Although the new BAP offices appear to be a perfect mesh between Fordist rationalization and high technology, most of the Latina welfare recipients interviewed for this study insisted on talking about the irrationality of the welfare system. Just as sociologist John Gilliom found in his study of welfare recipients in Appalachian Ohio, Latinas in Long Beach were acutely aware of the myriad ways that they were being surveilled by the welfare department.[10] They protested the impersonal and dehumanizing treatment they and other families endured from eligibility workers. They lamented that they no longer had an individual caseworker who knew them and their children. They talked of waiting for hours on the phone before being transferred to an anonymous caseworker who would then take another hour to get updated on the particularities of their case. They challenged the notion that computerized social services would assure "quality control" by citing example after example of how the computer had "messed up" their case, and how eligibility workers still retained the power to withhold applications, reject documentation, and kick them out of the office if they protested. And given the system's "irrationality" they returned time and again to the welfare office hoping to get a caseworker that would listen to them (which they sometimes did).

If some Latinas described the BAP offices as "nasty and rude," they spoke of the other face of welfare, the GAIN program, as *"bien pretty, pero puro mentiras* (real pretty, but all lies)." GAIN, or Greater Avenues for Independence, is the welfare-to-work arm of DPSS and the system's good cop. While BAP's persona rests on depersonalization, GAIN's fetishizes human personality as alternately the cause and cure of all social ills. Its modern, clean facilities resemble a cross between an employment agency and a psychoanalyst's office, with comfortable furniture, plants, and inspirational posters on the walls. ("What lies behind us and what lies ahead of us are tiny matters compared to what lies within us"; and "Even if you're on the right track, you'll get run over if you just sit there.") Here, "participants"—called "clients" in BAP offices—are assigned to an individual GAIN Service Worker (GSW), who will meet with them to design a personalized "Welfare-to-Work Plan" and later coordinate their "welfare-to-work activities." GSWs are trained to be welcoming, professional, and courteous with program participants, all part of GAIN's vision of motivating welfare recipients to achieve "self-sufficiency" and to regain "the same human dignity every working person enjoys."[11] However, GSWs have their own bag of tricks for disciplining welfare recipients, which include chastising them for their lack of motivation and self-esteem, and reporting them to their BAP worker, who has the power to reduce or cut off their benefits. And, while GAIN's slogan promises its participants "A Job. A Better Job. A Career," the program teaches welfare mothers that "any job is a good job" and directs them away from professional careers or skilled trades that require additional education or training. Thus, although the discourses of personal responsibility and self-reliance sit at the heart of GAIN, at base this program does not entirely trust welfare recipients to act in their own self-interest, and thus enforces a set of proscribed behaviors and choices through constant monitoring and surveillance.

These are the two components of welfare reform in Los Angeles County: One a hyperrationalized system for processing poor people, designed to deter them from accessing the welfare benefits they are entitled to under law; the other an equally rationalized effort to catalogue and normalize the various deficiencies of the welfare poor in order to "empower" them to help themselves. While BAP exercises its power directly on the bodies of welfare recipients by limiting their access to food, shelter, and medical care, GAIN strives to act upon their consciousness in order to align these women's personal desires and goals with the political and economic imperatives of post-Fordist capitalism.[12] The physical and economic coercion of BAP and the ideological reconditioning of GAIN work in tandem to materialize the messages behind welfare reform— principally, that being on welfare is bad—and to regulate poor women's subjectivities as workers, mothers, and citizens.

Numerous scholars have noted that welfare reform represses poor women, especially women of color, by policing their sexuality and motherhood and forcing them into exploitative labor arrangements. However, few have explained how the disciplinary power of welfare reform is codified and put into action through daily, small-scale discursive and administrative techniques, or analyzed the ways that welfare recipients interpret and move through this system of power. If we look closely at what political theorist Barbara Cruikshank calls "the messiness of small things [that] makes possible a large system like welfare," we see that, even in the era of welfare reform, punitive regulations and sanctions exist alongside efforts to promote self-sufficiency and personal responsibility among the welfare poor.[13] This discourse of self-empowerment is not an ideological ruse or form of false consciousness. Rather, as Cruikshank argues, it is central to a neoliberal system of governance that continues to depend on the consent and participation of poor people in their own "reform" and regulation. Current discourses of empowerment, self-esteem, and self-help not only contribute to the medicalization of poverty and its treatment as an individual pathology, but also transform the "question of governance" into one of self-governance.[14] The role of government is now to discipline the poor into governing themselves. This chapter, thus, presents an ethnographic case study of the micropolitics of case management, welfare-to-work classes, and job clubs in L.A. County. In these small and messy spaces of welfare reform, Latina immigrants are disciplined and pushed off the rolls through sanctions, contradictory rules, illegal actions by caseworkers, and "voluntary" decisions to disenroll. Paradoxically, through this same process, they are "empowered" to see and know themselves as the authors of their identities, choices, and actions within a fundamentally limited set of ideological and material restraints.[15]

Whose GAIN?

Building self-sufficiency through employment implies the strong belief that employment provides individuals and their families the independence to determine and accomplish their own physical, economic, social and health goals.

—Los Angeles County Office of Education Website

Lupe: They sent me to this "job club" shit. *Me mandaron a GAIN.* They say they are going to get you a job, but what they do is teach you to lie. Like, the lady there, she told us to put on our [job] application that, even if we take care of our kids at home, we should write that we have daycare experience. Or, if we have a little garden outside our house, we should put down "landscaping." That's lying! I mean, I don't think that's right. One of the men there in the room, he spoke out. He said that he's Christian and that he doesn't lie. . . . Man, I wanna get me some real training so that I can get a good paying job!

Norma: They just want you off welfare. That's the whole main point. . . . When we went to the [GAIN] meeting, I said, "So, in other words, you want everybody off, right?" And, she said, "Well, that's our goal, but we're not there yet." I said, "Okay, but have you thought about those people?"

As Mexican immigrants talk about their experiences under welfare reform, they speak over and over again about a program called GAIN. Most of the women in this study had learned about GAIN from a family member, neighbor, or friend who had participated in the program in the past. A few, including Lupe Jimenez, had themselves voluntarily enrolled in GAIN after their caseworker told them that it offered free childcare and help finding a good job. By the late spring of 1998, several women in the group had received a letter from the welfare office threatening to cut their benefits if they did not report to GAIN. Whether they found their way to GAIN voluntarily or under coercion, these Latina mothers entered the program with similar expectations. They had vast employment experience, yet were tired of shuttling between part-time, temporary jobs, and hoped that GAIN would connect them to stable work that could lift their families out of poverty. Most were attracted to the program by the promise of subsidized childcare; they wanted to work, but knew that they could not afford a babysitter on the low wages available to them, and worried about their children's welfare while they were at work. All understood the importance of education as a vehicle for social mobility, and they enrolled in GAIN with the expectation that the government would finally help them to attain a GED, study English, go to college, or learn a skilled trade.

Instead, these Latinas discovered in GAIN yet another welfare program that presumed their deficiency in most arenas of life, and told them how to dress, speak, take care of their children, use their time, and spend their money. Instead of professional careers, white-collar jobs, or skilled trades they were tracked into the same low-wage work they had been doing for years. Instead of academic schooling, they received soft-skills training in resume writing, interviewing techniques, and workplace attire. In lieu of access to quality and affordable childcare, they found themselves having to compromise their choice of childcare providers and to maneuver yet another maze of applications, contradictory eligibility rules, and lost paperwork. In the place of real opportunities for independence, they and their children were subjected to another set of arbitrary and harmful regulations.[16]

GAIN is the flagship of welfare reform in Los Angeles County. Participation in this welfare-to-work program is mandatory for adult recipients with children ages one and up. As of April 1998, all new CalWORKs applicants who pass the eligibility screening are referred to a GAIN Regional Office for an employment assessment, and then enrolled in Job Club. Between April and December of that same year, the county expected to phase in an additional 149,000 existing welfare clients into the program. Once enrolled in GAIN, a welfare recipient has 18 months to secure a full-time job or be assigned to unpaid on-the-job-training or "community service." Individuals who are not working (either for wages or a welfare check) by the end of the 18-month "work-trigger period" lose their cash aid and food stamps. Individuals who arrive late or inappropriately dressed, skip a meeting, refuse a job offer, or break any of the GAIN rules can be sanctioned with a portion or all of their benefits.

GAIN's 20-year history in California, and its transformation from an adult education to a work-first orientation, in many ways paralleled broader changes in American attitudes toward welfare and poverty. GAIN was created in the early 1980s as an experimental statewide program designed to encourage AFDC recipients to return to school. Recognizing the growing importance of education in California's information-based economy, GAIN encouraged welfare recipients to enroll in GED, community college, and four-year college courses through incentives like free tuition, childcare assistance, and transportation vouchers. Immigrants with limited English-language proficiency (one-third of L.A. County's GAIN caseload in the late 1980s) were enrolled in ESL classes and basic education programs. Although GAIN offered a job search component, this activity was not mandatory. Program staff stressed the idea that employment was a long-term goal for welfare recipients, who first needed to acquire the educational credentials and training that would enable them to secure good-paying jobs.[17]

In the early 1990s, faced with recession-driven cutbacks in social services and a vocal public backlash against welfare spending, California's policymakers decided that sending welfare recipients to work, rather than to school, could more quickly reduce the rolls—or at least show that the state was aggressively attacking the problem of "welfare dependency." In the words of then-Governor George Deukmejian:

> We need to give a hand to those who cannot help themselves for a short period of time, until they can make it on their own. In turn, those we help must help themselves. . . . GAIN should be transformed into a true "workfare" program, where the immediate priority is to remove people from welfare rolls and put them on payrolls as quickly as possible. . . . [All] participants should be required to look for jobs before being diverted into any education or training program.[18]

While GAIN's shift to a work-first approach was politically motivated, policymakers cynically justified it by claiming that they were acting in the best interest of welfare recipients, who wanted jobs not more schooling. This "hard-to-serve population," they argued, had never excelled in school and would be better served if GAIN instilled, as one administrator put it, "the old American work ethic" and pushed women to find a job. Under this new program, welfare as a way of life would be replaced by a working lifestyle, complete with a new set of cultural values and behavior. In 1995, a group of researchers contracted by DPSS to evaluate the new GAIN summarized its philosophy as follows:

Work is valuable
You will be better off financially.

As a working parent, you can be a working role model for your children.

Being on welfare is bad for your self-esteem.

Any job is a good job
The best way to get a good job is to first get your foot in the door.
Even a minimum wage job is better than no job at all.

You can get a job
With the proper attitude and job seeking skills, anyone can find a job in Los Angeles.

Continued education may also be valuable
You can get an education, but the best way is to get a job first, and then go to school in the evenings.

If you go to school as part of GAIN, it will be short term, with the goal of getting you into a job quickly.[19]

This new program, renamed "Jobs-First GAIN," stressed early job entry, even if the jobs were low paying, and even if participants didn't have a high school diploma or didn't speak English. Job Club participants were now taught to view low-skilled, entry-level, and part-time employment as the road to economic and social mobility, and advised to accept any job, regardless of pay level or work conditions. DPSS continued to offer transitional benefits, like subsidized childcare and transportation, to recipients who had found a job. However, those interested in GED, ESL, adult literacy, and job training programs were required to get a job first, and to pursue education or job training in night school or weekend classes. Furthermore, whereas the original GAIN had operated as a voluntary program, thanks to a 1993 waiver from the Clinton White House, participation in the Jobs-First program became mandatory for all "long-term" AFDC recipients (defined as having received three years of assistance in the past five years) with children ages three and up, and was strictly enforced through sanctions—about one-third of all Jobs-First GAIN participants lost some or all of their welfare benefits during their first year in the program.[20]

As the debate over welfare reform heated up in Washington, D.C., during the summer of 1996, Republicans and Democrats pointed to California's GAIN as a model initiative that was successfully transforming welfare dependents into productive workers. Much of this fanfare rested on an evaluation of GAIN commissioned by the state, and conducted by MDRC, which praised the program's work-first approach for increasing the employment and earnings of welfare recipients. Missing in congressional and media celebrations of GAIN, however, was any discussion of the fact that "GAIN's major success in this state had occurred in Riverside County, which has experienced a 3% job growth in each of the two years [when the study was conducted]. In Los Angeles County, with its far bleaker employment picture, welfare mothers who went through the GAIN program earned a mere $108 over a two-year period than those not enrolled in the program."[21] Nor did GAIN supporters address critics' concerns that by the end of MDRC's three-year study, two-thirds of the participants were not working, and almost half never worked during the entire three-year period. Thus, MDRC's research did not provide evidence that those people who had found a job while in GAIN remained employed and off of welfare, let alone that work was actually lifting them out of poverty. Yet despite these mixed and questionable findings, MDRC's endorsement of the work-first approach (one long favored by welfare critics) lent GAIN unprecedented legitimacy in policy circles and thrust the program into the center of state and national welfare debates.[22]

Predictably, then, the passage of PRWORA in 1996 was a major windfall for L.A. County's GAIN program. As they rushed to meet the federal and state guidelines, DPSS administrators fixed their sights on GAIN as the template for welfare reform. In 1997, in order to accommodate a mammoth explosion in the number of GAIN participants, DPSS allocated $140.4 million in federal and state funds and another $6.7 million in county funds to welfare-to-work operations (compared to a total $120 million for benefits administration) and created 245 welfare-to-work staff positions, including 108 new GAIN line staff.[23] Pumped up by tens of thousands of new participants and millions in federal and state welfare-to-work dollars, GAIN was transformed from a small experimental program into a mammoth, state-sponsored welfare-to-work conglomerate.[24] Embodying a new flexible model of government with an increasingly privatized public sector, GAIN's childcare services, Job Club, counseling, and career advisement services are contracted to government and nonprofit agencies outside the welfare department. Modeled after the corporate "performance incentive" system, the county now pays financial bonuses to agencies who send the most welfare recipients to work. In some agencies, caseworkers with the highest number of job placements are rewarded with free movie tickets and restaurant coupons.[25]

Today GAIN also functions as a state-subsidized temp agency, whose website for prospective employers announces, "When you're ready to hire, we're ready to help!" Indeed, GAIN's "employer services" confirm the worst fears of scholars like Steven Pimpare, who warned that welfare reform would manufacture a "compliant, docile, and dependent work-force for private companies with the use of public funds."[26] GAIN "pre-screens" job applicants, arranges for in-house interviews, works to assure a "good fit" between an individual and a job, and organizes "job fairs" where welfare recipients are on hand for immediate interviews. Although GAIN does not conduct formal drug tests or background checks, "during the pre-screening process all individuals are confronted on these issues." Up front about the private sector subsidies the government now provides, GAIN trumpets the rewards "to your company's bottom-line" because "we put you in touch with potential employees who have child care benefits and health care coverage in place when you hire." Hiring through GAIN saves employers money they would otherwise spend on advertising job openings and interviewing "random applicants." The website also highlights tax breaks for employers who hire welfare recipients, noting that "the Welfare-To-Work Tax Credit will provide your company with as much as $8,500 per employee, and there is no limit to the number of employees a company may hire." After the GAIN participant is hired, the employer assumes control over his/her employee—but rest assured that this individual will still have a "built in support system" with a GAIN Case Manager and other services, including mentoring, counseling, child-care, and more. Employers who receive rebates for hiring welfare work-ers at low wages are celebrated as part of the "national effort committed to helping families in our community become self-sufficient."

Twelve Steps to Self-Sufficiency

> Being on welfare affects your self-esteem, and it affects your kids. I felt like a failure when I was on welfare.
>
> —Ex-welfare recipient in GAIN orientation video

Many welfare recipients seem to need pressure from the outside to achieve their own goals. They seem to be looking for structure. The idea

of case managers monitoring people easily strikes the better-off as severe. . . . For the poor, however, supervision is often new and welcome.
. . . Said one [GAIN] supervisor in Riverside, [CA]: "It reminds them
that you *care,* and that you're *watching.*"
—Lawrence M. Mead, *The New Paternalism*

Employers who hire through GAIN enjoy real financial rewards. Yet,
when GAIN sends women like Lupe Jimenez to work, the program in-
structs them to compromise material gains like wages and health insurance for more elusive therapeutic benefits like improved self-esteem and
happier family lives. Like most self-help programs, GAIN is organized
into a series of progressive steps that are designed to lead the individual
toward the ultimate goal—whether it is defeating an addiction, surviving
sexual abuse, or, in the case of GAIN, moving from welfare to "self-sufficiency." Just as in Alcoholics Anonymous—where addiction is cured not
only by stopping the problem behavior, but also by training the individual to acknowledge, diagnose, and narrate himself or herself as a sick individual—GAIN's mission is to change the individual's behavior by getting her to understand herself as a welfare dependent and welfare as a deviant condition. Thus, Alcoholics Anonymous (AA) and GAIN are
similar in that they teach participants that they have enough control over
their lives to be held responsible for their dependency.

The discourse of welfare dependency both structures a way to read the
welfare recipient's past and provides her with an identity for the future.
The medicalization of welfare dependency provides the former recipient
with a teleological path of "recovery" in which to anchor her future, a
scar in her past that always already constructs the present as an improvement. Narration is central to the process of recovery, whether from
welfare or alcoholism. Indeed, much of the treatment in both addiction
and welfare-to-work programs involves "sick" people testifying about
their illness under the belief that improved self-knowledge itself is "good
medicine." Although Job Club participants are not required to provide
public testimonials as in AA, former recipients serve as motivational
speakers at the GAIN orientation and are featured throughout the program's promotional materials. Whereas in Alcoholics Anonymous the
primary mode of discipline is individual self-monitoring (reinforced by
group sessions), the surveillance at work in GAIN is more pervasive.
While the program trains welfare recipients to monitor themselves, it ultimately does not trust them to be responsible for their own "recovery"

and thus subjects them to constant monitoring by program staff through strict enforcement of tardiness, daily activity reports, and physical inspections.

The psycho-behavioral model that undergirds welfare-to-work programs like GAIN is emblematic of what Sanford Schram identifies as a pronounced historical shift in welfare administration in the United States. According to Schram, over the past three decades, welfare has been converted from an income redistribution program to a "behavior modification regime" that treats poor people as sick individuals who need to be cured of their bad personal habits (ranging from illicit drug use, to joblessness, to addiction to welfare). Schram locates this medicalization of poverty in the larger cultural anxieties over personal health and dependency (drug use, cigarette smoking, overeating, sexual addiction, etc.) that overtook American society in the late twentieth century. While the American middle class has long deployed a discourse of personal fitness, good habits, and self-discipline to distinguish itself from the "undeserving underclass," this has become an increasingly important tool of social and moral distinction under the intensified economic competition and individualism produced under late capitalism. Schram writes:

> Medicalization becomes even more important in the late-twentieth century postindustrial order where people are transformed into economic actors with less collective security than before from the family, community, firm, and government. . . . The need to embody the self-disciplined self is heightened and the failure to do so is seen as an even greater failure than previously.[27]

The medicalized lexicon of welfare dependency locates the causes of poverty in the individual characteristics and failings of poor people, while tying the personal health of the poor to that of society by turning welfare dependency into a social disease that must be aggressively diagnosed, quarantined, and treated. Charged with combating this threat to public health, the aim of welfare administration is no longer income maintenance, let alone poverty reduction. Rather, under the "new paternalism" championed above by conservative analyst Lawrence Mead, the public mission of welfare administration is to supervise and recondition the behavior of welfare recipients, who as "sick" and "damaged" people cannot be entirely trusted to act as responsible adults.

Entering the Welfare-to-Work Contract

This combination of self-discipline and external monitoring is evident in the first step of the GAIN program, a day of "Orientation and Motivation." In the morning session run by facilitators from the Los Angeles County Office of Education (LACOE) under contract with DPSS, crowds of up to 40 welfare recipients are informed of the new time limits and work requirements under CalWORKs and warned of the consequences if they fail to comply. An afternoon session of self-help advice and motivational activities follows—meant to, in the words of the LACOE website, "Reawaken old dreams. Set goals in order to make your dreams a reality. Begin to trust—and believe—that you have the power to achieve whatever you desire." Motivational activities are designed to be interactive and inspirational. Participants take turns reading aloud the GAIN materials and brainstorm collectively about the financial and emotional benefits derived from work, which are then listed on butcher paper and posted throughout the classroom. They watch videos that feature former GAIN participants who, in only a year, moved from welfare to jobs where they earn $18 an hour. They listen to heartfelt confessions from facilitators (many of whom are former welfare recipients) about their past problems with alcohol, depression, or abuse, and how faith and self-discipline allowed them to overcome these personal barriers to employment and self-sufficiency.

Following the orientation, each welfare recipient meets with a "GAIN Service Worker" (GSW), whose job it is to regulate her or his welfare-to-work activities. During this initial appraisal session, recipients are required to answer a set of perfunctory questions about their length of time on welfare and previous employment experience, and to read and sign a document entitled "Welfare-to-Work Plan: Rights and Responsibilities." Among the "rights" listed here is the right to "Receive direction and support from the county to help you improve your ability to get a job"—although what "direction and support" a person has a right to is never spelled out. Conversely, the recipient is informed of her/his responsibility to "Accept a job if you get an offer unless you have a good reason not to" —although what constitutes a "good reason" is left to the discretion of the GSW, not the recipient who is presumed to lack discretion. This Welfare-to-Work document is a legal contract between the welfare recipient and the state of California. However, as the document itself clearly states, refusal to sign does not relinquish an individual of her/his welfare-to-work rights and responsibilities. In other words, refusal to sign the contract is itself a violation of the contract and thus the "non-compliant" individual can be sanctioned with the loss of welfare benefits. Although always already constrained by the rules of engagement established by the state, the welfare recipient is nonetheless invited to make a "choice": to sign, or not to sign (which means s/he will be removed from public assistance).

The Spectacle of Job Club

After signing or refusing to sign the Welfare-to-Work Plan, an individual's "welfare clock" begins ticking—she now has 18 or 24 months to find a job, and the first step in this process is Job Club. This "job readiness" program functions like a boot-camp-meets-finishing-school to inculcate welfare recipients into the life skills, job search skills, and workplace rules and comportment deemed essential to finding and keeping a job. The first week of Job Club is dedicated to classroom instruction on topics ranging from how to compose a resume and fill out a job application, to interview techniques, to the importance of personal hygiene and physical fitness for success on the job. In Job Club welfare recipients are taught to brush their teeth before a job interview; as we heard from Lupe Jimenez above, they are instructed in "creative lying" techniques for resume writing; they are taught how to read the want ads in the newspaper and how to approach employers when asking for work; they are lectured on the importance of honesty, enthusiasm, and obedience in the workplace.[28]

Participants are expected to treat Job Club as though it were a paying job. Monday through Friday, they are lectured on the importance of orderliness, timeliness, and reliability. On their first day of the program, they are handed a list of Job Club rules:

> JOB CLUB RULES
> 1. Be on time—8:30 to 12:30
> 2. Dress for success
> 3. Full class participation
> 4. No criticisms
> 5. No food
> 6. No drink
> 7. No gum
> 8. Daily job search[29]

Those who arrive even a few minutes late are locked out of the classroom. Individuals who are absent or repeatedly tardy are reported to the BAP office for sanctioning. Norma Gonzalez, for example, was one of several women in this study who had been sanctioned for arriving late to Job Club. As she described:

> You have to be there exactly at 8 o'clock, or they lock you out. . . . I got locked out once . . . twice. Twice I got there at 8:15, I believe. Because it's kind of hard because I had to take my son to school, and then catch the bus and go all the way, this place was in Carson [a neighboring city]. So, I got here at 8:15, and I was like, "Well, open the door." And she was like, "You're late. I'm sorry. I'm going to have to write your worker a note." I said, "I'm only 15 minutes late. I had to take my son to school." She said, "Well, you should have gotten up earlier." And she closed the door and locked me out. . . . I was late about twice, so they cut me off.

Norma was removed from her family's welfare benefits, leaving her with less than $400 a month to support herself and her six-year-old son. Two months later, her benefits were reinstated and she was sent back to Job Club. She eventually found a job at the Cheap Bargains Warehouse, working four hours per week.

Strict dress codes are also enforced in Job Club, and breaking the dress code is cause for getting kicked off of welfare. In many GAIN offices, participants receive a handout on the "Mandatory Dress Code":

JOB CLUB MANDATORY DRESS CODE

MEN	WOMEN
Shirts and Slacks	Skirt and Blouse
Appropriate Shoes	Dress
Socks	Nylons (hose)
Neat and Clean	Neat and Clean
Clean Fingernails	Appropriate Shoes

ABSOLUTELY:

NO: Spandex pants	NO: Sun Dresses
NO: Short skirts (must be at least knee length	NO: Mid-rift tops
NO: Shorts	NO: Extreme hairstyles
NO: Theme tee shirts	NO: Tennis Shoes
NO: See-through tops	NO: Jeans/Levis
NO: Hats	

Appropriate dress is necessary to participate and be successful in your job!

When asked to describe the dress code, Margarita Gonzalez parodied the absurdly detailed requirements while highlighting the financial burden that this placed on program participants: "When you go to GAIN you have to wear closed shoes, stockings . . . skirts, [no more than] three fingers above the knees . . . shirts that are not low cut. . . . Only dress pants. And the men have to go with ties, suits. . . . But, a lot of people are poor." Because many welfare recipients cannot afford the "appropriate business attire" required for Job Club, some GAIN offices have partnered with the nonprofit organization "Clothes the Deal" to open on-site "boutiques" that offer free of cost "gently-used clothing for needy participants." And, for recipients who know to request the service, the county also offers a $50 clothing voucher for a welfare mother to buy a business suit and a pair of dress shoes. However, most of the Latinas in Long Beach reported that access to clothing—as well as bus passes, childcare vouchers, and other "employment-support services"—is tightly controlled by program staff, who dole out donated suits and vouchers to only certain recipients whom they deem the most deserving or promising. As Margarita elaborated, "They have clothing there at the office, but they don't give it to everyone. . . . I told them that I did not have clothes and they did not give me anything."

The dress code ranked high on Latina immigrants' list of grievances against GAIN. They protested that they were treated like low-class hillbillies devoid of common sense concerning basic rules of etiquette. Maria Sanchez, for example, pointedly commented on the "obviousness" of the job attire lessons: "*No tiene chiste* [there's no point to it]. I don't need to be told not to wear *chanclas* [flip-flops] when asking for a job." Similarly, Leticia Ramirez's husband refused to attend Job Club, noting that "I don't have the time to go and sit there for weeks, dressed all elegant, when I could be looking for a job." For many the dress code showed how out of touch GAIN was with their real opportunities in the labor market. At the same time that these welfare recipients were required to attend GAIN and go job hunting in business suits, they were sent to apply for jobs in factories, fast food restaurants, hospitals, and janitorial services. Many spoke of the humiliation of showing up "dressed up all elegant" to apply for a factory job. Because most women did not have the money to buy the clothing required by GAIN, they were forced to stretch their budgets to purchase office clothing they would have no use for once they started working.

Only one woman in this study, Norma Gonzalez, was informed by her GSW about the clothing services available to program participants. She received a $50 voucher for J.C. Penney's, a list of articles she was required to buy, and told to return to Job Club the next day with her receipts. As she explained:

> So, I went to the store, and the other girl who came with me, she said, "What are you going to buy with $50?" I said, "I don't know, but we better stretch it." So we were just looking. I got a skirt. It was 40-something [dollars], and I went back [to GAIN] and said, "I can only afford a skirt." She said, "You can. You can. I know it's hard, but you can't look at the classy stuff." . . . They want you to be presentable. They want you to be dressy, but then they want you to get the cheap stuff.

The dressing tutorial, how it functions, and how women theorize it, constitutes a microcosm of the GAIN program itself. These regulations police class—they set welfare recipients up as alien from the work and class culture they must aspire to and then they put them in their place once they do. "Dressing for success," then, becomes at once an empty exercise and a form of ritual humiliation because these women already know that the clothes they are being told to wear and buy are not appropriate for the jobs that are available. With very few in the group having even a high school diploma, they will not find jobs as executive secretaries or paralegals in L.A. County's competitive labor market. And they cannot wear suits to be janitors or home health care providers, factory workers, or domestic help. Moreover, these women already know what constitutes professional dress—and they know that $50 is not enough to purchase such an outfit. And then, when Norma buys such a skirt, her caseworker rebukes her. She has reached above her class position (even though she has been instructed to do so).[30]

For the Latinas in this study, the humiliation of Job Club was further compounded by the fact that they were offered limited assistance in finding a job. Following an initial week of classroom instruction in "life skills and job readiness," GAIN participants advance to Job Search. Each morning, they must report to the GAIN office (for the women in this study, this was a half-hour bus ride from their homes) before they are sent out to look for work; at the end of the day, they must once again return to GAIN with five job applications. Occasionally, job seekers are supplied with the classified sections of local newspapers or with information on job openings. More commonly, however, these women reported that they were instructed to drive or take the bus around town looking for "help wanted" signs or to cold-call businesses listed in the phonebook. Because few owned cars and because they were looking for jobs across the vast expanse of L.A. County, they often grouped together to ride the bus or chipped in to pay for gas when someone in their group owned a car. Once they collected the job applications, instead of filling them out and leaving them at the place of employment, they were required to return them to the GAIN office as proof that they had been out looking for work. (This system was tremendously inefficient as women traveled 25 miles to a potential workplace, once to pick up the application and then making a separate trip to drop off the application.) This continued every day for two weeks.

Margarita's account of the futility and arduousness of Job Search spoke to the frustration of other Latinas in the study:

> You have to go wherever to ask for applications . . . and those of us who don't have a car are walking or on the bus. One time I even fainted. . . . We had heard that a factory was hiring, so we went and there were a lot of people [asking for applications]. We got the application, and since I had not eaten and [it was very hot], I told my friend, "You know what? I think I'm going to faint. I feel very bad." . . . And the next day, I told the lady, the one who explained everything to us at the Job Club . . . I said, "Hey Maria, I fainted yesterday." She laughed and she asked why.

According to these Latinas' accounts, GAIN turns asking for a job into a public spectacle, where they are surveilled not only by the welfare state, but also by potential employers and sometimes other workers. Many women explained that Job Search made them feel branded as welfare recipients. Employers and workers would see a crowd of people dressed in business attire asking for applications at factories and supermarkets and know immediately that they had been sent by GAIN. A few women even reported that they had been sent away and told outright that the business was not hiring "people from the welfare office."

Not only did this system set welfare recipients apart from other job seekers, but it also further compounded the pressure these women were experiencing from GAIN to take any job they were offered, even if it was part-time or temporary. As Norma explained:

You have to have like a good, good reason not to take [a job] because they know. Like a lot of interviews that you go to, they know that you're going through this program that's called GAIN and everything, and if they [GAIN] find out that you didn't take a certain job, then you're in trouble because they want to know exactly why you didn't take that job. So, you're like being forced to take any job you can get. I mean you can't be picky.

Norma's observation that employers know when an applicant is from GAIN and know the rules of the program illustrates the ways that the surveillance of the welfare state radiates beyond the walls of the GAIN office, reminding recipients that they are being monitored at all times. It also echoes the objections raised by welfare rights advocates and labor unions that because employers know that welfare recipients are legally obligated to take any job offer, they are decreasing their entry-level wages and increasing their use of part-time and contingent labor.

Racial Steering: "Those of Us Who Speak Spanish Are Sent Directly to Work"

After three weeks of Job Club, individuals who successfully find 32 hours per week of employment advance to the final step of GAIN, its "post-employment services," which include "extended case management" (their GSW can, but is not required to, track them for up to one year), optional life skills and parenting classes, adult basic education and GED night courses, and services for the treatment of substance abuse, mental health problems, and domestic violence.[31] The GAIN participant who does not find a job is supposed to be referred to a day and a half-long "vocational and clinical assessment," where she takes a battery of personality and skills tests meant to match her natural abilities and vocational interests with "existing work opportunities," and to identify the services that she will need to find a job. The test results, along with an oral interview, will be used by the county to determine whether the individual will be reenrolled in Job Club, sent to a 6- to 12-month vocational program, or assigned to a "community service" (WEX) position at a public or nonprofit agency for unpaid "on-the-job" training.

However, all the Mexican immigrants in this study who had participated in GAIN endured a minimum of six weeks in Job Club before they found a job, were referred to a vocational assessment, or dropped off of welfare altogether. Margarita was sent through Job Club twice, applying for over 200 jobs, was sent home for a month, and then was ordered to take an English proficiency exam, which would determine if she qualified for computer classes. But as she recalled:

> My name sounds very Mexican. . . . I got there at 7:45 and my appointment was at 8:10. . . . I was the first on the list and all of the people below me on the list were called, but they did not call me. And it was 10:30 and I said, with the English that I know, I said, "They have not called me." She said, "Oh I'm sorry, I hadn't seen your name." But how could she have not seen my name? It was right on top and she jumped me and she went to the other ones because my name was Mexican. . . . So they apologized and told me that they were going to send me to another appointment and that I should go home. I asked if they could give me money for the bus because I had no money . . . so they gave me a dollar and I came home and I told my daughter. She said, "*Ay mami,* look at how they are treating you."

Margarita was scheduled for another assessment two weeks later, but in the interim she was offered and forced to take a part-time job cleaning rooms at the Hilton Hotel in downtown Long Beach. Margarita concluded that although she would have preferred to take ESL and computer classes so as to improve her opportunities in the labor market, "those of us who speak only Spanish, they are just sending us directly to work."

Margarita was not the only one to note a troubling pattern of discriminatory tracking between English and Spanish speakers in the GAIN program. Many of these women worried that GAIN was denying vocational training and basic education to Latino immigrants, especially to those who need it the most. Norma, for instance, attributed her eventual enrollment in a training program to the fact that she speaks fluent English and had already completed her GED. She described herself as "lucky" when compared to many other people, especially older immigrants, in her Job Club: "A lot of people have never been to school. They don't know how to read or write, and they [the GSWs] don't have any patience with them. There're like the people they cut off because they have no patience with them." In fact, the only two Latinas in this study who were approved by GAIN for job training, Norma and Lupe, were both bilingual speakers in their midtwenties who had completed some high school in the

United States. Conversely, the older women in the group—those with very limited literacy and English-language skills—were sent through Job Search over and over again until they found a job or dropped out of the system in frustration.

By steering foreign-born welfare recipients directly into part-time, temporary, and minimum wage jobs, GAIN contributes to the growth of a contingent immigrant laborforce, while denying immigrants one of the most fundamental hallmarks of U.S. citizenship: access to public education. Several studies of welfare reform in Los Angeles and other California counties have found similar evidence of racial steering and discrimination against non-English speakers in CalWORKs programs. A 2002 study conducted by the Economic Roundtable in L.A. County, for instance, found that although most Latino respondents said they needed ESL classes and job training, they were being tracked directly to Job Search and into low-wage jobs. Less than 1 percent of all welfare recipients interviewed for the study offered positive comments about CalWORKs services, whereas most described the program staff as disrespectful and rude and protested the lack of clear and accessible information about services like education, job training, and childcare.[32] Similarly, research conducted with Mexican and Vietnamese immigrants in Santa Clara County found that they had tremendous difficulty in obtaining information about CalWORKs services (program materials were printed only in English and there was a shortage of translators at DPSS offices), and that limited-proficiency English speakers were typically assigned to Job Search rather than educational and training programs.[33] Evidence of racial steering has been uncovered in welfare programs in other cities, prompting the U.S. Commission on Civil Rights to highlight "disparities in access to and utilization of services . . . [and] discrimination in the delivery of welfare benefits."[34]

The Meager Provisions of Education and Job Training

While this ethnographic research uncovered the need for more of a systematic survey of GAIN's tracking practices, this should not eclipse a closer scrutiny of the types of education and training programs actually promoted and subsidized under welfare reform. The 1996 federal law limited the educational component of "welfare-to-work activities" to training programs that directly prepare individuals for a job and that exceed no more than 12 months. This policy excludes most poor women from basic and higher education, and from higher-paying, male-dominated skilled trades that typically require more than a year of training. Even the short-term vocational programs approved under TANF (computer classes being the most popular choice among the Latinas interviewed) are not designed for real job training. Studies have shown that such programs fail to provide students with the technical skills they will need on the job and to connect students with stable jobs in the field once they finish their training. According to William Epstein, former policy analyst at the U.S. Department of Justice:

> Their meager provisions [are] seemingly intended more as a sop to participants and a symbol of charitability in the social dialectics of welfare than as a serious attempt to transmit skills. It takes more than a few months of cursory training to prepare a productive worker.[35]

Epstein's observation is supported by the examples of Leticia Ramirez and Angela Perez, who both attended a GAIN-approved computer-training program run by a large social service agency in Central Long Beach. Thirty-three-year-old Leticia enrolled in this program when she heard from a neighbor that it could get her excused from another round of Job Club (she had already gone through Job Club twice with no success in finding a job). Forty-eight-year-old Angela enrolled in this program on her own with the hope of training to become a home-based computer consultant like the Anglo woman whose house she cleaned on Fridays. Both women were satisfied with the specifics of this eight-month training program—it offered free, on-site childcare, the instructor spoke Spanish and was very supportive, and they learned the basics of how to operate a computer (turning it on, opening and closing files, using basic programs, etc.). Yet, the program left them no closer to a career in computers, or even a general office job, than when they began.

In large part, this was because this program failed to provide (or even acknowledge) the broader range of education and skills training that Leticia and Angela would need in order to successfully enter the white-collar workforce. Leticia has no formal schooling and does not read or write. Angela attended school in Mexico until the fifth grade, but like Leticia, her English fluency is limited to very basic transactions. Had GAIN simultaneously enrolled these women in adult literacy and ESL classes, and allowed them to continue on to learn more advanced computing skills, it would have given them a realistic chance of escaping low-wage, physical work for a desk job or even a professional career in computers. Instead, after completing the eight-month computer program, Angela went to work as a janitor, cleaning business offices at night for $6.25 an hour. Leticia could not find a job; worried that she would be forced to attend another futile and humiliating round of Job Club, she took her family off of welfare.[36]

Angela and Leticia's experiences were typical of the other Latinas in this study. Of the six women who participated in GAIN, three found paid employment while in the program. The first, Maria Sanchez, was referred by Job Club to a janitorial position at an aerospace factory. Yet, Maria left this job after three weeks because she was spending her entire paycheck ($200/week) to pay a neighbor to care for her five children while she was at work. The second, Margarita Gonzalez, endured two months in GAIN, applied for over 200 jobs, and finally found a job cleaning hotel rooms three days a week for $5.75/hr. For reasons we later address, Margarita immediately withdrew from the welfare system, even though there was little hope that a monthly paycheck of $552 would support her family of four, and even though she and her children were left without medical insurance. The third woman, Norma Gonzalez (Margarita's twenty-four-year-old daughter) had the most "successful" experience with GAIN in that she was the only one to leave the program with a stable, full-time job.[37]

However, a closer look at Norma's transition from welfare to work tells a different story. Norma was taking GED classes at Long Beach City College when she was ordered to attend GAIN in the summer of 1997. Forced to drop her classes because they did not fall under the state's definition of "welfare-to-work activities," Norma was enrolled instead in Job Club, where after three weeks, she found a minimum wage job as a cashier in a wholesale grocery warehouse. Like her mother, Norma withdrew herself and her child from cash and food stamp assistance because, as she put it, "I'm tired of dealing with them." This meant that she and her six-year-old son, who suffers from an acute intestinal disease that requires regular medical attention, were left without health insurance. With her average monthly earnings of $840, Norma could not afford the $50 copayment for the HMO plan offered by her employer, and although the family's low income continued to qualify them for Medi-Cal, their coverage was cancelled when Norma's TANF file was closed. Less than a year later, Norma had left her job and was back on welfare.

Conclusion

Today, GAIN continues to be widely celebrated as the winning formula for welfare reform. Policymakers and welfare administrators across the nation have requested help from GAIN representatives in setting up similar welfare-to-work programs in their states; MDRC has published a highly successful "how-to" manual that details a step-by-step procedure for implementing a GAIN-style, work-first approach; GAIN has been featured on the television news program *60 Minutes* and praised by major national newspapers for, in the words of the *Los Angeles Times,* "its dramatic gains in moving welfare recipients into jobs."[38] This despite the fact that DPSS's own data shows that GAIN's greatest success has been pushing poor people off of public assistance rather than helping them to find sustainable employment. In January 1999, DPSS reported a 42 percent increase in the number of GAIN-related sanctions over the past year. In the month of December alone, DPSS cut the aid of 11,397 persons, or 13 percent of its total caseload, because they allegedly had not complied with the GAIN requirements.[39] Similarly, an evaluation of the 5,469 persons mandated to participate in GAIN between April and August 1998 found that 26 percent had left the program, the vast majority because they had been kicked out and sanctioned or because they had dropped out. In contrast, only 22 percent of this cohort had found "full-time" (defined as 32 hours or more per week) employment while in GAIN, although it is not clear that GAIN actually helped them to find these jobs. DPSS data also disproves the agency's own contention that employment, no matter the wages or conditions, is a stepping stone out of poverty. An August 1998 survey of GAIN participants who were working showed that they were earning an average hourly wage of $6.48 an hour, or $233 a week, which meant that most "welfare-to-workers" continued to fall below the poverty line and to be eligible for, but often did not receive, public assistance.[40]

These program outcomes are not surprising when we consider that GAIN's principal mission is to promote the *concept* of "self-sufficiency through employment" to a welfare clientele in Los Angeles County that is made up predominantly of Latina, African-American, and Asian mothers. Although these mothers are held personally responsible for finding a job (and punished when they do not), GAIN does not assume responsibility for procuring sustainable employment for its participants, nor for providing them with the education and vocational training that would change their position in a regional labor market that is sharply bifurcated between high-skilled and low-skilled labor. This is because GAIN's definition of "self-sufficiency" is not contingent on the material effects of employment (such as income, shelter, nutrition, and access to medical care), but rather on the condition of being employed. In other words, a poor mother achieves "self-sufficiency" through the act of leaving welfare for a job—even if wage work leaves her with insufficient resources to provide for her family. "Self-sufficiency through employment" therefore only makes sense when placed in direct opposition to "welfare dependency," itself an overly laden signifier for cultural explanations of poverty. As Jamie Peck concluded in his evaluation of the GAIN program in Riverside County:

> While the Riverside program represents itself—to both clients and the outside world—in the language of "empowerment," "independence," and "self-sufficiency," there is also an important sense in which its methodology is about coercion, discipline and conformity. The foundation of [this] approach is a "basic work ethic," employment being viewed as a "gradual socialization process" to which GAIN's ostensibly dysfunctional and "welfare-dependent" clients must be subjected if they are to achieve "self-reliance."[41]

Proceeding from the assumption that welfare recipients do not know how to get and hold a job and that they do not value work more generally, GAIN translates the "culture of poverty" thesis into a set of moralistic lessons on the values of work, self-discipline, and individualism. These are conveyed to welfare recipients through practical instruction in time management, workplace comportment, and personal hygiene, and then reinforced through constant monitoring, surveillance, and sanction. Thus, by ignoring the reasons why welfare recipients are not working (when they are not), and the kinds of jobs they want, GAIN's approach to "job readiness" reifies the stereotype of poor people as socially illiterate and dysfunctional. By not offering women like Lupe Jimenez the real skills they say they need (like literacy and GED classes and access to college), the program's lessons on resume writing, interviewing techniques, and workplace attire make a mockery of the structural obstacles that Latina welfare recipients face by teaching them things they either already know or, as we will see in the next chapter, that are profoundly at odds with their lived experiences as mothers and workers.

4

The Myth of Welfare Dependency
Caught between Welfare and Work

The president keeps repeating the "dignity of work" idea. What
dignity? Wages are the measure of dignity that society puts on a
job. Wages. Nothing else. There is no dignity in starvation.
—Johnnie Tillmon, chair of the National
Welfare Rights Organization, 1972

While CalWORKs administrators, politicians, journalists, and public
policy analysts construct "welfare" and "work" as two opposing
lifestyles and choices, the Mexican immigrant women who appear in this
book use their own experiences as the grounds to challenge the false opposition between welfare and work. They assert that neither provides
them with sufficient material and social resources to raise their children
with dignity. Work dominates these women's oral histories, their memo-
ries of grandparents and parents with bodies scarred from physical labor,
of adolescent years spent scrubbing floors and hunched over sewing machines, of fathers, boyfriends, and husbands forced to travel north in
search of work, and of women left behind and just as often leaving home
to harvest crops, take in laundry, clean houses, peddle tamales, and solder computer chips in maquiladora plants. Women like Norma Gonzalez
and Maria Sanchez described wage work with a mix of pride, anger, and
defeat, peppered with stories of friendships and alliances on the shop
floor, of verbal and sexual abuse from male supervisors and coworkers,
of promotions and lay-offs, of days so long they couldn't see straight and
paychecks that fall short of paying the rent. Others like Margarita Gonzalez and Delia Villanueva spoke of "women's work," the sweeping,
washing, cooking, and singing lullabies that punctuate their days, refusing to distinguish between the work that welfare allows them to do for

their children versus the paid work they are expected to do in other people's kitchens and nurseries. Still others like Herminia Hernandez and Myrna Cardenas testified to the need to combine welfare and work, because "what they give you is not enough." They supplemented meager welfare checks with domestic labor and nighttime shifts counting inventory. When asked to imagine their futures, women like Lupe Jimenez pictured themselves as auto mechanics, truck drivers, and poets; others like Angela Perez dreamed of a career in computers and a home office. Their visions of their sons and daughters, someday grown up, also centered on work; they saw their children as nurses, doctors, lawyers, receptionists, and office clerks, and would do everything and anything in their power to make this possible. They despaired at the thought that their children might end up instead cleaning hospitals and office buildings or assembling burgers or plastic buckets.

A common trajectory runs throughout this group of Mexican immigrant women's life stories; one that takes different twists and turns due to individual circumstances, yet that directly opposes the life path constructed by most representations of the welfare poor. Public discourse on welfare reform assumes that poor women move from a culture unaccustomed to work and a work ethic, to dependence on welfare, to becoming self-sufficient workers through a government welfare-to-work program. Yet, these Latinas' oral histories paint an alternative picture of women, who have worked since childhood, who move into underpaid employment in the service and manufacturing sectors of a regional economy that is heavily dependent on their labor, who then move onto welfare programs because work alone does not provide them with sufficient means to support their families, and, finally, who leave the welfare system, because they are literally forced out or because welfare has become more "work" than it is worth. Throughout this entire cycle, neither working at jobs nor working at welfare—and, in several cases, working the double-shift of work *and* welfare—provides them with a real chance to move their families out of poverty.

These Latinas' oral histories also unsettle a number of pervasive myths about immigration. The political popularity of both Proposition 187 and welfare reform rested in part on public belief that immigrant women come to the United States with the explicit purpose of exploiting government handouts. However, none of the Mexican women in this study migrated to the United States in order to receive welfare—most lived and worked in this country for several decades before applying for aid, and yet still had to struggle to gain access to public assistance programs. At the same time that these Latinas disproved the myth of the pregnant immigrant mother who crosses the border and heads directly into the welfare office, they also challenged nativist rhetoric that lambastes immigrants for "stealing American jobs." If getting on welfare is not easy, these women asserted, neither is getting a job. Indeed, their firsthand accounts of labor market conditions in L.A. County show that competition for even entry-level, unskilled jobs is fierce, that most available positions are part-time and temporary, and that the "dirty work" assigned to Latinos in Los Angeles makes it possible for native-born whites to have better jobs. Contesting the belief that immigrants steal entitlements from American citizens, they argued that the hard work of immigrants enriches the standard of living of most Americans—and that immigrant workers were being robbed of their right to adequate shelter, nutrition, and medical care.

Finally, the life path shared by this group of Latinas disrupts the evolutionary narrative that structures most paradigms of immigration, in which newcomers start at the bottom and progressively work their way up into the American middle class. If we look at these women's histories and daily lives, they elicit all of the narrative tropes that we associate with "immigrant success stories": hard work, self-sacrifice, discipline, an unflagging commitment to their families, and a strong belief in education and individual self-improvement. Myrna worked up to 20 hours each day in order to pay for private school tuition for her two oldest children; Maria, Zoraida, and Herminia volunteered as teacher's aides in their children's classrooms and religiously attended parenting classes on Friday afternoons; Norma worked full days as a supermarket cashier, attended GED classes at night, and still made time to play video games or puzzle through math problems with her six-year-old son; Angela cleaned offices at night, cared for her preschooler during the day, and sang in her church choir on the weekends; Margarita and Leticia changed hotel bedsheets, scrubbed toilets, packed shampoo, while also going to school to learn English and computers. However, after an average of 15 years of living and working in the United States, none of these women had left the "bottom," let alone moved into the middle class.

These women do not normally compare welfare and work nor do they see welfare—or work—as a lifestyle. At some level, they treat them as intertwined. Welfare is a temporary measure, a necessity to protect their families but not enough to survive nor a permanent fixture in their lives.

Moreover, many of these Latina mothers asserted that it takes work to survive on welfare. They spent entire days on the phone trying to talk to a caseworker, driving around town trying to gather necessary documentation (children's school and health records, layoff slips, eviction notices), and sitting at the welfare office for hours at a stretch. Some women, like Carmen, described being on welfare as a "daily rhythm"—just like a job, surviving on welfare comes with its own schedule, set of tasks, and rules of conduct. Other women, like Norma, challenged the image of welfare recipients as free loaders: "People think, 'Oh you're on welfare, you get free money.' No. There's sometimes you go in, like say you have an appointment and the lady at the desk is in a bad mood. She's going to take it out on you." Abuse from caseworkers, endless waits at the welfare office, arbitrary cuts in their welfare checks, all of these involve not only the practical work of maintaining one's benefits but also the psychic work of surviving the denigration in the hands of the welfare system.

Work too is temporary and unpredictable, a necessity to support their families but never enough to do so in a sufficient and meaningful way. All but one of the women in this study worked in the past and were just as poor, or even poorer, than they are now. For three-quarters of these families, wage work is a crucial source of household income. Even before L.A. County began requiring welfare recipients to work, two of these women were working part-time, and another four had husbands who were employed but earning such low wages that their families still qualified for aid. Moreover, half of these women had to regularly depend on income or in-kind assistance from working relatives, boyfriends, or extended kin to make ends meet on a welfare check. For many, doubling-up was a strategy to be able to afford the rent as well as to obtain financial support with other household costs. Delia and her husband, for instance, rented out one of the rooms in their two-bedroom apartment to their children's godfather, who helped out with the phone bill and groceries. Similarly, Teresa and her two boys shared a three-bedroom bungalow with her brother and sister-in-law, employed as a machinist and a garment worker, respectively. Not only did the couple pay half of the rent, but they also paid all of the utility bills in exchange for Teresa taking care of their eight-month-old infant while they were at work. Most women also relied on cash loans and "gifts" of food, clothing, and furniture from their parents, siblings, and boyfriends. Lupe's older sister, a medical intake clerk at Long Beach Memorial Hospital, frequently visited with bags of clothing, groceries, and pampers for Lupe's children. Maria's neighbor, a construction worker, often appeared at her door with bags of groceries and *paletas* (ice cream bars) for Maria's kids. Therefore, for these Latino immigrant families, welfare exists as part of a larger household or family economy, where different family members produce different resources (whether it is a paycheck, household labor, or childcare) and where welfare serves as an inadequate yet essential supplement to low-wage, erratic employment.

While numerous scholars have demonstrated that poor people regularly cycle in and out of welfare and work, they have not systematically used these findings to dismantle one of the central premises of underclass theory: namely, that the urban poor live in neighborhoods devoid of stable working-class people and have become estranged from the habits and practices of working life. These Long Beach neighborhoods where these Latinas live—classified as "high-density poverty" areas—have a range of income levels and occupations. While some family members in this study were unemployed, or underemployed, this did not mean that they were isolated from the culture of work. Far from isolated, these Latina mothers were workers, their husbands and parents worked, their neighbors worked, shared job tips, watched the news for labor conditions, traded information, took care of each other's kids when they had job interviews or overtime work, and helped each other fill out applications. For these families, then, work had been ever present in their lives but had never been a means for material security or individual fulfillment.

Simultaneously, the culture of work had never isolated these families from poverty. The highest wage that any of the women in this study had *ever* earned (often encompassing a number of jobs over a period of decades) was $7.25/hour. Put another way, *not one* Latina immigrant in this group had ever held a job that lifted their families above the poverty line. The closest these women ever came to the "pink collar" was Lupe's two-month stint as a receptionist—two weeks unpaid for training.

Working Girls

For many of the older women, wage work began during girlhood or early adolescence in Mexico, after they were pulled from school because their families could not afford to buy books or needed them to work for additional income. Maria Sanchez left school in the sixth grade because, as she recalled, "I had to start working because my mother couldn't support all of us." By age fifteen, Maria got her first job in a shoe factory in Guadalajara; she continued working in the garment industry throughout her teenage years. Zoraida Jimenez had only three months of formal schooling. She spent her early childhood working on her family's *ejido* (small farm) near San Juan de los Lagos, in the state of Jalisco. When Zoraida was ten years old, her parents sent her to work for a middle-class family in a nearby pueblo, where she cared for two young children, cooked, and scrubbed floors on her knees for less than 30 pesos per month. Leticia Ramirez never went to school. As a young girl, she worked with her parents selling fruit to tourists on the streets of Mazatlan. It was there that sixteen-year-old Leticia, already married and mother to a twenty-two-month-old baby, met a Mexican-American couple from California: "They were looking for someone to clean their house over there, and that they would pay all the costs for me and the baby to come here. So, it was a good opportunity for me. I talked with my husband, and he was okay with it. Then when I was over here, I saved money and I sent it to him, my husband." Leticia spent the last of her teenage years as a live-in domestic in Long Beach, cleaning her employers' home and caring for their two young children, until she had earned enough money to hire a coyote to guide her husband north across the border.[1]

While all but one of the women who grew up in Mexico began working for wages when they were girls or young teenagers, most of the U.S.-raised *mexicanas* entered the wage labor market in their late teens and twenties, typically after dropping out of high school or separating from their boyfriends and husbands.[2] Yet, even these women's accounts of childhood are steeped in what sociologist Lisa Dodson calls "daughter's work"[3]—caring for younger siblings, doing the family laundry, cooking meals, and running errands while their immigrant parents worked double-shifts to make ends meet. Carmen Garcia was two years old when her family emigrated from Guadalajara to San Pedro, California, where her mother and father worked long days in the fish canneries. By age seven, Carmen was doing most of the housework and taking caring of her three younger siblings. As she recalled, "I was doing everything, you know, in the house. Cooking, cleaning, you know. Mainly everything. . . . My parents were working all of the time, and they didn't have time for me, to help me, encourage me, you know. So I just dropped out." Carmen left school in the ninth grade and ran away from home to live with an older sister in Long Beach. A year later, at age fifteen, she was married and became pregnant with her first child.

Like all of the high school dropouts in this study, Carmen blamed her youthful recklessness and "*cabeza dura*" (hard-headedness) for her decision to leave school. Yet, a different explanation begins to emerge if we listen closely to these women's accounts of their childhood and teenage years, of their struggles to balance the institutional demands of school with the responsibilities and pressures of trying to hold their families together in the midst of economic and emotional turmoil. Young women found it difficult to do their homework after school and were tired during the school day because they had to cook dinner, baby-sit their siblings, clean, shop for groceries, and care for other relatives. Once they started to fall behind on their schoolwork, they were tracked into remedial classes that did not stimulate them. The combination of these factors led them to withdraw from school.

Delia Villanueva was nine years old when her mother, Teresa Barragan, found a steady job at a Mexican restaurant in Los Angeles, where for the next eight years she waited tables and washed dishes for $25 in wages and an average of $15 in tips, per 12-hour shift. When interviewed for this study, Teresa described those years as follows:

> I was working like crazy, looking for the best for my daughters. . . . We lived by ourselves, and I controlled them daily through the telephone. . . . When I would get home late, or if they changed my work shift, I was checking up on them on the phone. This is why I wouldn't do any of the housework, so that they could arrive [from school] to work. [I would say], "Wash the dishes, tell your sister to throw out the trash, and do not go outside, and make the food because I'm going to arrive really hungry, pick up your clothes, and take a shower." I was on the telephone from work, every half an hour, in order to check up on them so that they would not feel alone, that they would not go out onto the streets.

Working seven days a week, Teresa agonized over how best to care for and protect her two daughters while she was at work. Like many single mothers, she turned to house chores as one of the few means at her disposal to keep her children safe and busy at home while she was at work. Although during her interviews for this study Delia was reluctant to talk at length about her childhood, her mother's description above gives us a brief glimpse at the tremendous family responsibilities and pressures that competed with Delia's schooling. By age nine, Delia was not only caring for herself and her younger sister, but was also catapulted into an adult world of insufficient paychecks and mounting bills, of single mothers on the brink of exhaustion and desperation. By age fourteen, Delia stopped attending school, and in order to help out with the family's finances, she spent her weekdays babysitting neighborhood children and her weekends as a salesgirl at the swap meet. By age eighteen, Delia was shut out of the labor market because she didn't have a high school diploma and was "working off" a General Relief check by cleaning public bathrooms. By age twenty-four, Delia was married and raising two children, yet her husband's wages were so low that the family depended on AFDC to make ends meet.

Delia Villanueva's story illustrates the ways that "daughter's work" becomes a pathway to "women's work" for Latina girls growing up in poverty. As they assume the role of babysitters, surrogate parents, part-time employees, house cleaners, errand runners, caretakers, and family protectors, girls in low-income families work to maintain the material and emotional well-being of their families. In the process, they are socialized into the practical knowledge and skills they will later put to work as waitresses, domestic workers, and office clerks, and as low-income mothers providing for and defending their own children. For single mothers like Teresa, "daughter's work" becomes a means to keep their daughters safe and off the streets, while also teaching them the crucial skills of independence and self-reliance that they can later draw on as grown women in a hostile world.

However, for daughters like Delia and Carmen, the independence and responsibility they learn at home too often is not nurtured at school with a curriculum that prepares them to go on to college. Too often, public school classrooms teach smart girls to be meek and lower their ambitions, and the "life lessons" on inequality, power, sexuality, and racism that these girls glean at home and in their neighborhoods are silenced or glossed over in high school textbooks.[4] And for many, the strain of juggling between the worlds of family and school is simply too much. As Dodson reminds us, while girls do the invisible work that "makes family life possible" at the bottom of America's economic structure, this work comes at tremendous personal and social cost:

> Specifically, 37 percent of female dropouts cited family issues as the cause of disconnecting from school, while this was only true for 5 percent of the male dropouts.[5]

From "Daughter's Work" to "Women's Work"

Work provides dignity, satisfaction, and self-respect. And, if you're employed, you can provide for your kids the things they need.

—Narrator in GAIN orientation video

Angela Perez, age 48
Work Experience: assembly-line worker, electronics *maquiladora* (Tecate); hotel maid (San Diego); live-in domestic and nanny (San Diego); hotel maid (Chicago); assembly-line worker, paper cup factory (Chicago); Avon and Jafra direct-sales (Long Beach); janitor (Long Beach)
Highest hourly wage: $5.75

Leticia Ramirez, age 33
Work Experience: street food vendor (Mazatlan); live-in domestic servant (Long Beach); farmworker (Orange County); packer, shampoo factory (Los Angeles); house cleaning (Long Beach); childcare (Long Beach); circular stuffer, newspaper plant (Los Angeles)
Highest hourly wage: $5.75

Angela Perez attended primary school in Mexico but did not continue her secondary education because "there was no money to pay." As she recalled, "I was very disillusioned because I wanted to be a teacher or something, but, no more [education]. I started working at an electronics factory. It was an American factory, but it was over there in Mexico." Angela entered the labor market in 1969, just four years into the Border Industrialization Project, a multibillion-dollar effort led by the Mexican and U.S. governments to transform Mexico's border region into an export-processing zone for foreign capital.[6] By the late 1960s, thousands of poor and working-class young adults, 80 percent of them women, were laboring behind sewing machines, microscopes, and conveyer belts in assembly plants, or *maquiladoras,* run by U.S. and Japanese corporations like Zenith, Toshiba, and Mattel. Fifteen-year-old Angela went to work in one of Tecate's first American-owned electronics plants, where she was paid 1,000 pesos a week ($80) to solder components for television sets that would be transported to the United States for packaging and retail distribution, and later shipped back to Tecate to be sold as imports. This job was Angela's entry into a lifetime of work. She lasted in the maquiladoras for a year until she obtained a border-crossing pass that enabled her to work as a hotel maid in San Diego.

Herminia Hernandez got her first job at the age of seventeen, working for a *patrona* who operated a food-vending cart outside the gates of Ciudad Juarez's *maquiladora* industrial parks. Throughout much of the 1970s, while her husband picked crops in the United States, Herminia supported herself and her five children by crossing the border each week to clean houses in El Paso; she later got a job soldering electrical wires in one of Juarez's auto assembly plants. After immigrating to California with her children in 1985, Herminia worked winters packing tuna fish in the San Pedro canneries and summers picking cotton and strawberries in northern San Diego County. During frequent bouts of unemployment, Herminia and her children collected aluminum cans and glass bottles from trash dumpsters outside Long Beach restaurants to sell for cash at recycling centers. In February 1998, forty-four-year-old Herminia was caring for two grandchildren (her daughter had been deported to Mexico) on a welfare check of $495, and $10 in food stamps. Until recently, she had supplemented her public assistance by working as a domestic servant for a man named Michael, cleaning his house and ironing his shirts and bed sheets for $400 a month. But, after seven years of service, Michael had replaced Herminia with a younger woman willing to work for less pay. Herminia was now looking for a night job, "so that I can take care of the kids during the day."

Angela and Herminia's stories are emblematic of the extensive work experience that characterizes the lives of Mexican immigrant women on public assistance. Their resumes directly repudiate the premises that GAIN is built on: they did not describe any of these jobs as a good job (indeed, most sought jobs different from and better than what they had had) nor did they say picking strawberries, cleaning hotel rooms, or stuffing ads inside newspapers had improved their self-esteem or family relationships. Sifting through the interview transcripts makes clear that low-wage labor is neither stable nor empowering, that having a job does not mean that you will get a better job, and that jobs are sporadic and not necessarily plentiful. The Latina women interviewed in Long Beach have worked most of their lives in jobs that are intensely physical and yet paradoxically deemed women's work. These immigrant women have extensive experience in the service sector as nannies, maids, cooks, and servers, where they performed tasks that mirrored the unpaid labor they do at home. Many had also worked in small factories as sewing machine operators, assemblers, packers, cutters, quality inspectors, and janitors; these nonunion industrial jobs were typically subcontracted through temp agencies, paid the minimum wage, and lasted for six months or less. This too is not aberrational given recent studies that show that Latinos make up more than half of the manufacturing workforce in L.A. County,[7] and that 35 percent of all women employed in direct production nationwide are Latina.[8]

Indeed, these immigrant women's individual work histories challenge theories that blame high poverty rates among Latino immigrants on their concentration in secondary sectors of the economy. Far from secondary laborers, Latina immigrants stand at the center of Los Angeles's economy. As they sew jeans, pack shampoo bottles, clean laser disks, and solder stereo parts, these women form the rank-and-file of what scholars Victor Valle and Rodolfo Torres identify as the "majority Latino industrial working class in the nation's largest manufacturing metropolis."[9] As they iron bed sheets, scrub floors, wash dishes, and change diapers in the homes of lawyers, investment bankers, and doctors, they facilitate the development of the region's burgeoning service economy and its growing leisure class.

These Latinas' work histories also dispute one of the most pervasive myths about welfare: that once poor people get used to the "good life" on a welfare check, they will never go back to work. In the spring of 1998, as politicians and welfare administrators debated the quickest way to push welfare mothers into the workforce, nearly half of the welfare recipients in this study were currently working or had worked within the past year. This ranged from regular, part-time employment to temporary stints of wage work during economic crises, to odd jobs and cash work, like babysitting, collecting cans, and selling Avon and handmade *recuerdos* (mementos) for weddings and baptisms.

After a caseworker reduced the Ramirez family's welfare check by $200 (under the false claim that Leticia and her husband are no longer eligible for aid because they are not U.S. citizens), Leticia applied for work at a Long Beach temp agency and was sent to work on the assembly line at a packing plant 15 miles away in Carson. She described her work assignment as follows:

> In the factory, there are a lot of tables, and the women are standing [there], and they give you a box of 24 shampoos, and you have to put them inside a special box . . . and then you seal it, and you put it on the

floor, and then they give you another one. But, it has to be like this [snaps fingers to signify speed].

Leticia worked eight-hour shifts on her feet, packing, sealing, and lifting boxes of shampoo, while supervisors patrolled the room, yelling at the female employees to work faster. Yet when she got her first paycheck, she discovered that she was only earning $32 per day, far below the minimum wage pay she had been promised. Leticia confronted her supervisor:

> I didn't think it was fair because [the job] was from three in the afternoon to eleven at night, and they only paid me that. So, when the supervisor asked me if I was going to return [the next week], I went and showed him my paycheck, and I said, "Look at how much my paycheck is. Do you think I will be able to pay the rent with that? Am I going to support my kids with that?"

Leticia spent the following eight months applying for minimum wage jobs in hotels, restaurants, factories, nursing homes, and hospitals, but she still had not found work. "There are no jobs," Leticia replied flatly when asked to describe the job market in Los Angeles. "I want a job where I can work every day, but there aren't any."

Twenty-six-year-old Lupe Jimenez, on the other hand, explained that

> there's lots of jobs out there, but they're like bad. You know, those that pay you low income. There're also jobs like computers and all that stuff, but for all that, man, you need experience . . . I mean, nobody was born with experience.

A few weeks before she was first interviewed for this study of welfare reform, Lupe had been working as a receptionist at an auto insurance company. As a precondition to employment, she endured an unpaid "training" period, during which she performed regular work tasks (answering phones and computer data entry) from noon to six, five days a week. After two weeks of working for free, Lupe was hired "off the books" for $110 a week, half of which she paid to her stepmother who took care of her kids while she was at work. Although Lupe was only netting $50 a week, she was initially optimistic about this job—because she was earning cash, she didn't have to report her income to her caseworker, and she could finally start repaying her sister the money she had borrowed to buy her kids Christmas presents. And, even though this desk job only paid the minimum wage, it seemed like a step-up from the fast food service and factory work she had done in the past. But, Lupe quickly discovered that entry-level office work comes with the same indignities as manual labor. As soon as the employer started paying Lupe for her time, he began to yell at and insult her in front of other employees and customers. Lupe quit after three weeks "because the boss was always putting me down."

Verbal abuse, disrespect from employers, and unstable employment was the norm, not the exception, among these Latina workers. While two women in this study had worked for the same employer for as many as 12 years, the majority had employment records listing dozens of part-time and full-time jobs that lasted anywhere from two weeks to six months. This rapid turnover in employment was partly the result of the way that Latinas accessed the labor market. Because of intense competition for jobs, and because many of these immigrant women lacked the English skills necessary to fill out job applications, they turned to Latino-owned or staffed temp agencies for help finding work. This meant that they had no direct contract with the employers for whom they worked, and that they were bounced frequently between work assignments and workplaces. Others found employment through word-of-mouth, typically in industries like food processing and apparel manufacturing, where flexible labor arrangements like irregular hours, lay-offs, piecework, and day labor are common.

In some cases, women turned to short-term employment or informal cash work during periods when they needed extra income, such as the holidays or the start of the school year. Others went to work when their husbands' work hours were cut back or if they were temporarily laid off. Still others explained that they moved from job to job with the hope that they might find a slightly higher wage or better working conditions. As we saw above, in the examples of Leticia and Lupe, quitting and leaving jobs are often individual acts of protest against the widespread exploitation and abuse in the labor market. However, this resistance inadvertently benefits an economy that thrives on high employee turnover and temporary labor. Moreover, once reports of these Latinas' irregular employment histories land on the desks of politicians and policymakers, they are not seen as workers' critiques of labor conditions but, rather, as evidence of the "weak laborforce attachment" of the welfare underclass and as fodder for proposals for work-first solutions to poverty.

Theorizing Race, Gender, and Work

Not just "subjects of experience," these Latina immigrants develop their own analyses of the structure of the labor market, the ways that race and gender position them within it, as well as a sharp critique of how others benefit from these structural arrangements. A number of women, for example, highlighted the contradiction between the ways that Latino immigrants are vilified by public discourse as criminals and welfare cheats, yet relied upon to do the "dirty work" that makes Americans rich. In the following quote, Herminia Hernandez overturns the dominant discourse that casts her as economically marginal:

> I don't understand why the United States can't stand Latinos. It's Latinos that are sustaining the United States. In Mexico, in Ciudad Juarez where I lived, I worked for a factory that made all of the wiring that goes into American cars. . . . But, how much does the United States pay Mexicans? Twenty. Twenty-five dollars [a week], I would say. If I were the president [of Mexico], I would send all of the factories back to the United States. Either way, they can't stand Latinos. As soon as they see a Latino here, they claim that we come and take away jobs from Americans. But, it's because Americans are really lazy. They don't want to work for the minimum wage. . . . And for us Latinos, they [employers] see that we are desperate and that we will work for whatever they pay us.

Herminia provocatively reverses the language of dependency that undergirds popular representations of U.S.-Mexico relations and of Mexican immigrant welfare recipients. While American political discourse portrays her and other *Mexicanas* as dependents, Herminia instead shifts the focus to U.S. economic dependency on Mexican labor.

While Herminia Hernandez turned the tables by recasting American workers as lazy and American employers as thieves who take advantage of Latino workers, Zoraida Torres played with the metaphor of theft through a recounting of the history of the U.S. annexation of Mexico:

> They took away the right to live here away from us supposedly. Because this was our country, right? So, it ended up, like the saying goes, "Who will come from the outside to kick you out of your own home?" We live here in our country and they kick us out like thieves. So as a right, it is

ours. . . . Why do they tell us to go home to our country, if we are from here?

Zoraida not only stakes a historical entitlement to Mexico's once-northern territories, but she also inverts the language of nativism, portraying Americans—not Mexicans—as the outsiders and criminals. Throughout her interviews, Zoraida grappled with the meaning of citizenship in a society where belonging and rights are structured in a system of racial inequality. For instance, when asked if she planned on eventually applying to become a U.S. citizen, the following conversation ensued:

> *Zoraida*: Well, from what I understand, being a citizen is something good, not because for what they give you but because you won't be hiding from anyone. . . .
> *Alejandra*: And do you think that once you become a citizen, things will change and people will look at you like you belong here?
> *Zoraida*: I don't think so. I think that people are racist everywhere. . . . When they ask at school, or when you fill out a paper, they ask if you are a resident or a citizen. And you say, "No, I don't have papers." Right away, they lower their heads as if to say [pause]. Well, it's something sad that they do to you. Now, if you're a resident, they doubt it. Let me see your greencard, to see if it's true or not. Your Social Security number? *Pruebas?* [connotes double meaning of "proof" and "test"]
> *Alejandra*: And when you become a citizen, will they ask you for proof?
> *Zoraida*: I think so. I think they will always ask because we are Latinos.

Zoraida Torres was one of several women in this study who challenged the rhetoric of assimilation by asserting that, no matter how hard they worked, or how many years they had been in the United States, or how much "proof" they accumulated, as Latinas they would always be positioned as undeserving outsiders. This group of Latinas spoke forcefully about the ways that race and nativity work together to exclude them from full membership and rights in U.S. society, and, in turn, how this political and social exclusion facilitates their economic exploitation.

A few women explicitly connected this exploitation to welfare reform, arguing that the work-first agenda would intensify the vulnerability of Latinas in the workforce. For instance, when asked to describe her job prospects in the post-welfare economy, Delia responded:

Well, I think that you can get a lot of jobs like in places where they don't pay you well. Like in sewing factories, in places where they exploit people. . . . And what's more, with the new changes in welfare . . . they're forcing people to take jobs where they don't pay them well and where they are being exploited.

Delia Villanueva's observation was echoed by a number of other women, whose responses included: "You're pretty much forced to take any job" (Norma), and "As a *mexicano,* you have to take whatever job they offer you" (Zoraida). When read alongside the above critiques of racial discrimination, these statements overturn the prevailing image of Mexican immigrants as supplicant workers, happily taking the least desirable jobs in order to get ahead in U.S. society. Indeed, these women rejected the ideology of free market individualism when assessing their location in the labor market. They asserted that as *mexicanas,* regardless of their immigration status or the length of time they have lived in the United States, they are limited to manual labor and low-skilled, low-wage jobs that offer them little opportunity to move up the socioeconomic structure.[10]

While these Latinas talked about race and racism in explicitly political terms, their critiques of the gendered division of labor tended to be more subtly embedded in their personal narratives. This theme emerged most prominently in the interviews with some of the older women in the study, whose husbands had first migrated alone to the United States for work but failed to send money home to the families they had left behind. Although these women did not directly challenge the model of the male-headed household, they shaped their oral histories in ways that recentered themselves as the economic actors and providers in their families. For example, between 1979 and 1984, Herminia's husband migrated back and forth to Los Angeles, leaving Herminia in Cuidad Juarez with their five children. As Herminia recounted, "He would go and return. He never lasted one full year. Not even ten months. But in six months, he would send money only once." Although her husband did not want her to work outside the home, Herminia defied him and went to work selling *gorditas* to workers in the city's *maquiladora* factories, and then later got a job inside one of the automobile assembly plants soldering electrical wires. With these wages, Herminia supported herself and her children and also saved enough money to purchase a small plot of land. Herminia describes one confrontation with her husband, following her decision to take a job as a live-in domestic in El Paso:

One day, since he didn't want to get a job, I left. But I didn't tell him that I left. I left him with the children. . . . And later he would scold me regularly, saying that I had abandoned them, that I left, and I don't know what else. One day, he said, "You were very comfortable [in El Paso]." I said, "No, as a matter of fact, I would go into my room all of the time, and I wouldn't eat anything." I said, "When you left, you had women in the United States"—because he had their pictures in his wallet. I told him, "You had other women, a place to sleep, food. I didn't. I came back after I got what I went for. You didn't want to return, so you should have stayed." I told him, "When you go to the United States with empty hands, that's how you return. Not me. Not to reproach you, but I paid the water bill. I had another room built for my daughters." After that, he didn't say anything again. I went [to the United States] to work. I didn't go to have a good time.

Herminia's story unsettles scholarly and popular portraits of Mexican immigration, in which men are represented as economic migrants, whereas women and children are treated as "secondary migration flows."[11] Herminia not only asserts a place next to her husband as an "economic migrant," but by casting herself as more responsible and successful in this role, she also contests a number of gendered representations. Herminia protests her husband's refusal to get a job by reversing the traditional gender roles—she migrates to the United States for work, leaving her husband at home with the children. Moreover, by stating that her husband went to the United States to "have a good time" and returned with "empty pockets," Herminia relocates him in the domestic and feminine sphere of comfort and leisure. In contrast, she explains, she went to the United States to work and returned to Cuidad Juarez with enough money to pay the water bill and build a room for her daughters. As she ties her earnings to her family's basic necessities (water and shelter), Herminia critiques the social construction of women's wage work as supplemental to the household economy. She locates herself in the public and masculine sphere of work while continuing to affirm her importance as a maternal caretaker.

Herminia Hernandez challenged the distinction between female domesticity and male productivity. Lupe Jimenez, on the other hand, questioned the gendered division of work and wages as she talked about her dream of becoming a car mechanic. As a young girl assisting her father while he worked on his car, Lupe discovered that "I love mechanics. . . .

I like to get my hands dirty. . . . If you're a woman mechanic, they give you top money. If you're a carpenter, a plumber, all of that, where you don't see women, they pay you top money." Yet, Lupe began to question her chances of gaining entry into this male-dominated field after a conversation with a mechanic at an auto body shop in her neighborhood:

> It's just that now, this man discouraged me, telling me that it was not good because I, that it wasn't convenient for me because I was a girl that had a bit more class. . . . And then I said to myself, "Man, what if I don't make it? What if I don't succeed? I fail the test and stuff like that. And, you know, there's going to be only men there. . . . Maybe they might say, "What is this woman doing here?" . . . They're going to say, "Man, look at this woman. She thinks she can do this or that." What if I can't prove them wrong, you know?

Lupe described herself as trapped between the masculine blue-collar jobs she wants to pursue—auto mechanics, carpentry, trucking, jobs that not only paid "top dollar" but that also conveyed to her skill, mastery, and power—and those that society deems more sexually respectable (higher "class") and better suited to her abilities as a woman. Over the next two years of the study, Lupe struggled to translate her vocational interests into "female appropriate" careers. She enrolled in a flower arrangement class at the community college, thinking that it might resemble the manual dexterity she enjoys in auto mechanics, yet dropped out midway through the semester because she was bored. After this experience, Lupe was determined to take courses in carpentry and mechanics the following semester. Six months later, upon the urging of her welfare caseworker and family members, she had instead enrolled in a medical assistant training program, a traditionally female career path that would lead her to feeding patients and changing hospital bed sheets.

By highlighting the ways that race and gender structure unequal access to opportunities in the labor market, these Latina welfare recipients rejected the notion that all it takes to get a decent job is a positive attitude. They argued instead that, as Latinas and as women, they are doubly disadvantaged in the workforce and therefore that education and experience are even more crucial to their getting hired and advancing into higher-paying jobs. All insisted that they had worked in the past, and that they planned to return to work in the future, but dismissed the idea that "any job is a good job." When asked to define a "good job," most women responded like Delia Villanueva: "Well, a good job is where they respect you. They respect you, they pay you well, that you have opportunities to grow as a person, and not just be working. If you're doing your job right, they have no reason to yell at you, or to disrespect you."[12] In these women's words, fair wages, respectful working conditions, and personal satisfaction are essential to their self-definition as workers, yet are in short supply at the bottom of a Los Angeles labor market that is sharply stratified by gender, race, and class.

From Work to Welfare

For most of the Mexican immigrant women interviewed in Long Beach, the decision to apply for welfare was contextualized in a lifetime of work but framed as the consequence of tragedy and upheaval in their personal lives.[13] Based on their firsthand experiences in the laborforce, these women understood that the entry-level jobs available to them did not pay enough to provide for their family's basic material needs, nor were these jobs stepping stones to better careers and wages. This is not to say, however, that they viewed welfare as a viable long-term alternative to work. Welfare did not pay enough for them to provide for their families, and it was a demeaning and abusive system. While these women turned to welfare for various reasons, they all did so reluctantly during a period of crisis or transition in their lives and after exhausting all other possibilities. Three narratives emerged to explain the move to welfare: they were divorced or leaving an abusive relationship; they needed to leave their jobs because they were pregnant or had to care for a sick child; or their husbands were laid off or hurt on the job.

Nearly half of the women in this study applied for AFDC following their divorce or separation from their children's father. In several of these cases, welfare served as the lifeboat for women escaping domestic violence. Emotionally traumatized, financially destitute, and unable and unwilling to press for child support from their abusers, these women had few places to turn for help. After seven years of marriage to an abusive alcoholic, Angela Perez sold everything she owned and fled from Chicago with her three children to a sister's house in Long Beach. Although she had worked for the past four years as a shift supervisor in a paper cup factory, Angela did not qualify for unemployment compensation in California. After several unsuccessful weeks of job-hunting, and with no money for a deposit on an apartment, Angela applied for emergency public assistance. Similarly, Norma Gonzalez turned to public assistance after her boyfriend beat her so violently that she was hospitalized with three broken ribs. At first, Norma moved in with her mother and cared for a neighbor's child for $50 a week, enough to buy pampers and milk for her three-year-old son. As Norma recalled:

> I wasn't on welfare at the time. I didn't want to accept that I had to be on welfare. . . . But later on he started threatening me that he was going to get married and that he was going to take my son from me because the court would give him to him because . . . I didn't have a job. I didn't go to school. And that he had a good job and made more money than I did. . . . So, I went and applied for child support and for welfare.

Norma struggled with the social stigma attached to public assistance, but ultimately recast the moral discourse by characterizing AFDC as proof of her worthiness as a mother. Like other Latinas in this study, Norma saw welfare as a means to ensure her own safety and to demonstrate to society that she is doing everything necessary to protect her child.

In other cases, welfare served as ballast against the financial and personal chaos that typically follows the breakup of a marriage. Myrna Cardenas and Carmen Garcia were both in their midtwenties when their marriages dissolved, and with no property or savings and no hope that their husbands could earn enough to keep up their child support payments, AFDC was one of the few resources they could turn to in order to provide for themselves and their children. During the course of her ten-year marriage, Carmen had held a number of temporary manufacturing jobs, from welding parts for an aerospace subcontractor to packing merchandise at a Tonka Toy factory, always working the night shift so that she could be at home with her children during the day, and her husband, a construction worker, could look after them at night. After her divorce, Carmen searched for a job that coordinated with her children's school hours but found that competition for daytime employment was fierce, and that most of these jobs required a high school diploma. Carmen could not return to working a night shift because she had no one to watch her children overnight and to take them to school in the morning, nor could she survive on erratic and increasingly miniscule child support payments from her ex-husband. Having exhausted her options and resources, Carmen applied for AFDC.

On the surface, stories like Norma and Carmen's seem to support the popular conservative contention that "broken families" are to blame for poverty and welfare dependency. Yet, as Dorothy Roberts points out, the myth that marriage is a safeguard against children's poverty fails to account for the "racial differences in paths to poverty for women."[14] Whereas divorce is a common trigger for white women's entry into poverty and the welfare system, women of color are likely to be poor *prior* to the dissolution of a two-parent household. Indeed, in each of the above cases, divorce was decidedly not the catalyst for these women's poverty—all were poor even when married and the loss of their spouse's crucial income thrust them deeper into economic crisis. Moreover, if we read Norma and Carmen's stories alongside those of other women in the study, single motherhood further recedes as the causal explanation for welfare use. Several of these Latinas had not applied for welfare until they were in their late thirties or early forties, decades after separating from their children's fathers; conversely, nearly one-third of the women in this study were married and living with their husbands at the time that they went on welfare.

Both Margarita Gonzalez and Teresa Barragan supported their older children as working single-mothers, and both had been recently employed when they first applied for welfare. As described above, Teresa raised two daughters as a single mother working double shifts in a restaurant. She was in her late thirties and had recently left a job at a garment factory when she began receiving AFDC. As she explained, "I went on welfare because this child was born premature, and I wanted to get him Medi-Cal because he had to stay in the incubator. . . . and the caseworker assigned to me asked why I wanted only Medi-Cal, why I didn't also want cash assistance." Teresa told the caseworker that she didn't want to go on welfare "because I didn't want any problems in the future," and that she was living with her younger children's father. The caseworker encouraged Teresa to fill out the AFDC application, and she and her baby were approved. Like Teresa, Margarita had also lived in the United States for nearly 20 years and raised two children on her wages as a hotel maid before she applied for welfare in 1997. At the time, she was thirty-eight years old, eight months pregnant, and had recently quit her job at the hotel because her body could no longer endure the physical strain of lifting mattresses and pushing vacuum cleaners. Because Margarita's employer, a major national hotel chain, does not offer paid maternity leave, she turned to the welfare system as a temporary safety-net while she cared for her newborn child.

Just as single motherhood did not cause Teresa and Margarita to apply for public assistance, the presence of a father in the household for nearly one-third of the families in this study did not provide insurance against poverty. These married couples also turned to the welfare state for those basic worker protections (disability, maternity leave, unemployment compensation, and health insurance) that they were denied in the private sector. For example, Leticia Ramirez first applied for AFDC after her husband Reynaldo, who worked for a company that cleans up oil spillage in the Long Beach harbor, suffered from severe chemical burns as a result of a workplace accident. Because Reynaldo was hired as an independent contractor, he was not covered under worker's compensation benefits— this despite the fact that he had worked for this same company for seven years and had not been provided with the protective gear required under federal and state OSHA laws. After the accident, as Reynaldo underwent reconstructive surgery, the couple relied entirely on AFDC to feed and shelter their five children. A few years later, Reynaldo went back to work part-time, yet his earnings were so low (between $200 and $600 a month) that the family continued to qualify for and receive public assistance. Similarly, Yasmín and Alberto Nuñez applied for AFDC for themselves and their five children in 1990, after the landscaping company that Alberto had worked with for ten years laid him off with no advance notice or severance package. Alberto found a new job on the carpentry crew of a Long Beach company that sets up film shoots and special events like parades and festivals. However, because he was hired as a "contingent employee," his family's income was dictated by the employer's needs. Some months, Alberto worked ten-hour days installing bleachers and building stages and set props and brought home paychecks as high as $1,500; other months he worked as little as ten days, and his earnings dropped to $600. Each month, Yasmín reported her husband's earnings to the welfare office, which then readjusted the family's welfare benefits based on the previous month's income.[15]

These families' paths into the welfare system thus blur the boundaries between the "welfare poor" and the "working poor." Over half of the immigrant families in this study combined welfare with reported income from work. Those who did not have a working parent relied on unreported assistance from employed family members in order to make ends meet on welfare. In this regard, they are no different from the estimated one million "working poor" in Los Angeles County. In the late 1990s, one in four workers in Los Angeles qualified for (but did not necessarily receive) public assistance, and 64 percent of all poor adults and children lived in a household in which at least one member worked full-time.[16] Nor are the immigrants who appear in this book different from other welfare recipients in California, where nearly 50 percent of all state and federal funding for public assistance programs goes to families with low-wage, working members.[17] For Mexican immigrant families, welfare reform did not offer a path to self-sufficiency—indeed, for those already working, it did not even offer a path to work—but rather it pushed many off of welfare and drove them deeper into poverty.

Pushed Off of Welfare

> *Alejandra*: How you heard about the new time limits on welfare?
> *Zoraida*: Well, I've always known these limits because whenever you go to a meeting with a social worker, they only meet with you for five minutes.

Latina immigrants challenged the "open door" image of the welfare system, asserting that it is neither easy to get on nor stay on public assistance. Even prior to the passage of welfare reform, many of these women—all legal permanent residents at the time that they applied for AFDC—had been wrongly informed that they were not eligible for welfare because they were not U.S. citizens; several were accused of possessing fake immigration documents, told to go back to Mexico, and threatened that they would have to repay the government for any benefits they received. Once approved, they constantly battled to stay on assistance in the face of a welfare department that chronically lost their paperwork, arbitrarily cut their checks and food stamps, and, in several instances, canceled a family's AFDC case or Medi-Cal coverage without notice or justification. These Latinas' experiences illustrate that the practice of pushing people off assistance is not a new phenomenon under welfare reform. Unlike other federal entitlement programs, like Social Security and Worker's Compensation, AFDC was purposefully designed with variable benefit levels, and discretion for caseworkers to determine eligibility. This was to deter single mothers, and particularly women of color, from applying for aid and making it nearly impossible for them to exist on welfare for very long. Moreover, as John Gilliom documents, the introduction of "quality control" and anti-fraud measures in the late 1970s had produced the current system that punishes counties for overpayment of welfare benefits, but not for underpayment or wrongful termination, and thereby encourages caseworkers to "deny first, and ask questions later."

This pattern of disentitlement was sharply intensified under the bureaucratic chaos and nativist climate that accompanied the implementation of welfare reform. When this research began in 1998, Long Beach community activists, teachers, social service providers, and residents reported that Latino immigrant families were being cut off of welfare, even though they were still legally eligible. In their early interviews for this study, Latinas complained about a pronounced rise in the level of intimidation and hostility in their dealings with caseworkers. They described the waiting room at the DPSS office, once packed with women and children, as eerily empty; they pointed out that this climate of intimidation and mass confusion silenced questioning and protest and made it easier for caseworkers to push people, especially noncitizens and non-English speakers, off the rolls.

These women's ground-level observations have since been corroborated by large-scale studies, which show alarming disparities between immigrant and citizen access to public assistance under welfare reform. A study of welfare records in L.A. County conducted by the Urban Institute, for instance, reported that the number of *approved* applications of legal noncitizen families for Medi-Cal and TANF dropped by 71 percent between January 1996 and January 1998, compared to no significant change among citizen applications.[18] Another nationwide study found that the use of public benefits (including TANF, SSI, General Assistance, Medicaid, and food stamps) among noncitizen households declined by 35 percent between 1994 and 1997, compared to only 14 percent among citizen households, and that neither naturalization nor rising incomes accounted for this drop.[19] Most analysts have cited these figures as evidence of the "chilling effects" of welfare reform, arguing that immigrants have become increasingly fearful of applying for aid. Yet, few analysts have addressed the systematic denial of applications from eligible immigrants, and widespread removal of existing immigrant recipients from the welfare rolls.

By the third year of ethnographic research in Long Beach, nearly two-thirds of the Mexican families in this study had lost some or all of their benefits. Many of these women were told incorrectly by caseworkers that they were no longer eligible because they are not U.S. citizens. For example, in April 1998, Leticia received a letter from the welfare department wrongly stating that she, her husband, and their oldest daughter (all legal permanent residents) no longer qualified for aid. Although the letter implied that Leticia's four U.S.-born children were still eligible, the entire family's cash aid and food stamps totaling $900 were cut off the following month. Three months later, however, Leticia received another letter ordering her to report to GAIN. When she called the welfare department to question why she had to attend GAIN if no one in her household was receiving aid, the eligibility worker reinstated cash and food stamp benefits, but only for Leticia's U.S.-born children. Whereas Leticia's family of seven had once received $900 a month in benefits, they now had to survive on $400. Similarly, in September 1997, Teresa received a letter from DPSS stating that, "I needed to become a citizen, or show documents that I have worked in this country for ten years since I arrived. And, well, like I told you, I have always worked as a waitress [where] they pay you in cash." Unable to provide paystubs that documented her more than 20 years of employment in the United States, Teresa was cut off entirely from public assistance, even though she was still legally eligible for cash aid and Medi-Cal. Although she still received aid for one child, the loss of the adult portion of her family grant dramatically impacted her household income; her monthly check dropped from $490 to $279, and her food stamps from $190 to $80.

While Leticia and Teresa received an explicit, although erroneous, explanation for why their benefits had been terminated, most of these immigrant women lost welfare income for reasons they did not understand and could not get an explanation for from their caseworkers. After discovering that her family's food stamps had been terminated, Delia called the welfare office several times and finally spoke to a caseworker who offered to reinstate a monthly food stamp allotment of $68 (she previously had received $260). As Delia recounted, she asked, "Why $68?" and explained to the caseworker that her family needed to eat. The caseworker responded, "You people, always are asking for help when you don't need it. You should be happy with what you have or go back to Mexico." Delia backed off, fearful that the caseworker would take away even the $68 in food stamps she had first offered.

For many of these *mexicanas,* the most frightening aspect of welfare reform was its unpredictability, particularly the lack of consistent rules and information. Because most had heard conflicting accounts from caseworkers, relatives, neighbors, and the Spanish-language news about the new eligibility rules for noncitizens, they did not know what to expect and were prepared for the worst. Herminia voiced a fear common among these women: "You don't know what to think, what to say, or what to do. Today they'll say one thing, and tomorrow another. You're left with your mouth open." The circulation of sometimes useful, but often incorrect information through word of mouth produced heightened fear, resignation, and acquiescence. People reported hearing that as a precondition to naturalization, legal immigrants were required to repay their children's benefits. Many also misunderstood that only U.S. citizens were eligible for both cash aid and food stamp assistance. Moreover, because many of these women were familiar with the case of another family whose benefits had been cut, they were less likely to ask questions or to file an appeal when their own benefits were cut. For example, Norma spoke about a friend who had gotten a letter from DPSS saying that she had hit her time limit: "She was left in the cold with no job or anything. But, I said, "How can it be five years? [From] '98, and we're in 2000?" Norma urged her friend to go to the welfare office and insist that her benefits be restored. Instead, her friend found a part-time job at the convention center, and although she didn't have enough to live on or medical insurance, she did not reapply for food stamps or Medi-Cal. As Norma concluded, "A lot of people just let it go because they don't want to deal with it no more. It's frustrating and it's a big ol' hassle and big ol' lines that you have to go through. It's awful." It is possible that Norma's friend's benefits were terminated because she had hit a work-trigger deadline. But this incident illustrates that welfare recipients do not understand the rules and that the bureaucratic apparatus discourages them from asking questions.

Even asking questions did not often provide the women in this study with a clearer understanding of how the new system worked. In some instances, caseworkers did take a second look at their case and made changes, but rarely in a consistent or intelligible way. As we saw above, Leticia's entire family was cut off from public assistance, yet she received a letter from GAIN ordering her to report to Job Club or she would lose her benefits. As Leticia explained:

> I called the [GAIN] worker and said, "Hey, if you already took the aid away from me, why do I have to go the program?" I also told her that I couldn't go to the GAIN program because I don't know how to read. I

don't know how to drive. During that time my husband was also working. And do you know what she said to me? That she didn't care. [She said], "I don't care how you get here, if you come on a bicycle, in a car, or in a bus, but you have to come to GAIN and if you don't, I am going to take your aid away from you."

When Leticia repeated that her family had not received benefits in over two months, the GAIN worker told Leticia that she and her husband would have to attend GAIN in order to repay the government for benefits they had received in the past. When Leticia insisted again, the GAIN worker called the BAP office, which reinstated benefits for Leticia's four U.S.-born children. Leticia, her husband, and their oldest daughter (also born in Mexico) continued to be denied assistance, but Leticia was told that she would have to participate in GAIN in order to protect her younger children's benefits. Leticia went through two "rounds" of Job Club, applying for over 200 jobs, but did not find a position. She obtained a temporary waiver from GAIN after enrolling in computer classes at a social service agency near her house. However, a few weeks later, Leticia's husband received a notice ordering him to attend GAIN:

> *Leticia*: And they sent him also to one of those programs, a club. And he didn't want to go, and he went personally to the lady . . . no, he called first. . . . He said, "Why should I be reporting to you that I go and look for applications? I get applications, and then to top it off I have to go and show them to you?" There's no use because I don't see any benefit [to GAIN]. There is no benefit.
>
> *Alejandra*: And, so how did he get out of having to go to GAIN?
>
> *Leticia*: The worker told him he had to go to [the GAIN office] personally, and so my husband went and he told her the same thing he had said on the phone: "I am not going to go through with this because I don't have the time to go and sit there for weeks, dressed all elegant, when I could be looking for a job." In other words, "I am not going to waste my time by sitting there when I could be looking for a job." My husband told her no, he was not going to go along with this and he didn't. So, they threatened him too. That if he didn't go [. . .] , they would take the aid away from him.
>
> *Alejandra*: But at the time he wasn't receiving aid?

Leticia: That's what he told them. He told them he was only getting Medi-Cal. But they said, you are the father of your children. That he had to pay for what his children were receiving.

In the end, convinced of the purposelessness of GAIN and tired of the harassment from caseworkers, Leticia and her husband withdrew their children from welfare.

In fact, under federal and state law, adults like Leticia and her husband who receive TANF only for their children are not subject to work requirements nor required to participate in welfare-to-work activities. But, as this research documented, many Latino immigrants in Long Beach who received welfare benefits for their children were nevertheless being threatened into participating in GAIN.[20] Whether this pattern is intentional, or a product of bureaucratic disorganization, it ultimately furthers the goals of welfare reform: to enforce the notion of welfare as a public debt and, ultimately, to reduce the rolls by any means possible. In California, where children make up the majority of welfare recipients and are not subject to time limits, federal demands for total caseload decline lead to a competing pressure for the state to encourage and harass parents to disenroll their children from welfare. Thus, California's child welfare protections are hardly a guarantee when they are undercut by the national political economy of welfare reform (where caseload reduction is paramount), which produces local-level and surreptitious actions to reduce child welfare rolls.

The case of Leticia's family also unravels the false distinction between voluntary and coercive paths off of welfare. Even though some women in this study were directly cut off of welfare (despite being legally eligible), more common was this process of "voluntary" disenrollment. Indeed, half of the women in this study took their families off of welfare because, like Leticia, they were frustrated with the arbitrary and discriminatory enforcement of new contradictory rules, the stepped-up harassment from caseworkers, and the futility and humiliation of welfare-to-work programs. And many, like Norma, directly explained their decision to disenroll through a critique of the increased surveillance and dehumanization of the new welfare system:

Yeah, because now they ask you like, "Are you running from the law? Are you doing drugs? Is anyone in your house?" . . . I got scared. . . . It makes you feel as it they're spying on you and they want to be sure that you're really reporting everyone that comes in and out of your house and everything. And I was like, "Mom why are they saying that to me, if I'm running from the law?" Plus, you have to go in and they like finger-print you through the computer so like your fingerprints are there for-ever and ever.

Thus, as we explore in the next chapter, the notion of "volition"—the existence of free and open choice—is extremely slippery and insidious within the TANF system.

5

"It's Not What You Choose, but Where They Send You"

Inside Personal Responsibility

> Even when they are overtly coercive, [welfare and other social pro-
> grams] work by getting the recipient to see her own interests in
> those control strategies. . . . She is, then, both the subject of and
> subject to welfare discourses, not merely their object.
> —Barbara Cruikshank, *The Will to Empower*

> By making every citizen an agent of his or her own destiny, we will
> give our fellow Americans greater freedom from want and fear, and
> make our society more prosperous and just and equal. . . . Self-gov-
> ernment relies, in the end, on the governing of the self.
> —President George W. Bush, Inaugural Speech 2005

Maria Sanchez has heard on television that the government is helping
welfare mothers to find a job. But as she explains, "It's a lie. If it's going
to be like GAIN, then I don't believe in that." Maria voluntarily enrolled
in GAIN in 1997 (before the program became mandatory in L.A. County)
after hearing from her caseworker that the program would help her to
find a good paying job and would pay for her childcare while she was
working. Maria is no stranger to hard work. At age fifteen she got her first
job as a sewing machine operator in a men's apparel factory in Guadalajara. Later, Maria and her sisters purchased a knitting machine and produced sweaters at home for a local manufacturer who paid them by the
piece. After migrating to Chicago to live with an older brother in 1986,
Maria spent five years working for the minimum wage in the inventory
department of an automobile plant. Most recently, she had held a string
of low-wage jobs, from sewing to merchandise inspection, in downtown

Los Angeles's garment industry. Tired of part-time, temporary work that "didn't even pay enough to pay the babysitter," Maria enrolled in a three-week Job Club, at the end of which she was sent to clean bathrooms in an aerospace plant from 4 P.M. to midnight. As she related:

> When I started working there, well, they would tell you they have good benefits and everything. And well, no, because they paid me the minimum, which was five dollars an hour. Five dollars an hour, but there are 18 bathrooms there . . . and each bathroom had an endless number of toilets! There are women who have been there for years, and they felt like that, so exhausted they couldn't even walk.

Although Maria had been told that GAIN would pay for her childcare while she was working, she never received a voucher from the state. After three weeks on the job, Maria realized that she was spending her entire paycheck ($200 a week) to pay a neighbor to take care of her five children while she was at work. She requested a switch from her evening shift to a morning shift, so that she and her husband could trade off childcare responsibilities, but her supervisor denied her request saying that everyone wanted a day shift. Maria resigned a week later: "I can't leave my kids alone and I can't leave them with [the babysitter] because I don't have the money to pay. And that was the reason why I left my job. I know that I was the one to quit."

Trapped in an impossible economy—between society's demand that she demonstrate "personal responsibility" and a low-wage labor market that eviscerates the margin between a paycheck and a childcare bill—Maria's critique of the system collapses into self-blame: "I know that I was the one to quit."

In August 1998, Margarita Gonzalez received a letter in the mail from the welfare department that, as she recalls, "congratulated me for being selected to participate in GAIN, [and said] that they were going to pay for all of my costs for my children." This letter informed Margarita that her participation in GAIN was mandatory; if she did not comply, her welfare benefits would be terminated. When she met with a GAIN service worker, Margarita explained that she had five years experience as a home care worker and another four years as a hotel maid. Tired of dead-end jobs, Margarita requested that GAIN allow her to enroll in ESL and computer classes at Long Beach City College. Instead, she was sent to Job Club where she was taught "how to look for jobs, how to fill out applications, what you have to put on them, how you have to ask for a job, how you have to dress, and things like that."

After five days of classroom instruction, Margarita was sent to look for a job, often armed with little more than the help-wanted section of the newspaper. For the following two weeks, she spent eight hours a day on foot and on public buses criss-crossing L.A. County in an aimless pursuit of job applications. Margarita applied for over 50 jobs—hotel housekeeping jobs, inventory and cashier positions at retail stores and supermarkets, work at a lamp factory and at a laundromat—but did not receive any calls for an interview.

Margarita was sent home for a month, and then reenrolled in GAIN at step one. This second time, she was assigned to a "community service" position at the county jail, 25 miles away in downtown Los Angeles. In order to continue receiving public assistance, she would have to perform custodial work at the jail from midnight to 7 A.M., five days a week. Margarita confronted her GSW:

> "But how am I going to get there? Are you going to give me a ride? If you are going to give me a ride, I'll gladly go." She said, "I can't give you a ride." I asked, "Then how do you expect me to go? On the bus? Busses don't run at that time. Who is going to give me a ride?" "Well, a neighbor?" "My neighbors don't even have cars, and not all neighbors are so good to take me to work in the middle of the night." [. . .] I said, "I'll go, I'll go but you have to take me." . . . She said, "I am going to report you to your [eligibility] worker." . . . I was crying because I was thinking that she would tell my worker, but now she did not tell her. Because, it's that everyone told her, "Maria, how is [she] supposed to go all the way over there?"

Thanks to the other people in the Job Club who came to Margarita's defense, the GSW excused Margarita from the workfare assignment with a warning that she could not refuse another job.[1] Shortly after this confrontation Margarita found a minimum wage job at the Hilton Hotel in downtown Long Beach, cleaning rooms three days a week. As soon as she got her first paycheck, she was going to cancel her and her children's welfare benefits, "so that they will leave me alone." Echoing the language of the GAIN program, she explained:

> Right now, I am going to start working, but little hours. I'll put up with it because that's how you start. You are at the bottom and then you go

up. They give me a few hours and a few days, but then they will add another day or more hours. How long I last there all depends on the quality of my work. . . . But now, I know how to do things and I know how to behave. That is why when you go for an interview, they ask you, "What are your qualities?" I didn't know what "qualities" were before [attending GAIN]. Now I tell them, I am very responsible, punctual, honest.

Margarita's sharp critique of the GAIN program was tempered by the discourse of self-discipline and upward mobility. She articulated her choice to get off welfare as a positive one (while concurrently noting that this is the only way "they will leave me alone"). Although there was little hope that Margarita and her children would be able to survive on the meager earnings from this part-time job, Margarita echoed the GAIN philosophy that her success from welfare-to-work depends on her willingness to see herself as a "responsible, punctual, and honest" employee.

Margarita protested, first by refusing a workfare assignment and then by leaving the welfare system altogether. But, how can we hear Margarita Gonzalez's protest inside a bureaucratic and political system in which leaving welfare, whether in protest or compliance, is narrated as a story of individual empowerment and as proof that welfare reform is a success?

This chapter analyzes the ways that social critique is itself disciplined by the ideology of personal responsibility (and its corollary effect of self-blame) promoted by welfare-to-work programs. During the course of this study, nearly two-thirds of these Mexican immigrant women were forced from the welfare rolls, and their families were faced with intensified economic and personal instability. However, these women narrated their exit from the welfare system as a personal choice and continued to assert the ideal of work as a marker of individual responsibility—this despite the fact their jobs (if they had jobs) were no more empowering, lucrative, or stable than welfare, and that working was making it difficult for them to fulfill their responsibilities as mothers. While these Latinas' remarks about choosing to get off welfare could be read as an endorsement of programs designed to push people off of public assistance, we offer an alternative reading by looking at the ways that Latina immigrants negotiate and redefine personal responsibility in a society that dictates and limits their choices, yet ultimately holds them responsible for these limitations.

Notably, while welfare dependency is typically described with a psycho-medical language of low self-esteem, addiction, and social dysfunction, this discourse was largely absent in these Latinas' self-narratives. While some women blamed themselves for their family's situation, and asserted that this situation would improve once they got off welfare, none talked about being on welfare as an "illness" nor poverty as a moral or individual failing. And, while these Latinas talked about leaving welfare as a personal choice, they nevertheless challenged the notion of free choice when talking about the coercive nature of the welfare system. Within their narratives of personal responsibility were vivid critiques of the welfare state's lack of responsibility and accountability, along with an assertion that true personal responsibility is only possible in a society that is responsible for all its members.

The Limits of Empowerment

As Maria's and Margarita's experiences attest, quitting and leaving become one of the few forms of resistance and empowerment available in a system built on enabling personal responsibility. Yet these forms of resistance are seen as "good choices" rather than as critique—recuperated as proof that welfare reform is working rather than unveiling how degraded and disempowering a system it is that women will risk further poverty to leave. In this system where women are made to feel simultaneously powerless and responsible in the face of their "dependency," the decision to leave welfare is constructed as a form of empowerment regardless of whether she has a job or sufficient means to support her family. However, these decisions ultimately boomerang back upon each woman; because she has made the choice to quit a welfare-to-work assignment or to disenroll her family from benefits, she is made further responsible for the consequences of her decisions. Because there is no clear way to hold the welfare system accountable (when it does not provide the childcare subsidy as promised), Maria holds herself responsible instead.

CalWORKs rests, then, on negative empowerment, on choice through opting out and giving up entitlement. GAIN's function and success as a public agency is measured not by finding people jobs but by teaching them how to look for work, not by people getting good jobs but by moving them into existing low-wage, entry-level openings in the laborforce and retraining their attitudes. Its work-first philosophy is premised on the "stepping stone" model of the labor market, on the idea that one's first job is inevitably bad but that each job is a "learning experience" and that incremental progress will be made if a person merely applies herself. Dean Curtis, cofounder of Curtis and Associates, the private consulting agency that designed GAIN's welfare-to-work package, elaborates this philosophy as follows:

> What people on welfare need are jobs and they need them right away. We believe that anyone can be successful with just what they bring in the door. . . . Self-sufficiency is what people really want. . . . The thing that welfare agencies have to do is change their attitudes about people, and to stop treating them like they are weak and wounded. Experience, age, education, appearance—none of that matters. It's attitude.[2]

Yet, underlying this sunny language on high expectations and good attitude is a "survival-of-the-fittest" model of the economy, one that presumes that the labor market will naturally and fairly select for the most talented and deserving workers. Margarita echoes this philosophy above when she asserts that it is purely her own attitude and performance on the job that will determine her future mobility.

Work-first programs like GAIN instruct welfare recipients to be "realistic" about the options open to them (subtly implying that their lack of realism has prevented them from taking the necessary steps to improve their lives), and promise that this realism will lead to greater rewards in the future. When women like Margarita ask to go back to school, they are met with a bureaucracy that praises their ambition and motivation in a general sense, but dissuades them in the specific by representing their educational ambitions as unnecessary to their success in the labor market. Thus, GAIN proceeds from the "realistic" assumption that Maria could never attend college because she has a fifth grade education and invites her instead to choose between five manual jobs potentially available to her. Since Maria is invited to choose, she is defined as the agent and thus responsible for her choices. While she has not constructed these choices, they have now become hers through this process of decision-making. The act of choosing invests Maria in the list of work options that GAIN defines as appropriate for her—she is now embroiled in the activity of deciding whether she is better suited to be a seamstress or a nursing home aide. As a result, Maria is distracted from imagining other choices not on the list.

Corresponding to the desire women have to be listened to, seen, and respected as people, GAIN focuses on and holds up the individual, not so that those individuals can literally have more options but to make them more responsible for their increasingly limited ones.

This discourse of personal responsibility rests on what Schram characterizes as a "particularly invidious form of individualism," which "reduces people to atomistic selves whose particular differentiating circumstances need not be taken into account."[3] Functioning as a tracking system, GAIN marks which choices are appropriate for certain people by representing the constraints on their lives as immutable, and social and economic inequality as natural—as a "reality" that welfare recipients must adjust to or as the logical outcome of their bad personal choices (like getting pregnant too young, dropping out of school, using drugs, etc.). In this way, Schram argues, "Personal responsibility organizes discrimination."[4] In normalizing discrimination, the discourse of personal responsibility silences poor women's critiques of the low-wage labor market, their demands for education and skills-training necessary to access better-paying jobs, and their accounts of racial and sexual harassment in the workplace. Because in GAIN the welfare recipient determines her own progress up the ladder of success, her critique of the system is dismissed as an excuse for not trying harder. This lack of "motivation" is then offered as evidence that welfare has destroyed her self-esteem, and that she needs a welfare-to-work program to teach her how to help herself.

Beyond the discursive level, personal responsibility is actualized in the mundane, day-to-day operations of what Cruikshank describes as an administrative system with "no clear lines of authority," and where "the relations of rule . . . are multiple, shifting, and often contradictory and insidious."[5] In this ever-shifting and diffuse system of power, the welfare recipient has only herself to look to for action or blame because all lines of authority ultimately cast her as the responsible agent. But this agency is exceedingly tenuous—for poor women are allowed no real authority in the welfare system yet are held responsible for their behavior, the behavior of those around them, and the workings of all the institutions they encounter (the bus must come on time, the post office must never lose their forms). One of the most persistent complaints about the welfare system voiced by these Latina immigrants was that it is never clear who is answerable for particular bureaucratic decisions or even if the decision is inconsistent with the law. When Norma Gonzalez and Leticia Ramirez confronted their caseworkers about unfair rules, the caseworkers responded that they were "just doing their job," a position that these Latina workers were sympathetic to. Similarly, Angela Perez had been informed at a CalWORKs orientation that people who left welfare for work would receive transitional benefits like food stamps and Medi-Cal. Yet, when she began working as a janitor, "They took away my Medi-Cal without telling me, or saying anything, or asking me." Angela spent three days on the phone with the welfare office but was not able to track down the caseworker responsible for terminating her medical coverage or someone in the office who was authorized to reinstate it.

Inside the bureaucratic tangle of welfare, mistakes become untraceable. As a result, the recipient is held responsible for all problems. Moreover, as we argued in the previous chapter, the arbitrariness of this system allows for nonarbitrary enforcement, for systematic denial of benefits and patterns of discrimination. Indeed, all of the Latinas in this study testified that their race and immigration status were constantly foregrounded in the ways they were treated within the CalWORKs system. Held personally responsible for a disorganized and discriminatory system in which they had little control, many of these women turned to one of the few things they had control over: leaving the welfare system, often at great cost to themselves and their families.

As numerous scholars have documented, the discourse of personal responsibility emerged in the 1970s as a backlash against the expansion of rights in the 1960s and as a way to co-opt black nationalist and feminist notions of individual and community empowerment.[6] In particular, it fueled a new direction in federal anti-poverty programs. With the individual now standing as the principal agent of social reform, government programs were created to reform individuals, not to reform society. Over the past 30 years, federal and state governments and nonprofit foundations have invested billions of dollars in efforts to retrain disadvantaged populations for reentry into the labor market.[7] As Epstein explains, this expansion in manpower training entailed a shift from structural attempts to correct inequities in the labor market to an "individual and subcultural approach to manpower":

> While structural approaches attempt either to anticipate the imperfections of the business cycle through macroeconomic fiscal policy or to compensate for its failures through public works programs and perhaps job retraining, training programs aim to overcome the impediments to employment that presumably reside in the individual. . . . [E]mployment and training programs for the welfare population and other low-income

groups are routinely ineffective against basic employment goals, let alone against grander hopes of alleviating poverty through adequate wages.[8]

As early as the 1960s, manpower development rejected higher education as a means to redress human capital inequities and focused instead on job readiness skills (such as attire, resume-writing, and interviewing skills) and cultural retraining (including timeliness, cleanliness, and attitude). We can see this stunted vision of manpower development at work in the case of Margarita, who got a part-time job as a hotel maid while in GAIN and who by current standards would be considered a GAIN success story. The GAIN program did not address any of Margarita's specific labor market disadvantages (a third grade education and very limited English skills). And when we consider that Margarita has worked most of her adult life as a hotel maid, is Margarita's recent "success" in the labor market really attributable to GAIN's lessons on interviewing skills? Was she able to get this minimum-wage hotel housekeeping job because GAIN taught her to say that she was "responsible, punctual, honest"?

Three decades of evaluations of manpower development programs have shown that they produce modest or negligible gains for participants. However, during this same period, federal and state officials, social scientists, foundations and many nonprofits have become more entrenched in their commitment to this approach, obscuring the concrete data in favor of a politically motivated rhetoric of individuals overcoming their own deficiencies. This has propelled a monumental expansion of these programs both in terms of dollars spent and people required to participate. But the travesty of manpower development is not simply that it wastes government dollars and poor people's time. Rather, what these negligible gains accomplish, as William Epstein argues, is that once participants fail in programs not designed to work, "they certify their own worthlessness and excuse social neglect."[9]

Indeed, most of these Latinas emphasized that participating in the GAIN program made them feel deficient and worthless. Because many had entered the program optimistic about the prospect of real job training and help finding work, they were profoundly demoralized by the purposelessness of Job Club and the ritual humiliation of aimlessly canvassing L.A. County in search of work while dressed in *"disfrases ridículos"* (ridiculous costumes) that publicly marked them as welfare recipients. Moreover, the sheer volume of jobs they were required to apply for (an enforced minimum of 50 per week) further exacerbated their sense of worthlessness when they never got called for an interview. This branding of welfare recipients as "worthless" begins at the individual level, making GAIN participants feel worthless when they do not get a job, and radiates out to the social level, as the public can feel good for providing a "hand up" for welfare recipients and also blame them when the program does not work. Because of the recent avalanche of positive publicity surrounding GAIN, those participants who do not find a job while in GAIN —no matter if they constitute the majority—are seen as individual failures and castigated for their lack of motivation and low self-esteem. This psychologizing function of GAIN ultimately facilitates the mission of welfare reform. In Los Angeles County, where there are not enough jobs to employ the existing number of welfare recipients, GAIN's success as a public agency rests on its ability to train welfare recipients to link their self-esteem to a personal and voluntary choice to get off of welfare.[10]

Inside the institutions of welfare reform, the construction of public assistance as an individual and voluntary choice operates as an ideological fetish or what Michelle Fine describes as "frames for papering over contradictory . . . pieces of institutional life, [which] persist way beyond evidence of their own inadequacy." Ideological fetishes, Fine writes, "obscure through partial truths," they advance irrelevant or misleading explanations of social phenomena that prevent a full understanding of the social and material relations that govern people's existence.[11] One of the primary ways that GAIN legitimizes its power over welfare recipients is by representing the receipt of public assistance as a free choice, rather than one that is inextricably enmeshed in gender, race, and class relations in U.S. society. According to social theorist Slavoj Žižek, in a liberal society premised on the appearance of free agency, choice is essentially symbolic:

> Every belonging to a society involves a paradoxical point at which the subject is ordered to embrace freely, as the result of his choice, what is anyway imposed on him (we *must* all love our country, our parents . . .). This paradox of willing (choosing freely) what is in any case necessary, of pretending (maintaining the appearance) that there is a free choice although in fact there isn't, is strictly codependent with the notion of an empty symbolic gesture, a gesture—an offer—which is meant to be rejected: what the empty gesture offers is the opportunity to choose the impossible, that which inevitably will *not* happen.[12]

We saw this fetishization of choice earlier in the example of the "Welfare to Work Plan," where recipients can choose not to sign yet are still subject to the contractual rules in the plan which stipulates that if they do not sign they lose their benefits. If a woman is threatened with her family's primary source of support, can we say that she has a free choice?

Still, unlike other social programs, like K–12 education (where participation is compulsory) and Social Security (where receipt of benefits is pro forma), there is an assumption that going on welfare is a discretionary choice, neither a fundamental right nor responsibility. A poor woman cannot be made to go on welfare as proof that she is a responsible mother, even though she can be forced to get her children immunized or even to go on birth control; she cannot be prosecuted by the state for not applying for welfare, but she can be prosecuted for not sending her kids to school. To guarantee her right to a fair trial, she is assigned a public defendant if she cannot afford a private attorney, but not food stamps if she does not have enough money for food. She will routinely receive a yearly statement of her Social Security benefits, but not an unsolicited letter from the government advising her that she is eligible for and entitled to public assistance.[13] There is a prima facie logic that constructs poverty not as an objective condition but a personal one, distinct, for instance, from getting old. Because poverty is individualized in American ideology and public policy, it is possible to represent a woman's entry into the welfare system as voluntary.[14]

Once a woman "voluntarily" goes on welfare, she is subject to a contradictory discourse of choice. A woman is told that she has given up her right to choice (forfeiting the hallmarks of U.S. citizenship such as privacy and due process) after "choosing" to go on welfare. At the same time, she is told that she can regain her right to choice if she demonstrates that she is capable of making "better choices" for herself and her children. Choice thus becomes a slippery and contested terrain inside the GAIN office, where welfare recipients are invited to see themselves as "participants," yet silenced or sanctioned when they question the social, economic, and institutional forces that constrain their agency. One of the few possible choices, then, is the choice the state wants them to make— refusing to participate and leaving welfare. However, while most of the Latinas in this study framed leaving welfare as a personal choice, they simultaneously articulated the ways that their choices were constrained, pre-manufactured, and policed inside the new welfare system. While wide-ranging, their critiques fell under two themes: "It's not what you choose but what they choose for you," and "How can I make impossible choices?"

Choice and Coercion: It's Not What You Choose but What They Choose for You

Throughout their interviews for this study, Latina immigrants grappled with the welfare state's contradictory discourse of choice, and more often than not substituted it with a language of coercion and terror.

> *Alejandra*: What happens if you can't participate, or if you refuse to participate, in GAIN?
>
> *Leticia*: They fine you. . . . No, supposedly they send you to jail.
>
> *Norma*: The bottom rule is that if you don't participate, you're automatically cut off. . . . They threaten you. . . . A lot of people don't know their rights, and they're scared. Just to hear the fact that they're going to cut you off, it scares them. . . . And, a lot of people do that. They take advantage because a lot of people don't speak out.

Both Leticia Ramirez and Norma Gonzalez directly challenged the language of free participation that runs throughout GAIN's official literature and activities. These women assert that GAIN is not voluntary and so they are not actually "participating" but complying with a punitive system of rules that has the power to take away their family's primary livelihood. This coercion is so powerful that many Latina immigrants in this study feared that there was more to lose than their welfare benefits. Leticia feared that she would go to jail. Other women feared that they could be deported or barred from becoming U.S. citizens. Still others feared that their children would be taken away from them. In these instances, when these women talked about going to GAIN, there was no reference even to Žižek's concept of an empty gesture of free will. In other words, although GAIN calls its welfare recipients "participants," these women talked about going to GAIN not as a form of participation but as a form of control.

Women talked not only about direct threats and dire consequences, but also how constant confusion and rule changes inside the system produced a climate of fear, defeat, and docility, as they attempted to satisfy an ever-changing set of requirements. These Latinas understood that the system ultimately was not accountable for its actions. We saw this in the previous chapter when Leticia was ordered to go to GAIN, even though her family had been cut off of welfare. Although Leticia knew that she should not have to attend GAIN, she nevertheless complied when her caseworker ordered her to go anyway. Similarly, when Margarita recounts the confrontation with her GSW over her workfare assignment, she does not frame this as a choice about whether or not to accept the position. Margarita does not directly refuse to comply with the assignment, but instead pleads with her GSW to find her a mode of transportation— "if you tell me how to get there, I will go." Both women, then, employ a language of coerced compliance, not participation.

"Choice" is built into each of the steps in the GAIN program. Welfare recipients choose a Welfare-to-Work Plan in consultation with their GSW; they choose the appropriate attire from the donation boxes at Job Club or from a retail store of their choice; they choose to apply for the jobs best suited to their talents and experience; and then they choose a set of classes and support systems from an array of post-employment services. Yet, these Latinas challenged the notion of free choice in each of these steps. Margarita, for example, pointed out the absurdity of the GAIN form on "employment goals":

> *Margarita*: There on the form, it asks you how much you want to earn, but it's the same for all jobs.
> *Alejandra*: And what do you write?
> *Margarita*: The minimum.

As Margarita points out, this request for her input on a desirable wage is an empty gesture: If all jobs available to her pay the minimum wage, then she has little choice about her earnings; if she lists a higher wage, then she will appear out of touch with the reality of the job market and in fact will receive little practical assistance from GAIN in reaching this goal. Moreover, the truth is that no matter what Margarita writes, she has no other choice but to accept any job she gets while in GAIN.

So, given the emptiness of this exercise, why does GAIN require its "participants" to fill out such forms? The function of this exercise is to symbolically enact the image of the welfare recipient as a self-determining agent inside a free labor market. Presumably, when Margarita writes that she wants to earn "the minimum," she consents to this wage. Also, in naming the minimum wage as a preference or "goal," the implication is that Margarita has realistically surveyed the options available to her and set her own personal goals. Whether or not she realizes these goals is now predicated on her motivation, discipline, and talents.[15] In getting Margarita to cite the minimum wage as her preference, GAIN also assures its own success—when Margarita gets a minimum wage job as a hotel maid, her employment aspirations and outcomes have been successfully aligned. Yet, through her comments above, Margarita Gonzalez denaturalizes the spectacle of consent; by pointing out that all jobs pay the minimum wage, she refuses this as a personal preference.

Similarly, although DPSS literature describes GAIN as an individualized program that is tailored to the aspirations and experience of each participant, most of the Mexican immigrant women challenged this fallacy of individual choice. For example, when talking about the welfare-to-work activities approved by GAIN, Norma Gonzalez noted that "some people are choosing to go to school." But seconds later she amended her response by saying, "It's not what you choose, but where they send you. If you're not one of the lucky ones, then you don't get to go to school." When asked how GAIN decides who goes to school, she replied:

> That's what I want to know, because I never got sent. I wanted to go but I never got sent. And I had asked, "You know, I want to go and get my GED and I want to do this." [The GSW] said, "Well, that's good that you're being motivated." She never sent me. . . . So that's why I got the job that I got.

Chastised by society for lacking initiative, Norma arrived at her GAIN orientation with a clear action plan to move her family out of poverty. In fact, she was already attending GED classes at Long Beach City College and wanted to continue in the program so that she could eventually enroll in nursing school. Instead Norma was forced to drop her classes and to participate in a Job Club that, as she notes above, resulted in a minimum wage job as a supermarket cashier. Determined to get her GED, Norma enrolled in a home study program and completed her coursework at night. After a year of work at the supermarket, Norma got pregnant and had to quit her job. She returned to welfare, was sent again to GAIN, and this time convinced the GSW to refer her to a job-training program. She was handed a list of short-term vocational programs from which she chose "medical assistant."

Lupe also chose the "medical assistant" track, although in her interviews she had talked about her love of poetry, her desire to go to college, and her lifelong dream of becoming an auto mechanic. Like many of the women in this study, Lupe believed that there was a job out there that fit her talents and interests. She wanted a career that would provide both personal satisfaction and opportunities for advancement. As she asserted, "I want to do something I like. I don't want to . . . take on a profession, you know, something, a career, and then later on I get bored and I don't want to do it anymore." Although Lupe had never before been interested in working in the medical field, after two excruciating and unproductive rounds of Job Club, she jumped at the opportunity to enroll in a GAIN-approved medical assistant training program.

In Norma's and Lupe's stories, we can see GAIN's tracking function. Although both women requested that they be enrolled in college classes that would lead to a professional career, they were handed a short list of vocational programs from which to choose. Here tracking is accomplished both by directly blocking women's plans and aspirations and by training them to change their aspirations themselves. In encouraging these women to "start small," in requiring them to go through Job Club before they qualify for vocational classes, and in making them feel fortunate when they are approved for any activity other than work, GAIN invokes an invisible form of coercion. When interviewed in the first year of the study, Norma wanted to study to become a Registered Nurse (a career path that requires college education and extensive training and thus is not an approved "educational activity" under welfare reform). Three years later, after being forced out of GED classes and into a minimum-wage job, Norma felt "lucky" to be training to become a medical assistant, a job that involves comparatively lower pay and less autonomy than nursing. Yet although Norma herself recognized that this training program represented a downgrade of her original career ambitions, she didn't describe it as a setback or compromise—she talked about it as her preference or choice.[16]

To suggest that Norma was merely "tricked" or forced into choosing the medical assistant path, however, misses the ideological effects of GAIN and the importance of limited agency in this system. According to sociologist Naila Kabeer, choices are not atomistic expressions of individual free will, divorced from the historical and socioeconomic contexts in which they arise; nor conversely are most choices forcibly dictated or determined by external structures.[17] In her study of Bangladeshi women's labor market choices in the global economy, Kabeer draws on Pierre Bourdieu's concept of "habitus" to theorize the ways that social class, cultural capital, gender, and race structure the contours of what is thinkable and therefore "chooseable" for this group of women workers.[18] As Kabeer elaborates:

> Because habitus generates aspirations and practices which reflect, and are compatible with, the objective range of possibilities available in given social contexts, it serves to delineate the improbable and the unthinkable within particular situations from what is possible, desirable or indeed inevitable. This "sense of limits" which a social order produces in its members, which is also their "sense of reality," underpins their adherence to the social order to "naturalising" some aspects of reality.[19]

In the above example, this "sense of limits" is produced when Norma's desire to become a Registered Nurse collides against her "objective range of possibilities," which is constructed by society and policed by GAIN, and eventually moves into the category of the "improbable and the unthinkable." Not only is it now unthinkable that Norma could become a Registered Nurse, but also the social and material underpinnings of this impossibility (for example, the fact that Norma is barred from attending college as part of her "welfare-to-work activities") disappear from view, as Norma actively participates in bureaucratic rituals like choosing from a predetermined list of options and signing a new Welfare-to-Work Plan.

Norma's "sense of limits" is also reinforced by a larger public discourse which asserts that welfare recipients need to be more realistic about their opportunities in the labor market. Where government programs to correct social inequality are now blamed for having produced a "culture of victimization," welfare recipients' demands for education and real opportunities for mobility are dismissed as excuses to avoid work and personal responsibility. So powerful is this discourse that it produces its own terms of dissent, as many welfare rights advocates, labor unions, and community groups have responded to welfare reform by arguing that recipients want to work but that they need a living wage. Although this campaign to "raise the floor" of the labor market is absolutely essential to the survival of poor families in the post-welfare economy, it nevertheless leaves unchallenged the belief that higher education and professional careers for poor women are "improbable and unthinkable."

In a related sense, we can see this "sense of limits" as it was produced in Alejandra's conversations with these Latinas about their labor market options. The interview instrument designed by MDRC and administered by ethnographers in the Urban Change research sites asked welfare recipients to rank "the qualities you look for in a job," and provided them with a list of criteria from which to choose (including wages, benefits, hours, distance from home, working conditions, access to a telephone, opportunities for advancement, etc.) This interview question not only typifies the "rational choice" model that undergirds most welfare research, but it also provides us with a concrete illustration of how these women's "sense of limits" was actively constructed in the interview process. By asking welfare recipients to choose from a predetermined list of work-related characteristics, the interview process communicated to these women that they must have a rational (limited) set of expectations of the labor market and that they needed to accept that they could not "have it all." Respondents like Delia and Yasmín were asked to choose whether they preferred a job that paid above the minimum wage *or* one with health benefits, between a workplace where the supervisor does not yell at employees *or* one where there is a telephone accessible to call their children. The class and gender underpinnings of these "choices" are all too apparent—it is improbable that an entertainment lawyer would have to select between salary and health benefits or that a male administrative assistant would be faced with a choice between respect on the job or access to a telephone. And yet, because this set of criteria bore sufficient resemblance to the objective conditions that these Latina workers face at the bottom of L.A. County's socioeconomic structure, it in effect naturalized the forces of their exploitation by representing the parameters of their choices as inevitable and routine.

Indeed, for this group of women accustomed to commuting 25 miles for a decent job or forgoing health benefits for regular employment, the task of weighing a limited set of options was not entirely strange.[20] Nor, in this regard, was it strange that most women identified working hours as their primary concern, explaining that they needed to work the night shift in order to care for their children during the day. As rational economic actors, these Latina mothers knew that the wages available to them are insufficient to pay for childcare and that they had to enlist unpaid childcare assistance from their spouse or a family member during the night when their kids were asleep. Although these Latinas most often turned to night work because they had few other options, most did not describe this decision in purely economic terms.[21] As they bemoaned the lack of affordable, quality childcare and grappled with the logistics of combining work and childcare shifts with their spouses or relatives, these Latinas explicitly linked their nighttime work to their identities as "good mothers"—an identity that is forged in direct opposition to their public portrayal as welfare queens. By working for wages at night and for their families during the day, these women explained, they were ensuring that their children excelled in school, stayed out of trouble, and "grew up knowing that their mother loves them."[22] For several of the married women in the study, working the night shift was also commensurate with their responsibilities as "good wives." By working at night and taking care of the children and housework during the day (often sleeping as little as three hours), they could not be accused by their husbands and other family members of shirking their domestic duties.[23] Still others discussed their nighttime work in the language of sacrifice, calling up the ideology of the American Dream, in which immigrant parents compromise their own immediate interests in exchange for a better future for their offspring. Standing on this precipice between realism and hopefulness, Leticia took a job stuffing newspaper circulars at night for the chance that her daughters might graduate from high school and advance to college. Myrna shelved inventory at Target stores from midnight to 5 A.M. so that she could drive her two older kids to school and spend the morning with her five-year-old before driving to Orange County for an afternoon shift on the plastics production line. Angela prepared dinner for her family and put her children to bed before reporting to work at a janitorial services agency to clean dental clinics and real estate offices.[24]

Contending with a profound lack of options to be able to care emotionally, physically, and materially for their children, most Latinas talked about the night shift as a "choice" because it allowed them to be both mothers and workers. What is sacrificed in this equation is the choice of caring for their own health and well-being, and even the recognition that this is a viable goal. Moreover, viewing the night shift as an individual decision does not adequately explain how it corresponds to the interests of employers, whose profitability rests on hiring immigrants and people of color for irregular shifts and overnight work. While "off hours" work used to pay more than a 9-to-5 shift, today most employers pay the same wage regardless of the time of day. None of the women in this study who worked at night earned more than they would in a day shift. To the contrary, because they often worked split shifts that spread across calendar days, their employers were not required to pay them overtime.

Thus, we can see the "choice" of working the night shift as both a product of and a response to welfare reform's ideology of personal responsibility, which instruct poor women that their "powerlessness" and lack of choices makes them subjects and not citizens. Inside this ideological hall of mirrors, these Latinas' recasting of limited options like nighttime work as personal choices must be read as a bid for the status of citizen, one of the few means by which a woman can imagine herself as an agent of her own fate.

Trapped in the Double-Bind of Welfare: "How Can I Make Impossible Choices?"

At the same time that Latina immigrants alternately appropriated the language of choice and critiqued the ways that their choices were constrained and forced upon them by the welfare state, they also protested the impossibility of choice inside this system. They found themselves faced with daily impossible decisions, most of which led to harmful consequences for their families. Seeing few opportunities for effective resistance or empowerment inside the contradictory web of welfare rules, many Latinas chose to resist by leaving the system altogether. Ultimately, however, leaving welfare was itself an impossible choice because the loss of supplemental income, food stamps, and medical coverage pushed these women and their families into a more precarious existence.

Numerous critics of the AFDC and TANF programs have talked about welfare as a series of impossible choices, specifically noting that benefit levels have been set so low and rules so stringent that the only way to continue existing inside the system is by breaking the rules.[25] Cruikshank, for example, notes:

> The worst double-bind followed from the fact that AFDC grants were made at levels well below the established poverty line. Everyone knew that welfare grants were not enough to live on and this fact more than any other created an atmosphere of fear and suspicion. Welfare recipients knew, probation officers knew, therapists and ex-boyfriends knew, fraud investigators knew: if you lived in one place and had well-fed and

well-cared for children, you were in all likelihood committing welfare fraud; if you were homeless or living in substandard housing, if your kids were poorly dressed and truant, then you were a likely candidate for child-protective services.[26]

The welfare recipient is always assumed guilty of fraud or parental neglect until proven innocent. Because most disciplinary actions take place at the hands of individual caseworkers and welfare review boards (not in civil or criminal court), the recipient is constituted as a unique political subject at the mercy of bureaucratic practices rather than the civil liberties that most Americans enjoy. Indeed, a number of Latinas in this study had been investigated for welfare fraud without the opportunity to confront their accusers. Myrna's home was twice raided by welfare officials following unsubstantiated, anonymous accusations that she had a live-in boyfriend and that she was physically abusing her children. As Myrna herself explained, she had no choice but to allow the fraud investigators to search her home and to answer their questions; refusal to cooperate would not only have been understood by the state as an admission of guilt, but it also would have been a violation of the rules of the welfare system and grounds for the termination of her benefits. Myrna was faced with an impossible choice: to forfeit her constitutional rights to due process and privacy or to forfeit the social entitlements that enable her to shelter and feed her family.

Even in cases where women were not directly investigated by the state, they nevertheless characterized life on welfare as a constant struggle to satisfy an ever-changing and contradictory body of rules and expectations. Over and over this group of Latina mothers explained that they were being judged according to a set of standards that always set them up for failure. This theme permeated their descriptions of the most mundane experiences, from dressing their children for school, to shopping for food, to interacting with teachers, doctors, and social workers. Herminia, for example, recounted a home visit from the Child Protective Services Department, when she was reprimanded by a social worker for buying clothing for her granddaughter that was "too nice." As she recalled:

When I showed her my granddaughter's dresses, the social worker told me, "Don't be buying her clothes like that all the time." . . . But I tell her that I have to have my granddaughter dressed nicely. . . . They give me money to take care of my grandchildren and I invest it in them. I don't want them to tell me [how to spend my money].

For Herminia Hernandez, this confrontation with the social worker exemplified the double-bind of welfare. She had proudly shown off her granddaughter's new clothing as proof that she was fulfilling her obligations as a guardian to the children in her custody—in fact, had the social worker determined that the child was not adequately dressed, Herminia could have lost custody rights. However, Herminia's attempt to satisfy society's standards of middle-class motherhood became an opportunity for the welfare state to police her private life and question the soundness of her choices. Just as Norma was scolded by her GAIN counselor for buying an expensive work outfit, Herminia was reprimanded for allowing her granddaughter to enjoy material comforts that, in the social worker's estimation, Herminia would not be able to provide in the future. Thus, despite the new TANF program's celebration of hard work and self-determination, it ultimately treats Herminia's class position as fixed and predetermined. Yet when women like Herminia protest the structural obstacles that stand in the way of their mobility, they are chastised and disciplined for their lack of motivation and self-esteem.

Other Latinas highlighted this double-bind by recounting the ways that they were being forced to "choose" between complying with the GAIN rules (which often conflicted with the best interests of their family) or privileging their family's well-being above the rules (which would ultimately result in the loss of their welfare benefits). Maria Sanchez, for example, described an incident in which she needed to take her sick son to the doctor, yet was threatened with sanctions if she missed a session of GAIN:

They don't care if you eat, if you sleep, if you're clothed, if you're shoeless, nothing. They don't care if you get sick. They don't. . . . I had to take one of my kids to the doctor. I called [the GAIN worker] and I told her, "You know, my son is very sick." "I don't care," she said, "I want you here at such and such hour." She said, "You can do it." I didn't say anything. I was quiet. So she said, "Obligations are obligations." I told her, "My son comes first."

Maria's GAIN worker demanded that she prioritize her "obligation" to the program above her son's health. Maria not only defied these orders, but she also justified her resistance to GAIN's inflexible regime of rules by appropriating the program's discourse of personal responsibility—"my son comes first." Our research documented countless stories like Maria's. Norma, for example, recounted a very similar confrontation that took place in her Job Club:

> Like this lady had a sick son, and she went in and told them, "You know, my son is sick. He is vomiting a lot and he has a high fever. So, I just came to sign in and to tell you that I can't stay in class today." The caseworker said, "Is your son dying? . . . Unless your son is dying and he has a life-threatening condition, then you can't leave or you'll be cut off." So then I told her, "Oh, if my son is sick and I leave, I don't care if I get cut off, because my son comes first.

Challenging a racist society that puts Latino children on the bottom, women like Maria Sanchez and Norma Gonzalez reasserted their fundamental right and responsibility to righteous motherhood by putting their children first.

However, while these Latina mothers critiqued these impossible choices, they did not entirely escape the self-blame and sense of failure that often accompanies being forced to make an impossible choice. Despite her condemnation of the inflexibility and heartlessness of the new welfare rules, Maria blamed herself for her family's disqualification from TANF and the eventual removal of her five children from her custody and into the foster care system. Similarly, Norma collapsed into self-blame when recounting how she and her mother carried her sick son three miles to the nearest hospital in the middle of the night because they could not afford a taxi:

> There was a time when my mom didn't have no money and I didn't have no money, so she walked with me and we took turns carrying Marvin to the emergency room. So you know, I feel really bad telling you about this. I feel . . . I don't know. It made me feel really, really bad that I was not doing my job as a parent.

Norma originally began telling this story to Alejandra in order to illustrate how "welfare is not enough." However, through the course of the interview session, Norma's critique of the system quickly turned inward into a critique of herself. When pressed by Alejandra to provide a specific explanation for her culpability (What exactly could she have done differently in this situation? What would a "better" mother have done?), Norma's response was tautological: She was a bad mother because welfare did not provide her with enough to be a good mother to her son. Rather than blame the system for placing her family in an impossible situation, she blamed herself for that situation.

Yet, even when Norma blames herself, she is claiming a certain degree of agency—eschewing a class defeatism ("this is just the way the world works") and nihilism ("nothing will ever change"). For many of the women, then, self-blame was closely aligned to a claim for power; if they could be responsible for the negative circumstances of their lives in the present, then they had sufficient power and self-possession to shape their destinies in the future. This is, however, a deceptive bind: Their claim to agency becomes articulated through a language of self-blame—potentially personally harmful—within a system predicated on their lack of agency. The discourses of choice and personal responsibility are effective tools of discipline in the welfare system precisely because they resonate with poor women's own desires for recognition, dignity, and agency.

Double-Consciousness and the Choice between Welfare and Work

Norma's self-narrative, like those of most of the Mexican immigrant women in this study, dances on the hyphen between moralizing individualism, self-blame, and social critique. From the same space that these Latinas challenged the racism of the welfare state, they launched an attack on African Americans who they claim are the "real welfare problem." In the same breath that these women asserted that work does not pay for those at the bottom of the economic structure, they affirmed their own work ethic and their willingness to accept any job, no matter the pay or conditions. They critiqued the impossible standards of motherhood that society imposes on women of color, and at the same time contrasted themselves to other black and Latina women in their neighborhood who "don't care about their children like I do." Although some engaged in small, daily acts of defiance (from not reporting cash income to refusing job placements), most continued to comply with the rules and to echo the ideologies of welfare reform—even as they voiced a broader critique of the welfare system and the low-wage labor market.

From W. E. B. Du Bois, we hear about how people objectified as "problems" exist on the margin between seeing themselves through the eyes of society and constructing their own identities:

> Between me and the other world there is ever an unasked question: unasked by some through feelings of delicacy; by others through the difficulty of rightly framing it. All nevertheless, flutter round it. . . . How does it feel to be a problem? It is a peculiar sensation, this double consciousness, this sense of always looking at one's self through the eyes of others, of measuring one's soul by the tape of the world that looks on in amused contempt and pity.[27]

Legal scholar Patricia Williams elaborates on this recurring self-regard when she writes, "What complicates this structure of thought insofar as racism is concerned, however is that the distancing does not stop with the separation of the white self from the black other . . . the black self is placed at a distance even from itself, as in my example of blacks being asked to put themselves in the position of the white shopkeepers [and DPSS workers] who scrutinized them."[28]

From the Latinas in this study, we learn about the multiple contradictions of negotiating this double vision inside the welfare state. In a system that tracks welfare recipients' movements through national data systems and launches surprise inspections of their homes, one's survival rests on avoiding being noticed. Yet, being seen as an individual still holds the elusive promise of humanization and empowerment. This individual self, however, is necessarily crafted in opposition to the "problem" other—to the bad mother who trades her food stamps for drugs, to the illegal immigrant cheating the system. Within a system where following and defying the rules produces harmful effects on one's family, these women understand that their choices will always be judged and limited by a society that constructs them as a problem. Composing a sense of self—even a self in opposition to the welfare queen—then, still requires seeing oneself through the eyes of a world that "looks on with pity and contempt."

It is only in the context of this double vision inside the welfare state, and the growing intimidation and insecurity brought on by welfare reform, that we can understand why most Latina mothers in this study said that work is better than welfare. Most of the Latinas did not see welfare and work as mutually defining alternatives. But in the course of the interviews, women were asked, "How does working compare to welfare?"

Angela: Well, with work, you are receiving a paycheck every 15 days or every week, and with welfare it's every month. And what they send you. . . . For example, if I didn't get any help from him [her fiancé] with $496 I would only be able to pay the rent. What about the bills, the children's clothing? And what they send us in food stamps is not enough for the whole month. It's only enough for 15 days of food. After the 15 days, what do we do?

Margarita: Sometimes I think that [my life] will improve because if I work, I can have credit anywhere. But right now I can't have credit because I'm on welfare. And if I work, the [creditor] is going to say, "Oh, she is working. She has someone to vouch for her." But if I'm on welfare, who is going to vouch for me?

Myrna: What's good is to make the people work. They should really try to work. . . . But I also understand that there're lots of people who have lots of kids, and to work just to pay the babysitter, that's real hard. . . . Also, like at the day care centers, you know, it's full. You have to sign up, wait your turn. You can't just get childcare right away. They have waiting lists. And for me, that I work the graveyard shift, it's hard because not just anybody can watch my kids.

Carmen: Working? I love it. I love it 'cause you feel better. Whether you get your paycheck every week or every two weeks, you do feel better because you know you are going to get that check . . . and not be waiting for a month. 'Cause can I say my [welfare] check is going to be there when I go pick it up? I've been through that. Like when I started working, there was some problem, and I didn't get my check and food stamps.

Norma: I think that working is always better because, you know, you don't have to sit around and wait, depend on them to send you something. Because you know that if you're working, you're going to get it [paid]. But, if you're depending on them to send it to you, and they *know* you're depending on them, they just send it when they want to?

Lupe: I would say [that], in a way, it's better, you know, for them to send people to work 'cause, there's just some people that just, you know, stay at home because they know, "Hey, my money's gonna come."

These Latina mothers asserted that working is better than being on welfare; they wanted to work and not be dependent on the government; their children would be "better off" if they were working; and although they themselves were honest and responsible, there were too many other people out there abusing the system.

Similar responses have been echoed by welfare recipients across the country, appearing in recent media coverage, social science reports and policy briefs, and promotional videos and brochures used by government programs like GAIN to sell the message of welfare reform to recipients. There are two predominant ways of reading welfare recipients' affirmation of the messages behind welfare reform. In most journalistic and applied policy accounts, they are framed as the transparent reporting of authentic experience. If welfare recipients say welfare reform is a good idea, then it must be true.[29] Other scholars reduce welfare recipients' dislike of welfare to the power of dominant ideology—welfare recipients as duped and further oppressed—rather than analyzing more closely what women are saying.[30]

Yet, what would it mean to read the above statements in another light? First, it would require hearing the variety of other things that Latina immigrants are saying alongside this. Although there was a continual allusion to bad women on welfare in the interview transcripts, there was also a notion of collectivity and solidarity. For these women, the humiliation of welfare was not just individual but collective. They built alliances in welfare offices and job clubs, shared rides, stuck up for each other, and protected each other's privacy. Myrna often gave part of her welfare money to her neighbor, who was undocumented and could not receive aid. Margarita counted on Angela to watch her children when she had a job interview or needed to run a quick errand. Norma helped other Latina immigrants in her Job Club fill out job applications in English and protested when one of her classmates, who suffered from epilepsy, was punished for leaving class early.

Moreover, through the course of the interviews, it became increasingly clear that these women were not talking about any literal person they knew; there was no actual welfare queen living next door or down the block and when pressed to name a woman they knew who "sold her food stamps for drugs," "who was lazy and had too many babies," they could not. This is because they were not, in fact, constructing an oppositional identity to other real women but to the welfare queen as a symbol—and in the process carving out a place for self-definition. Their discursive strategy illustrates the power of this anti-welfare ideology; women did not always attempt, and perhaps could not imagine, how to discredit the image wholesale. Rather what they were able to do was take the symbol as a counterpoint for who they were, who their mothers were, who their sisters and neighbors were. The symbol of the welfare queen opened up a space for talking about their motherhood, their morals regarding family, work, and responsibility, and their fears that other people—including the state—did not share this morality.

Similarly, when these Latinas praised work and its benefits, they were operating from the category of the ideal of work—set apart from their actual experiences as workers and their knowledge and expectations of the labor market. Even though they said they would feel better about themselves if they were working, their accounts of work provided substantive evidence to the contrary. They relayed stories of harassment and humiliation on the job, of jobs that left them physically exhausted, of mind-numbing boredom and continual stress. Many women said that work was better because they could count on getting a paycheck, whereas they could not count on getting a welfare check. But often, their actual work experiences did not bear out this belief. Their work hours were constantly changing (and usually never enough) and included jobs where they did not even get paid for the work they had done. And even though they held out the promise of a good job, their understanding of how the labor market functioned revealed that they did not believe any good jobs were available to them. Finally, although they emphasized the idea of respect on the job, most of their accounts of work highlighted the absence of dignity in low-wage jobs.

Conversely, these Latinas were not critiquing the concept of welfare but rather their lived experiences within the welfare system. All but one of the immigrant women in this study shared stories of harassment, discrimination, or unfairness from their caseworkers. Caseworkers regularly yelled at them, threatened to cut off part or all of their benefits, and told them that because they were not real Americans they didn't deserve any help from the government. All said that they wanted to get off of welfare because benefits were shrinking every day while humiliation and punishment were growing. Indeed, if we look at these women's comments above on the advantages of working relative to receiving welfare, nearly all framed this comparison in terms of the unpredictability and lack of accountability on the part of the welfare system.

Still, even though these women critiqued the discriminatory nature of the welfare system, they maintained a language of rights regarding the need for public assistance, and they asserted that welfare provided families with an important protection against hunger and homelessness. In the midst of saying that they wanted to be off welfare, women still asserted that welfare had been crucial to their family's survival. Margarita wanted to get off welfare so that "they will leave me alone. I will be tranquil and everything. They are not going to be sending me anywhere. . . . But if it wasn't for welfare can you imagine how I could have done it? Now that they take it away, how many children are going to go hungry?" Similarly, asked where she would be in five years, Carmen said she would be working and off of welfare. But then she interrupted herself saying, "I mean [welfare] does help. It helps families."

These Latinas could cast leaving welfare as a personal goal and claim its absolute necessity as social policy. They worried about the fate of other families in the wake of welfare reform and critiqued the hypocrisy and shortsightedness in cuts in social spending. For instance, Norma Gonzalez observed:

> Now, it's awful because all they think about is saving money. But they don't think about the kids. . . . I mean it's awful. They are going to have the biggest homeless state in all of the United States, because, you know, they're not really thinking about anything else except saving money. They're not thinking about the people that are going to be homeless. You know, kids are going to be homeless. And they're not thinking about the people that are going to go hungry.

Similarly, Angela Perez commented that her benefits had been reduced every year but that she had never received an explanation from the welfare office about these reductions:

> No, just that they were cutting because there was no money from the government. I would say, well why do they have money for . . . what is it that they are doing in Saudi Arabia, or sending airplanes to war and all of that? What are they doing that for? Instead of the government spending money on weapons and to kill people, what about the people over here?

The Mexican immigrant women interviewed for this study were initially attracted to welfare reform programs that promised job training, education, and English instruction, and they believed in the promise of equal opportunity trumpeted under welfare reform. Yet their experiences in these programs taught them that this was, in fact, a cheapened form of citizenship reserved for those groups who continue to be posited as racial outsiders to the national community.[31] Indeed, Zoraida Torres's fear at the outset of welfare reform implementation in L.A. County seems all too prescient: "Some days I get discouraged and think that as soon as they see that so many Latinos are becoming citizens, then they'll put another law in our way so that our citizenship doesn't mean anything anymore."

Conclusion: A New Americanization Program?

> Personally, I believe that the first essential is more and better education . . . of the bodies and souls, as well as the minds of people, to make them understand their place in the universe as efficient, useful, productive agents.
>
> —Rheta Childe Dorr, Americanization supporter, 1920

> The earnest Americanizers of the interwar years now appear dated. Not only would the idea of systematically instilling a rigorous form of Americanism constitute an improbable political agenda, but also the political developments since the 1960's effectively preclude such an approach.
>
> —Desmond King, *Making Americans*

One need only to talk to welfare recipients about their experiences in the GAIN program to question political scientist Desmond King's above assertion that Americanization is an impossible political agenda in the contemporary moment.[32] With their expansive network of government social welfare agencies, private charities, and social service providers extolling the virtues of hard work, discipline, and self-sacrifice, today's welfare-to-work programs bear a striking resemblance to Americanization campaigns in the 1920s.[33] Like these early twentieth-century programs, contemporary initiatives like GAIN strive to assimilate a group of impoverished and "culturally alien" mothers (native-born and immigrant women of color) into mainstream American society. As in past assimilationist efforts, GAIN promises its participants greater access to the American Dream, reinforcing central tenets of American ideology like individualism, meritocracy, and personal responsibility, while engaging them in a regimen of self-improvement and self-discipline. Just as Americanizers tracked Mexican women into work in garment factories and middle-class homes, GAIN rests on a set of gendered and racialist assumptions about the natural suitability of people for different types of labor. By preparing and channeling welfare recipients into low-wage, feminized work, under the guise of "helping" them to achieve self-sufficiency, this program ultimately reproduces the structural inequalities that restrict these women to second-class citizenship in the national community.[34]

The idea of cultural uplift was the fulcrum upon which welfare reform rested.[35] Indeed, Desmond King's above assertion that Americanization became an impossible agenda in the aftermath of the 1960s does not account for the ways that the now dominant paradigm of multiculturalism stands on a post–civil rights discourse of welfare queens, inner city gangs, deadbeat dads, and illegal aliens (understood as nonwhites) who threaten to unravel American culture. It misses the foundational role that race disguised as culture continues to play in the constitution of citizenship and belonging.

Like early twentieth-century Americanizers, social scientists, policymakers, and caseworkers today converge on the individual as the target of reform. And, as in the past, efforts to control socially deviant populations rest not on explicitly repressive measures and physical force, but in programs like GAIN which strive to educate their "bodies and souls, as well as the minds of people" by enacting their active participation in their own reformation. Reflecting the prominence of the psychological individual in contemporary American culture, programs like GAIN call on welfare recipients to "confront" their lack of motivation and low self-esteem, linking work to female empowerment and self-actualization. And because work is cast as intrinsically uplifting, welfare-to-work programs are not held publicly accountable for placing participants in stable living wage jobs, nor for providing them with substantive job training and education that will allow them to move up the employment ladder. By getting poor women to link their empowerment to getting off of welfare, regardless of the material effects on their families, welfare reform efficiently reduces the welfare rolls without having to take on the more costly work of addressing the problems in the labor market and the educational system. And by appropriating poor women's desire for self-determination through a slippery discourse of personal responsibility, American society effectively revokes its public responsibility to these women and their children.

The oxymoronic nature of choice and responsibility as it is articulated in these women's accounts is itself instructive. As these women's experiences reveal, their bid for citizenship and full and equal participation in

U.S. society engages them in an ideological shell game, where women's desire for control over their lives too easily slips into self-blame and societal castigation for circumstances beyond their control. In the final analysis, neither welfare nor work provide these Latinas with economic stability or personal empowerment. And so they struggle with the impossible choice between welfare and work inside a society that continues to deny them the right to develop their individual minds for their own talents.

Conclusion

The Emperor's New Welfare: Reassessing the "Success" of Welfare Reform

Fieldnote #39

I was not supposed to interview Zoraida Torres. She didn't fit into my sample, but she contacted me after seeing a flyer for the study and insisted that she had an important story to tell about life on welfare. As I started to tell her that she didn't qualify to participate in the study because she received welfare only for her kids, I saw the look of disappointment in her face. Here I was, another authority figure with a notebook and a list of criteria, reminding her that she wasn't eligible.

After four months in the field, I am still having trouble tracking down the "right kind" of welfare recipient for this study. I am supposed to interview Mexican immigrant women who receive TANF for themselves and their kids. Yet this seems to be the exception in Long Beach, where most immigrant parents are not eligible for welfare or have been denied access, kicked off, scared from applying. I have talked to residents, teachers, community organizations who have all told me that most Mexican families in Long Beach receive welfare for their children only. When I suggest to MDRC that I include these families in my sample, I am told that we are not studying adults in "child-only cases" because they are not required by federal law to go to work. This is a study of "welfare reform," which is, in fact, a study of welfare-to-work, which is thus not a study of the vast majority of immigrants who supplement their low pay from cleaning hotel rooms and sewing in sweatshops with meager welfare benefits for their kids. Today, in both research offices and welfare offices, "welfare" means "work," and the welfare of those poor people who cannot work or who are not mandated by law to work, but work nonetheless, is deemed irrelevant to social policy.

Even more troubling is the fact that many of these people are legal residents, who like Zoraida have lived in the United States for ten or more years. They are legally entitled to welfare under federal law, yet their ben-efits were cut off after 1996. When I report to MDRC that eligible immi-grants in Long Beach are being kicked off of welfare, my concerns are dis-missed. They have checked with their sources inside the welfare depart-ment who say this is not true, which means that the women I have talked to must be either confused or lying. When I suggest that welfare officials might be invested in saying that the system is working, I am accused of being an "advocate." This notion of "advocacy" pits the authority of DPSS against the subjective testimony of welfare recipients and commu-nity groups.

What is the purpose of ethnography here? To provide some nitty-gritty details about "a life in crisis," a few colorful quotations from the welfare poor, that will enrich but not substantially reformulate the conceptual framework that MDRC constructed before the ethnographers even set a foot into the field? How can this be an evaluation of the new rules under welfare reform if we are not to evaluate whether those rules are being fairly applied?

> The social science of poverty is impoverished in its ability to provide structural or even poststructural critique of the current state of affairs. . . . [It] is conducted in ways that largely constrain its ability to be a source of alternative policy approaches. The net result is that existing welfare policy, with all its limitations, is affirmed in general even as it is challenged in the specific.
> —Sanford F. Schram, *Words of Welfare*

Public policies do not merely redress or solve social problems; they pro-duce the justification for their way of defining, evaluating, and managing the problem. As we have argued throughout this book, the 1996 welfare reform legislation rested on a number of faulty premises regarding the construction of welfare as a social problem. First, the PRWORA viewed welfare receipt as a contributing cause, rather than effect, of poverty. Fol-lowing from the belief that welfare produces a set of values and behaviors that are at odds with economic mobility, policymakers and program op-erators assumed that once people traded welfare for a paycheck (no mat-ter how much they were earning or under what conditions), they would progressively lift themselves out of poverty. Paradoxically, this legislation also treated welfare dependency as a social problem that exists apart from poverty. Attempting to legislate family morality and to inculcate in recipients the "value of work," the PRWORA defined welfare recipients as a distinct subpopulation of the poor with a different set of values and behaviors that needed to be corrected—even if these people remained poor. According to this definition, welfare was coterminous with dependency; an individual could not receive public assistance without being dependent, and conversely, getting off of welfare (regardless of the consequences to a person's emotional or physical well-being) was intrinsically an act of independence and personal empowerment. Thus, the principal goal of welfare reform was not to change the economic conditions of poor people's lives, but rather to transform the moral and psychological deficiencies of the poor themselves. And because the new TANF program established dependency as the central problem with poor people, it could be hailed as a successful anti-poverty program simply by getting millions of people off the welfare rolls.

When welfare reform passed in August 1996, it specified that TANF would have to be evaluated and reauthorized by Congress in 2001. However, the legislation made few provisions for the federal government to collect the data necessary for reauthorization. Welfare reform thus set off a scramble among universities, foundations, and nonprofit research institutes to document the implementation of the PRWORA, and, in particular, to examine what was happening to poor families in the aftermath of reform. While social science research and U.S. welfare policy have long been intertwined, this mutually dependent relationship flourished after 1996. Just as research had driven the passage of the PRWORA, the fate of reauthorization would come to rest largely with social science, as congressional leaders and the American public looked to researchers for an authoritative evaluation of the effectiveness of the new law. In post–civil rights America—where the elimination of the safety net was sold as a way to make all Americans more safe and free—"objective" social science was necessary to illustrate that welfare was being dismantled for people's own good. Because most studies of welfare reform were conceived with reauthorization in mind, researchers often took the pragmatic tactic of collecting data on specific policy measures that could be improved, such as childcare, job training, and transportation programs. As a result, most studies of welfare reform have called for limited changes to the TANF program, while affirming in general its goal of "ending dependency."

Since 2001, Congress has not succeeded in reauthorizing TANF but instead has passed a series of extensions. Not surprisingly, the congressional debate over reauthorization has centered on a bipartisan celebration of its success, while Democrats and Republicans have battled over limited changes to the TANF program (the former pushing for expanded childcare, transportation, and education, while the latter lobbying for increased work participation requirements and more money for marriage and faith-based initiatives). At the time of this writing, both the Senate Finance Committee and the House Ways and Means Subcommittee on Human Resources had passed separate reauthorization bills, which are expected to go before a full Congress in fall 2005.[1] These bills make a handful of limited improvements on the existing TANF program: allocating more money for childcare, requiring that more child support collected go directly to families rather than to state and federal agencies, and extending Transitional Medicaid for five years. Nonetheless, they leave intact the major provisions of TANF while increasing work requirements and funneling hundreds of millions of dollars into marriage promotion and responsible fatherhood programs.[2] Both bills require states to develop a "self-sufficiency plan" for every adult TANF recipient, mandating penalties for the entire family if the plan was not followed, and maintain the anti-immigrant provisions of the current TANF program.[3] Fueled by widespread consensus about the success and soundness of welfare reform reauthorization promises to further entrench a work-first model of social welfare, force people into low-wage jobs, and maintain the gap between citizens and immigrants.

This chapter critically examines the social science research that has helped to shape the public consensus over the success of welfare reform. The Mexican immigrant women who appear in this book participated in one influential study of welfare reform: the "Project on Devolution and Urban Change" (UCP). Undertaken by MDRC, a Manhattan-based non-profit research organization and leading voice in the field of welfare policy, the Urban Change Project proposed to track the effects of welfare reform in four urban counties—Los Angeles, Miami-Dade, Philadelphia, and Cleveland-Cuyahoga County—across a period of five years, beginning in 1997. Financed with over $26 million in research grants from private foundations and some government funds, the UCP employed a virtual army of demographers, economists, planners, and ethnographers across the country in an effort to understand the multiple aspects of welfare reform, from local policy and administration to urban neighborhoods and institutions to individual recipients and their families.

A multimethod study, the Urban Change Project was organized into five interrelated but methodologically distinct components: the *Imple-*

mentation Study; the *Individual-Level Impact Study*; the *Neighborhood Indicators Study*; the *Institutional Study*; and finally, the *Ethnographic Study*, which proposed to "illuminate the effects of changes, in depth and over time, how approximately 40 welfare-reliant families in each site (L.A., Miami, Philadelphia, and Cleveland) cope with the new rules and policies."[4] Whereas MDRC research staff undertook the first four components, the ethnographic research was subcontracted to a team of university faculty and graduate students in each of the four cities under study. MDRC provided each ethnographic team with guidelines on selecting the neighborhoods for the study, specifications on who was to be interviewed, and an official protocol of interview questions to be administered to study participants across a three-year period (this protocol was the same for all four cities).[5] Local ethnographers were responsible for recruiting a sample of respondents that fit MDRC specifications; conducting an annual in-depth, tightly structured interview with each respondent; and tracking changes in between the annual interviews through phone conversations and informal visits to recipients' homes. In Los Angeles County, for example, a team of faculty and graduate students based at UCLA's Center for the Study of Urban Poverty conducted the ethnographic research. Each ethnographer was assigned to study one racial group (African American, Chicano, Mexican immigrant, or Cambodian) and responsible for a sample of 10 to 14 welfare recipients within a designated neighborhood. The ethnographic findings collected in all four sites were provided to MDRC in two ways: as coded data using a database system designed by MDRC and in summary reports following templates provided by MDRC. At the same time, ethnographers retained the full rights to the research they had conducted to publish as they saw fit.

Regarded in research and policy circles as one of the most comprehensive studies of welfare reform, the Urban Change Project's findings have received widespread attention from national and local media and have entered into the congressional record through the testimony of MDRC staff and other researchers associated with the project. The data collected for the UCP has also informed an ongoing series of reports and policy briefs issued by MDRC. These reports have highlighted dropping caseloads and increased employment among welfare recipients to advance a largely positive assessment of the TANF program and its work-first orientation (a policy shift that MDRC has endorsed for over a decade). Thus, the Urban Change Project merits closer consideration because its findings have contributed to the public consensus over the "success" of welfare reform and will influence congressional proposals for reauthorization.

Numerous scholars have examined MDRC's research methodology and powerful role in influencing welfare policy in the years leading up to the passage of the PRWORA. This chapter picks up where others have left off, looking at MDRC's research after 1996. In particular, we conduct a detailed analysis of the ethnographic research undertaken in the Urban Change Project. We look at the assumptions that guided the ethnographic study's design and execution, the type of data that was collected, and how this data was interpreted. The decision to include in this book an analysis of the research process itself followed from several years of critical reflection on the ideological and methodological problems of the UCP and social science research more broadly—and its potential effects on the women who had trusted us and other ethnographers to record and represent their voices and experiences.[6] In particular, the ways this study reproduced many of the assumptions of welfare reform policy, and was being used by MDRC and policymakers to affirm—with recommended improvements—the general soundness of welfare reform, convinced us of the urgency of turning the analytical gaze on poverty science itself. This chapter, then, presents an exploration of why the story that we tell about welfare reform in the preceding chapters differs markedly from that being told by MDRC.

The previous chapters have shown that Mexican immigrant families were being illegally kicked off the welfare rolls; that racial and gender inequities structured the job opportunities and social services available to these women; that women had worked long before welfare reform, and worked, and worked, but could not earn enough money to get out of poverty; that these women said that they needed real educational opportunities to get ahead but were constricted to short-term and dead-end vocational training; that they could not afford childcare on their wages and had to work night shifts and odd hours in order to have time with their children. Our ethnographic research lays out fundamental flaws in the construction of the legislation itself, discrimination in its enactment, lack of access to the services promised, and deepening poverty for many families with growing advantages to businesses who have access to a ready supply of low-wage labor. Yet, when these research findings, and those collected in other Urban Change sites, appeared in reports published by

MDRC, they were either squeezed into a work-first framework or thrown aside because they did not fit within the rubric that MDRC had constructed for the Urban Change Project.

In critically analyzing the methodology of the UCP, our intention is not to single it out as an exceptional example of problematic research. Rather, we treat the UCP as a *representative case* of applied poverty research, which provides an important window onto the broader epistemological frameworks and institutional arrangements that produce poverty knowledge and public policy in the contemporary moment. Most critiques of applied poverty research provide a bird's-eye view of the research industry rather than a ground-level analysis of the process by which these mega-studies are designed and data is collected, interpreted, circulated, and validated. Because these critiques lack detailed analysis, and because they rarely come from researchers who participate in these mega-studies, they are too easily dismissed as politically motivated attacks waged by "outsiders" who lack practical experience in the field. Moreover, the assumptions behind these large-scale studies get naturalized—as if this were the only way to conduct a systematic study of the effects of welfare reform.

This chapter, thus, attempts to bridge the gap between the practice and critique of poverty research. The reluctance of poverty researchers to speak publicly about the myriad forces that constrain our work, and to engage in a detailed critique of our assumptions and methods, not only impoverishes the poverty knowledge that we produce, but also puts at risk the people we claim to represent through our work. Often missing in poverty research are the voices of poor people, who continue to be treated as passive objects of research and not as experts on social issues. We know little about the ways that poor people themselves grapple with, contest, and redefine their representation in scientific and popular discourse, particularly as they challenge the very terms of the studies they are participating in. Some of the immigrant women interviewed in Long Beach explicitly criticized the framework of MDRC's study, challenging us to justify why certain immigrants were excluded from the sample. Others implicitly critiqued the faulty assumptions embedded in the study, and in social and political discourse about welfare recipients more broadly, by evading or outright refusing to answer particular questions (especially those regarding welfare cheating and their spending patterns) and by redirecting the oral interview to topics not included in the official protocol (such as the denial of benefits to needy families and racial discrimination in the labor market). Yet, within the confines of mainstream policy research and discourse, these Latinas' words would be held up as evidence, cited as case studies, brought in for color. But these same women would not be treated as sophisticated theorists and policy experts who could contribute to a fundamental rethinking of welfare reform policy.

By stressing the typicality of the UCP, by outlining the ways it could have been done differently, and by situating it within its historical and discursive contexts, we hope to underscore that this chapter not be read as a targeted critique of MDRC, nor of the deeply committed researchers who contributed to the study. As education scholar Michelle Fine reminds us, critiques of state institutions, discourses, and policies too often rest on, and are obscured by, an evaluation of the intentions of individual actors. As she notes:

> That these educators and personnel are well intentioned, caring, and at moments even subversive for students' sake does not undo the damage brought by the structures, policies and practices that they implement. The reproduction of social inequality persists easily, without malintent.[7]

Like the school administrators and teachers that Fine encountered while conducting research on New York City public schools, the researchers working on the UCP, including Alejandra, other members of the L.A. ethnographic research team, and MDRC staff, were well intentioned and strongly committed to rigorous and meaningful social science. Despite good intentions, however, the study failed to disrupt, and in many cases reinforced, the systems of power that constrain the very poor people that it intended to help. In critically analyzing the myriad forces that constrained this research project, we do not question the validity of the data collected under the UCP, but the deeply entrenched paradigms that delimited what researchers could see and hear in the field, how the data could be interpreted, and what would make it to the write-ups. It is only by reflecting critically on the specifics of our research and on the contexts and structures that shape the choices we make as poverty researchers that we can begin to imagine and shape an alternative praxis.

This chapter interweaves three threads of analysis and argumentation: First, it looks at the ways that the poverty knowledge industry constructs the problem of poverty as one of welfare dependency, not political economy, and then carries out such research. As Sanford Schram and others have documented, since the late 1970s, poverty researchers have abandoned a structural analysis of poverty, favoring instead a "rational choice" paradigm, where welfare receipt is conceptualized as a problematic "choice" and set of behaviors that need to be corrected under the tutorial gaze of social science and the welfare state.[8] Within such research, ethnographic data functions to help the public get inside the heads and lives of recipients, and particularly as compelling evidence of individual psychology and behavior. Like most large-scale evaluations of welfare reform, the UCP sought to isolate the effects of new policies, like time limits and work requirements, on the behavior of welfare recipients. By focusing on recipients' responses to the new system of incentives and punishments introduced after 1996, yet failing to account for the structural context of recipient's lives and choices, this study reinforced the prevailing view of poverty as an individual condition that must be treated through behavioral, rather than societal, reform.

Second and relatedly, this chapter critiques the prevailing representation of applied policy research on welfare and poverty as politically neutral and value-free by examining the mutual dependencies that exist between social science and the welfare state—from funding streams, to shared epistemologies and sources of data, to politicized circuits for legitimating and disseminating information. Increasingly dependent on the government for funding and information on welfare populations, the poverty knowledge industry has taken a decidedly technocratic turn over the past three decades, and today plays a key role in assisting the state in the development and evaluation of programmatic strategies to change the behavior of the poor. MDRC's study of welfare reform and its inclusion of ethnography provides an ideal case study of this technocratic trend in poverty research. As we elaborate below, because this study was explicitly designed to collect data that would assist government officials in the successful implementation of the PRWORA, it adopted and legitimated many of the problematic approaches of welfare reform policy itself. Moreover, because MDRC had produced much of the initial research that supported a work-first approach to welfare reform (particularly in California), the institution's reputation for reliable research was inextricably tied to its evaluation of the PRWORA. Empowered to evaluate a policy that MDRC had, in part, helped to shape, the Urban Change study affirmed the general soundness of welfare reform, even while challenging certain specific limitations.

Finally, this chapter questions the very terms set by researchers, policymakers, and the American public for evaluating the success of welfare reform. Reducing welfare rolls and moving clients from "dependency" to work are too narrow and vague a criterion. We cannot have a real evaluation of the success of welfare reform without looking at whether work pays enough or is stable enough to move a family out of poverty, whether jobs are decent or demeaning, whether a family's well-being is compromised because of leaving welfare, whether people are able to enact long-term goals of self-sufficiency, and whether people are given equal access to services and educational opportunities. Getting off of welfare, in many cases, is a positive step but only if it does not compromise health, nutrition, or safety. Thus, drops in the welfare rolls cannot be celebrated as a success without a welfare policy that facilitates self-sufficiency, economic well-being, and educational opportunity.

A View from Inside the Poverty Knowledge Industry

The Urban Change Project was one among a number of "mega-studies" of welfare reform undertaken in the late 1990s. As one of the nation's most established poverty think tanks, the Manhattan-based MDRC was well positioned to take the lead in this research. Created in 1974 to run a large-scale urban employment demonstration project funded jointly by the Department of Labor and the Ford Foundation, MDRC quickly became what historian Alice O'Connor characterizes as a "standard-setter in social policy demonstration and, more generally, for policy-related research."[9] Over the next decade, MDRC created its own niche in the poverty research industry, partnering with county and city governments to design and evaluate experimental job readiness programs (also known as "demonstration programs"). Its "how-to" manuals for welfare administrators circulated widely in congressional hallways, governors' offices, and local welfare and planning departments. The research organization's success in large part was fueled by its focus on the culturally based behaviors of the "hard-core" poor (an umbrella term used by MDRC and others to include criminals, drug addicts, long-term recipients, teenage mothers, and high school dropouts), which conformed to underclass theories popular in Washington, D.C., and sociology departments across the nation and reflected the increasingly conservative mood in national politics.[10]

A number of public policy experts have credited MDRC with producing the large body of data that influenced federal and state welfare reform initiatives in the late 1980s and early 1990s and the 1996 national legislation. In particular, the 1987 publication of former MDRC president Judith Gueron's book *Reforming Welfare with Work*—released the year prior to the passage of the Family Support Act (FSA)—firmly established MDRC as a powerful supporter of work-first approaches to welfare reform. A 1988 *New York Times* editorial on the FSA singled out MDRC for having "created the data base that convinced Republicans and Democrats that welfare recipients are willing and capable of working." One Senate staff member explained, "In all the years I worked on welfare reform, we never had a body of data that showed what worked. Now we had it."[11] William Epstein also highlights the influential role of MDRC's research in the passage of the FSA but argues that this followed from political, not scientific, interests: "[MDRC and others] were following popular tastes for conservative welfare reform rather then the dictates of their own experiments."[12]

Following the passage of the FSA, MDRC undertook another project that would later be described by *New York Times* poverty reporter Jason De Parle as the "most influential study of the end-welfare age."[13] From 1988 to 1993, MDRC ran six demonstration programs in California—one in Riverside County directed that recipients take the first job they could find, while the other five favored training and education before sending recipients into the workforce. The Riverside project was seen to have more successful results than the other five. These results led L.A. County to move completely to a work-first model. As De Parle explains, "Turning the conventional wisdom—train first, then work—on its head . . . [t]he Riverside philosophy quickly became the philosophy nationwide: work first."[14] Numerous researchers, however, have raised serious questions about the methodology and conclusions drawn from MDRC's demonstration research in California. In 2003, the nonpartisan research organization Economic Roundtable released its own analysis of work-first policy in L.A. County. Finding that "most families have not become self-sufficient after participating in the county's welfare-to-work program," the Roundtable critiqued MDRC's interpretation of its own research regarding welfare-to-work programs, the ways that such misinterpretation undermined educational initiatives for recipients (which had been shown to provide significant earnings increases over time), and the consequences of that misinterpretation for recipients in L.A. Country. While treated by policymakers as providing conclusive evidence, MDRC's research was shown to be more questionable than previously understood.[15]

MDRC's growing authority in public policy circles in the 1980s and 1990s signaled a closer alignment between the poverty researchers and the state and, in particular, the use of research to assist the welfare state in running more efficiently. Not just a trend follower, MDRC also pioneered a number of monumental changes in the poverty knowledge industry during this period. The most significant change was spurred by an internal backlash within research networks against the community-action models of the 1960s, and a move to scale back the goals of poverty research. At the forefront of this backlash, MDRC's directors claimed that poverty knowledge during the Great Society era had become too entangled with advocacy groups and political interests, and called for a return to "data-driven" and "politically-neutral" research. Whereas earlier research institutes had been "dedicated to no less than finding the 'causes, consequences, and cures' for poverty, MDRC very consciously claimed the more limited objective of testing out incremental policy changes with modest, precisely delineated goals."[16] Yet, as O'Connor concludes, the new body of poverty knowledge produced by think tanks like MDRC "was not apolitical in actuality, but instead merely devoted itself to what was already politically sanctioned—and to what lent itself to testing with quantitative, analytic techniques."[17]

By the mid-1980s, poverty knowledge was reborn as "big science," dependent on government contracts and guided by a reinvigorated mission to count, classify, and correct the poor. In their respective works, O'Connor and Michael Katz cite a number of factors to explain this seismic shift toward quantitative research and market-based models, including the academic backgrounds of institute directors and researchers, the development of new research technologies (which facilitated the aggregation and manipulation of large data sets), and the expanding role of the federal government in collecting poverty data. Both scholars stress that the "capture of the social science agenda by government" increased dramatically during the Reagan years.[18] As the White House purged liberals from federal research agencies and pressured universities and private foundations to do the same, poverty researchers embraced the Reagan administration's market-driven worldview and abandoned in-depth qualitative analysis in favor of large data sets and controlled experiments. Bombarded with statistics, charts, and econometric formulas, those outside the scientific community had few tools to challenge the methodological weaknesses of poverty research.

The quantitative turn in poverty research was lamented by Nathan Glazer, one of the postwar era's leading voices on issues of poverty and welfare. In a 1986 editorial, Glazer criticized fellow researchers for their overdependence on market-based models and economistic analysis and called for a return to ethnographic studies of poverty. Like many of his liberal contemporaries, however, Glazer did not view ethnography as a means to critique the prevalent pathologicalization of poverty, but instead as a *better tool* for understanding and remediating the defective values and behaviors of the poor. As Glazer argued in this influential article, only in-depth qualitative methods could shed light on what he characterized as the cultural-behavioral nature of poverty in contemporary U.S. society:

> We are entering a period—we are in it now—when, I believe, these kinds of [cultural] differences are going to play a larger and larger role in poverty and poverty research. [. . .] And if the single largest change in the character of American poverty escapes economic analysis and large-scale correlations and regressions in our efforts to understand it, we have a good argument for other kinds of research on poverty.[19]

Glazer's cultural model of poverty came to define ethnographic and journalistic portraits of poverty in the 1990s.[20] While attempting to give a more sympathetic "human face" to poverty by detailing poor people's personal histories and daily lives, ethnographic works like Elijah Anderson's *Streetwise*, Mitchell Duneier's *Slim's Table*, and Alex Kotlowitz's *There Are No Children Here* nevertheless obscured the structural causes of poverty by emphasizing the themes of individual motivation and "adaptive" and "self-defeating" cultural strategies in the urban ghetto. Rather than challenge the market-based paradigms of most quantitative research on poverty, ethnographic research validated this approach.

This brand of poverty research found ardent support in the presidency of Bill Clinton. A firm believer in knowledge as the engine of progress and opportunity, Clinton publicly positioned himself as an advocate of data-driven public policy and included prominent academics like Harvard sociologists David Ellwood and Mary Jo Bane in his inner circle of advisors. Clinton's presidency also reverberated with the behavioral discourse at the heart of welfare research. Nowhere was this more evident than in the

Clintonian spectacle of the nationally televised town-hall meeting, where citizens' questions and comments were preselected and where democratic voice could be reduced to two-minute sound bites. While providing a modicum of controlled exposure to individual concerns, the scripted nature of Clinton's town-hall politics did not lead the White House to formulate new policies to address these concerns. Rather, the therapeutic and confessional nature of the Clinton presidency worked to psychologize the social and economic issues facing the nation through a language of dependency and empowerment, personal responsibility and self-realization.

In several regards, the UCP was a product of the political moment in which it was born (Clinton himself was a public supporter of MDRC's welfare-to-work experiments); yet it also marked a significant departure from MDRC's business as usual. Unlike MDRC's usual reliance on government research contracts, the UCP was primarily funded by private money from a veritable "who's who" list of key players in the world of nongovernmental public policy, including the Ford Foundation, the W. K. Kellogg Foundation, and Pew Charitable Trust. Thus, while MDRC's preestablished relationships with local welfare agencies in each site meant better access to administrative records, the stream of private funding also initially promised to lend more autonomy to the study. Second, whereas MDRC's previous work had focused on small-scale demonstration projects, federal welfare reform expanded MDRC's purview to the national level. No longer limited to evaluations of local policy initiatives under "controlled" conditions, researchers at MDRC now had a national laboratory in which to compare welfare reform outcomes. Lastly, and most significantly, MDRC included an ethnographic component in its Urban Change Project, indicative of this new political moment where the President would "feel your pain" in order to pass the most dramatic rehauling of welfare in the twentieth century. This inclusion of ethnographic research in a multimethod project was not unique to MDRC, but typical of a number of large-scale studies of welfare reform, including William Julius Wilson's Three-City Study based at Johns Hopkins University. Ethnography, in a very limited sense, was now understood as a necessary component of poverty knowledge.

Mainstreaming Ethnography

While there is a growing body of scholarship on the ideological and methodological problems of quantitative research in the poverty knowledge industry, the emergent use of qualitative methods like ethnography has received relatively little critical attention from policy scholars.[21] In the mainstream social sciences, ethnography often takes on an almost statistical quality as individuals are selected and studied for their generalizability, classified as representative "cases," and then mapped along a grid of normative social types and patterns.[22] This fetishization of human measurement is particularly pronounced in the specialized subfield of welfare policy research, where ethnography must be reconciled with scientific empiricism and humanistic concerns are believed to contaminate the integrity of the study.

What is referred to as "ethnography" in the subfield of applied policy research is, in fact, a style of qualitative research that utilizes tightly controlled surveys and very limited participant-observation on the part of the interviewer, along with a rigid, predetermined system for coding interviews in order to create a measurable set of attitudes and behaviors that are analyzed in relation to a set of factors like employment, barriers to work, and family well-being. This is not what most anthropologists and sociologists define as ethnography—a naturalistic method rooted in the researcher's deep embeddedness and regular participation in the daily routines and life of the community under study. As anthropologist and poverty scholar Karen Curtis describes:

> Most ethnographic research is conducted by living in or regularly being present in a selected community, organization, or interaction point, over an extended period, providing opportunities for continual data collection, analysis, and comparison, to refine constructs "and to ensure the match between scientific categories and participant reality."[23]

Recognizing that researchers will unavoidably bring a set of biases to the field, rigorous ethnographic method entails a constant reexamination of the researcher's constructs and the parameters of the research endeavor itself. Ethnography works, as Curtis affirms, when it is honest about those biases and allows for a rich picture of how people negotiate and understand the world around them.

The inclusion of ethnography within a large multivariate study such as the UCP could have been used as a corrective, to "ensure a match between scientific categories and participant reality." Ethnographic findings could have been used to augment and revise what was being found through quantitative methods and to generate questions that could have then been investigated using the administrative and demographic data collected through the other components. But the UCP did not function this way. The ethnographic component was endowed with little scientific power within the project, and instead was used to support the data produced in the other components of the study, not to amend or expand it. In most Urban Change reports published by MDRC, long and complex interviews with ethnographic participants have been chopped up into colorful sound bites and reduced to two-dimensional cases that supported the "hard data" provided by random surveys, statistical databases, and welfare administrators. Indeed, as we illustrate below, the ethnography functioned as *vérité,* as authenticating data to support the paradigms MDRC had from the outset and the basic conclusions drawn from the quantitative methods.

Defining the Problem and the Ethnographic Sample

> Certain forms of knowledge and control require a narrowing of vision. The great advantage of such tunnel vision is that it brings into sharp focus certain limited aspects of an otherwise far more complex and unwieldy reality. —James C. Scott, *Seeing like a State*

MDRC's study of welfare reform sought to evaluate the effectiveness of the TANF program, and specifically to help policymakers and administrators improve the policies and practices that were advancing the goals of welfare reform. We can see this clearly in the mission statement for the Urban Change Project, which explicitly places its research goals in the service of welfare administration:

> By examining welfare reform as it plays out in big-city neighborhoods— where the nation's caseload is increasingly concentrated—the project aims to inform policymakers' and program operators' efforts to fully realize the 1996 law and its reauthorization and to identify and address service gaps.[24]

In order to accomplish this, MDRC created a research project compatible with the welfare state's modes of organization. Mired in what Reed has called the "technicist mystique" (the belief that science can arrive at a better set of knowledge and management techniques to solve social problems), the UCP was designed using the state's definition of the "welfare problem," particularly the view of dependency, rather than poverty, as the primary problem to be tackled by welfare reform, and the emphasis on work as the main solution to dependency.[25] Despite its mission to evaluate the implementation of new welfare rules, the UCP did not conduct an independent assessment of the fairness of implementation, doing no analysis of sanction or eligibility rates and relying primarily on welfare administrators to describe how the program was working.

Just as the PRWORA was not designed to alleviate poverty, the UCP was not conceived as a study of urban poverty. This can be seen through its construction of the sample of study participants.[26] The ethnographic sample did not include poor urban residents who did not receive welfare —whether because they had not applied, or because they had applied and been denied assistance. Nor did ethnographers interview people who had left welfare prior to 1996 (curiously, former recipients were included in other components of the UCP, but not the ethnography).[27] The focus on current recipients limited the types of questions that ethnographers could ask and investigate. Because ethnographers did not interview poor people not receiving welfare and nonpoor residents (both groups in fact comprised the majority of residents in most neighborhoods studied by Urban Change), there was no comparative basis on which to support claims about the welfare poor versus other poor and working-class people in urban communities. Without examining the broader range of work experiences among neighborhood residents, for example, researchers could not ascertain which job-related characteristics are unique to welfare recipients and which are structural problems shared by recipients and nonrecipients. Similarly, without interviewing the nonwelfare poor about their attitudes toward work, the study could not accurately generalize about work values and attitudes among the welfare poor.

Even if we accept the UCP's narrow focus on welfare recipients, the ethnographic component included only the most predictable image of this group: single mothers who receive cash benefits for themselves and their children. While ethnographers in each of the four sites were not prohibited from interviewing male recipients, the interview protocol was written explicitly for single mothers, and men present in the household were not expected to participate in the interviews. Nor did ethnographers interview lesbian or gay parents,[28] and the interview schedule was based on a heteronormative model of sexuality with questions like, "What do you think of men in general?"[29] The sampling criteria for this study thus mirrored the assumptions behind the federal legislation, which posited the welfare recipient as an unmarried mother and did not reflect the diversity of households receiving welfare in the United States.[30] Indeed, among the Mexican immigrant families who participated in the Urban Change ethnography in Long Beach, over half were headed by two parents, and most of the single mothers in this sample relied on assistance from male partners and male family members.[31] Yet, because the official interview protocol excluded Mexican immigrant men from the conversation about welfare reform, the study failed to challenge the prevailing wisdom that blames urban poverty on male absenteeism and broken families. And it failed to learn what could have been useful to the emerging public interest in marriage about the interplay of work, welfare, poverty, and marriage for many American families.

Similarly, when designing the ethnographic sample, MDRC chose not to include households where parents receive welfare benefits only for their children (referred to in public policy circles as a "child-only" case or a "zero-parent family"). Figures show that nationwide the number of "child-only" welfare cases has grown steadily over the past decade—in California, for instance, they comprised one-fourth of the total welfare caseload in 1996, and by 2002, they were nearly 40 percent of the TANF caseload nationwide. This is particularly true for immigrant communities where noncitizen parents are not eligible or reluctant to apply for benefits.[32] MDRC excluded child-only cases from the ethnographic sample for the UCP under the rationale that parents in such households are not required by federal law to participate in welfare-to-work activities and, thus, fall outside the study's principal mission of evaluating TANF as a work participation program.[33] Yet, including child-only cases in this study could have raised important questions about the work-based models at the heart of welfare policy. Because parents in child-only households are typically employed but still need government assistance for their children in order to make ends meet, these households challenge the distinction between the working poor and the welfare poor. A study of welfare reform that looked at child-only cases might lead policymakers to see the inadequacy of work as a prophylactic against poverty and to rethink the necessary role the welfare state plays in mitigating the most severe effects of the labor market.

The ethnographic sample of the UCP suggests that this was a study of the stereotypical welfare underclass: single mothers on welfare who live in big cities. In most descriptions of the project, underclass discourse pervades the descriptions of the people being studied—"large caseloads, which have posed difficult management and implementation problems," "long-term dependent persons who face multiple employment barriers, [and are] more likely to be people of color and immigrants." Although the UCP was promoted as a study of cities grounded in local neighborhoods, the parameters of the study, which treated each welfare recipient as an individual story, made it not in fact a study of poor neighborhoods. A study of unconnected individuals living in the same geographical space and affected by the same bureaucratic changes, the UCP looked at community factors only as a set of demographic criteria—poverty and welfare use rates, unemployment levels, racial makeup of population, percentage of foreign-born residents, etc. Typical of most underclass research, the UCP did not consider neighborhood as a collective and dynamic process, but rather as a static and bounded site in which individuals could be located and their behaviors tracked.[34]

The Urban Change study also involved very limited investigation into the political economy of each of the four cities included in the project. Most UCP literature describes these cities in broad economic terms as "deindustrialized" or "immigrant gateways," but lacks detailed analysis of the specific economic structure, changes in industry, and labor market conditions in each city. This problem was particularly pronounced in L.A. County, where ethnographic samples were drawn from two different cities—Mexican immigrants and Cambodians in Long Beach and Chicanos and African Americans in the city of Los Angeles. Little research was conducted on the unique dynamics of each city to explain how these local particularities shape the experiences of the neighborhoods and individuals being studied.

For each city, Urban Change researchers first determined the "races" to be studied and then selected a neighborhood for each racial population[35] using a statistical formula of high poverty concentration and high welfare use, that closely followed William Julius Wilson's spatialized model of urban poverty.[36] By picking a census tract to represent an entire racial group, the study presumed and reified residential segregation, often at odds with the demographics and daily life of the neighborhood being studied. In Central Long Beach, for example, Asians, Latinos, and blacks live side by side.[37] But the UCP's designation of some Long Beach neighborhoods as Cambodian and others as Mexican (and the explicit directive that different census tracts had to be picked to represent each population) failed to capture the city's diversity. It missed not just the actual demographics of the population, but more important the ways that Central Long Beach residents come to define themselves, each other, and the geographical and social space they share through the kaleidoscopic lens of race.[38]

As is true for most contemporary poverty research, the UCP did not analyze *race* per se but instead included people of color in its survey. Race and ethnicity were not understood as socially constructed categories but, rather, as natural, self-evident demographic variables — "white," "African American," "Asian," "Puerto Rican" (in Philadelphia), "Hispanic" (in Miami), and "Mexican Immigrant" and "Chicano" (in Los Angeles). Because each ethnographer was assigned to study one racial group, s/he decided which potential respondents fit into that racial category. The interview protocol did not ask study participants how they identified themselves racially or conceptualized race. Nor was this a study of the racial barriers imbedded within the welfare system and the job market. The interview protocol did not include questions about respondent's experiences with racial discrimination in the welfare bureaucracy (eligibility review, benefit determination, tracking, etc.) or in the workplace (hiring, job assignment, wages, etc.). Questions like these could have established specific data on discrimination patterns and challenged the view that securing a job or getting on or off welfare is entirely within the individual recipient's control.

The category of "immigrant" similarly functioned in the study as a demographic variable, not as a sociopolitical experience or racial label in need of interrogation.[39] At the start of the study, Alejandra was instructed to compose an ethnographic sample of women who were born in Mexico and receiving welfare for themselves and their children. The rationale for dividing the ethnic Mexican population in L.A. County into two separate research samples—immigrants in Long Beach and Chicanos in Boyle Heights—seemed logically to rest on issues of nativity and citizenship.[40] Upon closer scrutiny, however, the definition of "immigrant" employed by the UCP did not match that of "qualified immigrant" under the 1996 law (where benefit eligibility is determined by criteria like naturalization, date of arrival, military service, and work credit). Because immigrants were selected for the study based on nativity rather than citizenship status, the "Mexican immigrant" sample included naturalized citizens who are legally entitled to the same welfare benefits as U.S.-born Chicanas. MDRC's insistence that undocumented immigrants be excluded from the study (under the rationale that they are not subject to federal work requirements because they receive welfare only for their children) produced a very limited portrait of the impact of welfare reform on Long Beach's Mexican immigrant community. Furthermore, by not interviewing legal immigrants who are eligible for welfare but only approved for their children, the study could not systematically document patterns of anti-immigrant discrimination inside the welfare bureaucracy.[41]

Notably, European immigrants were not included in the ethnographic study, even though Russian refugees and other Eastern European immigrants have relatively significant rates of welfare use. This coloring of the immigrant population in the United States by the UCP is entirely consistent with the current political moment, in which immigration has become a new code word for nonwhiteness. By excluding white immigrants from its sample, the study not only reinforced the slippage between immigration and race, but it also failed to investigate race and racism as factors that are distinct from other "barriers" (like language ability and cultural adaptation) that all immigrants face. Although the UCP interview protocol did not include questions for immigrant welfare recipients about racial discrimination, most of the Mexican women interviewed in Long Beach insisted on talking about the widespread racism and nativism they had encountered in the welfare system and the labor market. As we saw in previous chapters, most of these women asserted that, as Mexicans, regardless of their citizenship status and length of time in the United States, they would always be treated as racial outsiders and second-class members of American society. Thirty-six-year-old Carmen, for example, noted that she is still treated like an immigrant in the welfare office, despite the fact that she has lived in the United States since she was three years old and has been a naturalized citizen since the age of twelve. When asked to describe how the welfare office treats her like an immigrant, Carmen responded, "I mean the racial thing that they're doing, you know, against Hispanics and all that. You know, I don't feel that comfortable because, you know, how they treat a Mexican." Reponses like Carmen Garcia's shed light on the deeply entangled nature of racism and nativism in American public institutions, and how these forces shape the experiences of Latino immigrants under welfare reform. However, as we illustrate below, these women's far-reaching and complex understandings of race and immigration as sociohistorical processes grounded in unequal power relations were marginalized in the Urban Change Project. Rather, race and immigration status were reduced to descriptive adjectives that sorted between different "samples" of women in the study.

Data Collection: How an Inexhaustible
List of Questions Is Not Thorough

Nineteen pages in length with over 400 questions on topics ranging new child immunization rules to their relationships with coworkers to changes in the look of the welfare office to their use of contraception, the Urban Change interview protocol covered a seemingly endless array of topics. It was not only the vast number of questions asked but also their level of detail that made the interview resemble more an extended survey rather than the textured and open-ended exchange that is characteristic of ethnography. The highly scripted nature of the interview protocol[42] and its uniformity across cities provided limited opportunity for organic conversation and little space for ethnographic respondents to define the themes important to them.[43] Nor did women's responses to these questions and to the experience of the interview itself (indeed, many of the women complained that it was invasive and too long) lead to any systematic reevaluation of the research approach. MDRC convened no national meeting after the completion of the first round of interviews to reassess the interview protocol and change the questions based on what ethnographers had heard from women. Instead, ethnographers were instructed to ask the same questions across the three years of the study (in year two, the protocol remained the same, but a supplemental section was added with questions about health). Still, individual researchers did adapt the protocol on an ad hoc basis, particularly probing further in areas like welfare administration, life and work histories, and working conditions. The conversations between ethnographers and respondents often spilled beyond the study protocol. Yet these findings often did not make it to MDRC headquarters in New York because of the narrow system for coding ethnographic data established by MDRC before the research began and the rigid reporting templates provided to ethnographic teams in each site.

With its inclusion of immigrant populations, its five integrated components, and its massive accumulation of data, the UCP gave the impression of depth and completeness. But in fact, it looked only narrowly at the social and economic structures that affect poor people's lives.[44] The multiple constraints on these families (lack of jobs, unaffordable housing, overcrowded schools, and few childcare options) were taken as the baseline for the ethnographic study, and the researcher's job was to document the behavioral responses to these conditions. For example, the study looked only cursorily at recipients' previous educational experiences, the barriers they encountered or continued to encounter in pursuing an education, and their future educational goals. Like a statistical survey, it assigned a level of education to each recipient, which was then used to explain her location in the labor market. In other words, the study treated recipient's educational backgrounds as fixed and finite; the concern for researchers and policymakers was not how to increase these women's educational levels but how to match their educational background with an appropriate job. In sidestepping the centrality and mutability of education in poor women's lives, the study affirmed the underlying logic of current "welfare-to-work" policy, which also treats educational opportunity as peripheral to the task of reform.[45]

Also like the PRWORA, the UCP was organized around the assumption that getting off of welfare was the most desirable outcome for each recipient. The design of the ethnographic component and proscribed set of interview questions framed the issue of public assistance as an individual one. Interview questions like *"Where do you see yourself in five years?"* resonated with the message of welfare reform, communicating to the study participants that the primary concern was their getting off of welfare. Amidst a cluster of questions about respondent's individual barriers to employment—like, *"What would lead you not to take a job?"*— there was only one question—*"What's the job market like these days?"* —that asked welfare recipients about the inadequacies of the labor market. Poor women's analyses of welfare policies and the economy were outside the scope of this study, except when cited as evidence of recipient "attitudes."

If we examine the types of questions included in the interview protocol and MDRC's interpretation of the ethnographic data, we find two overlapping and sometimes conflicting paradigms at work. On the one hand, the interview protocol was based on a rational choice model, which posits individuals as self-maximizing actors whose behavior is primarily determined by economic stimuli.[46] The interview questions were intended to assess how recipients were responding to the new set of incentives and punishments introduced under welfare reform, thereby collecting information that would enable the welfare state to better manage the behavior of its clientele. Some questions—like, *"Are there new procedures for getting clothing vouchers?"*—sought to gauge how successfully welfare agencies were communicating the message of reform and information about new work incentives to clients. Others—like, *"Have your views about abortion changed as a result of the new welfare rules? Do you think you are more likely to get an abortion now?"*—investigated whether the financial disincentives of family cap rules would change a woman's reproductive choices. And another body of questions—like, *"What kinds of things do you consider (the costs and benefits) when making a decision about taking a particular job? Wages? Hours? Benefits?"*—attempted to identify the economic factors that influence women's job decisions in order for administration to better design programs that facilitate these women's entry into the labor market.

At the same time, there was a psychological model of human personality and behavior informing the interview protocol. In contrast to, but often working in tandem with, the economistic model above, many of the questions were directed toward an exploration of women's attitudes and feelings about topics like welfare, work, motherhood, and family life. For example, in the interview section on "Work Incentives and Disincentives," inquiries about women's labor market choices were coupled with questions that sought to catalogue their attitudes toward work more generally—*"How do you think that work will affect your family life? What do you think makes a job a good job?"* Similarly, at the same time that the study attempted to determine whether women were more or less likely to marry in response to the financial incentives introduced under welfare reform, it also sought to construct a portrait of poor women's attitudes toward marriage, with questions like, *"What are your views on marriage? Some people don't get married but live together—how do you feel about that?"*

There are a number of troubling problems with this style of ethnography. Poor women were constructed as psychological subjects capable of having attitudes and feelings, but not of possessing grounded, empirical knowledge about the world. Thus, when welfare recipients were asked about the types of wages and jobs available, these questions were not intended to arrive at an "objective" portrait of the labor market in each city (this would be provided by census data), but instead to understand how these recipients' "opinions" influence their choices about and motivation to work. Even if we accept this psycho-behavioral approach, the survey-like nature of the ethnographic component prevented the UCP from achieving an in-depth understanding of each woman's personal background. Rather, the individual respondent was reconstructed as a compilation of social characteristics identified as meaningful to studying welfare recipients (age, race, number of children, depression, work experience, educational level, domestic violence, etc.), compared to other "individuals" for generalizability, and held up as a representative "case" or "type."

Equally problematic were the types of questions *not* included in the Urban Change interview protocol. In a nineteen-page interview schedule, with over 400 detailed questions regarding jobs, wages, and childcare, there was only one open-ended question that asked women to describe "life on welfare." The official protocol did not ask welfare recipients about the process of getting and staying on welfare, the presumption being that the difficulty was getting off rather than accessing one's entitlements. The interview protocol included questions asking women to describe in detail the new rules and procedures of the TANF system, but not if these rules were actually being followed by caseworkers. There were no explicit questions regarding procedural violations, harassment, or discrimination at their local welfare office. Women were never directly asked whether public assistance had improved their quality of life, nor invited to openly consider a range of public policies, such as an increase in welfare payments or housing subsidies, which might facilitate their family's movement out of poverty.

The ideological framework of the UCP research protocol comes into sharp relief when we compare it to another study of welfare reform conducted in L.A. County during the spring of 2002 (at the same time that MDRC was running the third round of ethnographic interviews of the UCP in Los Angeles). The Los Angeles County Children's Planning Council commissioned the Economic Roundtable to work with a broad array of community organizations to design a study to learn "directly from families who receive public assistance about the kinds of help they need to become economically self-sufficient." The Economic Roundtable study provides one example of a large-scale evaluation of welfare reform that frames welfare receipt as an issue of poverty rather than dependency. The study included 8,536 survey respondents (4,075 current CalWORKs recipients, another 675 that had received CalWORKs within the past two years, and the rest low-income Californians not receiving public assistance) plus 22 focus groups using a semistructured interview format.[47] Open-ended questions including *"How is your relationship with welfare-to-work staff?"* and *"Is the welfare-to-work program difficult to understand or difficult to comply with?"* allowed respondents to talk extensively about how they were being treated in the welfare office. Centered on client's needs, questions like *"What services do you need that the welfare-to-work program does not provide for you?"* and *"In your experience and in the experience of others you know well, what kinds of problems do people face in getting a job that can support their family?"* invited respondents to theorize their own experiences in order to design effective social policy. Notably, the study did not focus on personal barriers to employment but on how the program could better serve poor families, evidencing a significantly different model for assessing welfare administration. The survey was organized around the needs of the respondent, and the onus of responsibility was put on the County, not just on the recipient. This type of survey joins personal responsibility with social responsibility—with questions such as *"What are the most important things that the County should do so you can get a job that will support your family?"* and *"Please identify two problems you have right now that keep you from having a good-paying job."* It not simply focused on getting people off of welfare but on having them find "good-paying" jobs, and allows for a different set of policy initiatives that are focused on the expertise and key priorities of low-income families.[48]

Seeing Like a State/Not Seeing Discrimination

Although designed to assist policymakers and welfare officials to "fully realize the 1996 law and its reauthorization," MDRC's Urban Change Project did not seek to investigate whether the new federal rules were being applied fairly at the local level. At the time that the UCP was initiated, and increasingly through its three-year duration, there were numerous complaints from civil rights and welfare groups across the nation and a mounting roster of successful legal suits against welfare agencies, all of which suggested that welfare reform had produced a sharp increase in disentitlement and discrimination inside the system. Nevertheless, the UCP ethnographic component did not include interview questions inviting women to talk specifically about their relationship with welfare staff, or about problems with procedural violations, maltreatment, or discrimination. Nor did other components of the project systematically collect and review data for potentially disparate patterns of administrative action (such as diversion, sanctioning, and service provision) in the four Urban Change sites. The issue of discrimination was left out of the Urban Change research agenda—despite reports from welfare recipients participating in the study that racial hostility and harassment in the welfare office had risen precipitously after 1996.

Indeed, from the moment that ethnographers in L.A. County stepped into the field, it became apparent that issues of access and rights to welfare were crucial to understanding the impact of welfare reform on poor people's lives. In Long Beach, Alejandra heard numerous accounts from recipients, teachers, and community leaders that Latino immigrants were having tremendous difficulty getting on welfare and were frequently being forced off the rolls. Even though most of these immigrants were still legally eligible for aid, they had been wrongly informed by welfare caseworkers that only U.S. citizens could receive welfare, or that they needed proof of ten quarters of employment to receive cash aid, or that they should "just go back to where they came from." Many of the Mexican women who agreed to participate in the study did so because it provided them with a forum to publicly testify about the systematic disentitlement in the welfare system and how this had worsened since 1996. Although all of the women in the Mexican immigrant sample were still receiving welfare when they joined the study in 1998, the vast majority had recently experienced cuts in their welfare checks, a decrease in their food stamp allotment, or had been cut off of Medi-Cal, and in many cases could not get an explanation from their caseworkers for these changes. However, because this information could not be confirmed by welfare administrators in L.A. County (who, when asked about it by MDRC, denied any wrongdoing), the issue was not further investigated or reported.

Most large-scale evaluations of welfare reform, including the UCP, have not been concerned with whether poor people have been accessing the rights and services they need, but instead whether TANF was moving them off of welfare in an efficient and timely way. This stems from a culture of political realism in the poverty research industry, which accepts the prevailing wisdom that public assistance is not a realistic solution to poverty. As Schram explains:

> Poverty research as a special field of applied social science exists because it was created to serve state managers and existing political-economic

arrangements. From government grants and contracts to a political realism that reinforces the need to impress those in power, the discursive practices of poverty research anticipate the prevailing structures of society writ large.[49]

Typical of most applied policy research, MDRC's Urban Change Project did not study welfare as a political institution with its own bureaucratic practices, institutional needs, and political or economic motivations. Rather, welfare was studied as a problematic "lifestyle" among the poor that could be corrected through better program design and management. Because MDRC operates more like a semiautonomous business consultant than an independent auditor of the welfare state, the types of programs and management strategies it will consider are proscribed by the institutional framework and interests of the state. In turn, MDRC's success as a research institution lies in this semiautonomy, assuring it access to information and funding from state agencies yet with the veneer of sufficient objectivity for its research to be taken seriously by policymakers and other researchers.[50]

The welfare state was a trusted source of data, as MDRC relied upon administrative records, statistical charts, and interviews with federal and local welfare authorities to construct an account of the implementation and effects of welfare reform. Because they did not regard recipients as a trusted source for evaluating welfare bureaucratic practices and because they constructed no other independent way to analyze welfare administration, they could only rely on welfare staff to report on themselves, using quotes from caseworkers and administrators as to how the programs were working. For a research organization dedicated to controls, methodological rigor, and objective analysis, this is a troubling but telling omission. In this regard, MDRC is once again emblematic of problems pervasive throughout the poverty knowledge industry. Because researchers are dependent on welfare offices for information on the welfare population, there is often an accompanying pressure on them not to be too critical of the welfare state for fear of losing access.

Accordingly, Urban Change reports and press releases have reported the number of respondents who have left welfare but do not describe the process by which they got off of welfare. Such reports are concerned with the ways that welfare agencies are communicating information about the new rules and programs but not how they may be miscommunicating information about these rules to deter people from applying for benefits or to push them off of welfare. In its Miami report, MDRC offered its strongest critique of welfare reform implementation, noting "the poor quality of services being delivered" and "the highest sanctioning rate for noncompliance that MDRC has ever observed in a welfare-to-work program" (MDRC's research found more people were sanctioned in Miami-Dade than actually participated in welfare-to-work programs). Yet, they did not investigate for patterns of discriminatory treatment or bureaucratic illegality. Indeed, the report notes this finding as something almost commendable—high sanctioning rates "underscoring the seriousness with which the county enforced work participation rules." Most of the women interviewed in Miami complained, according to the report, about being sanctioned "when they felt unprepared for it or thought they did not deserve it." Many women "did not speak positively about their interactions with welfare staff" and most described those "disrespectful" interactions as reasons for wanting to find a job. Yet these complaints are treated as subjective accounts, not evidence of systematic procedure. In a section entitled "Perceptions and Experiences of Former and Ongoing Welfare Recipients," half of the 119 people interviewed in MDRC's second interview had been sanctioned; yet this alarming figure is downplayed by the report, which notes that this sample picked up "many individuals who were noncompliant." In this report, MDRC seems to be sending a mixed message. On the one hand, the report states that "high sanctioning was to some degree a reflection of administrative problems and inconsistent case management practices" and calls for independent oversight and "if necessary, corrective administrative action." On the other hand, MDRC still persists in characterizing Miami's program as "tough": "Clearly, the new policies and programs did not create a 'user friendly' system that made people want to prolong their stay on cash assistance."[51]

Numerous studies, including a review by the U.S. Commission on Civil Rights, have shown significant racial disparities in the implementation of welfare reform. When asked about this research, MDRC president Gordon Berlin explained the difference with MDRC's study, "We didn't set out to do a study of discrimination. We set out to do a study of welfare reform. We didn't set out to do an audit of welfare reform; we set out to find out what difference [the implementation was having]."[52] Yet Berlin maintained, "If we picked up [evidence of discrimination], we reported it." (In fact, there had been reports of racial disparities in sanctioning and illegalities in service provision from Mexican immigrants in the study.)

Indeed, the fact that MDRC reports do not use the word "discrimination," nor cite evidence of discrimination as welfare reform was being implemented, can be explained by Berlin's contention that a study of discrimination was distinct from a study of the impact of welfare reform. As he explained, "If [discrimination] was the main purpose, we would have designed the study differently." MDRC instead had set out to study "the impacts of welfare reform." Unwilling to grant that researchers studying the impacts of welfare reform might find it incumbent to look at disparate and discriminatory impacts, Berlin alleged that researchers who report discrimination in the welfare system "must have set out to study discrimination in the welfare system." MDRC's approach embodies a post–civil rights model for welfare research, professing a commitment to reporting discrimination when it exists; refusing to see it where it exists; and constructing it as a separate and tertiary research agenda rather than a crucial component to understanding the effects of the PRWORA.

MDRC's professed mission to study welfare agencies in order to improve their performance and efficacy is, in fact, premised on a very limited model of what can be studied, critiqued, and improved. Indeed, while part of their described mission is evaluation of the welfare system, this assessment does not extend to an analysis of who is being sanctioned and why, which would require detailing the "administrative problems" that led to these sanctioning rates. Administrative problems and inconsistency in Miami led to people being sanctioned who were not supposed to be, yet MDRC understates these findings by characterizing it as "poor service delivery." MDRC's dependent relationship with the state (revealed above in Berlin's insistence that MDRC was not doing an "audit of welfare reform"), thus, compromised its ability to produce sound academic analysis of the nature of sanctioning in Miami-Dade County.

MDRC's report on welfare reform in Miami is consistent with most evaluations of PRWORA produced by mainstream think tanks, which look only at dropping caseloads and the experiences of welfare leavers as the standard for judging the efficacy of welfare policy. Largely missing from evaluations of PRWORA is a systematic investigation of the diversionary tactics used by states to prevent eligible people from applying for benefits and of the discriminatory application of eligibility rules and sanctions. The Mexican immigrant women who appear in this book challenged the current focus on welfare leaving by refocusing their interviews on their struggles to get on welfare and to hold on to the benefits that they and their children are entitled to under law. Myrna's account of the welfare system—of erratic and unpredictable fluctuations in her monthly benefits, of racial discrimination from welfare officials, of confusing and contradictory rules and paperwork—was echoed by most of the Mexican immigrant women interviewed in Long Beach. For these women, the idea of "welfare dependency" stood in stark contrast to their actual experiences in the welfare system. How could they become dependent on welfare, these women asked, when they could never count on a steady welfare check from month to month? As they insisted on talking over and over again about how hard it is to get on and stay on welfare, these women redefined the "problem" of welfare, shifting the focus from individual pathology and dependency to issues of civil rights, entitlement, and social justice.

This was framed most strongly in the following passage from Zoraida Torres:

> They don't treat you right, many caseworkers do not treat you right. Because people don't defend themselves, they feel as though they owe [the caseworkers] something. But everyone has a natural right to be treated fairly. . . . I had one social worker who would say that the help that I received was only for my two daughters, and not for the rest of us. She would always say that the food stamps were for them and not for us. She was very racist because why did it matter to her? Even if we weren't citizens, [my daughters] were and they deserved it.

Zoraida's description of the welfare system as racializing, dehumanizing, and discriminatory was one of the most persistent themes in the interviews with Mexican immigrant women for this study. Sometimes these *mexicanas* talked about how specific rules had been violated by caseworkers (yet when asked why they didn't pursue a grievance or appeal, dismissed this as a "waste of time"). In other instances, they grounded their right to welfare in broader philosophical principles of human decency and equality—"they only think about saving money, not about how it's affecting people."

Although welfare procedures suggest a uniform set of standards being applied when determining eligibility and benefit levels, in fact, the standards are often inscrutable—even to caseworkers. Moreover, the subjective nature of the oral interview used to determine eligibility endows the individual caseworker with the power of evaluation and judgment. Despite the welfare state's attempt to systematize and regulate the eligibility procedures, interviews with Latinas in Long Beach suggested that this process plays out in local welfare offices through an incredibly complicated web of individual caseworkers' prejudices, staff shortages, insufficient training, inconsistent practices, and lost paperwork. Yet such bureaucratic confusion—and the idea that the success of welfare reform might lie with such confusion—rested outside MDRC's empiricist approach, which adheres to strict rules of evidence for the specific rule that was violated. Moreover, this approach maintains a notion of the state as interest-free, forgetting that states now had tremendous incentive to remove people from the rolls and little oversight to prevent them from doing it by any means necessary.

The interview instrument designed for the UCP did not aim to capture the systematic violations on the part of the welfare bureaucracy in the aftermath of welfare reform. The ethnographic component did not include a set of explicit questions about discrimination and rights abuses inside the welfare office. Ethnographic reports related to deterrence practices, erratic benefit cuts, and discrimination were treated as marginal to the scientific mission of the study, and administrative records were not examined for racial patterns in benefit administration or sanctioning. However, women like Zoraida, Norma, and Herminia insisted on talking between the gaps and silences of the UCP. Throughout their interviews, these Latina immigrants returned again and again to the subject of rights and entitlement by protesting the ways that they had been insulted, harassed, and cheated at the welfare office. And, in doing so, they challenged the epistemological myopia of the very study that had promised to document their experiences under welfare reform.

Writing Up Welfare Research: How a Positive Story Is Told from Troubling Findings

At the time of this writing, MDRC had released a number of reports and press releases based on findings from the Urban Change Project, including city-specific reports on welfare reform in Philadelphia, Cleveland, and Miami (the report on Los Angeles was released in September 2005 as this book was going to press). Whether read individually or together, these publications tell a largely positive story of welfare reform, highlighted by dropping caseloads and slight increases in employment and earnings among former recipients in the Urban Change sites. While acknowledging some "troubling findings"—including persistent poverty, widespread lack of health care, high rates of job turnover, recidivism among former recipients, and bureaucratic mismanagement—the main story promoted by MDRC is that welfare reform has decidedly not led to the disastrous effects that critics had predicted. As early as April 1999, a report on preliminary findings from the UCP concluded that "the worst fears of PRWORA's critics have not come true at the Urban Change sites. The states in which the study's counties are located have not used their new freedom to shape policy to impose a draconian regime on their poorest citizens."[53] This message of ungrounded fear has been reiterated in each subsequent Urban Change report—most recently in the June 2004 report on Miami, which assails critics that "harsher aspects of welfare reform . . . did not lead to the social disintegration that some . . . feared."[54] Attempting to situate MDRC as a reasonable, nonpartisan voice in a polarized political debate, several Urban Change reports also call for a measured language of evaluation, characterizing the PRWORA as a "qualified success," and warning that the positive effects documented by the UCP may derive from a temporary upswing in the nation's economy and thus that the potentially worst effects of welfare reform have yet to be seen. Despite these qualifications, however, the persistent invocation of an unrealized "doom and gloom" scenario effectively bolsters MDRC's positive spin on welfare reform while casting a long shadow of doubt on ongoing critiques waged by researchers, community groups, and welfare recipients.

In telling a story of welfare reform, MDRC has consistently employed three narrative techniques in its the presentation of Urban Change research findings: (1) foregrounding the positive; (2) underreporting troubling (and, to its government backers, potentially discomfiting) findings; and (3) treating the data collected from the ethnographic sample as less authoritative on matters of welfare administration, labor market analysis, and racial discrimination, but rather as indications of behaviors, attitudes, and perceptions among recipients.

Most Urban Change reports foreground positive research findings, while burying negative or contradictory evidence later in the text in a muted or convoluted narrative. This is evident in the first UCP report published in April 1999, *Big Cities and Welfare Reform*, which culled data from the institutional and ethnographic research in all four Urban Change sites. The report commends welfare agencies in all sites for "making significant strides in communicating a new welfare message, mandating participation in welfare-to-work services, and designing new institutional structures" (followed by the less positive finding that "much work remains to be done"). While reporting that, "to date, the sites have not seen a fraying of their 'social safety nets,' " the authors also note that "the participants in the ethnographic study were in favor of many of the welfare reform provisions but expressed anxiety about their consequences."[55]

To accentuate this last point, several of the chapters open with a quotation from a welfare recipient that affirmed the goals and ideology of reform. The chapter on L.A. County, for example, opens with the following quote from an ethnographic study respondent: "I would prefer to work and stop dealing with them, deal with them on an every blue moon basis. It does not make you happy or proud that you are on it. It is a steppingstone. It pushes you more so to get out there and get [a job] if that is what your mind is calling for. If your mind ain't on it, you ain't going to do it."[56] However, because the chapter does not provide a discussion or analysis of this quotation but instead launches directly into a description of welfare policy in L.A. County, this woman's words are severed from any meaningful context. Readers are not provided with information about this woman's past experiences with the welfare bureaucracy, and thus have no context in which to understand her desire to "stop dealing with them" nor have a sense of the specific conditions (type of job, working conditions, and childcare supports) under which she would prefer work to welfare. Ultimately, then, the above ethnographic quotation functions in the report to authenticate the message behind the PRWORA—even welfare recipients agree that getting off of assistance is in their best interest and that their own attitude determines their success in the labor market. This use of welfare recipients' words to legitimate the goals of welfare reform can be seen again later in this chapter in a section on "Respondents' Attitudes." Although acknowledging that the ethnographic study documented a "mixture of attitudes" among recipients, this section first focuses on the minority of respondents with positive views of welfare reform: "Seven of the 17 women in the ethnographic sample viewed welfare reform as a positive step." Only later does the report reveal that "the majority of the women in the ethnographic study, however, were not optimistic about the impending changes and expressed great concern, even anger."[57]

Other Urban Change reports similarly employ this technique of putting "positive" findings first and then moving on to discuss less positive or more qualified findings. This is enacted literally in chapter 4 of the report,

Welfare Reform in Miami, which begins with a discussion of positive findings under the heading "Good News," followed by a battery of more negative findings under the heading "The Troubling News." In the preface to the Miami report, MDRC writes, "Like the Cleveland and Philadelphia reports that preceded it, the Miami report tells a largely positive story. Welfare rolls are down, employment rates are up, and most people who left welfare for work appear to be doing better financially."[58] Yet, one hundred pages later, readers learn that Miami's welfare reforms "moved people off the rolls slightly faster but increased recidivism by a small amount,"[59] "the number of respondents neither working nor on welfare increased from 16.4 in 1998 to 28.7 in 2001";[60] and most survey respondents who worked "did not receive a wage that lifted their family above the poverty line, nor did their employer provide benefits."[61] Moreover, one of the most significant findings of the Miami study was the importance of education in determining recipients' experiences in the labor market: "[H]aving a high school diploma or GED certificate was the single most important factor in determining whether these women found work and the conditions of the work they found"[62] Yet while this conclusion should call for a radical reassessment of the work-first approach of TANF, it instead led MDRC to a very limited policy recommendation that some basic education instruction be included in occupational training programs.

Thus, while some Urban Change reports include fairly devastating findings, these are always framed in a measured tone that continues to praise the PRWORA for having made some "advances" and calls for "more supports," but not a major rehauling of welfare reform policy. This measured tone in part stems from MDRC's reluctance to be too critical for fear of being associated with advocacy research and also compromising its mutually beneficial relationship with welfare agencies. As MDRC concludes in the preface to the Miami report, "If there is a negative side to the Miami story, it concerns the poor quality of services that were offered to help welfare recipients prepare for work."[63] By the use of "if," by the backgrounding of the negative, these findings are treated as less central and, by extension, not the story that needs to be highlighted about the effects of the 1996 legislation. The Miami report is quite critical in parts of the ways that welfare was administered in Miami-Dade County. But the tone is not uniform, and evidence of "administrative failure" is treated as arising from particular problems in Miami, not as indicative of flaws within PRWORA itself. Still, by referring to some of the more negative findings, MDRC fulfills its claims to balance. It has included disparate findings and not simply engaged in partisan approval. Other scholars looking at the same data or doing similar studies cannot accuse them of ignoring the issue. Critical theorists Michael Apple and Linda Christian-Smith refer to this narrative technique as "dominance through mentioning."[64] By mentioning legacies of racism in the job market, by noting administrative problems within welfare offices, and by alluding to loss of health care for some recipients or lack of safe childcare, research organizations such as MDRC fulfill their responsibility to demonstrate negative findings, without giving those findings the kind of analysis and presentation needed for them to be noticed, further researched, or acted upon. They have presented the "full story"—even if parts of the story are put front and center, while other parts must be hunted for later in the text.

Equally troubling are the ways that the ethnographic data is used in these reports as colorful quotes and anecdotes to support conclusions drawn from other components of the study (particularly the implementation and survey data). In most Urban Change reports, welfare recipients do not appear as complex social subjects with rich experience and expertise in the labor market, welfare policy, and poverty. Rather, these women's life histories and perspectives, as captured in hundreds of hours of long and intricate oral interviews with ethnographers, are reduced to short quotations that presumably illustrate a particular theme; often in these reports, several quotations from different ethnographic respondents appear in a separate text box under a heading ("On time limits"; "On dealing with the welfare office"; "On work") with no additional context or analysis. In other instances, women's responses to preselected interview questions are quantified and sorted into "patterns" or "types." For instance, in a 2001 UCP report on the work experiences of current and former welfare recipients, responses to a health questionnaire were classified as "barriers to employment" alongside other traits such as English fluency, lack of high school diploma, and child under the age of three. Each respondent was assigned a number of barriers out of a total of 13, and this number was correlated to her employment stability.[65] While individualizing each respondent, the ethnographic data was also aggregated into a general schema that could later be used by other researchers and policymakers to predict and manipulate labor market outcomes for different "types" of welfare recipients.[66]

Not only does this technique of typing blur the lines between ethnography and statistics, but it also involves a process of assembling a set of traits to embody each individual and a class of individuals that is both arbitrary and ideological. As Reed writes of underclass research more broadly:

> This process involves a number of discrete, ideological moves that, for instance, reify freeze-frame incidents in individual life trajectories under the static rubric, "behavior." Someone who is unemployed or a drug user at the moment when that piece of her life is collected as a data point may not be a year or two later. . . . Construing [such incidents] as definitive behavior snatches them out of that context of dynamic life processes and the webs of interaction in which they are shaped and take on meaning. Instead, analysts impose meanings on them from the outside by interpreting them through very specific social theoretical prejudices.[67]

We can see this process at work in the above mentioned list of "barriers to employment," which equates such disparate characteristics as depression, domestic violence, GED, health problems, English fluency, and substance abuse, but does not provide an explanation for how these are related. Are dropping out of high school and drug addiction similar barriers to employment? Does a woman with limited English-language skills face the same challenges in the labor market as one who is clinically depressed? Does domestic violence always lead to employment instability or is it equally possible that abuse at home would make someone more likely to stay in an abusive job? In compiling this list, the authors of the report did not need to distinguish structural conditions like unemployment and education from problems like substance abuse and depression nor provide empirical evidence of their impact on an individual's employment experiences. These disparate traits could be matter-of-factly grouped together because they resonate with the widely held assumption in both social science and popular discourse that poverty is caused by the personal deficiencies of the poor.

In another example, an Urban Change report on the working poor framed its research findings around a table listing a representative sample of respondents, their demographic characteristics, employment histories, and "other background."[68] The "other background" column included a grab bag of personal details on each woman: About Kathryn, all we learn is that she "passed away from cancer on March 30, 2001." The only detail provided about Myrna's background is that she "had legalized her immigration status in 1996 but was having difficulties obtaining benefits to which she was entitled."[69] Sarah "had been on welfare for a total of 6 years; and felt that work both improved self-esteem and contributed to depression," while Tina had "dropped out of high school because of difficulty concentrating (older brother was sexually abusing her); second husband was also abusive." Never does the report provide an explanation for how such details about the "other background" of these women are comparable or relevant. Did Tina decide that this history of being sexually abused was central to her current experiences or did the writer of the report?[70] Should we assume that Kathryn and Sarah were never sexually abused because this is not mentioned in the "other background" column? Without being contextualized within the full trajectory of women's lives and their own self-understandings, these intensely personal details— whether dying from cancer or being sexually abused or being on welfare for six years or legalizing one's immigration status—tell us little about the women who participated in the UCP. Rather, much like the list of employment barriers described above, this report aggregated a random and ideologically predetermined set of characteristics into a composite portrait of an underclass of welfare recipients, who are marked through a set of behaviors that illustrate some of the "ongoing challenges" of welfare reform.

Finally, the treatment of the ethnographic data in UCP reports reflects the disparate weight given to welfare recipients than welfare officials. Whereas welfare recipients were scrutinized for their attitudes and behavior, a similar measure of scrutiny was not employed for data collected from welfare staff and administrators. Welfare officials appear in UCP reports as possessors of facts, not attitudes, and as unmediated sources of information about program implementation and procedures.[71] Indeed, Myrna's tremendous difficulties in accessing her benefits is characterized as "personal background" rather than evidence of how the current welfare system is working or not working.

In September 2005, MDRC released its final report from the Urban Change Project, *Welfare Reform in Los Angeles: Implementation, Effects, and Experiences of Poor Families and Neighborhoods*. While the ethnographic component was backgrounded in most Urban Change publications, this is most pronounced in the L.A.-specific report, which cites the ethnographic data sparingly and only as decontextualized quotations and case examples that bolster conclusions drawn from the survey and administrative data. One of the central ways that the report engages the experiences of poor women is to frame them as confused. Ethnographic accounts of the unjust and, at times, unlawful treatment that recipients received from the welfare office turn up as "complicated stories" that show women's "confusion" and "erroneous" beliefs. On page 65, the report asserts, "Myrna, an immigrant from Mexico, told ethnographers a complicated story about her attempts to get Medi-Cal coverage after her cash benefits ceased. At various points in the story, Myrna reported that she had been denied coverage, that she needed to apply for coverage, and that she had always been covered but "with [another] district." By saying that "Myrna told ethnographers a complicated story," Myrna's statements are implicitly transformed into a tall tale spun by a bewildered immigrant. The seriousness of her situation, the persistent misinformation she received, and the denial of her legal entitlements are side-stepped; the use of confusion as an administrative practice to reduce the welfare rolls is not considered. Myrna is not the only confused recipient who is made responsible for her disentitlement: "Several immigrant Latinas in the ethnographic study also reported that they were not receiving transitional benefits and were unsure whether their problems were related to immigration status. Some believed (erroneously) that the county no longer could provide benefits to immigrant families." Yet Latinas had reported that the welfare office was one of the main sources of misinformation about immigrant entitlements—a significant and troubling finding that is obscured by this statement and never addressed in the report. A more rigorous evaluation of welfare reform in Los Angeles might have investigated why women were being given this misinformation and why certain groups were more regularly denied benefits, rather than remind the reader that these beliefs are "erroneous."

Other discrepancies uncovered by the Urban Change–Los Angeles study are similarly glossed over. The report persistently characterizes CalWORKs policy as providing "generous supports" like protections for children, earned income disregards, and extensive post-employment services, yet MDRC's own research also uncovered that these supports are not available to the vast majority of recipients in L.A. County. Buried deep in the report are alarming figures: less than 2 percent of recipients in the county had received special services for substance abuse, mental health, or domestic violence problems (yet the majority of women interviewed reported domestic violence); less than a quarter of all caseworkers were familiar with the state's earned income disregard policy; and the vast majority of women interviewed for the study reported that they were treated disrespectfully by staff, that Job Club had not helped them to find employment, and that they were pushed by GAIN to take a low-paying job. While these findings point to systematic administrative failure in L.A. County, and a startling disconnect between CalWORKs policy in theory and implementation in practice, MDRC only advances a limited recommendation of more training for welfare staff and draws the following conclusion on page 69: "the overall picture that emerges of clients' experiences with CalWORKs shows that the enthusiasm of DPSS staff did not translate into clarity and optimism on the part of recipients." Throughout this report, as in other Urban Change publications, the onus of responsibility is placed on recipients who lack "optimism," are "confused" about the rules, and fail to avail themselves of services—despite ample evidence from the ethnography that women often did ask for services but were turned down and that much of the confusion documented by the study originates in the welfare office. And whereas most recipients in Los Angeles said that they needed more education to achieve self-sufficiency and many had explicitly asked their caseworkers to go to school, MDRC seems puzzled that "very few clients do so, perhaps because staff do not encourage it." Despite the fact that MDRC's data showed that education had a significant impact on improved employment outcomes over time, the report does not call for a radical reform of L.A. County's work-first approach that would allow education to count as a work activity and provide more supports for a broad base of recipients to go to school.

Indeed, one would be hard-pressed in the ethnographic sample to find a welfare recipient who would characterize the county's welfare policy as adequate and fair—let alone "generous" and "lenient." Yet MDRC's use of this language is consistent with the organization's approach to welfare research, which fundamentally embraces the worldview of policymakers and welfare administrators while marginalizing the perspectives of poor people. By adopting the vision of welfare policymakers, MDRC can claim the "steady progress" of welfare reform in Los Angeles but simultaneously note that most welfare leavers are in unstable jobs with no health insurance and remain poor or nearly poor.

Conclusion

On March 12, 2002, then MDRC Senior Vice President Gordon Berlin testified to Congress about the reauthorization of the TANF program. Basing his testimony on what he characterized as "unusually reliable" research on the impact of the PRWORA, Berlin credited the 1996 reforms in part with "declines in welfare dependency and the rise in employment [that] exceeded all expectations." While Berlin worried about approaching time limits and cautioned lawmakers against increasing work participation levels, his comments to Congress largely highlighted the success of welfare reform: "Most important of all, we should not let the remarkable accomplishments of the last five years get lost in the details or the politics of reauthorization. It isn't broken; it could be improved; the challenge is to adapt TANF to the changing environment while building on its success."[72] Commanding a national platform to highlight its findings on the effects of welfare reform, MDRC affirmed the "remarkable" accomplishments of this legislation.

Hailing welfare reform as a success rests on the conviction that definitive assessments of the effects of the legislation are available. Despite Berlin's confidence in the "unusually reliable" data collected by MDRC and other policy think tanks, there are still many questions unanswered about welfare reform: What has happened to people who disappeared from the rolls but are not working? What will happen to poor families and communities when time limits hit? How has the low-wage labor market been affected by the shift to temporary welfare (i.e., impact on wages, benefits, job stability)? What are the long-term effects to families who have substandard childcare and no health care? Have family separations and foster care referrals risen under TANF? As we have argued throughout this chapter, these gaps in our knowledge do not merely reflect the scope of the task of evaluation but, rather, are the product of strategic silences in the poverty knowledge industry. The solution, we argue, is not simply more of the same style of research. Rather, scholars, foundations, think-tanks, community groups, and poor people must work together to develop a new research agenda for evaluating welfare reform. A rigorous evaluation of welfare reform would take seriously the role of political economy in structuring economic inequality; unravel fixed categories of analysis (examining European as well as Latino immigrant welfare recipients, poor fathers as well as poor mothers); undertake a substantive analysis of welfare administration, including patterns of access, services, and sanctioning; and promote sustained investigation that is founded on the experiences and expertise of poor people themselves. Such research must begin by interrogating the fundamental tenets of the welfare reform legislation rather than approach it as a done deal with only limited modifications possible.

This book also argues that what we do know about welfare reform is deeply troubling. In these pages, we have taken a closer look at the "remarkable" success stories of welfare reform—of what the drop in rolls and the rise in employment look like on the ground. Two years after the implementation of welfare reform in L.A. County, two-thirds of the Mexican immigrant women interviewed for this study had left the welfare system. Yet, this was not because they had traded their government checks for "self-sufficiency." These women had been directly forced off the rolls through sanctions and intimidation; or they had voluntarily disenrolled from TANF because they were tired of the heightened surveillance and disrespect from the welfare office. Those Latinas who had found employment were working temporary and part-time jobs in the service and light-manufacturing sectors, for earnings that hovered around the state minimum wage of $6.75 per hour, no medical benefits, and scarce opportunities for job advancement. In order to make ends meet, some of these working mothers continued to supplement their low wages with welfare benefits as little as $100 per month. Yet while these wage supplements were essential to these families' survival, the ongoing receipt of benefits pushed them closer to their five-year lifetime limit. Many were caught in a no-win situation; they needed welfare now to stave off hunger and eviction, but time limits meant that they would have nothing to turn to in future emergencies. In most cases, these families' food stamp and Medi-Cal coverage had been cancelled when they left the TANF rolls, and most did not reapply even though they were still eligible. More than half of these families were two-parent families—yet marriage was no antidote to poverty. *Most important, not one welfare-to-worker in this study had found a job that lifted her family above the poverty line or even an employment path that promised to in the future.*

The findings from this study of Mexican immigrants were echoed by Urban Change researchers looking at African Americans, Mexican Americans, and Cambodians across L.A. County. Most of the welfare recipients interviewed in L.A. County were deeply disappointed with the GAIN program, having found little help in locating work, assistance in pursuing their educational goals, or access to childcare subsidies. Many had found welfare administrators to be disrespectful in how they treated them and at times dismissive of their attempts to secure education and training. While a number were working, very few had found a job through GAIN. Women who were working were largely employed in temporary positions that often ended, and most were anxious about their childcare arrangements. Across L.A. County, women talked about the lack of job opportunities, the barriers to sustainable employment, and the importance of their job as mothers that they felt needed to be factored much more substantively into the shape of welfare policy. Not one family in the L.A. County ethnographic study had permanently left poverty, and many had been thrust deeper into financial and personal insecurity.

In sum, what we do know about how families are faring in the aftermath of 1996 provides significant evidence about the failure of the legislation. Nevertheless, through congressional debate and on the pages of our nation's newspapers and best-selling books, welfare reform is affirmed as anti-poverty policy, without actually having to address poverty or account for families falling deeper into poverty. It is praised as empowering people through work when actual wages and working conditions are degrading and erratic. It is celebrated as profamily when many families have been thrust further into poverty and report increasing food shortages and insecure childcare. It is touted as egalitarian opportunity despite the fact that it has been discriminately enacted and has had unequal effects.

With access to a different array of services, whites have left the welfare rolls in much larger numbers, and today people of color constitute the majority of welfare recipients. As the U.S. Commission on Civil Rights reports, "numerous studies have found that white recipients are more likely to be encouraged to pursue an education, are less likely to be sanctioned, and are more likely to receive child care subsidies."[73] Such racially disparate practices make welfare reform a clear example of the success of the post–civil rights political agenda. Public officials used a racially coded language to portray welfare as morally bankrupt and sold welfare reform as a way to extend American opportunity to people on the margins. Yet the "hand up" promised by PRWORA was never substantive or equally extended to people of color.

Lurking beneath the public celebration is an unacknowledged reality: Americans benefit from the elimination of the safety net by paying cheaper prices for goods and services. A ready supply of vulnerable workers shreds the labor protections at the heart of the New Deal. By providing a floor that employers would have to surpass, by providing a choice so that Americans would not be forced to take any job at any wage, by providing a standard of living that no one could fall below, the New Deal instantiated a social citizenship under the rationale that all Americans would be more secure. The PRWORA unraveled that commitment to social citizenship. And in the process it created a national form of dependency: that any service can be procured affordably, that consumers of all classes need not spend prohibitive amounts for the latest fashion or electronic gadget. Work is such a positive form of self-improvement that the nation need not concern itself with the technicalities of wages, conditions, and benefits. (Indeed, only one question in the 2004 presidential campaign debates even touched on the issue of the minimum wage.) Welfare now functions as a temporary government subsidy to businesses and consumers, in the form of unemployment insurance for temporary work and wage supplements for low-paid labor. Taking a cue from American agribusiness, which has long relied on the availability of public assistance to supplement seasonal work, today multinationals like Wal-Mart encourage their employees to apply for welfare and Medicaid to offset their low wages, irregular hours, and lack of benefits.

The celebration of welfare reform—and the construction of welfare use as dependency—has closed off discussion of public assistance as fundamental to American citizenship. As a nation, we hold fast to the belief that hard work produces opportunity and that degradation is not the price of survival in a democratic nation. Yet, the structure of the U.S. labor market and the elimination of cash assistance chips away at this promise. Americans—including immigrants—must depend on welfare, at times, to survive economically, to raise healthy children, and to prevent a variety of deprivations (homelessness, abusive relationships, oppressive or unsafe work situations, deteriorating health). Yet, to assert this need is now a renunciation of one's citizenship. As conservative attacks on immigrant entitlement have mounted, regrettably the progressive response has largely been to assert that immigrants work hard and do not rely on welfare. And indeed, most immigrants before and particularly after 1996 do not receive welfare, even though need has increased and many are eligible. Since 1996, even fewer eligible immigrants apply for and receive welfare and food stamps, despite studies showing that immigrants are reporting significant food insecurity and deep poverty. Yet as we have shown here, welfare plays a crucial role in the life of those immigrants who do access it—often the difference of adequate food, school supplies and clothing, bus fare, phone cards, and toiletries.[74] And thus, we cannot afford to treat immigrant welfare use as some shameful secret rather than the measure of justice in a democratic nation.

Welfare reform held up a promise of freedom through new opportunity but actually put forth a limited notion of freedom as the choice between being dependent or not being dependent. It pledged a hand up but proved to be a sleight of hand, offering poor people the spectacle of job assistance, education, and childcare subsidies rather than the actual goods. It told immigrant women to imagine the road to self-sufficiency but then made a mockery of those visions by refusing them access to higher education, job training, and English classes. And it degraded American citizenship, trading the federal protection against deprivation for an empty gesture of personal empowerment through work.

Notes

1. Robert Fogelson was one of the earliest scholars to write about this relationship between architectural design and ideologies of urbanism in Los Angeles. See chapter 7 of his now classic 1967 work, *The Fragmented Metropolis* (Berkeley, 1967). For a lucid social history of architecture in Los Angeles, also see Merry Ovnick, *Los Angeles: End of the Rainbow* (Los Angeles, 1994).

2. While Alejandra Marchevsky conducted the ethnographic research on Mexican immigrant welfare recipients that appears in this book, the analysis and writing was a collaborative process. The singular voice ("I") appears in Alejandra's fieldnotes.

3. Personal Responsibility and Work Opportunity Reconciliation Act of 1996, PL 104-193 (HR 3734), in *Congressional Record,* July 31, 1996.

4. Sharon Hays, *Flat Broke with Children: Women in the Age of Welfare Reform* (London, 2003), 8.

5. Institute for Women's Policy Research, *Combining Work and Welfare: An Alternative Anti-Poverty Strategy* (Washington, D.C.: Institute for Women's Policy Research, January 1995). This study found that one out of four welfare recipients combine work and welfare. Even among those labeled "more welfare reliant" (those who worked at a paid job for less than 600 hours in a two-year period), the study found that 7.4 percent were working limited hours and receiving welfare, and another 23.4 percent were actively looking for work. Notably, the authors of the study concluded that this tactic of using AFDC as a wage supplement was the only feasible long-term route out of poverty for single-mothers in the low-wage labor market.

6. Prior to the passage of the PWRORA, there was a large body of research disputing the myth of the welfare queen. See the article in *MS* magazine, May/June 1995 issue, entitled "Welfare: Fact and Fiction," for a succinct summary of these findings.

7. Hays, 11.

8. Children's Defense Fund (http://www.childrensdefense.org/pressreleases/040322.aspx).

9. The Census Bureau, by its own admission, undercounts undocumented im-

migrants, and thus these poverty figures do not adequately reflect all persons living in the United States.

10. Pamela Loprest, *Families Who Left Welfare: Who Are They and How Are They Doing?* (Washington, D.C.: Urban Institute, 1999); Robert A. Moffit, *From Welfare To Work: What the Evidence Shows. Welfare Reform and Beyond: Policy Brief #13* (Washington, D.C.: Brookings Institute, 2002).

11. Loprest, 5.

12. Ibid.

13. Melissa Healy, "More Ex-Welfare Recipients Are Working But Still Poor," *Los Angeles Times,* May 29, 1999, A2. A National Governor's Association also found that only half of former recipients found any work and that work paid $5.50 to $7.00, not enough to lift a family out of poverty. Lisa Dodson, *Don't Call Us Out of Name: The Untold Lives of Women and Girls in America* (Boston, 1999), 223.

14. Gwendolyn Mink, *Whose Welfare?* (Ithaca, 1999), 3.

15. Randy Capps et al., *How Are Immigrants Faring after Welfare Reform? Preliminary Findings from L.A. and N.Y.C.* (Washington, D.C.: Urban Institute, March 2002).

16. M. Greenberg et al., *Welfare Reauthorization: An Early Guide to Issues* (Washington, D.C.: Center for Law and Social Policy, July 2000). This surpassed earlier predictions that restrictions on immigrant eligibility for TANF, food stamps, old-age pensions (SSI), Medicaid, and public housing would account for 44 percent, or $23 billion, of the net savings of welfare reform.

17. Randy Capps et al. See also Michael Fix and Jeffrey S. Passel, *Trends in Noncitizens' and Citizens' Use of Public Benefits Following Welfare Reform: 1994–1997* (Washington, D.C.: Urban Institute, 1999).

18. A review of Illinois administrative records from this period shows disproportionate cancellations (by a factor of two) of welfare benefits to immigrants. Although the foreign-born comprised only 2 percent of the state's TANF caseload, they were 4 percent of all cancelled cases between July 1997 and April 1999. Rob Paral, "Disparate Welfare Needs and Impacts of Welfare Reform among Illinois Immigrants," in *Immigrants, Welfare Reform, and the Poverty of Policy,* edited by Philip Kretsedemas and Ana Aparicio (Westport, CT, 2004), 98–100.

19. This sharp decline in food stamp receipt among immigrants from over 140,000 to fewer than 60,000 took place during a five-month period, from May to September 1997, when the Texas Department of Social Services undertook a review of food stamp eligibility among legal permanent residents. Despite partial restoration of immigrant food stamps by Congress in 1998, the number of immigrants receiving food stamps in Texas never exceeded 60,000 by June 1999. Randy Capps, Jacqueline Hagan, and Nestor Rodriguez, "Border Residents Manage U.S. Immigration and Welfare Reforms," in *Immigrants, Welfare Reform, and the Poverty of Policy,* 240.

20. Jason DeParle, *American Dream: Three Women, Ten Kids, and a Nation's Drive to End Welfare* (New York, 2004), 326.

21. Sanford Schram and Joe Soss, "Success Stories: Welfare Reform, Policy Discourse, and the Politics of Research," in *Lost Ground: Welfare Reform, Poverty, and Beyond,* edited by Randy Abelda and Ann Withorn (Cambridge, MA, 2002), 65.

22. The National Organization for Women reports that "only 64% of parents who had left welfare [in 1999] were employed, with a median hourly wage of $7.15. Only 33% or fewer welfare leavers had employer-sponsored health insurance. About 20% of former recipients had simply 'disappeared'—not working, not having a working spouse, and not receiving government benefits. In 1999, 41% of former TANF recipients lived in poverty. [. . .] For those still receiving benefits, the story is worse. By January 2000, the TANF benefit for a typical family of three had fallen to less than half the $1179 monthly poverty guideline in all but six states, and the $421 median state benefit was but 36% of the guideline. The combined TANF and Food Stamp benefit was less than two-thirds of poverty in all but seven states, and the $669 median combined benefit was only 57% of the guideline. Over three quarters of welfare families experienced serious hardship and over a third experienced critical hardship, defined as being evicted, having utilities disconnected, doubling up in others' housing due to lack of funds, or not having enough food to eat" (http://www.nowldef.org/html/issues/wel/welfareworking.shtml).

23. Michael Katz, *The Price of Citizenship: Redefining the American Welfare State* (New York, 2001), 31.

24. By widening the eligibility gap between citizens and noncitizens, PRWORA laid the legal and ideological groundwork for the broader assault on immigrant rights that we have witnessed in the current Bush administration's war on terrorism. As legal scholar David Cole observes, the USA PATRIOT Act, signed by Congress in September 2001, rests on an unconstitutional double standard of rights extended to U.S. citizens versus those denied foreigners. He writes, "Under our Constitution, the rights at stake—political and religious freedom, due process, and equal protection of the laws—are not limited to citizens, but apply to all "persons" subject to our laws" (11). Furthermore, we can see undercurrents of the PATRIOT Act's subordination of individual privacy to national "interest" in the massive welfare fraud surveillance systems which were instituted in the 1970s and culminated in the information-sharing provisions of the PRWORA. Indeed, welfare recipients were the "test case" for the dismantling of American civil liberties in the post-9/11 climate. David Cole, *Enemy Aliens: Double Standards and Constitutional Freedoms in the War on Terrorism* (New York, 2003).

25. Dorothy Roberts, "Who May Give Birth to Citizens? Reproduction, Eugenics, and Immigration," in *Immigrants Out! The New Nativism and the Anti-*

Immigrant Impulse in the United States, edited by Juan F. Perea (New York, 1997), 205.

26. Cited in Syd Lindsley, "The Gendered Assault on Immigrants," in *Policing the National Body: Race, Gender, and Criminalization,* edited by Jael Silliman and Anannya Bhattacharjee (Cambridge, MA, 2002), 189.

27. Quoted in Leo R. Chavez, *Covering Immigration: Popular Images and the Politics of the Nation* (Berkeley, 2002), 163.

28. For a critique of this argument, see Maria Patricia Fernández Kelly and Saskia Sassen, "Recasting Women in the Global Economy: Internationalization and Changing Gender Definitions," in *Women in the Latin American Development Process,* edited by C. Bose and E. Acosta-Belén (Philadelphia, 1995), 99–124. In their study of Hispanic immigrant women in the garment and electronics industries, the authors conclude that "economic internationalization has not abolished older patriarchal definitions but transformed them instead to meet the requirements of global competition" (113). For a critique of "global feminism" see Inderpal Grewal and Caren Kaplan, eds., *Scattered Hegemonies: Postmodernity and Transnational Feminist Practices* (Minneapolis, 1994).

29. In 2000, we published "Welfare Reform, Globalization, and the Racialization of Entitlement," *American Studies* (Summer/Fall 2000).

30. Long Beach was selected as one site for the ethnographic study because it had the highest rates of poverty and welfare use among Mexican immigrants in L.A. County and because welfare was administered on a county basis, which placed Long Beach within the L.A. County Department of Public and Social Service's jurisdiction.

31. This focus on work in the literature on immigration reflects a broader shift in the ways that academics and activists are tackling poverty in the contemporary period. From the revitalization of the labor movement in the 1990s, to academic studies of immigrant nannies in Los Angeles and displaced industrial workers in Detroit, calls for a living wage have highlighted the ways that work does not pay in the global economy, while inadvertently constructing work as separate from welfare and positing the rights and protections of workers as possible without the existence of a welfare state.

32. A selected list of scholarship on immigrant workers and economic restructuring in the United States includes: Louise Lamphere, ed., *Newcomers in the Workplace: Immigrants and the Restructuring of the U.S. Economy* (Philadelphia, 1994); Marta Lopez-Garza and David R. Diaz, *Asian and Latino Immigrants in a Restructuring Economy: The Metamorphosis of Southern California* (Stanford, 2001); Ruth Milkman, *Organizing Immigrants: The Challenge for Unions in Contemporary California* (Ithaca, 2000); David Naguib Pellow and Lisa Sun-Hee Park, *The Silicon Valley of Dreams: Environmental Injustice, Immigrant Workers and the High-Tech Global Economy* (New York, 2003); Jennifer Parker Talwar, *Fast Food, Fast Trade: Immigrants, Big Business, and the*

American Dream (New York, 2002); Roger Waldinger and Michael I. Lichter, *How the Other Half Works: Immigration and the Social Organization of Labor* (Berkeley, 2003).

33. Two pioneering ethnographic works in this field are: Maria Patricia Fernandez-Kelley, *For We Are Sold, I and My People: Women and Industry in Mexico's Frontier* (Albany, 1983); and Aihwa Ong, *Spirits of Resistance and Capitalist Discipline: Factory Women in Malaysia* (Albany, 1987). Two useful reviews of the migration literature include Sylvia Pedraza, "Women and Migration: The Social Consequences of Gender," *Annual Review of Sociology* 17 (1991): 303–325; and Pierrette Hondagneu-Sotelo, "Gender and Contemporary U.S. Immigration," *American Behavioral Scientist* 2, 4 (January 1999): 567–577.

34. Sociologist Grace Chang's 1999 book, *Disposable Domestic: Immigrant Women Workers in the Global Economy* (Boston, 2000) is one of the few works to explore directly the subject of welfare among immigrant women in the United States. Although Chang persuasively demonstrates how the social construction of Latina and Asian immigrant women as "public burdens" facilitates their exploitation in the labor market, she nevertheless problematically posits work and welfare as distinct arenas. Her ethnographic data is divided into two groups of women of color, native-born welfare recipients and immigrant service workers, whom she represents as having conflicting interests. None of the immigrant nannies and health care workers who appear in her book are welfare recipients, and most are distrustful of people on welfare, whom they perceive as lazy and opportunistic. While Chang's final chapter centers on the impact of welfare reform on immigrant communities, she again casts immigrant women as the workers of the story who are being displaced from their jobs by native-born (though also exploited) African-American, Chicana, and Puerto Rican women in workfare programs.

35. Notable exceptions are the research on immigrants and welfare use conducted by Wendy Zimmermann and Michael Fix at the Urban Institute and the collection of essays on immigrants and welfare reform edited by Kretsedemas and Aparicio.

36. Capps et al., 4.

37. Pierrette Hondagneu-Sotelo, *Gendered Transitions: Mexican Experiences of Immigration* (Berkeley, 1994).

38. There is a large body of writing on citizenship and immigration in the wake of globalization: William Rogers Brubaker, *Nationalisms Reframed: Nationhood and the National Question in the New Europe* (London, 1996); William Rogers Brubaker, ed., *Immigration and the Politics of Citizenship in Europe and North America* (Lanham, MD, 1989); Stephen Castles and Alastair Davidson, eds., *Citizenship and Migration: Globalization and the Politics of Belonging* (New York, 2000); Georgie Anne Geyer, *Americans No More: The Death of Citizenship* (New York, 1996); David Jacobsen, *Rights Across Borders: Immigration*

and the Decline of Citizenship (Baltimore, 1999); Claudia Sadowski, ed., *Globalization on the Line: Culture, Capital, and Citizenship* (New York, 2002); Saskia Sassen, *Guests and Aliens* (New York, 2000); Peter H. Schuck, *Citizens, Strangers, and In-Betweens: Essays on Immigration and Citizenship* (Boulder, CO, 2000).

39. Duke Hefland, "Citizenship Surge Sweeps Southland," *Los Angeles Times,* June 20, 1996, A3.

40. Joseph Nevins, *Operation Gatekeeper: The Rise of the "Illegal Alien" and the Remaking of the U.S.-Mexico Boundary* (New York, 2001).

41. Border patrol, according to Michael Kearney, "is *not* to make the U.S.-Mexico border impermeable to the passage of 'illegal' entrants, but rather to regulate their 'flow,' while at the same time maintaining the official distinctions between the 'sending' and 'receiving' nations, i.e., between different kinds of people, that is, to constitute classes of people in both the categorical and social sense." Michael Kearney, "Borders and Boundaries of State and Self at the End of Empire," *Journal of Historical Sociology* 4, 1 (March 1991): 52–74. Christian Parenti advances a similar argument in *Lockdown America*; the INS's "interior enforcement" campaigns, from the agency's raids of immigrant workplaces and neighborhoods to its computerized databases and surveillance systems, constitute a form of labor discipline, ensuring that they remain a docile and exploitable laborforce. Christian Parenti, *Lockdown America: Police and Prisons in the Age of Crisis* (London, 1999), 139–160.

42. Here, we are drawing on Michel Foucault's theory of governmentality, which asserts that modern regimes of power operate through a mix of "technologies of domination" and "technologies of the self." Foucault's writing illuminates the ways that the modern state regulates human conduct through direct force and repression but, more important, by rational, technical means that induce self-control in the individual. Michel Foucault, "The Subject and Power," in *Michel Foucault: Beyond Structuralism and Hermeneutics,* 2nd ed., ed. Herbert L. Dreyfus and Paul Rabinow (Chicago, 1983), and *Discipline and Punish: The Birth of the Prison* (New York, 1977). Political theorist Barbara Cruikshank expands Foucault's theory to look at how such "productive" power is exercised through social scientific knowledge about the poor, private philanthropy, and government-run job training and self-esteem programs. Barbara Cruikshank, *The Will to Empower: Democratic Citizens and Other Subjects* (Ithaca, 1999).

NOTES TO CHAPTER I

1. Proposition 187 consisted of five major provisions: (1) barred illegal aliens from public education and required public schools to verify students' immigration status; (2) required providers of public, nonemergency health services to verify immigration status and refuse services to illegal aliens; (3) required welfare de-

partment to verify applicant's immigration status; (4) required service providers to report "suspected illegal aliens" to the state attorney general and the INS; (5) made it a felony to make, distribute, or use false immigration documents in an effort to obtain public services or monies.

2. For an insightful analysis of Proposition 187, see Pierrette Hondagneu-Sotelo, "Unpacking 187: Targeting Mexicanas," in *Immigration and Ethnic Communities: A Focus on Latinos,* ed. Refugio Rochin (East Lansing, MI, 1996), 93.

3. Kim Moody defines "neoliberalism" as "a mixture of neoclassical economic fundamentalism, market regulation in place of state guidance, economic redistribution in favor of capital (known as "supply-side" economics), moral authoritarianism with an idealized family at its center, international free-trade principles (sometimes inconsistently applied), and a thorough intolerance of trade unionism. [. . .] Neoliberal ideology attributes to the market almost mystical powers to cleanse a sick world economy. It does not hesitate to use the state to affect economic trends, but it does so in ways that free up market forces rather than restrain them." Kim Moody, *Workers in a Lean World: Unions in the International Economy* (London, 1997), 119–120.

4. Frances Fox Piven concludes that "when labor market effects are taken into account, 'welfare reform' is more likely to weaken families than to restore them." (84) Welfare reform will not only force low-income women to compete in a saturated low-wage labor market, but also drive down the wage floor, particularly in states like California and New York with large welfare populations. Frances Fox Piven, "Welfare and Work," in *Whose Welfare?* 83–99.

5. The ways welfare reform limited and thus reinscribed social citizenship provided a "wage of whiteness"—to apply David Roediger's useful formulation —in the face of globalization. David Roediger, *The Wages of Whiteness: Race and the Making of the American Working Class* (London, 1991).

6. We draw on the theory of narrative analysis that views media narratives as constitutive of societal power relations. Literary critic Wahneema Lubiano, for instance, has argued that categories like "black woman" and "welfare mother/queen" are social narratives (or "stories") that naturalize ideological beliefs as "common-sense" and disguise relations of power. Wahneema Lubiano, "Black Ladies, Welfare Queens, and State Minstrels: Ideological War by Narrative Means," in *Race-ing Justice, En-Gendering Power,* ed. Toni Morrison (New York, 1992), 323–361. For an expanded analysis of anti-welfare discourse, see Angie-Marie Hancock, *The Politics of Disgust: The Public Identity of the Welfare Queen* (New York, 2004).

7. In Los Angeles County, for example, officials adopted a policy of denying pensions to Mexican-American women under the rationale that the "feudal" background of Mexican immigrants made it difficult for them to "understand and not abuse the principle of a regular grant of money from the state." Gwendolyn

Mink, *The Wages of Motherhood: Inequality in the Welfare State, 1917–1942* (Ithaca, 1996), 49–52.

8. Cited in Valerie Polakow, *Lives on the Edge: Single Mothers and Their Children in the Other America* (Chicago, 1993), 56.

9. One southern welfare supervisor explained, "The number of Negro cases is few due to the unanimous feeling on the part of the staff and the board that there are more work opportunities for Negro women and to their intense desire not to interfere with local labor conditions." Dorothy Roberts, *Killing the Black Body: Race, Reproduction, and the Meaning of Liberty* (New York, 1988), 207.

10. While the law mandated the federal government to pay beneficiaries on Social Security a fixed amount, it provided much more discretion for caseworkers and administrators in determining who got ADC and how much a family received. Roberts, 205.

11. Jill Quadagno, *The Color of Welfare: How Racism Undermined the War on Poverty* (New York, 1994), 19–24.

12. Michael Katz, *In the Shadow of the Poorhouse: A Social History of Welfare in America* (New York, 1986), 260.

13. Quoted in Teresa Amott and Julie Matthaei, *Race, Gender, and Work* (Boston, 1996), 178. For a provocative analysis of how the NWRO appropriated the discourse of domesticity to argue in favor of welfare entitlements for black women, see Eileen Boris, "When Work is Slavery," in *Whose Welfare?* 36–55. NWRO activists asserted poor women's right to a sustainable income while they stayed at home to raise their children, challenging the racial and class underpinnings of work and domesticity. Premilla Nadasen's *Welfare Warriors: The Welfare Rights Movement in the United States* (New York, 2004) provides an illuminating history of the NRWO, particularly of conflicts over political ideology and strategy between the organization's middle-class leadership and its membership of welfare recipients.

14. The NWRO also challenged public perceptions of welfare recipients. In 1968, when Senator Russell Long refused to let female welfare rights leaders testify to Congress and called them "brood mares," Johnnie Tillmon and the organization responded with what she termed a "brood mare stampede," picketing welfare centers, government offices, and the homes of legislators themselves. Deborah Gray White, *Too Heavy a Load: Black Women in Defense of Themselves, 1894–1994* (New York, 2000).

15. *La Raza Yearbook* (September 1968), 45.

16. Sandra Ugarte, "Welfare," *La Raza* (April 1972), 16.

17. Rudy Acuna, *Occupied America: A History of Chicanos* (New York, 1988), 395.

18. Katz, *In the Shadow of the Poorhouse*, 275–276. Katz contends that the expansion of social welfare in the post–World War II period drew on the language of racial equality, yet also fulfilled the Keynesian mission of regulating economic

competition. Proponents of increasing AFDC benefits argued that more generous income maintenance programs would discourage the welfare poor from looking for work and thereby protect American workers from unfair competition that would lead to lower wages.

19. Although scholars like Lewis emphasized the sociohistorical context of supposed cultural patterns among the poor, the emphasis on the cross-generational transmission of this "culture" and contention that the "culture of poverty" would reproduce itself even in the face of marked socioeconomic improvements, reified older theories of poverty as an innate trait.

20. Quoted in Lisa McGirr, *Suburban Warriors: The Origins of the New American Right* (Princeton, 2001), 82.

21. Created in 1960 by Orange County businessman Walter Knott to disseminate anti-communist literature to his employees, the CFEA quickly grew into one of Southern California's premier New Right institutions with the support of local conservatives, from actors Ronald Reagan and Pat Boone to businesses like Carl's Jr. Burgers and Technicolor Corporation. By the mid-1960s, the CFEA's focus had shifted from anti-communism to opposition to Washington's liberal "establishment," tackling issues from taxes and welfare spending to the spread of dangerous liberal ideas (like evolution and family planning) in public school curricula. See McGirr, 99–101.

22. McGirr, 100.

23. Suburbanization was also an effective tool for labor control. Breaking with the prevailing norm in city planning, which placed industry in the central city, Los Angeles officials in the early twentieth century actively encouraged the industrialization of outlying areas and the construction of adjoining working-class housing tracts. Spreading the working-class population across the region into de facto "factory towns" gave employers greater discipline over the social life of their workers, while posing formidable obstacles to labor organizing. In 1935, attracted by Los Angeles's "open shop" policy, the Ford Motor Company built a large assembly plant in the city of Pico Rivera. General Motors followed suit one year later, opening an assembly plant in South Gate. Throughout the decade, this southeastern region developed into the rust-belt of Los Angeles County, as Bethlehem Steel opened its factory doors in Vernon, and rubber manufacturers like Goodrich, Goodyear, and Firestone built major plants in South Gate, Lynwood, and Pico Rivera. By 1936, the auto and rubber industries employed more than 40,000 men, who found shelter in the new suburban housing tracts alongside the factory gates. Aided by HOLC "redlining" practices, L.A.'s southeast cities developed as exclusively white factory suburbs. Becky M. Nicolaides, *My Blue Heaven: Life and Politics in the Working-Class Suburbs of Los Angeles, 1920–1965* (Chicago, 2002).

24. McGirr, 201.

25. McGirr, 204.

26. Ibid.

27. McGirr, 205.

28. Polakow, 59. One of Reagan's favorite stories lambasted a black Chicago mother with "80 names, 30 addresses, 12 Social Security Cards and a tax-free income of over $150,000." Yet Reagan's infamous "welfare queen" had actually cheated the state of $8,000. David Zucchino, *The Myth of the Welfare Queen* (New York, 1997), 75.

29. Ibid.

30. David Harvey, *The Condition of Postmodernity* (Cambridge, 1990), 153. For a discussion of the effects of "flexibilization" on the African-American working class, see Robin Kelley's *yo mama's disfunktional: fighting the culture wars in urban america* (Boston, 1997); for a case-study of Latina workers in the New York and Los Angeles apparel and electronics industries, see Maria Patricia Fernandez Kelly and Saskia Sassen, "Recasting Women in the Global Economy: Internationalization and Changing Definitions of Gender," in *Women in the Latin American Development Process*.

31. Karin Stallard, Barbara Ehrenreich, and Holly Sklar, *Poverty in the American Dream: Women and Children First* (Boston, 1983), 6–7.

32. Saskia Sassen, *The Global City: New York, London, Tokyo* (Princeton, 1991), 13. See also Manuel Castells, *The Informational City: Information Technology, Economic Restructuring, and the Urban Regional Process* (London, 1989).

33. Andres Torres and Frank Bonilla, "Decline Within Decline: The New York Perspective," in *Latinos in a Changing U.S. Economy*, eds. Rebecca Morales and Frank Bonilla (London, 1993), 85–108.

34. Barry Bluestone and Bennett Harrison, *The Deindustrialization of America: Corporate Restructuring and the Polarizing of America* (New York, 1982); Antonia Darder, Rodolfo D. Torres, and Henry Gutierrez, eds. *Latinos and Education: A Critical Reader* (New York, 1997) 52.

35. Leo R. Chavez, "Immigration Reform and Nativism: The Nationalist Response to the Transnationalist Challenge," in *Immigrants Out! The New Nativism*, 442.

36. Rebecca Morales and Paul Ong, "The Illusion of Progress: Latinos in Los Angeles," in *Latinos in a Changing U.S. Economy*, 55–84. In a recent study, UCLA geographer William Clark found that the earning power of Mexican and Central American immigrants, even among those who have been in the United States for over 20 years, has decreased dramatically since the 1970s. For instance, between 1970 and 1995, Mexican immigrant men and women earned nearly $2,000 less per year in adjusted constant dollars. Even when tracking the same immigrant cohort from 1970 to 1995, Clark found a similar drop in average yearly earnings, suggesting that long-term settlement in the United States does not

equal higher wages for Mexican immigrants. William Clark, *The California Cauldron: Immigration and the Fortune of Local Communities* (New York, 1998), 74–87.

37. Morales and Ong, 57.

38. Sheryl Cashin, *The Failures of Integration* (New York, 2004), 115–116.

39. Victor Valle and Rodolfo Torres, *Latino Metropolis* (Minneapolis, 2000), 19.

40. Rob Cling, Spencer Olin, and Mark Poster, *Postsuburban California: The Transformation of Orange County since World War II* (Berkeley, 1995), 75.

41. Lauren Berlant, *The Queen of America Goes to Washington City: Essays on Sex and Citizenship* (Durham, NC, 1997), 2.

42. Most historians agree that a "tradition" of self-help never existed in the United States. For a convincing refutation of the idea, see chapter 4 of Stephanie Coontz's *The Way We Never Were: American Families and the Nostalgia Trap* (New York: 1992).

43. Katz, *In the Shadow of the Poorhouse*, 330.

44. Katz, 296.

45. Katz, 297.

46. Parenti, *Lockdown America*, 40.

47. John Gilliom, *Overseers of the Poor: Surveillance, Resistance, and the Limits of Privacy* (Chicago, 2001), 30.

48. Gilliom, 30–31.

49. Parenti, 137.

50. Under the FSA, one parent in a two-parent family was required to perform work in the private or public sector for a minimum of 16 hours per week. The legislation also extended new work incentives to single-parent families and required states to enroll part of their caseloads in job search and training programs. However, as Katz concludes, "Sponsors of the FSA assumed the availability of jobs for AFDC clients. They did not want to create jobs, and they permitted state welfare departments to design programs without serious analyses of local labor markets or consultation with labor departments." Moreover, even the limited expansion of entitlements like childcare and education under the FSA ran against public sentiment in the late 1980s, which called on the federal government "to cut benefits, not extend them." Katz, 309.

51. Katz, 330.

52. William Julius Wilson, *The Truly Disadvantaged* (Chicago, 1987), 137–138.

53. The slippage between poor blacks and the underclass is notable throughout Wilson's work.

54. Wilson uses statistical indices on poverty and family patterns to support his claims about the changing social organization and cultural disintegration of

high-poverty black neighborhoods. Numerous qualitative studies have refuted Wilson's claims about black community dissolution. For example, see Steven Gregory, *Black Corona: Race and the Politics of Place in an Urban Community* (Princeton, NJ, 1998); and Katherine Newman, *No Shame in My Game: The Working Poor in the Inner City* (New York, 1999). Even if we accept that poor people living in high poverty areas are more likely to interact with other poor people than those living in low poverty areas, the alarmist labeling of this phenomenon as "social isolation" is not only scientifically false but also politically charged because it assumes that interacting with poor people is inherently a problem. As this research found, Latinas in Long Beach are not socially isolated, as they move throughout the Southern California region on a regular basis. For example, Delia's sister lives 25 miles away in downtown Los Angeles; Lupe's mother and younger siblings live in South Gate, located about a 20-minute freeway drive from Long Beach. Also, most women shopped for food and clothing outside the immediate vicinity of their neighborhood.

55. Wilson, 7.

56. Wilson, 21.

57. Coontz, 250.

58. These include highly regarded works like Elijah Anderson's *Streetwise: Race, Class and Change in an Urban Community* (Chicago, 1990); Alex Kotlowitz's *There Are No Children Here: A Story of Two Boys Growing Up in the Other America* (New York, 1991); Carl Nightingale's *On the Edge: A History of Poor Black Children and Their American Dreams* (New York, 1993); Mitchell Duneier's *Slim's Table: Race, Respectability and Masculinity* (Chicago, 1992); and David Simon and Edward Burns's *The Corner: A Year in the Life of an Inner-City Neighborhood* (New York, 2000).

59. Joan Moore and Raquel Pinderhughes, eds., *In the Barrios: Latinos and the Underclass Debate* (New York: Russell Sage Foundation, 1994).

60. Alejandro Portes and Min Zhou, "The New Second Generation: Segmented Assimilation and Its Variants among Post-1965 Immigrant Youth," *Annals* 530 (1993): 81.

61. Portes elaborates this argument in his most recent work, coauthored with Ruben G. Rumbaut, *Legacies: The Story of the Immigrant Second Generation* (Berkeley, 2001). In this large sociological study of second-generation immigrant youth in San Diego and Miami, Portes and Rumbaut draw on qualitative life history interviews with young people as well as statistical data (on educational outcomes, employment patterns, etc.) to argue that assimilation into "inner-city culture" is a major deterrent to social and economic mobility for second-generation immigrants.

62. Nowhere is the "mainstreaming" of sociological theories of segmented assimilation more problematic than in Linda Chavez's *Out of the Barrio: Towards a New Politics of Hispanic Assimilation* (New York, 1991). Chavez blames the

U.S. welfare system for the social and economic "isolation" of Puerto Ricans from mainstream society, contending that welfare has destroyed traditional family values and the work ethic among Puerto Ricans in the United States. Foreshadowing the discourse of personal responsibility that would later undergird the PRWORA, she writes, "If anything, Puerto Ricans have been showered with too much government attention, but of the wrong kind. Citizenship, which should have enhanced Puerto Rican achievements, may actually have hindered it by conferring entitlements, such as welfare, with no concomitant obligations. The state has functioned like an anonymous *patrón,* dispensing welfare checks that allowed recipients to avoid the responsibilities of autonomous adults" (159). Chavez's association between the welfare state and the *patrón* system in Latin America echoes the argument advanced by welfare officials earlier in the century that Mexicans should not be eligible for welfare because their "feudal background" made them susceptible to long-term dependency on government handouts.

63. Wilson, 19.

64. Mike Davis, *City of Quartz: Excavating the Future in Los Angeles* (London, 1990), 156.

65. Donald Kinder and Lynn Sanders, *Divided by Color: Racial Politics and Democratic Ideas* (Chicago, 1996), 92–127. Tellingly, in another poll conducted by the *New York Times*/CBS News, two-thirds of Americans said there was too little assistance for the poor. But when asked about welfare and those who receive it, only 23 percent said that the assistance was too little. Farai Chideya, *Don't Believe the Hype: fighting cultural misinformation about african-americans* (New York, 1995), 36.

66. We are building on Reeves and Campbell's critique of the "new racism" that developed in the Reagan era. Jimmie L. Reeves and Richard Campbell, *Cracked Coverage: Television News, the Anti-Cocaine Crusade, and the Reagan Legacy* (Durham, NC, 1994), 97–102.

67. Seminal examples of this approach include Thomas Sowell's *Ethnic America* (New York, 1981); Milton Gordon's *Assimilation in American Life* (New York, 1964); Nathan Glazer and Daniel P. Moynihan's *Beyond the Melting Pot* (Cambridge, MA, 1969). For critiques of ethnicity paradigms of U.S. race relations, see Michael Omi and Howard Winant, *Racial Formation in the United States from the 1960's to the 1980's* (New York, 1986), and Alan Wald, "Theorizing Cultural Difference: A Critique of the Ethnicity School," *MELUS* 14 (1987): 21–33.

68. Peter Brimelow, *Alien Nation: Common Sense about America's Immigration Disaster* (New York, 1996), 52.

69. Ibid., xii.

70. Georgie Anne Geyer, *Americans No More* (New York, 1996).

71. The issue of immigration caused division within Republican Party ranks and forged unusual alliances between conservatives and Latin American multina-

tionals. As the debate over Proposition 187 heated up, William Bennett and Jack Kemp took out a two-page advertisement in the *Los Angeles Times,* urging fellow Republicans not to broaden "legitimate concerns about illegal immigrants . . . into an ugly antipathy towards all immigrants." In this ad, paid for by the Mexico City–based Univision Television Group, Bennett and Kemp wrote, "[Immigrants] tend to live in strong, stable families; possess impressive energy and entrepreneurial spirit; have a deeply rooted religious faith; and make important intellectual contributions to the nation. Most come to America in large part because they believe in traditional American ideals." *Los Angeles Times,* November 6, 1994, A28–29. The moral typology between "good" and "bad" immigrants is reflected in ambivalent (if often contradictory) American attitudes concerning proposals to restrict immigration. For example, in several 1996 Roper polls, the majority of people polled supported the idea of a five-year moratorium on immigration. Yet, only 21 percent said that they viewed legal immigration as a major problem. Furthermore, in a 1995 Roper poll, 61 percent disapproved of eliminating the preference for family reunification in U.S. immigration policy. Cited in Debra DeLaet, *U.S. Immigration Policy in an Age of Rights* (Westport, CT, 2000), 114.

72. The language wars of this period were also intensely racialized, as campaigns for English-Only were targeted explicitly at speakers of Spanish and Asian languages, not French or Russian.

73. On the historical shift in American popular media discourse on immigration from the 1960s to the present, see Leo Chavez's *Covering Immigration.*

74. Etienne Balibar and Emmanuel Wallerstein, *Race, Nation, Class: Ambiguous Identities* (London, 1991), 21.

75. Paul Gilroy, *Against Race: Imagining Political Culture beyond the Color Line* (Cambridge, MA, 2000), 69.

76. It is not surprising that the birthplace of Proposition 187 was Orange County. Orange County filed for bankruptcy the same year the Proposition was on the ballot. The fact that Orange County drew its laborforce from around the world, that its globally integrated capital rivaled that of major cities and nations throughout the world, that it had the fourth highest rate of immigration in the United States, and that it also spawned the slow growth movements in the 1970s all ask that we take more seriously the historical relationship between suburbanization, globalization, and racialized nationalism.

77. Both media sources cited in Chang, *Disposable Domestic,* 6.

78. Ibid.

79. Pfaelzer's ruling overturned most provisions of Proposition 187, leaving intact only those imposing state criminal penalties for making, distributing, and using false immigration documents. Then-Governor Wilson appealed this ruling and passed on the appeal to his Democratic successor Gray Davis. Although Davis campaigned as a supporter of immigrant rights and won the election

thanks to the backing of the state's civil rights groups and labor unions, he refused to drop the appeal and instead sent the matter to arbitration. Finally, in
1999, Davis agreed to drop the appeal due to intensive lobbying from labor, immigrant rights groups, and from members of his own party (most visibly State Assembly Speaker Antonio Villaragosa and Lieutenant Governor Cruz Bustamente).
See Chang, 6–7.

80. In fact, most welfare recipients were white, lived in the suburbs, were in
their twenties and thirties, and had two kids. Michael Moore, *Downsize This*
(New York, 1997), 69.

81. "Welfare: Facts and Fiction" in *MS* (May/June 1995), 93; U.S. Census,
"Selected Characteristics of the Foreign-Born Population by Year of Entry and Selected Countries of Birth," 1990.

82. Comparing Mexican immigrants to Middle Eastern and Asian immigrants
in California, William A. V. Clark found that Mexicans have the highest poverty
rate and the lowest welfare dependency rate of all three groups. Clark, *California
Cauldron*, 76. Similarly, after examining U.S. Census data from 1990 (ibid.), we
found that Mexican immigrants received AFDC at a slightly higher rate than
Russian immigrants (3.1 percent to 2.4 percent, respectively), but that Russians
received "other welfare" (SSI, food stamps, etc.) at a much higher rate than Mexicans (7.5 percent compared to less than 1 percent). Furthermore, the percentages
are significantly higher for Vietnamese, Laotian, and Cambodian immigrants in
part due to the connection between public assistance and refugee resettlement
policy.

83. Numerous studies have shown that women on welfare want to work and
do so when they can find jobs. "Over a two-year interval . . . the typical mother
held 1.7 jobs during that period. Forty-four percent held two or more jobs."
Zucchino, 64.

84. Kathryn Edin and Laura Lein, *Making Ends Meet: How Single Mothers
Survive Welfare and Low-Wage Work* (New York, 1997).

85. "Welfare: Facts and Fiction," 93.

86. Such caricatures were so symbolically powerful that the new TANF system seemed to be designed with them in mind. For example, although faced with
evidence that teenage mothers make up a small minority of all welfare recipients,
welfare policymakers nonetheless concentrated their efforts on combating teen
pregnancy.

87. Vanessa Tait, " 'Workers Just Like Anyone Else': Organizing Workfare
Unions in New York City," in *Still Lifting, Still Climbing: African American
Women's Contemporary Activism,* ed. Kimberly Springer (New York, 1999),
304–305.

88. While most unions did not break with Clinton or Congress over the legislation, since its passage, new coalitions and organizing efforts have begun to
form. A number of SEIU and AFSCME locals as well as community groups such

as the Kensington Welfare Rights Union have begun the work of bringing together welfare recipients and union workers to see their common interests.

89. Tait, 314. Under the Work Opportunity Tax Credit, employers who hire a TANF recipient can claim up to 40 percent of that employee's first-year wages (not to exceed $2,400). Under the Welfare To Work Tax Credit, employers who hire an AFDC or TANF recipient who has received welfare for at least 18 consecutive months can claim 35 percent of that employee's first-year wages, and 50 percent of that employee's second-year wages.

90. Adam Cohen, "When Wall Street Runs Welfare," *Time Magazine* (March 23, 1998). Valerie Polakow cites a similar example of Lockheed Martin, the weapons industry giant and now private welfare administrator, in *A New Introduction to Poverty*, ed. Louis Kushnik and James Jennings (New York, 1999), 168.

91. Audrey Singer, "Welfare Reform and Immigrants: A Policy Review," in *Immigrants, Welfare Reform, and the Poverty of Policy*, 22–25. Singer notes that this new citizenship criterion departs from past U.S. policy and international standards; in most industrialized democracies, permanent residents are eligible for the same benefits as citizens.

92. While the work documentation requirement would be hard for any citizen to meet, it was nearly impossible for an immigrant population concentrated in informal and seasonal employment.

93. During the summer of 1997, due largely to the efforts of immigrant advocacy groups and, interestingly, agribusiness lobbyists (who sought to protect a steady supply of cheap immigrant farm labor), Congress passed the Balanced Budget Act. This legislation restored limited food stamp benefits to "pre 8/22" legal immigrant children, seniors, and disabled persons, Hmong Vietnam era veterans, and extended benefits to refugees and asylees from five to seven years. Congress also changed the PRWORA's provision that prohibits states from using federal funds to aid legal immigrants to allow states to *purchase* federal food stamps for legal immigrants. Numerous states with large immigrant populations provide limited food stamps to legal immigrants under this provision. California and New York, for example, have used state funds to purchase federal food stamps for children, elderly, and disabled legal immigrants. Texas provides such benefits to elderly and disabled legal immigrants. See DeLaet, *U.S. Immigration Policy*, 108–109.

94. Immigrants who arrived in the United States after the passage of PRWORA were ineligible for food stamps and SSI until they became naturalized citizens. This changed under the Farm Security and Rural Investment Act of 2002, which established a five-year waiting period for "qualified immigrants," exempted children from the waiting period, and made "qualified immigrants" eligible for disability-related insurance, regardless of their date of entry.

95. California Immigrant Welfare Collaborative, *Immigrants and Welfare in California* (Spring 1998), Section B, 1–36. Even prior to the passage of the

PRWORA, federal legislation moved toward restrictions on immigrant eligibility for public benefits. The 1990 Immigration Act required that sponsors sign an "Affidavit of Support" stating that they will support the immigrant at 125 percent of the poverty line until that immigrant becomes a U.S. citizen or works for 40 "qualifying quarters." Under such affidavits, sponsors also assume financial responsibility for any public costs incurred by the legal immigrant under their sponsorship.

96. Lynn H. Fujiwara, "Asian Immigrant Communities and Welfare Reform," in *Whose Welfare?* 125.

97. By December 1997, there were reports that INS officials were unlawfully stopping legal immigrants at the border and at airports and making repayment of legally obtained public benefits a condition for reentry into the United States. See, for example, December 17, 1997 letter from the U.S. Department of Health and Human Services to State TANF Directors regarding this matter. *Immigrants and Welfare in California,* Tab H.9.

98. The USA PATRIOT Act passed by Congress with little debate in October 2001 permits the detention of noncitizens for mere suspicion of "terrorist" involvement, expands terrorism laws to include "domestic terrorism," denies readmission to the United States of foreign nationals for engaging in free speech, and allows the indefinite detainment of noncitizens in six-month increments without meaningful judicial review. As legal scholar David Cole writes in *Enemy Aliens,* "[F]or purposes of regulating immigration, "terrorist activity" is defined much more expansively, to include support of the otherwise lawful and nonviolent activities of virtually any group that has used violence, and any use of threat to use a weapon against person or property ("other than for mere personal monetary gain"). . . . With the stroke of the pen, President Bush denied foreign nationals basic rights of political association, political speech, due process, and privacy" (58).

99. Kretsedemas and Aparicio 9. Parenti advances a similar argument in chapter 7 of *Lockdown America.*

100. There has been much less coverage of the rising activism in the face of these devastating changes. From workfare organizing in New York City, to the Economic Human Rights campaign of the Kensington Welfare Rights Union, to community protests in the Mission Hill section of Boston, the activism of former welfare recipients and their allies has not fit with the prevailing celebration of welfare reform and thus received little media attention.

101. Lisa Dodson in *Don't Call Us Out of Name* cautions, "When we find one of the many low-income mothers who has found a better place, more education, a decent job, a chance to develop, let us all recall history . . . the vast majority of families on welfare have always moved on, moved up through their own tenacious determination, with the help of their family and decent programs for real education and opportunity" (224).

102. James Gerstenzang, "Clinton Touts Welfare-To-Work Progress," *Los Angeles Times,* August 4, 1999, A-3.

103. Beginning in the mid-1980s, and culminating with the passage of the PRWORA, numerous states had been carving away at cash and food stamp assistance, making it easier for caseworkers to terminate clients' benefits and imposing strict work requirements and behavioral rules. Even before the federal overhaul in 1996, over half of the nation's recipients were covered by state welfare rules that, without the waiver program implemented by the Reagan administration in 1986, would have violated federal law.

104. Barbara Vobejda and Judith Haveman, "Sanctions Fuel Drop in Welfare Rolls," *Washington Post,* March 23, 1998, A01.

105. Sharon Hays, *Flat Broke with Children,* 41.

106. U.S. Commission on Civil Rights, 1.

107. Mark Weisbrot, "Welfare Reform: The Jobs Aren't There," http://www.rtk.net/preamble/welfjobs/fulltex.2.html. Cited in Mink, *Whose Welfare?* 2.

108. Don Lee, "L.A. County Jobs Surge Since '93, but Not Wages," *Los Angeles Times,* July 26, 1999, A-1.

109. John MacArthur, *The Selling of "Free Trade": NAFTA, Washington, and the Subversion of American Democracy* (New York, 2000), 19. See, for example, the Urban Institute's study of welfare reform's labor market effects on 20 metropolitan areas: Robert Lerman, Pamela Loprest, and Caroline Ratcliffe, "How Well Can Urban Labor Markets Absorb Welfare Recipients?" (New York: Urban Institute, 2000).

110. Piven, 88.

111. Stephen Pimpare, *The New Victorians: Poverty, Politics, and Propaganda in Two Gilded Eras* (New York, 2004).

112. Gilliom, 103.

113. See, for example, the website of the Welfare-to-Work Partnership (www.welfaretowork.org), a nonprofit organization created and governed by the CEOs of corporations like United Airlines, Burger King, Sprint, Monsanto, and UPS.

114. This language describing NAFTA is drawn from a 1995 *Los Angeles Times* 16-article special section entitled "The Melding Americas." Claiming that the borders between the Americas are dissolving through free trade and the democratization of Latin America, most of the *Times* stories focused on the "The Cultural Ties [That] Mend Continental Divide." The transnationalism celebrated in this special section was one undergirded by a "universal" (American) consumer ethic, as article after article glowed over the success of U.S. performers (Gloria Estefan, Edward James Olmos, and Jean-Claude Van Damme) and other consumer commodities in the Latin American market. A similar blend of "global Ameri-

canism" was evident when President Clinton lauded NAFTA as an opportunity to export American ideals throughout the continent. *Los Angeles Times*, "Special Section: The Melding Americas," July 18, 1994, Section D.

115. On the day President Clinton signed the PRWORA, he extolled how the new law would restore "America's basic bargain of providing opportunity and demanding in return responsibility." *New York Times*, August 23, 1996, A1.

116. For varying renditions of this argument, see: Linda Basch, Nina Glick Schiller, and Cristina Szanton Blanc, *Nations Unbound: Transnational Projects, Postcolonial Predicaments, and Deterritorialized Nation-States* (Amsterdam, 1994); Brimelow, *Alien Nation*; Brubaker, *Immigration and the Politics of Citizenship in Europe and North America*; Geyer, *Americans No More*; and Peter Schuck and Rogers Smith, *Citizenship without Consent: Illegal Aliens in the American Polity* (New Haven, CT, 1985).

NOTES TO CHAPTER 2

1. Nancy Paradise, "The Long Beach Public Library: The Mark Twain Neighborhood Library: A Collection Study" (unpublished manuscript, 2003, available at the Mark Twain Public Library in Long Beach).

2. Stephanie Coontz convincingly elaborates this point in *The Way We Never Were*.

3. There is a small body of academic work that looks at Latino immigrant suburban communities. See, for instance, Sarah Mahler, *American Dreaming: Immigrant Life on the Margins* (Princeton, NJ, 1995); Sarah Mahler and Nancy Foner, *Salvadorans in Suburbia: Symbiosis and Conflict* (New York, 1996); and Raymond Rocco, "Latino Los Angeles: Reframing Boundaries/Borders," in *The City: Los Angeles and Urban Theory at the End of the Twentieth Century*, edited by Edward Soja and Allen J. Scott (Berkeley, 1997), 365–378.

4. While nearly every work on contemporary Los Angeles foregrounds the region's new "Latino majority," there have been surprisingly few ethnographic studies of Los Angeles, and, in particular, its Mexican and Central American communities. For an analysis of this absence of ethnographic research, see T. Monahan, "Los Angeles Studies: The Emergence of a Specialty Field," *City & Society* 14, 2 (2002): 155–184.

5. Work by sociologists, cultural geographers, and urban planners has illuminated the importance of locality under globalization but undervalued the centrality of suburbs in the emergent global system role. For instance, see: Saskia Sassen, *Cities in a World Economy* (Thousand Oaks, CA, 1994); Janet L. Abu-Lughod, *New York, Chicago, Los Angeles: America's Global Cities* (Minneapolis, 1999); and Sharon Zukin, *The Cultures of Cities* (London, 1995).

6. Victor Valle and Rodolfo Torres remind us that, "[T]he social and eco-

nomic transformations needed to facilitate the economies of global efficiency have progressively reduced the control of local communities over their own political institutions." *Latino Metropolis,* 19.

7. Published scholarly literature on Long Beach is extremely thin and limited to works by "booster" historians. In this regard, we are especially indebted to Kaye Briegel for conversations on Long Beach history and for sharing her unpublished paper, coauthored with Gary Peters, "The Black Experience in Long Beach, California." We are also very grateful to James Elmendorf for sharing his unpublished undergraduate honor's thesis, "The Military and the Mall: Society and Culture in Long Beach, California" (Hampshire College, Spring 1995).

8. Virginia Carpenter, *As I Look Back.* Oral History Program, CSULB 1989. Larry Meyer and Patricia Kalayjian, *Long Beach: Fortune's Harbor* (Tulsa, 1983).

9. Walter Case, *The History of Long Beach and Vicinity, Volume 1* (Chicago, 1927), 69.

10. Case, 90.

11. Prohibition was actively enforced by Long Beach residents, who formed an armed blockade to prohibit one businessman from selling alcohol on the beach. The city's "prominent residents" informed this businessman that his "presence would not be tolerated in the city," and he was run out of town. "Modern Block to Supplant Oldest Landmarks in City," *Press-Telegram,* August 29, 1912, 3.

12. Elmendorf, 46.

13. Robert M. Fogelson, *The Fragmented Metropolis: Los Angeles, 1850–1930* (Los Angeles, 1993), 144–145.

14. "Long Beach Pike: 1902–2001," *Los Angeles Magazine,* July 2001, 32. Peter Theroux, *Translating L.A.* (New York, 1994), 57–58.

15. Don Ryan, "Long Beach, California: Farmer's Rest," *Nation,* February 20, 1924, 205. Cited in Elmendorf, 51.

16. Case, 155.

17. The Long Beach–San Pedro port, today the largest in the United States, did not occur naturally (like the San Francisco Bay) but required billions of federal dollars to readjust the natural landscape.

18. Elmendorf, 59.

19. Elmendorf, 81.

20. Bill Hillburg, *Long Beach: The City and Its People* (Carlsbad, CA, 2000), 68.

21. Throughout the 1920s and 1930s, these picnics drew crowds of over 60,000 participants, who divided the city's parks into picnic tables sporting the names of various Iowan counties.

22. A 1943 issue of *Douglas Airview,* the company newspaper, proclaimed, "A man or woman could be born in any one of the company's mammoth factories, spend a lifetime within its confines and never suffer for lack of the normal

accessories and advantages available to his fellow citizens outside." "Long Beach File" in History Collection of the Los Angeles Public Library.

23. Bill Hillburg, "Long Beach, Calif., Grew Along with McDonnell Douglas Corp." *Long Beach Press Telegram,* August 3, 1997, B3.

24. Hillburg, 86–87.

25. Ann Markusen and Robin Bloch note, "These [defense] communities are marked by relatively conservative, patriarchal and promilitary cultural attitudes. They may be adjacent to older metropolitan centers, but form few interconnections with them, coexisting as distinct labor markets and cultural enclaves. In essence, they are industrial 'cities' of an entirely new type, anti-cosmopolitan, anti-labor, anti-liberal." As quoted in Elmendorf, 75.

26. Hillburg, 87; The Junior League of Long Beach, "The 1950's: War ends with a boom," in *Long Beach Heritage.* "Long Beach File" in History Collection of the Los Angeles Public Library.

27. U.S. Census Bureau, "Census of Population and Housing," Long Beach, California: 1960.

28. Hillburg, 95.

29. Hillburg, 96.

30. Colette Marie McLaughlin, "Blighted Partnerships: Unsustainable Redevelopment Practices" (Ph.D. dissertation, University of California, Irvine, 2003).

31. Usha Sripalee Welaratna, "The Presence of the Past in Conflicts and Coalitions among Cambodians, African-Americans, and Hispanics in Central Long Beach" (Ph.D. dissertation, University of California, Berkeley, 1998), 14.

32. Popular among black and Chicano men in the 1940s, zoot suits soon became the object of white hysteria over urban criminality and aggressive youth subcultures. By 1942, zoot suits had become "an explicitly un-American style . . . because fabric rationing regulations instituted by the War Productions Board forbid the sale and manufacturing of zoot suits." Robin Kelley, *Race Rebels* (New York, 1994), 166.

33. Census figures show that, as late as 1970, nearly half of Long Beach's black population had been born in the South. U.S. Census Bureau, "Social Characteristics for Negro Population for Areas and Places: 1970."

34. These figures are taken from an analysis of Spanish-surnamed people listed in the Long Beach City Directory in 1943. This significantly undercounts Latinos living in rural areas around Long Beach. Moreover, the city directory shows a significant number of Latino men employed as shipdock workers, in what could be defense-related jobs.

35. Spencer Crump, "Negro in West, North Also Has Problems," *Press-Telegram,* March 25, 1956, A5-1.

36. "Service Corps Offers Negro Housing Plan," *Press-Telegram,* June 28, 1944, B1-4.

37. Welaratna, 26. The Terry family faced continual harassment while living

in Bixby Knolls. Rocks were thrown into the house, there were attempts to tap the family's phone, and a letter was circulated to Bixby Knolls residents, linking blacks moving into the neighborhood with "communist plots" and urging residents to write down license plates of any blacks seen in the neighborhood. "Cowardly Vandals," *The Independent,* June 24, 1958, A2; "Vandalism Assailed by Group," *The Independent,* June 27, 1958; and "New Case in Negro Housing," *Press-Telegram,* September 21, 1958, A-10-2. See also Hillburg, 123.

38. "Vandalism Assailed by Group," *The Independent,* June 27, 1958.

39. George Robeson, "Negroes Limited to 2 L.B. Areas," *Press-Telegram,* September 13, 1963, B1.

40. Robeson, B2.

41. "LB Negroes Housing Views Analyzed," *The Independent,* January 17, 1964, A18.

42. Ibid.

43. For all employed African-American workers in Long Beach, the three top occupations in 1970 were service workers (nonprivate household), operatives (most in durable goods manufacturing), and craftsmen. The median earnings in 1969 were $6,534. In this same year, 16.9 percent of all black families in Long Beach reported income less than 75 percent of the poverty line, suggesting that this was an extremely poor community. U.S. Census Bureau, "Occupation and Earnings for Negro Population for Areas and Places: 1970," and "Social Characteristics for Negro Population for Areas and Places," Long Beach, CA: 1970.

44. U.S. Census Bureau, "Ethnic Characteristics for Areas and Places," Long Beach, CA: 1970.

45. Ibid. In 1970, out of a total of 9,677 Latino workers in Long Beach, 3,782 were employed in professional, technical, and managerial positions. Another 4,861 were employed as craftsmen, operatives, laborers (except farm), and service workers. Curiously, the census counted only 28 Latino farm workers in Long Beach in this year, casting doubt on the accuracy of these figures. Indeed, the Census Bureau during this period was notoriously poor at counting migrant populations (including farm workers, homeless, and undocumented immigrants). Moreover, many historians have pointed out the difficulty of using census figures to track Mexican-American populations in the United States due to the use of shifting, ambiguous, and arbitrary ethnic and racial designations. In the 1970 Census, for example, Latinos might appear as "Spanish language persons," "Other Persons of Spanish surname," "Persons of Spanish origin," and "Puerto Rican."

46. U.S. Census Bureau, "Occupations and Earnings of Persons of Spanish Language or Spanish Surnames for Areas and Places," Long Beach, CA: 1970.

47. For a detailed picture of economic restructuring in the greater Los Angeles region, see Rebecca Morales and Paul Ong, "The Illusion of Progress: Latinos in Los Angeles," in *Latinos in a Changing U.S. Economy,* 55–84.

48. Jerry Miller, "Long Beach, California: A Model Military Re-Use Plan,"

Economic Development Commentary, Spring 1994. Cited in Elmendorf, 95. The Naval Station reopened in 1979 and then closed permanently in 1994.

49. Elmendorf, 115.

50. Mark Drayse, Daniel Flaming, and David Rigby, Synopsis of "Economic Restructuring in Long Beach: Opportunities and Challenges in a Post-Aerospace Economy" (Los Angeles: Economic Roundtable, 1999), 1.

51. Ibid.

52. James Sterngold, "Latest Series of Base Closings a New Setback for California," *New York Times,* February 26, 1995.

53. www.cnn.com/SPECIALS/cold.war/experience/the.bomb/route/08.long .beach.

54. The city's second largest industry, the Port of Long Beach, employed only 3,000 workers in 1992. Drayse et al., 1.

55. Proposition 13, which severely restricted municipalities from collecting property taxes, was propelled by the same probusiness interests that fueled redevelopment. However, these two strategies worked at cross-purposes in terms of city budgets; redevelopment could not provide the financial backbone the city sought, in part because of the limits that Proposition 13 placed on the collection of property tax from business.

56. As William Fulton documents in *The Reluctant Metropolis: The Politics of Urban Growth in Los Angeles* (Point Arena, CA, 1997), part of the appeal of retail to California municipalities was sales tax. In the wake of Proposition 13 many cities, including Long Beach, hoped to cultivate retail as a way to compensate for the significant loss of city income from property taxes. In 1978, prior to the implementation of Proposition 13, property tax revenues constituted 28 percent of Long Beach's General Fund, which funded most of its traditional city services like public works, human services, fire, police, etc. Twenty years later, property tax revenues constituted 14 percent of the city's fund. Rich Baenen et al., *Banking on Blight: Redevelopment in Post-Proposition 13 California* (Los Angeles, UCLA Urban Planning Department, 1999), 38–39.

57. George Weeks, "Redevelopers Adopt Free Enterprise Policy," *The Independent,* May 11, 1962.

58. Numerous African Americans wrote letters to the city council opposing this Redevelopment Agency. One from Sidney S. Watts read, "I don't believe this is the American way of government where if an area seems undesirable to some citizens or they would like to see it improved, to do it in this way." Transcript of September 26, 1961 Long Beach City Council Hearing on Urban Renewal. "Urban Renewal—1960s" folder, Long Beach Collection, Long Beach Public Library.

59. "Long Beach to Get $60 Million U.S. Aid," *The Independent,* January 28, 1979.

60. The increasingly popular belief that city government could not solve the

city's economic problems gave rise to nongovernmental redevelopment agencies like the Long Beach Economic Development Corporation (LBEDC), formed in 1974, and the Long Beach Community Partnership (LBCP), created in 1994. Funded in part by millions in public dollars, these organizations have been concerned with fostering a business-friendly environment within the city. Unlike city government, which must hold public meetings and seek citizen approval, nonprofit community corporations like LBEDC and LBCP are exempt from requirements for public accountability.

61. "Long Beach to Get $60 Million in U.S. Aid."

62. Elmendorf, 20.

63. Legal Aid Foundation of Los Angeles (http://www.lafla.org/news/november2001.asp).

64. Deborah Belgum, "Long Beach's Redevelopment Plans Running into Trouble," *Los Angeles Business Journal,* August 7, 2000.

65. McLaughlin, 29.

66. The city had allowed this debt to accrue by permitting Hyatt to default on its payments to the city with a 10 percent interest penalty per year. In 1999, a research team of graduate students from UCLA's Urban Planning Department conducted a comparative study of urban redevelopment in four California cities that included Long Beach. Their report, *Banking on Blight: Redevelopment in Post-Proposition 13 California,* strongly criticized Long Beach's redevelopment strategy for its "risky" and often unsuccessful investments in unstable industries like retail and tourism, and its promotion of low-paying service sector jobs. For a more detailed look at the Hyatt case, pages 41–47, this report.

67. For critical evaluations of Long Beach redevelopment, see *Banking on Blight*, and McLaughlin's *Blighted Partnerships*.

68. Elmendorf, 22.

69. One city publication from the 1980s read: "Social services should be designed and delivered, to the extent possible, in a manner which will not attract more dependent households." *Issues for the '80's,* cited in Elmendorf, 110.

70. John W. Cox and Sean Kearns, "Boeing Proposes Major Land Redevelopment Project for Long Beach, Calif.," *Press-Telegram,* February 16, 2000.

71. McLaughlin, 28

72. McLaughlin, 53.

73. Ibid.

74. McLaughlin, 29.

75. McLaughlin, 61.

76. McLaughlin, 58.

77. For a critical analysis of the high-technology industry, see Allen Scott, *Technopolis: High-Technology Industry and Regional Development in Southern California* (Berkeley, 1993).

78. Elmendorf, 99.

79. U.S. Census Bureau, "Census of Population and Housing," Long Beach, CA: 2000.

80. Janet Wiscombe, "Cambodians in Long Beach: Beyond the Killing Fields," *Long Beach Press-Telegram*, December 10, 1989; A1.

81. City of Long Beach Planning and Building Department, *Long Beach '90: U.S. Census Report No. 1*, 1992.

82. Women volunteered this information; the interview protocol did not ask women directly about their immigration status.

83. This is not surprising given that this was a study of welfare recipients. The vast majority of immigrants on welfare are, in fact, long-term permanent residents with U.S.-born children.

84. According to 1990 Census data for the Central Long Beach area, 11 percent of residents were non-Hispanic white, 17 percent African American, 13 percent Asian, and 55 percent Hispanic or Latino. Forty-two percent of residents in this area were foreign-born, with nearly half (42 percent) having entered the United States within the past ten years. Of these immigrants, nearly 65 percent were Mexican, 8 percent were other Central Americans, and 20 percent Southeast Asian.

85. These figures add credence to the critique of many social scientists that the federal government's formula for setting the poverty line does not accurately measure the economic circumstances under which families survive. The federal government's formula assumes that families will spend a third of their income on rent and another third on food. But 36.5 percent of families in Long Beach report spending over 35 percent on rent.

86. The city's at-large voting system that had frustrated the chances of candidates of color to be elected to the School Board was finally changed in 1988 to a district system. Teacher union activists, parents, and civil rights activists had fought and won a city charter proposal to change the voting system. Latina Jenny Oropeza (who would go on to be elected to the California State Assembly) and African American Bobbie Smith were elected to the School Board in 1988 as a result of these changes.

87. Janet Wiscombe, "Carrying the Burdens of Loss and Change, Immigrants Adapt," *Long Beach Press-Telegram*, December 10, 1989.

88. Hillburg, 128.

89. G. M. Bush, "Cease-Fire in Asian-Latino Gang War," *Press-Telegram*, October 18, 1994.

90. Reeves and Campbell elaborate the purpose of such stories as rites of inclusion and exclusion. "Rites of inclusion are not centrally about Us vs. a marginal Them but, instead, are devoted generally to the edification and internal discipline of those who are within the fold. . . . News reports that operated in this domain emphasize the reporter's role of maintaining the horizons of common sense by distinguishing between the threatened realm of Us and the threatening realm of Them" (39, 41, 42).

91. Elmendorf, 29.

92. Chris Woodyard, "Los Angeles Times Poll Results: Voters in Long Beach View Crime, Drugs as City's Top 2 Problems," *Los Angeles Times,* May 15, 1998, B-1. In 1989, a series of articles on Long Beach's Cambodian community in the *Long Beach Press-Telegram* provoked an angry outcry from readers. Irene Matthews wrote, "I think you should change the name of your paper to Cambodia Press. Why doesn't this Dorothy Korber write up about the USA? We have American families that are homeless. . . . The Cambodia people come into this country and have been given the red carpet. But people born in this country who have paid taxes get nothing. I'm sure sick of the whole thing." Another reader, D. Douglas, wrote, "Didn't you just over the summer complete a series on the Long Beach Cambodians? Come on! There has to be more news out there." *Long Beach Press-Telegram,* December 21, 1989, B-10.

93. Cited in Elmendorf, 15.

94. Darryl Kelley, "Population Pressure Point," *Los Angeles Times,* June 7, 1987.

95. Sharon Hormell, "Poor Called a Blight," *Long Beach Press-Telegram,* April 3, 1992. This and above citation appear in Elmendorf, 100.

96. Lindsay Isaacs, "Her Kind of Town," in *America City and County* (November 2004), 38. O'Neil was reelected in 1998 and then again in 2002 as a write-in candidate. Long Beach charter limits mayors to two four-year terms but provides that they can be elected to additional terms as write-in candidates.

NOTES TO CHAPTER 3

1. Created in the same year as CalWORKs, California's Cash Assistance Program for Immigrants (CAPI) overrides the federal five-year waiting period for cash aid to legal immigrants who arrive after August 1996. The California legislature also restored food stamps for legal immigrants who arrived before August 1996, and to all legal immigrants below the age of 18 and over age 65, regardless of date of entry.

2. Applicants have 18 months to find employment; current welfare recipients have 24 months.

3. The Maximum Family Grant (MFG) rule applies to all families who have been on cash aid for ten concurrent months, regardless of whether the mother of the newborn is herself receiving cash aid. All CalWORKs recipients are required to sign a sworn declaration that they had received notice of the MFG rule. But like most DPSS regulations, the number of rules and exemptions is dizzying. Consider, for example, a partial list of cases where the MFG does not apply: "If your family was off cash aid for at least two months in a row during the ten months before the birth of a child"; "If the child was conceived because of rape or incest. *You must report the rape or incest no later than three months after the birth of a child*

to a medical or mental health professional, or social services agency, or law en-forcement agency"; "If the child was conceived because of failure of one of these kinds of birth control: IUD (an intrauterine device), Norplant, Depo-Provera, or the sterilization of either parent. *You must give medical proof of any failure of a listed birth control method."* These latter two exemptions exemplify the guiding principle of welfare administration in the United States: Welfare recipients are guilty until they prove themselves innocent. California Department of Social Services, CW 2102, "The Maximum Family Grant (MFG) Rule for Recipients of Cash Aid," August 2000 (emphasis added).

4. Janet Quint, Kathryn Edin, Maria L. Buck, Barbara Fink, Yolanda C. Padilla, Olis Simmons-Hewitt, Mary Eustace Valmont, with Stan L. Bowie, Earl S. Johnson, Jill E. Korbin, Carol Dutton Stepick, Alex Stepick, and Abel Valenzuela Jr., *Big Cities and Welfare Reform: Early Implementation and Ethnographic Findings from the Project on Devolution and Urban Change* (New York, MDRC, 1999), 140. See also the August 1997 policy brief by the Center for the Continuing Study of the California Economy, entitled "The California Economy and Developing Annual Goals for Moving Welfare Recipients into the Workforce." This study determined that overall job growth in the state would not keep pace with the number of both welfare recipients and nonrecipients in need of work, and that welfare reform would intensify job competition and unemployment rates at the bottom of the labor market.

5. Quint et al., 140.

6. The City Jobs program grew out of a campaign led by the Los Angeles Metropolitan Alliance, a regional alliance of unions, community groups, and faith-based organizations, which met in 1995 to formulate a proactive response to federal plans for welfare reform. Over the next three years, the Metro Alliance mobilized around an Action Plan that advocated public sector job creation and high-wage job growth that would address the economic and public service needs of low-income communities. In November 1998, the Los Angeles City Council approved the Alliance's proposal for a small-scale experimental City Jobs program to provide welfare recipients with subsidized training for careers in public service and eventually place them in unionized employment with the city. By August 2002, the program had trained a total of 237 participants and placed 71 percent of these participants in permanent, full-time public jobs. Participants began earning a living wage ($9.38/hr.) while in training, and after transferring to a permanent position, their pay went up to $13.71/hr. with full medical and dental benefits. The program also gave women of color an avenue into jobs, like street reconstruction, garbage collection, and heavy machinery operation, from which they have historically been barred. Although the City Jobs program was widely praised by local politicians and welfare administrators for its success in moving poor people into stable and well-paying careers in public service, it has been plagued by a lack of consistent funding. Between 2001 and 2003, funding dropped from $4.2 to $1 million. See

Yardeena Aaron, Jennifer Ito, and Pronita Gupta, "The Los Angeles City Jobs Program: Lessons from a Career-First Program That Works" (Los Angeles, Community Institute for Policy, Heuristics Education and Research, December 2002).

7. Quoted in Manuel Moreno, "Evaluating CalWORKs in Los Angeles County," a 1999 study jointly directed by the Los Angeles County Urban Research Division, the Chief Administrative Office, and the Department of Public Social Services. URL: http://dpss.co.la.co.us.

8. For a critical history of the use of computer technology in welfare administration, and especially in fraud detection, see Gilliom's *Overseers of the Poor: Surveillance*; Rickie Solinger's *Beggars and Choosers: How the Politics of Choice Shapes Abortion, Adoption, and Welfare in the United States* (New York, 2001); and Barbara Cruikshank's *The Will to Empower*.

9. This "class interest" also plays itself out in growing resentment among BAP staff toward their GAIN counterparts, who are paid more, enjoy nicer offices and better resources, and on the whole tend to have more education than BAP staff. In the late 1990s DPSS transferred many of its most experienced eligibility workers to the GAIN division, which pays its employees higher salaries than BAP and receives a disproportionate percentage of DPSS resources. Evidence suggests that DPSS is evolving into a two-tier system, with growing material and status inequalities between BAP and GAIN, which mirror the broader ideological distinction between welfare receipt and welfare-leaving. For more on this two-tier system and growing tension among DPSS staff, see "Evaluating CalWORKs in Los Angeles County."

10. Gilliom, *Overseers of the Poor*. Like the Appalachian women in Gilliom's book, the Latina immigrants in this study also talked about the law as "exclusive, threatening, and mean-spirited." However, we read their verbal protests against racial and gender discrimination in the welfare system and the labor market as a form of "rights talk" that is grounded in group (rather than individual) claims to full citizenship.

11. Quote from "Job Developer" featured on GAIN's website for prospective employers. URL: http://www.ladpss.org/dpss/gainservices/default.cfm

12. Here, we draw on Michel Foucault's theory of "bio-power," which describes the myriad ways in which modern "disciplinary regimes" engage the individual in his/her own self-regulation. For Foucault, the ideological conditioning of the human "soul" (or consciousness) is inextricably connected to practices that discipline the physical body. Michel Foucault, *Discipline and Punish: The Birth of the Prison* (New York, 1979). Indeed, the bodies of welfare recipients stand at the center of "social welfare regime," as these bodies are constructed and policed as sites of race and gender difference, sexuality, biological reproduction, and labor power.

13. Cruikshank, *The Will to Empower*, 48.

14. Cruikshank, 232.

15. For Foucault, subjection and subjectivity are two complimentary, and inextricable, effects of what he calls "disciplinary technologies." The "individual" is simultaneously subjected to the authority of another, and "empowered" to discipline him or herself. In *Discipline and Punish*, 194.

16. At the outset of the Urban Change Project, as one measure to protect the anonymity and privacy of the study participants, ethnographers were instructed to avoid all contact with the welfare office. This meant that Alejandra did not conduct participant-observation research at the DPSS office that serves Long Beach, nor did she interview welfare caseworkers about their job responsibilities and their perspectives on welfare reform. Our account of the workings of the welfare system, and GAIN in particular, thus derives from the firsthand descriptions and experiences recounted by the welfare recipients who participated in this study. In order to fill in and (to the extent that this was possible) verify these women's accounts, we also reviewed official DPSS materials, such as program brochures and handouts, the program's website, as well as numerous evaluations of GAIN conducted by other researchers. These published works are cited throughout this and subsequent chapters.

17. For a description of the original GAIN program, and its transformation to a work-first model, see Evan Weissman, *Changing to a Work-First Strategy: Lessons from Los Angeles County's GAIN Program for Welfare Recipients* (New York, MDRC, 1997), 17.

18. Quoted in Jamie Peck, *Workfare States* (New York, 2001), 191. Later in his book, Peck quotes one of the program managers from Riverside County's GAIN: "If you have an automobile that does not start, do you pull the engine out and put a new engine in, pound the dents out, paint it and put new tires on it? Or do you just look at the spark plugs and the points and do the most minimum thing to make the car run? . . . Why should we do more if that's all it takes to get someone a job?" (174).

19. Weissman, 27.

20. Stephen Freedman, Marisa Mitchell, and David Navarro, *The Los Angeles Jobs-First GAIN Evaluation: Preliminary Findings on Participation Patterns and First-Year Impacts* (New York, MDRC, 1998).

21. Robert Scheer, "Mothers Lose in Wilson's GAIN Plan," *Los Angeles Times*, May 20, 1993. In the early 1990s, MDRC evaluated GAIN programs in six sites across California and concluded that Riverside County's work-first approach was far more successful than that of GAIN programs in Oakland and Los Angeles which focused on "human capital" development (including basic education and job training). MDRC's endorsement of the work-first approach rested largely on its finding that participants in the Riverside experiment group earned $20 a week more than those in the control group. Even more attractive to politicians was MDRC's claim that for every dollar invested in the Riverside program, $2.84 was gained in the form of reduced welfare costs and increased tax receipts.

As soon as it was released, MDRC's endorsement of Riverside's work-first approach came under heavy critique from other social policy experts, who noted that the evaluation did not account for the unique characteristics of Riverside County that contributed to its high job placement rate. As noted above, this semi-rural, suburban county experienced unusual economic growth during the course of the MDRC study (by contrast, in economically depressed Tulare County, GAIN participants earned $115 less than those not enrolled in the program). Moreover, Riverside's welfare population was largely white and therefore did not face the same labor market discrimination as black and Latina welfare recipients in other urban counties. Lastly, critics noted, Riverside's GAIN program made little improvement on wages paid to former recipients, either in the short or long term. In contrast, counties with a human capital approach, like Alameda, showed a significant increase in wages paid to participants. This latter point was conceded by MDRC President Judith Gueron: "[T]he downside to Riverside is that families weren't moved out of poverty. People didn't get better jobs. If that's your goal, you have to make a larger investment to get there." Peck, *Workfare States*, 204.

22. In 1993, Governor Pete Wilson proposed to increase state funds for GAIN, while slashing welfare payments to needy families by 19 percent. As support for his proposal, Wilson cited the MDRC evaluation of GAIN, stating that welfare mothers could make up the difference in income by working. By the early 1990s, most counties in California, including Los Angeles and Alameda, had been pressured to give up their human capital approach and to adopt the Riverside model. By the mid-90s, the GAIN model had been adopted by states across the nation. For a fascinating account of the "Riversidization" of welfare-to-work policy, see chapter 5 of Peck's *Workfare States*.

23. Compare to the proposed $74.9 million in spending for childcare, and a mere $5.3 million for substance abuse treatment. See Appendix IV, "CalWORKs County Plan Budget," in the County of Los Angeles Department of Public Social Services CalWORKs Implementation Plan, December 3, 1997.

24. Notably, as the county diverts significant financial and human resources from benefits administration to welfare-to-work operations, the social stigma attached to "welfare dependency" is made palpable through BAP's inferior facilities, its underpaid personnel, and its declining status inside the DPSS bureaucracy.

25. Weissman, 37.

26. Stephen Pimpare, "No Relief: The Politics of Welfare Retrenchment, 1873–1898 and 1973–2002" (Ph.D. dissertation, Graduate Center of CUNY, 2002).

27. Sanford F. Schram, *After Welfare: The Culture of Postindustrial Social Policy* (New York, 2000), 67.

28. Reminiscent of prison license plate programs, LACOE also runs an optional service it calls the "Plaque Business," which teaches GAIN participants how to create customized plaques, certificates, and various personal items. These

name plaques, awards, and certificates manufactured by welfare recipients are then sold to LACOE employees at a discount.

29. Cited in Peck, 175.

30. GSWs are well aware that they are sending recipients to apply for minimum wage jobs where business attire is unnecessary and often inappropriate. The kind of rationale behind the dress code, then, is a mixture of military-inspired discipline with the inculcating of recipients in good lessons for the future.

31. On paper, GAIN reflects some of the best and most current ideas in the field of social welfare policy: It includes provisions for subsidized childcare and transportation for working mothers; it creates a broad array of "post-employment services," from free counseling, career advancement seminars, and other services designed to facilitate job retention to subsidized job training and postsecondary education to aid former recipients in increasing their skills and wages; it also enacts safeguards to protect those people in the system who are most vulnerable, including work- and time-limit exemptions for the disabled, the elderly, pregnant women, and victims of domestic violence. A ground-up view, however, reveals that these programs are largely inaccessible to recipients, because caseworkers do not advertise them to clients (possibly for fear of encouraging opportunists who would fake domestic abuse or illness just to be exempt from the work requirements), because recipients have to reveal details about their personal lives that they would not even know to reveal or want to share in order for a caseworker to give them the information, or because in order to gain access to these services, recipients must complete an additional mountain of paperwork and another round of scrutiny into their private lives. Thus, the "supported work programs" as implemented serve a largely ideological, rather than practical, function; they exist to prove that the system has safeguards. There is no commitment or widespread practice to ensure that people needing the services available actually have access or are using them, despite the fact that the GAIN contract promises every signer the "direction and support . . . to help you improve your ability to get a job."

32. Daniel Flaming, Patricia Kwon, and Patrick Burns, *Running Out of Time: Voices of Parents Struggling to Move from Welfare to Work* (Los Angeles, Economic Roundtable, Summer 2002). Although this study was partially commissioned by the L.A. County Board of Supervisors, the Board has yet to respond to or act on the policy recommendations advanced in the Economic Roundtable report.

33. Doris Ng, "Welfare Reform in Santa Clara County: The Experiences of Mexican and Vietnamese Women," in *Immigrants, Welfare Reform and the Poverty of Policy,* 159–183.

34. "A New Paradigm for Welfare Reform: The Need for Civil Rights Enforcement," Statement by the U.S. Commission on Civil Rights (August 2002).

35. William M. Epstein, *Welfare in America: How Social Science Fails the Poor* (Madison, 1997), 180.

36. Other studies have also found that the short-term job training programs offered under CalWORKs typically do not lead welfare recipients to better job opportunities. The Economic Roundtable, for instance, found that the vast majority of recipients interviewed said they needed more education and training, and the few that had been sent to training were disappointed by the brevity and superficiality of the programs. One woman, for instance, had been sent to training for one week and then told by her caseworker that she now was ready to find a job. Several others commented that short-term training would not improve their opportunities in the labor market and called on GAIN to provide intensive ESL instruction, GED courses, and assistance in attending college. In her study of Mexican and Vietnamese women in Santa Clara County, Ng similarly interviewed women who had to convince their caseworkers to send them to job training programs, but after completing these short-term programs, they did not find a job and were reenrolled in Job Search. See Flaming et al., 2002; and Ng, 171–172.

37. When Norma first started this job, she was only assigned to 4 hours per week. It was only after a month of work that she was promoted to a full-time schedule.

38. Carla Rivera and Melissa Healy, "L.A. County Succeeding in Bid to Get Poor Off Aid," *Los Angeles Times*, August 20, 1998, A-1.

39. Another 817 welfare recipients were sanctioned for not giving paternity data, not showing proof of immunizations, and not verifying their children's school attendance. See Manuel Moreno, "From Welfare to Work and Economic Self-Sufficiency: A Baseline Evaluation of the Los Angeles County CalWORKs Program" (January 1999).

40. Ibid.

41. Peck, 175. The author cites a Riverside DPSS manual which asserts, "Employment, however modest, teaches GAIN clients employment discipline, such as setting the alarm clock, getting to work on time, learning to complete tasks, accepting supervision, and a chance to learn that they can be useful and successful."

NOTES TO CHAPTER 4

1. The fact that Leticia migrated before her husband and financed his migration disrupts the classical immigrant narrative and U.S. immigration law which both presume that the primary migrant is a male head of household and treats women and children's migration as secondary.

2. Among the U.S.-raised women in the sample, Delia Villanueva was the only one who turned to wage work immediately after dropping out of high school. The other women in this group either married in their teens and spent anywhere from one to ten years as full-time homemakers or lived in the homes of relatives or friends, where they performed unpaid labor like babysitting, cooking, etc. However, national statistics on employment rates for Latino/a youth show that this is

atypical. In 1990, Latino/a youth were more likely to be employed year-round than white and black youths and earned the lowest wages of all racial groups.

3. Lisa Dodson, *Don't Call Us Out of Name: The Untold Lives of Women and Girls in Poor America* (Boston, 1998), 14–49.

4. While numerous studies of high school dropouts have made this observation, none have done so more insightfully and powerfully than Michelle Fine's *Framing Dropouts: Notes on the Politics of an Urban High School* (Albany, 1991).

5. Michelle Fine and Nancie Zane, "Bein' Wrapped Too Tight: When Low-Income Women Drop Out of High School," *Women's Studies Quarterly* 19 (Spring/Summer 1991), 80. This gender gap is further amplified in the labor market, where female dropouts earn considerably less than their male counterparts. In California, female dropouts earned 58 percent less than male dropouts in 1996. See Deborah Reed, Melissa Haber, and Laura Mameesh, *The Distribution of Income in California* (San Francisco: Public Policy Institute of California, 1996).

6. For background on the *maquiladora* industry, see Maria Patricia Fernández-Kelly, *For We Are Sold, My People and I: Women and Industry in Mexico's Northern Frontier* (Albany, 1983); and Leslie Sklair, *Assembling for Development: The Maquila Industry in Mexico and the United States* (Boston, 1989).

7. Valle and Torres, *Latino Metropolis,* 16. In 1990, Latinos comprised more than half of the manufacturing laborforce in L.A. County, even though they constituted just over a third of the county's population. Specifically, Latinos made up 44.9 percent of workers employed in durable goods manufacturing, and 66 percent of workers employed in nondurable goods manufacturing. Additionally, Allen Scott's detailed analysis of L.A.'s manufacturing economy shows a clear pattern of gender division within this sector, with Latino males concentrated in "industries characterized by heavy materials-handling labor process and often noisy or dirty working conditions, such as wood products and metallurgical industries," and Latina females concentrated in "labor intensive craft industries, marked by small establishment size" (clothing, textiles, and leather product industries). Allen J. Scott, "The Manufacturing Economy: Ethnic and Gender Divisions of Labor," in *Ethnic Los Angeles,* ed. Roger Waldinger and Mehdi Bozorgmehr (New York, 1996), 215–244.

8. Fernández Kelly and Sassen, "Recasting Women in the Global Economy," 102. In Los Angeles County, nonwhite women comprise 70 percent of all "operators, fabricators, and laborers"; of that group, 76 percent are Latina.

9. Valle and Torres, 16.

10. This observation is confirmed by a 2001 study of wages, income, and employment trends in L.A. County, which found that Latinos on average earn the lowest wages. According to the California Budget Project, Latinos earn a median hourly wage of $10.00, up 1 percent from 1995, compared to the median hourly wage for whites of $19.73, up 7.3 percent; for Asians of $16.33, up 5.7 percent;

and for blacks of $15.06, a 2.9 percent decrease. See "The State of Working California—Key Findings and Summary of Forthcoming Report" (Sacramento, California Budget Project, 2001). Research conducted by sociologist Vilma Ortiz similarly concludes that nativity and length of time in the United States play a minimal role in determining the economic and social mobility of the Mexican-origin population in L.A. County. See Ortiz, "The Mexican-Origin Population: Permanent Working Class or Emerging Middle Class?" in *Ethnic Los Angeles*.

11. For a thorough critique of the literature on male economic migrants and household economy theories of Mexican immigration, see chapter 1 of Hondagneu-Sotelo's *Gendered Transitions*.

12. Ethnographer Jennifer Johnson reports similar findings from her interviews with white working-class women, who ranked respect from employers as the most important characteristic of a "decent job." Johnson's distinction between "job-satisfaction" and "work-satisfaction" is especially relevant to this discussion (97–100). When asked to describe a good job, the Latinas in this study used criteria like wages, respectful working conditions, benefits, work hours, and compatibility with their childcare responsibilities. However, when discussing different types of *work* they might enjoy, many Latinas stressed the importance of personal fulfillment. Several said that they would ideally like jobs where they could work with people and help others, like nursing (Norma) or working as a teacher's aide in an elementary school (Delia and Norma). Others, like Angela and Lupe, dreamed of technically skilled jobs in auto mechanics or computers, which they associated with mastery, autonomy, and prestige. This issue of personal fulfillment, or "work-satisfaction," is largely absent from welfare-to-work debates and policies, which narrowly focus on improving job conditions like wages and benefits. Personal satisfaction from work is the privileged domain of middle- and upper-class women workers, whereas poor and working-class women are expected to be happy with a "decent job." Missing from Johnson's analysis, however, is a critical analysis of how race and racism shape these white working-class women's experiences. The Latina women in this study had a keen understanding of how their race restricted them to certain jobs and tasks in the U.S. labor market. Most notably, while a significant percentage of the white working-class women that Johnson interviewed were employed as low-wage clerical workers and other service positions where they had extensive contact with the public (waitressing, sales, etc.), only one of the Latinas in this study had ever held a desk job, and the vast majority had worked at physically strenuous jobs, where they were typically out of the view of the public. See Jennifer Johnson, *Getting by on the Minimum: The Lives of Working-Class Women* (London, 2002).

13. This could be read as an effect of the social stigma attached to welfare in U.S. society. Just as poverty discourse in the United States eschews a structural analysis in favor of individual and moral explanations for welfare use, these

women strategically framed their own use of welfare in moral rather than structural terms.

14. Roberts writes, "While about half of poor white single mothers became poor at the time that they established a single-mother household, only a quarter of Black women did—the Black mothers were poor already. . . . Moreover, Black children living with two parents are still more likely to be poor than white children in female-headed households." *Killing the Black Body,* 224.

15. Like all the families in this study who reported employment income to DPSS, the Nuñez's welfare benefits fluctuated radically from month to month. March 2000, for example, was an exceptionally lucrative month for Alberto as he earned $1,500, nearly three times his average monthly pay of $600. As a result, in April, the family did not receive any food stamps (in April they had received $220), and only $282 in cash assistance (down from $680). DPSS's system of calculating benefits based on the previous month's earnings posed a disadvantage to the working families in this study, whose income from work varied widely from month to month, and who were paid by the week rather than at the end of the month. This made household budgeting incredibly complicated, as one month a family might have a combined income (from work and welfare) of over $2,000, whereas the following month, the same family's income could drop to just $500. Moreover, none of the people interviewed understood DPSS's inscrutable formula for adjusting benefits to income level, which meant that they had no way of predicting how much cash aid and food stamps they would receive each month, nor any means to contest errors in the calculation of their benefits. Indeed, this made it impossible to definitively track the effects of welfare reform on each family's welfare income. Nearly all the families in this study lost income during the three-year span of this research; yet because these families were accustomed to unexplainable changes to their benefits, it was often impossible to determine whether their income had been reduced as a result of employment earnings, sanctions, or administrative error.

16. Paul More, Patrice Wagonhurst, Jessica Goodheart, David Rusten, Enrico Marcelli, Pascale Joassart-Marcelli, and John Medearis, *The Other Los Angeles: The Working Poor in the City of the 21st Century* (Los Angeles, LAANE, 2000), v–vi.

17. Carol Zabin, Arindrajit Dube, and Ken Jacobs, *The Hidden Public Costs of Low-Wage Jobs in California* (Berkeley, UC Berkeley Labor Center, 2004).

18. Wendy Zimmermann and Michael Fix, "Declining Immigrant Applications for Medi-Cal and Welfare Benefits in Los Angeles County" (New York: Urban Institute, July 1998).

19. Wendy Zimmermann and Michael Fix, "Trends in Noncitizens' and Citizens' Use of Public Benefits Following Welfare Reform: 1994–1997" (New York: Urban Institute, March 1999).

20. While recruiting women to participate in this study, Alejandra visited a GAIN-run computer class at Long Beach City College and discovered that most

of the Latina women in the class were receiving assistance only for their children. When asked how they had come to enroll in this class, all responded that they had been ordered to do so by their caseworker and threatened with the loss of their children's benefits. Later that year, Gilbert Contreras, another member of the Los Angeles research team, had the opportunity to interview the director of this program. When asked why the program was enrolling participants who were not legally required to fulfill the state's welfare-to-work requirements, the director asserted that he did not decide who should participate in GAIN—that was up to the discretion of caseworkers—but that he was happy to "help" any person who walked through his door.

NOTES TO CHAPTER 5

1. Interestingly, the community of other welfare recipients did not function as a form of policing and evangelism (as they do in Alcoholics Anonymous) but as a source of solidarity and resistance against the values and practices of the GSW and GAIN itself.

2. Quoted in Peck, *Workfare States*, 180.

3. Sanford F. Schram, *After Welfare: The Culture of Postindustrial Social Policy* (New York, 2000), 45.

4. Schram, 46.

5. Cruikshank, *The Will to Empower*, 116.

6. See Robin Kelley, *yo mama's disfunktional*; Jill Quadragno, *The Color of Welfare*; and Adolph Reed, *Stirrings in the Jug*. For rich historical work on the rise of conservatism, see Rick Perlstein, *Before the Storm: Barry Goldwater and the Unmaking of the American Consensus* (New York, 2001); Thomas Byrne Edsall and Mary D. Edsall, *Chain Reaction: The Impact of Race, Rights, and Taxes on American Politics* (New York, 1992); and Dan Carter, *From George Wallace to Newt Gingrich: Race in the Conservative Counterrevolution, 1963–1994* (Baton Rouge, LA, 1999). For a critique of post-feminism, see Susan Douglas and Meredith Michaels, *The Mommy Myth: The Idealization of Motherhood and How It Has Undermined Women* (New York, 2004), and Susan Faludi, *Backlash: The Undeclared War against American Women* (New York, 1992).

7. Perhaps not surprisingly, the federal government is now spending more money on TANF than on welfare, just putting it to a different use.

8. Epstein, *Welfare in America*, 141–142.

9. Epstein, 142.

10. Cruikshank's *The Will To Empower* provides a fascinating look at the California Task Force to Promote Self-Esteem and Personal and Social Responsibility. Created in 1983, this task force was composed of prominent state legislators as well as academics, and marked the marriage of psychological paradigms of individual self-esteem and governmental strategies to correct social ills. As the

Task Force declared in a 1985 report: "Self-esteem is the likeliest candidate for a social vaccine, something that empowers us to live responsibly and that inoculates us against the lures of crime, violence, substance abuse, teen pregnancy, child abuse, chronic welfare dependency, and educational failure. The lack of self-esteem is central to most personal and social ills plaguing our state and nation as we approach the end of the twentieth century." Cited in Cruikshank, 119.

11. Fine, *Framing Dropouts,* 180–181.

12. Cited in Schram, *After Welfare,* 31.

13. Here, the question not only rests on whether a right/entitlement is universal and guaranteed, but also whether it is actively promoted and facilitated by the state.

14. Indeed, this functions as a hermeneutic circle: Not only does the individualization of poverty enable the receipt of welfare to be cast as voluntary, but once a woman "chooses" to go on welfare, this also proves that her poverty is individual. We saw this ideology surface in Latinas' own narratives of their path to welfare. While most talked about the labor market in terms of structural obstacles and discrimination, their narratives of going on welfare were framed in a language of individual circumstance and hardship.

15. This is yet another example of the bizarre mismatch between the actual job seekers that GAIN is responsible for and the skilled, middle-income job seeker that most of its exercises are modeled after. If some people have the power to negotiate their salary, is it not a form of degradation to have to admit in writing that you have no choice in your wage?

16. In *Democracy in America,* Alexis de Tocqueville foresaw the invisible and nonviolent subjection that accompanies self-government in a liberal democracy when he wrote, "Subjection in petty affairs is manifest daily and touches all citizens indiscriminately. It never drives men to despair, but continually thwarts them and leads them to give up using their free will." Alexis de Tocqueville, *Democracy in America* (New York, 1969), 667.

17. Naila Kabeer writes, "We can see why the extremes of methodological individualism in economics and methodological structuralism in sociology have not proven particularly useful in grappling with the problems of structure and agency in the real world. One portrayed economic actors as abstract ciphers, undifferentiated by context or biography, the bearer of 'one all-purpose preference ordering' which applies to all decisions in their lives, regardless of how trivial or momentous. The other presented the individual as a 'cultural dope' whose practices, purposes, and perceptions were blurred and out of focus because of the relentless occupation with overarching structures." Naila Kabeer, *The Power to Choose: Bangladeshi Women and Labor Market Decisions in London and Dhaka* (London, 2000), 46–47.

18. Habitus describes the "socially-structured aspect of subjectivity," that is, the way that individual behavior and beliefs are structured by the collectivities in

which they live. Writing about French society in the 1970s and 1980s, Bourdieu's work is largely concerned with social class as the site for the reproduction of structural inequities. A number of scholars, including Kabeer, have since expanded his discussion of "habitus" to include other axes of social differentiation, such as race, gender, and nationality.

19. Kabeer, 43–44.

20. By virtue of being structured into the interview, however, the activity of evaluating job characteristics was far more formal and performative than what would normally occur in their everyday lives.

21. As a number of feminist scholars have observed, ideologies of race, class, and gender are central to the social production of Third World women as "cheap" and "flexible" labor. For an especially lucid elaboration of this argument, see Chandra Talpade Mohanty, "Third World Women and Capitalist Scripts," in *Third World Women and the Politics of Feminism,* ed. Chandra Mohanty, Ann Russo, and Lourdes Torres (Bloomington, IN, 1991).

22. Indeed, when asked what their children would lose when they went back to work, most women responded, "Their mother." Delia, for example, replied, "What am I going to lose? Well, watching my kids grow up, interacting with them, spending more time with them."

23. While Leticia said that she had always preferred to work at night, she also admitted to suffering from extreme physical and mental exhaustion. When she returned home after a night shift, she was expected to prepare breakfast, prepare the older children for school, clean the house, care for her two toddlers, and cook dinner for that evening. Leticia took to hiding in the closet—the only quiet place in the family's small two-bedroom apartment—for brief naps during the course of the day. Other Latinas, like Zoraida, talked about women's domestic role not in terms of other people's expectations but as the "natural" order of the world. As she explained, "If it were up to me, I would stay at home with my family and take care of my children. Who is going to give my child his medication? If I go [to work], who is going to take care of the child?" They asserted this cultural norm of "motherwork" or "*familia*" as a counterpoint to social policies forcing welfare recipients into the labor market.

24. Angela's work always begins in the late evening hours and can stretch into one or two in the morning, depending on how many offices she is assigned to clean. She is required to drive her own car and to pay her own auto insurance and gas expenses. Although she sometimes earns as little as $400 a month, Angela considers this a good job because she works alone at her own pace, and no one is looking over her shoulder: "I mainly like this job because there is no one ordering me around. I do have my manager, but he never goes to check how I leave the offices because he knows that everything is fine if nobody calls to complain." When Alejandra asked her to describe a "bad job," she responded: "Well, if I were pressured to meet a certain quota in a certain amount of time. . . . Like in

the *maquiladoras,* they have to make a certain amount of things in a determined time." Angela's "preferences" are defined within the "sense of limits" produced by habitus. This is apparent when she favorably compares her janitorial work to one of the only other options she can imagine, the *maquiladora.*

25. Gilliom notes that because welfare benefit levels are set so low, the system itself produces an inevitable struggle between recipients (who break the rules by working under the table, taking in boarders, etc.) and welfare administrators constantly trying to catch them. Mundane acts of resistance give welfare recipients a sense of autonomy and agency as women carve out private spaces outside the view and reach of the welfare state.

26. Cruikshank, 116.

27. W. E. B. Du Bois, *The Souls of Black Folk,* 1–3.

28. Patricia Williams, *The Alchemy of Race and Rights* (Cambridge, MA, 1991), 62.

29. Ironically, this is one of the rare times that poor women get to be the experts on their own lives; in most articles, the many other things that women say do not get taken up in policy formulations.

30. More recently, we have seen attempts by scholars to balance a discussion of the repressive effects of the welfare state with more empowering images of collective political resistance. Grace Chang's *Disposable Domestics,* for example, intermixes ethnographic interviews with Latina and Asian immigrants with case studies of contemporary labor and welfare rights activism. Chang's narrative flattens immigrant women into illustrative "stories" of Third World women's subjugation in the global economy, which are then used to offset or frame local organizing drives and political campaigns.

31. Writing about public efforts to Americanize Los Angeles's Mexican immigrants in the 1920s, historian George Sanchez concludes that, "Rather than provide Mexican immigrants with an attainable picture of assimilation, Americanization programs could offer these immigrants only idealized versions of American values. In reality what was presented turned out to be little more than second-class citizenship." George Sanchez, *Becoming Mexican-American* (Oxford, 1993), 105–106. Sanchez tells us that while Mexican immigrant women earlier in the century were originally attracted to Americanization's promises of inclusion and equality, it did not take them long to realize that they and their families were being assimilated into the bottom of a racially stratified society.

32. Desmond King, *Making Americans: Immigration, Race, and the Origins of the Diverse Democracy* (Cambridge, MA, 2000), 257.

33. This discussion of Americanization programs in the 1920s draws on the following works: Cruikshank, *The Will to Empower,* 43–66; King, *Making Americans,* 85–126; Mink, *The Wages of Motherhood*; and Sanchez, *Becoming Mexican-American,* 87–107.

34. In both the 1920s and the 1990s, social reformers targeted women as the

source of the nation's problems and as the vehicle through which these problems could be corrected. In the 1920s, progressive public officials, philanthropists, social workers, and citizen volunteers focused their efforts on Americanizing immigrant women with the belief that women's natural reproductive abilities and maternal qualities positioned them uniquely to shape the nation's future citizens. Yet, although Americanization professed to value female maternalism and domesticity, in practice, these programs prepared and channeled immigrant women, and particularly Mexican women, into low-wage employment outside the home. Home instruction in "American" domestic skills like handiwork, sewing, and cooking trained immigrant women for jobs in the nation's sweatshops while also meeting the rising demand for domestics in middle-class homes.

Welfare reform policies in the contemporary era similarly target poor women principally as mothers who have the responsibility to transform their family's position in U.S. society. But the ideologies of maternalism and domesticity prevalent in the 1920s have been retooled to fit a different set of economic imperatives and gender ideals at the end of the twentieth century. Whereas earlier Americanization efforts asserted the importance of women's role in the home and their economic dependence on a male wage earner (while also expecting that women of color and white working-class women work outside the home), welfare-to-work initiatives draw on a post-feminist language that celebrates the "working mom" and the two-earner family as a national ideal, but provides working mothers with few resources to effectively juggle work and family life. Poor mothers who stay home to raise their children are stigmatized for their "dependency," and their worthiness as American citizens now rests, not on their identities as mothers, but as wage earners who assume financial responsibility for their families.

35. Another significant parallel between Americanizers in the 1920s and proponents of welfare reform in the 1990s lies in the cultural understanding of race that lurked beneath the claims of both groups to be rising above the racism and nativism of their respective eras. With its assimilationist mission, Americanization indeed marked a significant change from the virulent biological racism and restrictionism that had been growing steadily in American politics since the late 1800s. Responding to the rising prominence of the science of eugenics and the passage of a series of laws limiting the immigration of undesirable foreigners, progressives in the 1920s mobilized around a more inclusive model of American identity, and they earnestly sought to help immigrant families better adapt to U.S. society. However, this quest to improve the immigrant's status in America failed to radically challenge nativist ideas, as Americanization continued to affirm the superiority of Anglo-Saxon culture and the deprivations of immigrant cultures. Thus, while these progressive programs seemed to widen the arena for citizenship to include new immigrant groups, this citizenship was ultimately predicated on the willingness of the immigrant to renounce his old ways and embrace a more enlightened way of life.

NOTES TO THE CONCLUSION

1. Anti-poverty advocates fear that reauthorization will instead be folded into a budget reconciliation bill in Fall 2005. This could potentially have terrible consequences, leading to a reneging on proposed improvements to TANF (including money for childcare) and overall cuts to the TANF budget, while instituting dramatically increased work rates and further punitive measures into the program with little debate.

2. While both bills passed in spring 2005, there were significant differences between the two. The Senate bill reflected some bipartisan consensus as well as the input of state governors, while the House bill was essentially a Republican proposal that had been previously introduced in 2002. Both bills increased work requirements to 70 percent of a state's caseload (up from 50 percent), provided $300 million for marriage promotion (though the Senate includes protections related to the voluntary nature of these programs and to domestic violence), and upped work rates to 34 hours per week under the Senate bill and 40 hours under the House bill. The Senate bill proposed $6 billion new dollars for childcare while the House increased funding by only $1 billion. Whereas the Senate bill maintains the discretion of states to sanction only the adult portion of the grant, the House bill mandates that the entire family be sanctioned (which would have a monumental impact on California, where children are currently exempt from sanctions). The Senate bill includes some crucial protections for welfare recipients and their children: it requires that states make a good-faith effort to contact recipients before penalizing them for not following their "self-sufficiency plan"; requires that more money collected through child support payments go directly to the family; and includes exemptions to recipients with disabilities, including chemical dependency, and to parent caring for children with disabilities. Most notably, the Senate expands the educational activities allowable in TANF. Unlike the House bill, which allows vocational education for three months in any two-year period or if the TANF recipient also is working 24 hours per week, the Senate bill retains the current standard, which allows states to count vocational education as a stand-alone activity for up to 12 months. The latter also gives states the option to create a "Parents as Scholars" program to count postsecondary or vocational education as work activity for more than 12 months for up to 10 percent of the state's caseload.

3. The Senate bill's softer nature comes at the partial expense of the immigrant working poor. The Senate increase for childcare would partially be funded through an offset that would deny the Earned Income Tax Credit to families in which one (or both) immigrant parent does not have work authorization—even if the other parent is a U.S. citizen or work-authorized immigrant. Moreover, while TANF currently allows that refugees and other humanitarian immigrants

can receive SSI after being in the United States seven years, the Senate bill would extend this to nine.

4. The *Implementation Study* examined welfare reform policies in each of the four research sites, looking at how these policies were implemented and communicated at local welfare agencies. The *Individual-Level Impact Study* analyzed countywide administrative data, along with a randomly sampled phone survey of each county's welfare population, to "measure the impacts of new policies on welfare, employment, earnings, and other indicators of individual and family well-being." The *Neighborhood Indicators Study* analyzed demographic and statistical data to construct a portrait of economic and social changes in each urban county and in neighborhoods with "high concentrations" of poverty and welfare recipients. The *Institutional Study* surveyed local small businesses, nonprofit agencies, schools, churches, informal food banks, community-based organizations, and informal day care centers to assess the effects of new welfare policies and funding streams on economic institutions in poor neighborhoods in each of the four counties. URL: http://www.mdrc.org/project_25-3.html

5. One exception was the phone survey with welfare recipients, for which MDRC contracted a survey company in each city.

6. Historian Sonya Rose reminds us that social science discourse is not a politically autonomous and open field of representation, but rather one in which certain interpretations are imbued with explanatory power that exerts tremendous influence over ordinary people's lives: "When these interpretations are built into public policies they directly constrain people's lives. When they are articulated by particularly powerful people . . . they assume greater significance and wider currency than alternative interpretations by those who lack public prominence. In addition, they motivate or suppress action by defining or constructing the subjects to which the discourse applies." Sonya O. Rose, *Limited Livelihoods: Gender and Class in Nineteenth-Century England* (Berkeley, 1992), 8–9.

7. Fine, *Framing Dropouts*, 183.

8. Sanford F. Schram, *Words of Welfare: The Poverty of Social Science and the Social Science of Poverty* (Minneapolis, 1995), 4.

9. O'Connor, *Poverty Knowledge*, 236.

10. MDRC's Board of Directors has included prominent liberal social scientists like William Julius Wilson and Harvard professor Mary Jo Bane, Clinton's welfare policy advisor who was extremely influential in shaping the administration's position on work-based welfare reform.

11. Michael Katz, *The Price of Citizenship*, 72–73. Sociologist Peter Szanton reached a similar conclusion after interviewing politicians and federal welfare officials involved in the design of the FSA, noting that "a major shift in the nation's social policy seems to have been shaped largely by research and analysis." (Cited in Katz, 72.)

12. Sanford Schram, Alice O'Connor, and Jamie Peck have all waged

broader, theoretical critiques of MDRC's use of scientific authority and technocratic knowledge toward political ends, while analyzing the ways that research by MDRC and other liberal social science think-tanks were crucial to the passage of the PRWORA. See: William Epstein, *Welfare in America: How Social Science Fails the Poor* (Madison, 1997); Schram, *Words of Welfare*; Alice O'Connor, *Poverty Knowledge: Social Science, Social Policy, and the Poor in Twentieth-Century U.S. History* (Princeton, 2001); and Jamie Peck, *Workfare States* (New York, 2001). For scientific critiques of the design and execution of MDRC's research, also see P. L. Szanton, "The Remarkable 'Quango': Knowledge, Politics, and Welfare Reform," *Journal of Policy Analysis and Management* 10 (1991): 590–602; and S. J. Oliker, "Does Workfare Work? Evaluation Research and Workfare Policy," *Social Problems* 41 (1994): 195–213. Both Szanton and Oliker argue that the design of MDRC's workfare demonstration experiments favored laborforce attachment models over human-capital models.

13. Jason De Parle, *American Dream: Three Women, Ten Kids and a Nation's Drive to End Welfare* (New York, 2004), 111.

14. De Parle, 112.

15. The Economic Roundtable also criticized MDRC's evasion of human subjects' protocol—in the demonstration programs that MDRC had conducted, participants were selected for mandatory participation without their consent.

16. O'Connor, 232.

17. O'Connor, 236.

18. The quote comes from Katz, *The Undeserving Poor* (New York, 1990), 122.

19. Nathan Glazer, "Poverty and Poverty Research, Then and Now," *Focus* 9 (Summer 1986): 16–17. Cited in Schram, *Words of Welfare*, 45. Glazer's essay is especially interesting because it is an early example of the linkage between immigration and welfare in poverty debates. Glazer contrasts the economic success of recent immigrants with the ongoing poverty of U.S.-born blacks and Latinos to build an argument for the cultural nature of poverty.

20. These works followed a well-established culturalist trend in ethnographic studies of poverty, which began in the postwar period with the publication of Herbert St. Clair Drake and Horace Cayton's *Black Metropolis* (1945), and Oscar Lewis's *Five Families: Mexican Case Studies in the Culture of Poverty* (1959). In the 1960s, a flurry of sociological tracts on "ghetto culture" rose to national prominence, notably Herbert Gans, *The Urban Villagers* (1962); Elliot Liebow, *Tally's Corner* (1967); Ulf Hannerz, *Soulside* (1969); and Lee Rainwater, *Behind Ghetto Walls* (1970). In these and subsequent works, teenage pregnancy, joblessness, drug addiction, informal economies, domestic violence, and ultimately poverty itself are categorized as "behavior," determined by the individual psyche and group values and catalogued and remediated by social science.

21. Two exceptions are Schram's *Words of Welfare,* and Loic Wacquant's "Scrutinizing the Street: Poverty, Morality, and the Pitfalls of Urban Ethnography," *American Journal of Sociology* 107 (May 2002): 6.

22. Mark Seltzer argues that statistical studies "provide models of individualization: models for the generic, typical, or average man—what we might describe as the production of individuals as statistical persons." For Seltzer, the same fallacy of representation behind "statistical personification" can be found in realist ethnography, which emphasizes individual "cases" and representative "types." See Mark Seltzer, "Statistical Persons," *Diacritics* 17 (Fall 1987): 82–98. Cited in Schram, 46.

23. Karen Curtis, "'Bottom-Up' Poverty and Welfare Policy Discourse: Ethnography to the Rescue?" *Urban Anthropology* 28, 2 (1999): 109.

24. The mission statement also delineates four major sets of questions to be answered by the UCP: (1) How would welfare agencies respond to the new law? What "messages" and services would they put in place? How would they implement time limits? (2) What would be the effects of TANF on welfare caseloads? How would it alter patterns of welfare receipt and employment? (3) How would low-income families adapt to time limits and other dimensions of welfare reform? What would be their experiences in the labor market? Would they be better or worse off financially? (4) How would welfare reform affect social conditions in big cities? In particular, would conditions in poor neighborhoods improve or worsen? URL: http://www.mdrc.org/project_25-3.html.

25. Adolph Reed, *Stirrings in the Jug: Black Politics in the Post-Segregation Era,* (Minneapolis, 1999), 15.

26. MDRC's focus on welfare reform in urban communities (despite the fact that the majority of recipients across the nation do not live in cities) reifies longstanding associations between welfare and urban dwellers. In its many descriptions of the Urban Change Project, MDRC offers a shifting set of rationales for the focus on cities, from the intransigence of large urban welfare agencies to reform, to the concentration of poverty in cities, to the deficient "characteristics" of urban residents themselves. Often when talking about cities, MDRC is actually making claims about people who live in cities. See, for example, the introduction to MDRC's report on the Urban Change findings in Cleveland, which states that, "In terms of recipients' characteristics, environmental conditions, TANF policies, and program implementation, the big cities are disadvantaged on several counts." The paragraph goes on to focus on the shortcomings of urban residents as the major obstacle faced by cities when implementing welfare reform. Thomas Brock et al., *Welfare Reform in Cleveland: Implementation, Effects, and Experiences of Poor Families and Neighborhoods* (New York, MDRC, 2002), 6.

27. Paradoxically, the administrative data and phone survey components of the project incorporated a much broader sampling of low-income people, including those who had never received welfare and those who had left welfare prior to

the enactment of the 1996 reforms. Most subsequent reports from the UCP include a number of caveats that the changes that the UCP detected around increased employment and decreased welfare use could not necessarily be traced to the new legislation (and many seemed to predate 1996). Yet these caveats were not the main story that MDRC was promoting, and thus the reports generated from the UCP data could continue to mark the decisive changes under welfare reform.

28. None of the study participants were identified at the start of the research as gay or lesbian, nor did they identify themselves as such during the course of the interviews. This would have been difficult given the heteronormative nature of the interview questions.

29. The last of set of questions on "Children and Marriage" presumed a normative heterosexuality among respondents with questions like: "Under what conditions would you consider getting married?"

30. This is apparent in the publication on the working poor published by MDRC in November 2001, which drew on interviews from both survey and ethnographic respondents. While the report is framed around the issue of single mothers raising children alone, the actual data reveals that a number of participants in the UCP were not single (many were married or had long-term live-in partners) and that an even greater number were not raising children alone (they had substantial help from partners and/or relatives who helped to pay the bills, shared in childcare responsibilities and other housework, provided transportation, and helped to fill out paperwork). This disjuncture between the framework of the report and the empirical data reveals the potency of the dominant paradigm in welfare policy research. Denise Polit et al., *Is Work Enough? The Experiences of Current and Former Welfare Mothers Who Work* (New York, MDRC, 2001).

31. The predominance of two-parent families was even more pronounced in the Cambodian study in Long Beach, where all but one of the women in the sample were married.

32. Child-only welfare cases comprise one-quarter of all welfare households nationwide and are concentrated in two populations: First, "mixed-status" immigrant families, where the parents are not eligible for welfare due to their immigration status or where they are reluctant to receive welfare for themselves because it might jeopardize their later chances for naturalization or for sponsoring relatives for immigration. Second, cases where children are living with non-parental guardians who are not eligible for aid (for example, because they own their home) but the children under their care are eligible. For a discussion of the growth of such cases over the past ten years, see Nina Bernstein, "Child-Only Cases Grow in Welfare," *New York Times,* August 14, 2002, A1. For an important study of "mixed-status" immigrant households and their significance to social welfare policy, see Michael Fix and Wendy Zimmermann, "All Under One Roof: Mixed-Status Families in an Era of Reform" (New York: Urban Institute, June 1999). Fix and Zimmermann found that in 1998, 85 percent of immigrant

families (i.e., those with at least one noncitizen parent) were mixed-status families, and that such families are more likely to be poor than other families. In California, for instance, mixed-status families comprise 40 percent of low-income households with children; and in New York City, one-third of poor children live in mixed-status families. As the authors argue, these high percentages are in part attributable to the recent curtailment of noncitizen entitlements. Not only are noncitizen adults in such families less likely to apply for public assistance for their citizen children, but when they do apply, they also receive significantly lower benefits than families with citizen parents.

33. Most MDRC publications tied to the study have focused on issues of employment rates, barriers, and stability among former recipients.

34. This was evidenced in the use of a snowballing technique to recruit respondents into the study; ethnographers were instructed to build their local sample by asking women who had already agreed to participate in the study to provide the names of other welfare recipients who might also be willing to participate. Yet, the research protocol paid little attention to the social networks and human relationships that made these "snowball samples" possible in the first place. Ethnographers did not conduct group interviews with the women in their sample, nor were they expected to undertake in-depth and systematic observational analysis of family and community life.

35. The groups picked for Philadelphia included African Americans, whites, and Puerto Ricans; in Cleveland, African Americans and whites; in Miami, African Americans, Haitians, and Latinos (which included immigrants of varying statuses from all over Latin America); and in Los Angeles, African Americans, Chicanos, Mexican immigrants, and Cambodian immigrants. For Chicanos in Los Angeles County, the L.A. team studied the Boyle Heights neighborhood of East L.A.; for African Americans, the "Westmont-West Athens" area (located in the southwestern corner of the city, outside of historically black South L.A.); and for recent Mexican and Cambodian immigrants, two different neighborhoods in Long Beach. Once the neighborhoods were selected, the ethnographer assigned to that neighborhood was responsible for compiling a "snowball sample" of 12–14 women. In order to qualify to participate in the study, women had to fit a demographic profile. They had to live inside the census tract boundaries of the neighborhood being studied, they had to represent the racial group that presumably corresponded to that neighborhood, and they had to be receiving cash assistance for themselves and their children.

36. Wilson developed a statistical benchmark for identifying underclass neighborhoods—census tracts with a 30–40 percent poverty rate were labeled "high poverty areas" and those with a 40 percent or higher rate were rated as "extreme poverty areas," which was used in the neighborhood selection criteria for the UCP. When choosing neighborhoods in each of the four urban counties, MDRC used statistical data to locate census tracts that had a 40 percent poverty

rate and 20 percent welfare use rate. This selection criterion proved to be a problem in Los Angeles County, where very few census tracts met the "extreme poverty" index of 40 percent, whereas a significant number of tracts had poverty rates of 25–30 percent. For the L.A. ethnographic team, this interesting discovery suggested that poverty is not concentrated but rather spread throughout the county, and that poor people in Los Angeles are overwhelmingly likely to live in neighborhoods where the vast majority of their neighbors live above the poverty line. MDRC, however, responded pragmatically to this dilemma by lowering the poverty index for L.A., but not critically reevaluating the paradigm of urban poverty and social isolation that undergirds the UCP. Additionally, there was a lack of discussion over the implications of a "neighborhood study" that, in fact, studied only a small minority of neighborhood residents (and did not talk to the 75 percent who lived above the poverty line and those poor people who did not receive welfare).

37. The census tracts designated as the "Mexican immigrant neighborhood" for this study had very similar racial demographics to those of the adjacent area chosen as the "Cambodian immigrant neighborhood."

38. This problem surfaced differently in Boyle Heights, where the census tract being studied was home to both U.S.-born and immigrant ethnic Mexicans. Yet, because this was designated a "Chicano neighborhood," it meant not interviewing immigrants and thus excluding a significant portion of the area's residents from the ethnographic study.

39. Generational and cultural differences within immigrant populations that came up within the interviews, however, were not directly examined as a significant variable by the UCP. For instance, there were very few questions in the interview protocol concerning language skills and employment opportunities. MDRC did not survey employers in each of the four urban counties in order to determine whether language or nativity is a salient factor in their hiring decisions —this despite the mission statement for the UCP, which explicitly identified cultural capital as a key disadvantage that foreign-born recipients would face in welfare-to-work efforts. Even if MDRC could not have predicted that generational difference would be a key factor in shaping the experiences of immigrant welfare populations, by the end of the first year of ethnographic research, this had emerged as a key research finding for the ethnographic researchers in L.A. and Miami. However, the official interview protocol for subsequent years was not revised to investigate this issue more deeply.

40. Curiously, though, this was not the model in the Miami study, where immigrants from countries as diverse as Cuba, Nicaragua, Puerto Rico, and Colombia were grouped together under the racial category "Hispanic."

41. This research in Long Beach suggests that new federal "public charge" policies are leading some legal immigrants to get off of public assistance because receiving welfare could impede their path to citizenship and their ability to spon-

sor relatives for immigration. For example, Angela voluntarily took herself off of welfare in September 1996 out of fear that the government would reject her citizenship application. Other immigrants also made reference to the fact that receiving welfare could negatively impact their family's future eligibility not only in the arena of citizenship and immigration law, but also when applying for other government programs, like student loans for their children.

42. Ethnographers were instructed to closely follow the official interview protocol—that is, while ethnographers could change some of the wording of the questions, they were not to change the sentiment and were directed to ask every question. However, because of the length of the questionnaire and the inappropriateness of some of the questions, many of the ethnographers involved in the UCP, including Alejandra, changed questions, omitted others, and significantly altered the wording of many questions.

43. For example, under the section of the protocol entitled "Institutional Questions," women were asked about 40 different types of services they might have received in the past year, the name of the organization, and the organization's address. Like many other sections of the protocol, this produced a series of "yes or no" responses from the study participants rather than a discussion about the kinds and quality of social services that they were receiving or needing in the wake of welfare reform. This section ended with more open-ended questions (like "are there services your family needs but isn't receiving?"), but after ten or more minutes of responding either yes or no to the list of possible services and trying to remember the addresses for community organizations they had visited in the past year, most of the Mexican women who participated in the Long Beach study were alienated or intimidated by the rigid nature of the interview.

44. The UCP measured changes in "neighborhood indicators" like poverty level, unemployment, per capita income—all of which are effects of social and economic processes but tell us little about the causes.

45. Indeed, MDRC affirmed its own recommendations made years earlier that California move to a work-first rather than a human capital model—recommendations that pivotally shaped GAIN's work-first orientation.

46. This incredibly exhaustive set of questions about poor women's income and personal spending most palpably illustrates the slippery line between social science research and the surveilling gaze of the state. In fact, many of the budget questions in the Urban Change protocol bore an uncanny resemblance to those asked by caseworkers in the welfare eligibility interview and those included in the monthly report that all recipients must mail to the welfare office each month. In her recent ethnography of the welfare office, *Flat Broke with Children*, sociologist Sharon Hays provides the following synopsis of the resource-related questions asked at a typical eligibility interview: "*Do you have any cash right now, like in your purse, at home? Do you have a checking account, or a savings account? Do you have your recent statements? Do you have anything like stocks or*

bonds, U.S. savings bonds, retirement plans? Any houses or land? . . . In the last two years have you traded, sold or given away any of the resources we talked about or listed on the application? Any lawsuits you might be receiving a settlement on?" (p. 45). Compare these questions with those included in the budget section of the Urban Change interview protocol: *"Do you have a bank account? Checking? Savings? How much do you have in each account now? How much do you usually have in each account? Did you receive any interest payments from any source in the past year? Do you have any IRAs? Do you have any CDs? Do you own any stocks or bonds? Do you have any other assets I haven't mentioned? Have you received any cash from a legal settlement in the last year? Have you sold any personal property, like a house or a car? For how much? What did you do with the proceeds?"* These questions became all the more invasive as they moved outside the specific context of the welfare system, where women understood that their answers would be used to calculate their monthly benefits and to track down "cheaters," into the presumably separate and different terrain of social science research, where it was not at all clear to respondents why this information was being collected or how it would be used. The system of reproduction that we are describing here must be understood outside of the intentionality of the specific researchers who worked on this project.

47. "Running out of Time" includes numerous disclaimers to the research and tremendous transparency of the interview instruments. It also provides more quotes from respondents (5–6 quotes per point) along with an appendix with longer quotes.

48. Out of these surveys, the Roundtable made a list of key priorities for low-income families, in order of importance: "affordable childcare"; "program staff disrespectful and unhelpful"; "more education and job training"; "and make program requirements more feasible." Daniel Flaming, Patricia Kwon, and Patrick Burns, *Running Out of Time: Voices of Parents Struggling to Move from Welfare to Work* (Los Angeles, Economic Roundtable, Summer 2002).

49. Schram, *Words of Welfare,* xxviii.

50. MDRC's role as business consultant to the welfare state is evident in its treatment of the PRWORA as a seismic shift in welfare policy, one that would presumably produce a new set of attitudes and behaviors among the welfare poor. While TANF has constituted a monumental change and reorganization in welfare offices themselves, welfare recipients did not echo this sense of change. In the ethnographic interviews, when repeatedly asked to compare the "old" and "new" welfare systems, many women were confused by this distinction. While noting that specific time limits and work requirements were new, they did not see the spirit of welfare reform as all that different—or that much more draconian—than the welfare system they had experienced prior to 1996. Accustomed to surprise inspections by caseworkers, to filing monthly reports detailing their income and expenses, to requests for signed affidavits from landlords and doctors, to constant

changes in their eligibility and benefit levels, to negotiating the complicated maze of welfare and work, Mexican immigrant women said that the new system introduced under TANF was simply *"lo mismo que siempre"* (the same old thing). MDRC did not refine its questions—or adjust its analysis—based on these assessments by recipients in the study.

51. Thomas Brock, Isaac Kwayke, Judy C. Polyné, Lashawn Richburg-Hayes, David Seith, Alex Stepick, and Carol Dutton Stepick, *Welfare Reform in Miami: Implementation, Effects, and Experiences of Poor Families and Neighborhoods* (New York, MDRC, June 2004).

52. These quotes are taken from a meeting between Jeanne and Gordon Berlin on November 17, 2004 at MDRC's offices, in order to clarify the philosophy, scope, and findings of the UCP.

53. Janet Quint et al., *Big Cities and Welfare Reform*, 180.

54. Thomas Brock et al., *Welfare Reform in Miami*, xiii.

55. Quint et al., *Big Cities and Welfare Reform*, ES-5.

56. Quint et al., 73.

57. Quint et al., 109.

58. Brock et al., xiii.

59. Brock et al., 100.

60. Brock et al., 115.

61. Brock et al., 104.

62. Brock et al., 115.

63. Brock et al., xiii.

64. Michael Apple and Linda Christian-Smith, *The Politics of the Textbook* (New York, 1991), 61.

65. The concept of "employment stability" here refers only to the number of months in a year during which a respondent is employed. For example, a woman who had worked 19–24 months in two years was classified as having "high employment stability," whereas someone with less than seven months would be labeled as having "low stability." According to the definition offered by Polit et al., the term "stability" does not refer to the worker's economic conditions nor to job stability. Someone could have changed jobs eight times in the same year and made less than the minimum wage, and still be considered as having "high employment stability."

66. According to the tautological logic of this matrix, someone with three or more "barriers" could be expected to demonstrate low employment stability, whereas someone with no barriers would experience high stability.

67. Reed, *Stirrings in the Jug*, 32.

68. Denise Polit et al., *Is Work Enough?* 11–13.

69. In many regards, the stunted and seemingly arbitrary details provided about each respondent are the by-product of a report written by authors, who, in fact, did not conduct the actual ethnographic research but instead relied on sum-

mary accounts from the ethnographers who had talked at length with these women. Ethnographers in each site were provided with a list of questions and themes and instructed to compose brief biographical sketches and vignettes from the ethnographic data that could be included in the report. Thus, there was a significant gap between the actual practice of ethnographic research and the write-up of the ethnographic findings.

70. As we learned about Myrna in the introduction, her being shut out of the welfare office is what drives her to a series of unstable, low-paying jobs; thus, the denial of benefits is actually a facilitator of work. When we meet her later in the same report, this "difficulty in obtaining welfare benefits" has been completely erased from her story, and instead we are simply told that she has juggled welfare with a full-time job at Target (not that she was forced to take this job at Target because DPSS denied her application for welfare).

71. Indeed, for the Miami report, MDRC gave a copy to the Department of Children and Families to review before it was published but did not do the same for the welfare families who participated in the study.

72. Testimony of Gordon L. Berlin before the U.S. Senate Finance Committee, March 12, 2002. For the full text of Berlin's remarks, see http://www.mdrc.org/testimony/TANF_CongressionalTestimony/TANF_Testimony_Berlin.htm.

73. "New Paradigm for Welfare Reform: The Need for Civil Rights Enforcement," a Statement by the U.S. Commission on Civil Rights (August 2002).

74. Most studies of welfare and immigrants post-1996 have focused on food stamps and health care. While this is based in part on immigrant representation in different welfare programs, it effectively ignores and stigmatizes those who receive cash assistance.

Index

ACORN, 114

Affirmative action, 16, 18, 40

African American, 16, 111-112, 218-219; ADC restrictions, 36; cultural pathology, 49; discrimination in defense industries, 84-87; housing segregation and racial covenants, 84-87; Long Beach, 70, 83-87; poverty, 87, 138; social pathology, 49; underclass theory, 48-54; as "welfare cheats," 57, 191

Aid for Dependent Children (ADC), 36; change to AFDC, 35; restrictions to black women and Mexican-Americans, 36

Aid to Families with Dependant Children (AFDC), 3, 6, 9-10, 13, 20, 24, 35-37, 40-41, 45-47, 54, 63, 147, 158-162, 187; change of eligibility under Johnson, 38; change to TANF, 5; creation of GAIN, 120-121; dismantling, 46-47; neo-liberal claim of "cultural deprivation," 38; undermining capitalism and civil liberties, 39; undocumented alien restrictions, 61. *See also* Temporary Assistance to Needy Families (TANF)

AGENDA, 114

Alcoholics Anonymous welfare reform resemblance to, 125

American ideology, 14; American Dream, 1, 8, 103, 186; American entitlement, 9, 33

Americanism, 66; American values, 7, 14, 53; behavior as distinction, 126; pitfalls of liberalism, 7; race, 16, 21; wage disparity, 21; work ethic, 121, 202

Anderson, Elijah, *Streetwise*, 212

Antiterrorism and Effective Death Penalty Act, and labor market benefits, 61. *See also* Illegal Immigration Reform and Immigrant Responsibility Act of 1996 (IIRIA)

Aparicio, Ana, 61. *See also* Kretsedemas, Philip

Apple, Michael, on "cognitive dissonance," 235

Asia, 43, 57, 74, 95-96

Asian-Americans, 17, 138, 219; as model minorities, 52, 103; Chinese exclusion, 16, 78

Australia and narrowing of social assistance, 63

Avon Cosmetics, 148, 150

Balibar, Etienne, on racism without races, 53

Bane, Mary Jo, 48, 212; resignation, 47

Bangladeshi women, study of lack of labor market choices for, 183-184

Bayer, Lynn W. (DPSS director), 115

Berlin, Gordon (MDRC president), 228-229, 239-240

Bifurcated labor markets, 21-22, 33, 87, 94, 104, 135, 138

Bilbray, Brian, promotion of images of pregnant Mexican women on welfare, 55

Bixby, Jotham, 78

Bixby Knolls, 81

Bixby Park, 81

Boeing Corporation, in former Douglas aircraft plant, 94

Border Industrialization Project, 148

Border Patrol, 26, 66

Bourdieu, Pierre, 184

Boyle Heights Chicanos, 219

Bracero Program, 16-17, 24, 26, 27

Brimelow, Peter, and *Alien Nation* threat of unskilled Third World immigrants, 53

Brooks, Joseph, 86. *See also* National Association for the Advancement of Colored People (NAACP)

Brown, Pat, 40

About the Authors

Alejandra Marchevsky is Associate Professor of Liberal Studies at California State University, Los Angeles.

Jeanne Theoharis is Associate Professor of Political Science at Brooklyn College of the City University of New York. She is most recently coeditor of *Groundwork: Local Black Freedom Movements in America*, also from NYU Press. She is coauthor of *These Yet to Be United States: Civil Rights and Civil Liberties in America since 1945* and coeditor of *Freedom North: Black Freedom Struggles Outside the South, 1940–1980*.